Elizabeth Stone

Turkey Old and New

Historical, geographical and statistical. Vol. 1

Elizabeth Stone

Turkey Old and New
Historical, geographical and statistical. Vol. 1

ISBN/EAN: 9783337299163

Printed in Europe, USA, Canada, Australia, Japan

Cover: Foto ©ninafisch / pixelio.de

More available books at **www.hansebooks.com**

TURKEY OLD AND NEW:

Historical, Geographical and Statistical.

BY

SUTHERLAND MENZIES,

AUTHOR OF "ROYAL FAVOURITES," "POLITICAL WOMEN," "HISTORY OF FRANCE,"
"HISTORY OF GERMANY."

VOL. I.

LONDON:
W^M. H. ALLEN & CO., 13, WATERLOO PLACE, S.W.
PUBLISHERS TO THE INDIA OFFICE.
1880.

LONDON:
WOODFALL AND KINDER, PRINTERS,
MILFORD LANE, STRAND, W.C.

TO THE MEMORY OF

VISCOUNT STRATFORD DE REDCLIFFE, K.G., G.C.B., P.C.,

"THE GREAT ELTCHI"

WHO DIED, AS HE LIVED, FULL OF HONOURS AS OF YEARS,

AND

IN HIMSELF WAS AN EPITOME OF THAT MIGHTY PROBLEM (THE EASTERN QUESTION)

WHICH STILL DOMINATES THE POLITICAL HORIZON,

This Work is Dedicated.

PREFACE.

THE momentous events recently occurring in the East of Europe were the sequel and consequence of revolutions which have agitated that part of the world for several centuries. To thoroughly understand the facts now being accomplished from day to day, it is necessary to follow in its principal features, general results, and most important revolutions, the history of the formation, grandeur, and decadence of the OTTOMAN EMPIRE. In tracing the historical development and ethnical peculiarities of the Turks, the author has endeavoured to give a clear idea of the institutions, manners, races, peoples, and religions of the Empire, composed of so many different elements; and also as far as practicable an accurate knowledge of the geography of those still imperfectly known countries. This last-named feature, it is hoped, will be of great service to geography as well as history, and of the utmost interest to all who follow with serious attention the progress of events affecting what in this country is broadly and generally known as the EASTERN QUESTION.

The statistics of the Ottoman Empire are derived from the most trustworthy sources. For these the Author has been greatly indebted to recent researches—notably those of M. Vladimir Jakschitj, Director of the Statistical

Department of Servia, and of Mr. J. W. Redhouse, the well-known Turkish scholar, as also Herren Behm and Wagner.

The sources to which recourse has been made in the historical portion of the work are too numerous to cite here, but which have been acknowledged either in the text or in the foot-notes.

SUTHERLAND MENZIES.

Comrie,
 Alexandra Road,
  South Hampstead.

CONTENTS.

VOL. I.

BOOK I.

Introduction 1

CHAPTER I.

1. Antagonism of the East and West 6
2. Mahomet, the Korân, its Dogmas and Precepts 7
3. Errors of the Korân 11
4. Death of Mahomet. Arab Conquests 15
5. The First Khalifes, the Ommiades and Abbassides 19

CHAPTER II.

FROM THE ADVENT OF THE SELJUKIDES TO THAT OF THE OTTOMANS.

1. Origin of the Turks. Decadence of the Khalifate 25
2. Invasion of the Mongols 37
3. Sequel of the Mongol Conquests. Destruction of the Khalifate of Bagdad. Summary of the six preceding centuries . . . 39

CHAPTER III.

THE OTTOMAN TURKS TO THE REIGN OF AMURATH I. (1231-1360).

1. Origin of the Ottomans. Orthoguel 44
2. Reign of Othoman 51
3. Reign of Orchan 56
4. Early Contests of the Turks and Greeks in Europe . . . 62
5. History of Servia, Bosnia, Albania, &c. 66

CHAPTER IV.

REIGNS OF AMURATH I. AND BAJAZET I. (1360-1402).

1. Amurath I. Organization of the Janissaries 71
2. Acquisitions in Asia Minor. Feudal organization of the Sipahis . 77
3. New Conquests in Europe and Asia. Battle of Iconium . . 79

CONTENTS.

SECTION	PAGE
4. Battle of Kassova. Death of Amurath	81
5. Bajazet I. Abasement of the Greek Emperors. Acquisitions in Asia Minor. Conquest of Wallachia and Bulgaria	83
6. Submission of Asia Minor. Battle of Nicopolis. Conquest of Greece	86
7. Conquests of Tamerlane	91
8. War between Timour and Bajazet. Battle of Angora. Death of Bajazet	94

CHAPTER V.

REIGNS OF MAHOMET I., OF AMURATH II., AND OF MAHOMET II. TO THE CAPTURE OF CONSTANTINOPLE (1403-1453).

1. Interregnum. War between the sons of Bajazet (1403-1413) . . 98
2. Reign of Mahomet I. (1413-1421) 101
3. Amurath II. (1421-1450). Civil War. Siege of Constantinople. Submission of the Turkish States of Asia Minor . . . 105
4. Wars in Albania, Wallachia, and Servia. Hunyade Corvinus. Defeat of the Ottomans 109
5. Battle of Varna. Scanderbeg. Battle of Kassova . . . 112
6. Reign of Mahomet II. Siege and Capture of Constantinople . 115

BOOK II.

FROM THE CAPTURE OF CONSTANTINOPLE TO THE PEACE OF CARLOWITZ (1453-1699).

CHAPTER I.

REIGN OF MAHOMET II. FROM THE CAPTURE OF CONSTANTINOPLE (1453-1481).

1. Condition of the Greeks after the Conquest 125
2. The Conquest of Servia 128
3. Subjection of the Morea. War against Scanderbeg. Conquests in Asia 131
4. Conquest of Wallachia. Cruelties of Wlad *the Devil* . . . 133
5. Conquest of Bosnia. War with the Venetians and in Albania . 136
6. Conquest of Karamania 139
7. War in Moldavia. Conquest of the Crimea 142
8. Capture of Croïa. Siege of Scutari. Peace with the Venetians . 144
9. Expeditions into Hungary and Italy. Siege of Rhodes . . 145
10. Character of Mahomet II. His Institutions 148

CONTENTS. ix

CHAPTER II.
REIGN OF BAJAZET II. AND OF SELIM (1481–1520).

1. Revolt and Adventures of Djem 159
2. Expeditions in Hungary, Moldavia, and Asia Minor . . . 163
3. First Relations with Russia. War with the Venetians . . . 165
4. Revolt of the Sons of Bajazet. His death 167
5. Selim I. (1512–1520). War with Persia 168
6. Conquest of Egypt. Death and Character of Selim . . . 173

CHAPTER III.
REIGN OF SOLYMAN I. 1520 TO THE YEAR 1535.

1. First Acts of Solyman. Capture of Belgrade and of Rhodes . 179
2. The Grand Vizier Ibrahim. Troubles in Egypt, in the Crimea, in Wallachia 183
3. New Policy of France with Relation to the Ottoman Empire. Francis I. asks aid from Solyman. The Sultan's Letter . . 184
4. The Battle of Mohacz 190
5. Revolts in Asia 192
6. New Relations of Francis I. and Solyman 193
7. Second Expedition into Hungary. Siege of Vienna . . . 195
8. Third Expedition into Hungary. Embassy of Francis I. Siege of Güns. Peace with Austria 199
9. War with Persia. Capture of Bagdad. Chaireddin-Barbarossa. Capture of Tunis by Charles V. 204
10. First Capitulation of the Porte with France 207

CHAPTER IV.
REIGN OF SOLYMAN FROM THE CAPITULATIONS WITH FRANCE TO HIS DEATH (1536–1566).

1. Sequel of the Franco-Turkish Alliance. War with Venice . . 212
2. Affairs of Hungary. Capture of Buda 214
3. New Alliance between Turkey and France 216
4. War in Asia 221
5. Affairs of Hungary. Siege of Erlau. Sequel of the Franco-Turkish Alliance 223
6. War with Persia. The Sultana Roxalana. Death of Mustapha . 226
7. Affairs of Hungary. Revolt and Death of Bajazet . . . 228
8. Peace with Austria. Naval Affairs. Siege of Malta . . . 229
9. Renewal of the War in Hungary. Siege of Szigeth. Death of Solyman 231

CHAPTER V.

REIGNS OF SELIM II. AND AMURATH III. (1566–1595).

SECTION   PAGE

1. Selim II. surnamed *the Drunkard* (1566–1574). Revolt of the Janissaries. Peace with Austria 241
2. Relations with France 243
3. Expedition to Arabia 245
4. Conquest of Cyprus 246
5. Battle of Lepanto 249
6. Embassy from France. Peace with Venice 251
7. Capture of Tunis. Affairs of Poland and Moldavia. Death of Selim 253
8. Amurath III. (1574–1595). First Acts of his Reign . . . 255
9. War with Hungary. Relations with France 257
10. War with Persia 262
11. Relations with France, England, Venice, &c. Peace with Persia . 264
12. Revolts of the Janissaries and troubles in the Provinces. War renewed in Hungary. Death of Amurath III. . . . 268

CHAPTER VI.

REIGNS OF MAHOMET III. AND ACHMET I. (1596–1617).

1. First Acts and Character of Mahomet III. Revolt in Asia. Independence of Wallachia 271
2. War in Hungary. Treatment of the Christians by the Viziers. Michael the Brave 274
3. Relations of the Porte with France 276
4. Decadence of the Empire 280
5. War and Treaty with Persia. Treaty of Sitvatorok . . . 283
6. Mission of Savary de Brèves. Influence of France in the East . 286

CHAPTER VII.

REIGNS OF MUSTAPHA I., OSMAN II., AMURATH IV., AND IBRAHIM I. (1617–1649).

1. Reigns of Mustapha and Osman II. (1617–1622) 294
2. Restoration of Mustapha I. Amurath IV. (1623) . . . 299
3. Character of Amurath IV. State of the Army . . . 301
4. Relations with France 303
5. Depredations of the Barbary Corsairs 307
6. Ibrahim I. (1639). War against Venice 310

CHAPTER VIII.

REIGN OF MAHOMET IV. UNTIL 1669.

1. Insolence of the Janissaries; Revolts in Asia. War in Transylvania, Servia, and Moldavia 313
2. Diplomatic Rupture with France. Death of Kuproli I. . . 317
3. War in Hungary. Intervention of France. Battle of St. Gothard. Treaty of Vasvar 320
4. Hostilities against the Barbary Pirates 323
5. France succours Candia. Capture of that place 328
6. Fresh disagreement with France 332
7. The Embassy of Nointel. New Capitulations 335

CHAPTER IX.

FROM THE CAPTURE OF CANDIA TO THE PEACE OF CARLOWITZ (1669–1699.)

1. State of the Ottoman Empire after the Capture of Candia. Submission of the Cossacks. War in Poland. Treaty of 1676 . 342
2. Death of Ahmed-Kuproli (1676); Kara-Mustapha succeeds him. War with Russia. Peace of Radzin (1681) 346
3. War in Hungary. Policy of Louis XIV. Siege and Relief of Vienna 349
4. Power of France in the Mediterranean 359
5. War against the Holy Alliance. Deposition of Mahomet IV. (1687) 363
6. Solyman II. Continuation of the War. Vizierate of Kuproli-Mustapha 367
7. Reign of Achmet II. and Mustapha II. Peace of Carlowitz . 375

Historical Index 381

LIST OF ILLUSTRATIONS.

Portrait of Abdul Hamid		*Frontispiece.*
Arch of Chosroes		*Face page* 29
Bagdad		„ „ 41
Bayazid		„ „ 87
Servian Country People		„ „ 128
Scanderbeg		„ 132
Scutari		„ „ 145
Mahomet II.		„ 149
Harbour of Rhodes		„ 181
Lake and Fortress of Van		„ „ 204
Famagosta		„ „ 247
Harem		„ 293
Mount Ida, in Crete		„ 331

(The greater number of the Illustrations are from drawings taken by a German artist during the late Russo-Turkish war.)

TURKEY OLD AND NEW.

INTRODUCTION.

THE recent war waged between Russia and Turkey is only the latest episode in a great conflict of races which has lasted in Europe for more than five centuries, and the origin of which has to be traced back through a good many more than a thousand years into the obscurity of primitive and barbaric life in Central Asia. A brief review of this ancient feud will help us to understand the essential conditions of the strife that has so long existed between the two nations, and also serve as a fitting introduction of the following history of the Ottoman Empire.

Long ages before Greece or Rome existed, ethnologists tell us, two widely different races occupied the more habitable parts of the great Asiatic Continent, and as soon as they became too numerous to follow their nomadic ways of life without coming into collision with one another, began to struggle for the mastery. One of these races, the Mongolian, spreading westward from China, helped to displace the other race, the Aryan, already breaking into rival fragments, and branching out into independent nations and clusters of nations. From the Aryan stock sprang the Hindoos to the south of the Himalayas, and the successive colonies of Kelts, Teutons, Italians, Greeks, and others, who gradually took possession of the chief portions of Europe. The Slavonic tribes, more numerous but less open to civilizing agencies than most of the others, formed one of these families. The vast tract of country now known as European Russia was in course of time appropriated by them, before or during the period of the Roman Empire, and at a later date some branches of them stretched southward, and established themselves among the ruins of the Byzantine Empire that had succeeded to the effete rule of Rome in the East. Meanwhile, the Mongol race had in its turn broken up into separate nations and clusters of nations, of which the Tartars were the most lawless and daring. The newly-founded religion of Mahomet, especially favoured by them and their kinsmen, gave cohesion and increased ferocity to these Tartars, and after various nations of them had overrun and mastered the territories between the Himalayas and the Mediterranean, we find some tribes crossing the Caucasus and encroaching on the Russian Slavs, while the most desperate and adventurous of them all, the Ottoman Turks, aspired to the conquest of the European provinces still under the nominal sway of the Byzantine emperors, and also now protected by the Slavs. Hence it was that the far more remote struggle between Mongols and Aryans in Asia was reproduced in Europe by their descendants, the Tartars and Slavs.

The new struggle began in the thirteenth century. The Russian, or Muscovite, Empire dates from the year 862; but it had no solid existence till seven hundred years later. Grand dukes, grand princes, and kings, without number, ruled, or attempted to rule, over the disorganized barbarians who were thinly scattered over the immense territory, but it was really torn asunder by rival factions of freebooters and military aggressors, who swarmed in every generation. Indeed, the solidification of the nation only began in consequence of the necessity of union among the Slavs to resist the Tartar invaders, and the resistance was not successful until they had endured the Tartar oppression for more than two centuries. The Golden Horde, as it was called, invaded Muscovy, and burnt Moscow in 1240. It swept over all the central and southern parts of the country, conquered Poland, ravaged Hungary, and was barely prevented from seizing Germany as well. The then Grand Prince of Russia only secured for himself a continuance of nominal authority by becoming a tributary of the Tartar conqueror, and his successors had to submit to this galling yoke until 1481, when the revolt of Ivan the Threatening was successful, and the last Khan of the Golden Horde was killed in battle. Ivan the Threatening's grandson, Ivan the Terrible, was the first Czar of Russia, and from his time to the time of Peter the Great, amid frequent civil war and almost constant anarchy, the nation slowly grew; but more than that century and a half were needed for its recovery from the oppression which left in the mind of every patriotic Russian a bitter hatred of all Tartars, and all of the Tartar's kindred and religion. It is not strange that the chief objects of that hatred should have been, and should still be, the Turks, who had in the meanwhile conquered Constantinople, and established in Europe a dominion which extended to the Russian frontier, and that, along with their hatred of the Turks, should have been maintained a yearning to deliver from Turkish tyranny their own less fortunate kinsmen and fellow religionists south of the Danube.

It was in 1321, about eighty years after the invasion of Russia by the Golden Horde, that the Ottoman Turks crossed the Bosphorus to make their first raid in Europe. It took them 130 years to conquer Constantinople; but before that final exploit was achieved they had overrun and mastered nearly all the country from the Black Sea to the Adriatic, from the Ægean to the Danube. The Moldavians and Wallachians, the Bulgarians, Servians, Bosnians, and others—most of them being of Slavonic origin, or containing a large admixture of Slavonic blood, and all belonging to the same religion as the Russian Slavs—had made far greater advances in civilization than their northern kinsfolk; but perhaps this civilization made their conquest all the easier, and they fell quickly under the dominion of the invaders. Of what nature that dominion was during the first three centuries or so, we shall read in these dark pages of Turkish history, and in the records of travellers' visits to the country. What it has continued to be in those provinces left to the uncontrolled authority of the Turks, the proccedings in Bulgaria and Bosnia some two or three years since show us only too vividly and painfully. Considerable modifications in the lot of the communities subject to the Ottomans have taken place, however, during the past century or more. This has been mainly due to the spread of civilizing influences from Western Europe, affecting to some extent the Turks themselves, and to a greater extent their rivals and enemies. Before the time of Peter the Great—that is, till about a century and a half ago—the Eastern half of Europe was European only in name. Under his hand the huge unwieldy Russian Empire first took some sort of orderly shape, and since his day it has steadily increased in size, and yet more in power. One consequence of its development has been the havoc committed by it among the disorganized communities outside its borders. Turkey furnished one cluster of these communities, till then very loosely bound together under the central authorities of the Sultans in Constantinople. The immediate effect of Russian aggrandizement upon the Porte has undoubtedly been to compel it to adopt a more vigorous policy— whether more prudent and statesmanlike, or more reckless and tyrannical, we need not say—towards the inhabitants in the several provinces under its own set of statesmen or tyrants; the result has been a gradual breaking off of those provinces in which the aggravated misgovernment, instead of strengthening the allegiance of the inhabitants, has bred so much fresh resistance and confusion that they could no longer be controlled by the central authority, and which, invoking and obtaining Russian aid, have secured their partial independence.

It is not to be supposed that the aid thus given by Russia to the Moldavians, Wallachians, Servians, and Greeks has been wholly disinterested, or based exclusively upon sympathies of race and religion; but, whatever may have been the motives prompting the Czars and statesmen, it is evident that sympathies of race and religion, joined

INTRODUCTION. 5

with hatred and jealousy of the Turks, have always been powerful among the Russian people. From the earliest times of which we have records about them, the Slavonians in Russia have looked upon the whole country from the White Sea down to the Black Sea as theirs by right. As far back as the year 904 we find them invading Constantinople, and before any separate Slavonic communities had been planted south of the Danube, aiming to gain possession of the district. When the Greek Empire had crumbled away, and the Russian grand princes became the heads of the Greek Church, their desire to gain the holy city of their religion gave new zest to their political ambition. Ever since they have freed themselves from Mahometan oppressors, and have seen Constantinople in the hands of Mahometans, their ambition, religious as well as political, has been yet further intensified. Ivan the Threatening's triumph over the Golden Horde, and his expulsion of the Tartars from Russia, were followed, as a matter of course, by Ivan the Terrible's victories over the Tartars in their own territories, and his invasion of the Crimea, at that time no part of Russia. All his successors who were not too much absorbed in internal quarrels carried on, or tried to carry on, the work, and Peter the Great most zealously of all. Peter's most sacred legacy to the nation that he really built up was the overthrow of Turkey. Catherine II. conquered the Crimea in 1771, and acquired Azoff in 1774. What Nicholas did, and attempted, during his long reign is well known. By the treaty of Akermann in 1826 he obtained Russian protection for Moldavia, Wallachia, and Servia. In conjunction with England he secured the independence of Greece in 1830. He embarked on the Crimean war in 1853. That there should have been so long a pause as one-and-twenty years in the conflict between Russia and Turkey is the fact to be wondered at, rather than that war should have been resumed so soon. It is a feud of races that, extending from time immemorial, can only terminate with the utter overthrow of one or other of them. As to which of the two is destined to be overthrown, that is a problem by no means easy of solution.

BOOK I.

CHAPTER I.

THE ORIGIN OF ISLAMISM—THE KORAN—ARAB CONQUESTS—THE EMPIRE OF THE KHALIFES TO THE ADVENT OF THE SELJUKIDES.

1. *Antagonism of the East and West.*

THE East and the West form two distinct worlds of populations, manners, beliefs, between which there has been perpetual hatred and strife, which have sought, down to the present time, to invade and dominate each other. The remote ages saw that antagonism marked chiefly by the invasions of the Persians into Greece, invasions gloriously repulsed by the European victories of Salamis and Marathon; then came the reaction of the West upon the East by the conquests of Alexander, which was continued and completed by the Roman domination. Western Asia seemed then for ever acquired to civilization; barbarism, driven back within the unknown table-lands of Thibet, was henceforward impotent to invade Europe; the Mediterranean, that sea which unites and separates the East and the West, became solely an European sea; finally, Christianity, given by the conquered to the conquerors, in uniting them by the surest of all bonds, appeared to have consummated for ever the work of pacification commenced by arms. That pacification was not, however, definitive : neither the Roman power nor the Christian faith had succeeded in blending those two natures so opposed to each other, and when the Roman world divided itself into Eastern Empire and Western Empire, the struggle commenced.

It manifested itself at first by the creeds: Christianity

separated itself into rival Churches ; that of the East was speedily vitiated by the sophistical and disputatious spirit, the subtle and allegorical imagination, the frivolous and corrupt manners of Greece ; it wandered into the most dangerous controversies, into errors which caused the human race to relapse into the paths of the past; finally, it became the mother of numerous sects, daughters of ancient philosophic schools, and which seemed all to have one thought in common, the negation more or less veiled of the divinity of Jesus Christ. That fatal thought, which made of Christianity only a non-revealed and an invented religion, with the mental reservation that a better-inspired legislator might some day bring forward one more perfect, was destined to give birth to a supreme heresy or new religion—*Islamism*, for Islamism is no other than a bastard Christianity, incomplete and barbarous, the offspring of the heresies of Arius, Eutychus, and Nestorius.

2. *Mahomet, the Koran, its Dogmas and Precepts.*

A man of marvellous genius, Mahomet, born in 570, having seen that state of the East, announced himself as sent from God to explain the laws of Moses and of Christ, and to continue their work ; he said that the Gospel had been the way of salvation during six centuries, but that, the Christians having forgotten the laws of their founder, he was the *Paraclete* whose coming had been predicted, the last and most perfect of the prophets ;* consequently, he resumed in his doctrine the Arian, Nestorian, and Eutychian heresies, mixed them up with Jewish practices, adjusted them to Arab manners, and proclaimed the *Unity of God alone*. It was not a new religion that he announced, but the old religion of Moses and of Jesus, purified and transformed.

Mahomet at first had in view, when he founded his doctrine, only Arabia, his native country, then plunged into the wildest idolatry, and that religion was, in fact, an

* The *seal* of all the prophets, says the Koran.

immense benefit to it, as for all the barbarous countries that adopted it. " What you said of our poverty, of our divisions, of our barbarous condition," said an Arab deputy to the Persian King Yezdedjerd, "was just formerly. Yes, we were so miserable, that men amongst us were seen to sustain themselves upon insects and serpents, some put their daughters to death to avoid sharing their food with them. Plunged in the darkness of superstition and idolatry, lawless and uncurbed, for ever enemies of one another, we were only occupied with mutually pillaging and destroying ourselves. That is what we have been; we are now a new people. God has raised up in the midst of us a man, the most distinguished among Arabs by the nobility of his birth, by his virtues, by his genius, and has chosen him to be His envoy and His prophet. By the organs of that man, God has said to us: 'I am the One Eternal God, Creator of the Universe. My benevolence sends you a guide to direct your steps; the way that he points out to you will save you from the punishments which I reserve in another life for the impious and the cruel, and will lead you near Me in the regions of bliss.' We have believed in the prophet's mission; we have recognized that his words were the words of God; his commands the commands of God; the religion that he announced to us the only true religion. He has enlightened our minds, he has extinguished our hatreds, he has united us in a society of brotherhood under laws dictated by divine wisdom."* The truth of that eulogium bestowed by the Arab people upon its benefactor cannot be denied: Mahomet civilized Arabia. Religion, morals, legislation, society, all was contained in the scattered chapters of the Koran, source of all law, principle of all duty; Mussulman society sprang from it in its entirety. Therefore do the Mussulmans profess the most profound veneration for that sacred book; they never open it but with tokens of respect; they read it, they cite and apply it, unceasingly; they inscribe verses from it everywhere upon the walls of their mosques and in the interior of their houses; it is the guide of all their

* "Tabari," ii. 272.—Ibn-Khaldoun, f. 194.

actions, the constant rule of their whole life, their sole book. And the hundred and fourteen chapters or *surat* revealed to the prophet are not only graven in the memory of the believers: their spirit breathes in all their institutions, manners, thoughts. The Koran is for the Mussulmans very nearly what the Bible was for the Hebrews, and much more than what the Gospel is for the Christians: it embraces all the relations of political life, civil and religious, and regulates alike the conscience of individuals and the duties of the State, the government of nations and the details of the household.

Islamism encloses, in reality, only a single dogma, the unity of God, a dogma which dominates and fecundates all the new religion, and which must have appeared like light itself at that epoch, when the Greek heresies had obscured and even dishonoured it. "God is one," said Mahomet, "and the God eternal. He has not begot and is not begotten. He has no equal." In placing Jesus in the front rank of prophets, in acknowledging his miracles and his divine mission, in treating his mother as a *holy and immaculate virgin*, he rejects as idolatry the Trinity of the Christians.

To the dogma of the unity of God, Islamism adds the immortality of the soul and future rewards. The tortures of hell, the joys of paradise, are represented, in the Koran, by coarse imagery; but, after having described the material delights reserved for the just man, Mahomet adds: "The most favoured of God will be he who shall behold his face night and morning: that is a happiness which transcends all the pleasures of the senses, as the ocean surpasses a drop of dew."

The worship is, like the dogma, of an extreme simplicity: no mysteries, no altars, no images of any kind, not even priests.* The practice of Islamism consists solely in prayers, alms, fasting, in ablutions which are hygienic obligations appropriate to the climate. Prayer is an essential duty: it is offered up five times daily—at sunrise, at

* "No priesthood in Islam," the Koran says formally. We shall see how a clergy was formed with the *ulemas.*

noon, at three o'clock, at sunset, at night. The *muezzin* proclaims the hours of those five prayers by crying from the top of the towers or minarets of the mosques: "God is great! I attest that there is only one God! I attest that Mahomet is God's prophet. Come to prayer! Come to salvation! God is great!" It is the formula of announcement, *edhan*, adopted by the prophet. The face of the Mussulman in prayer must always be turned towards Mecca. Finally, circumcision, borrowed from the Jews, the sanctification of Friday, the fast of Rhamadan, resembling the Christian Lent, abstinence from wine, from blood and the flesh of pork, are other external practices imposed upon Mussulmans.

But Mahomet did not reduce religion to those external signs. "The flesh and blood of victims," he said himself, "ascend not up to God; it is your piety that reaches him."*

"Virtue consists not in turning one's face during prayer towards the East or the West, but believing in God and the last day, in the Book and the prophets; in giving for the love of God, in succouring one's parents, the indigent and the traveller, in ransoming captives, in observing prayer, in doing charity, in keeping one's engagements, by showing oneself patient in adversity, in times of hardship and violence. Those who do thus are just and God-fearing."†

"Prayer," said the Khalife Omar, "conducts us half-way towards God; fasting leads us to the gate of His palace; charity allows us to enter therein." Alms are obligatory; they are fixed for each individual at a tenth (*zecat*) of his possessions. Those whose liberalities are conferred through ostentation will derive no profit from their work. Praiseworthy if they exercise charity publicly, believers will be the more so every time that they practise it in secret.‡ Hospitality is in the same way prescribed by law and practised with the same simplicity.

The consequence of that universal charity, to be found

---

* Surat xxii. v. 38. † Surat ii. v. 172.
‡ Surat ii. v. 266 and following.

in every page of the Koran, is a feeling of equality and fraternity which is as profound in the manners as in the law, and the basis of all Mussulman society. "There are neither princes nor beggars in Islamism," said the first Khalife; "there are only Mussulmans." No nobility, no castes, no classes, no privileges, no distinctions; the lowest and poorest of believers ascends quite naturally to the highest functions of the State by his intelligence or his virtue; he descends thence without shame, and thus returns simply into his poverty.

Thus, as will be seen, the morality of the Koran is the morality of the Gospel, and in all questions which do not touch upon dogma, that book is almost always accordant with Christianity: it recommends the forgiveness of injuries, love of one another, good faith even towards infidels; it curses pride, anger, and especially hypocrisy; but with a contradiction that is not rare in its code, it admits of revenge, the *lex talionis*, evil for evil. Notwithstanding that, and to sum up, it may be said that the law of Mahomet is only a plagiarism of the Gospel accommodated to the barbarous manners of Arabia. "Thus," remarks an historian of the Middle Ages, "it would be more exact to call its votaries heretics than unbelievers; but custom has prevailed." *

3. *Errors of the Koran.*

If Mahomet approaches Christianity through its morality, he separates himself from it by three grand errors, which dominate and characterise his doctrine, which open an abyss of separation between Christians and Mussulmans, which are the cause of the immobility of the latter in face of the progressive advance of the former, which in short includes the whole secret of the destinies of Islamism. Those three errors are: the confusion of the civil and the religious law, fatal predestination, the abasement and plurality of women.

* Jacques de Vitry, "Histoire des Croisades," liv. i.

1. The Koran is asserted to be a work inspired by God, perfect and immutable, and, as it is a political and civil as well as a religious code, it follows that nothing can be changed in the social order, such as the Koran has regulated it, without impiety and sacrilege.* What Christianity has separated, God and Cæsar, the spiritual power and the temporal power, is thus found reunited and confounded, and the concentration of those two powers has brought about despotism. Moreover, the Koran having only been announced by Mahomet in fragments, and during a space of twenty-three years, contains numerous contradictions; and its interpretation is not confided to a supreme and infallible authority, but to the judgment of the *ulemas*, learned or literate, whom the Khalifes, overwhelmed by temporal affairs, have charged with religious and judicial functions which they can no longer fulfil: those ulemas, which have become a very powerful body, have every interest to let the civil law be confounded with the religious, and, consequently, are opposed to any change and all reform.

2. Fatal predestination is inscribed even in the name of the religion, *Islam*, "abandoned of God," and in that of his votaries, *Moslem*, resigned to God. "The elect, as the reprobate," says Mahomet, "is predestined to happiness or woe eternal, being yet the one and the other in the bosom of their mother." "Among mankind, many a one will be reprobate, many a one blessed." "Man dies only by the will of God, according to the book which fixes the term of his life."† And that terrible dogma regards not only individuals, but nations. "Every people has its time," says the Koran; "when the term has come, men can neither recede nor advance." It is this dogma which must inspire its votaries with the blind spirit of conquest, contempt of death, fanaticism; but also with the stolid submission to despotism, political apathy, the

* Numerous examples might be cited. Thus, in these recent times, the Ottoman Government could only introduce vaccination and quarantine into the Empire by combatting popular prejudices through the aid of an interpretation more or less exact of the Koran.
† Surat xii. v. 32.

resistance to all reform, immobility. The *ulemas*, however, relying upon the authority of the old *imans*, have repeatedly declared that predestination regards only the future life, and that the Koran leaves man all his freewill; but that belief is instinctive in the manners and ideas of the Mussulmans; it pleases them, it agrees with their careless nature, with their innate recklessness, their oriental life; it gives them, moreover, in adversity, a singular dignity, and inspires the poor and unfortunate with contentment with their lot, the absence of all envy, a resignation which has something of the evangelic.

Mahomet counsels, as laudable, the restricting oneself to one wife, but he permits the taking of four legitimate, and as many illegitimate or slaves as can be supported. The offspring of those diverse unions were equal.* Women might be purchased; they were repudiated at the will of the husband; they lived continually shut up; they received no instruction; they had no dowry; they were, in short, only instruments of pleasure. Polygamy, doubtless, is only practised in the East by comparatively a few men —those only capable of supporting the expenses and luxury of a *harem;* but the principle of the abasement of women shows itself not the less in the manners, with all their consequences—that is to say, in the imperfect condition of the family. However, it must be owned that Mahomet ameliorated the condition of women, who, before him, were, in Arabia, treated as animals. "Men," said he, "you have rights over your women, and your women have rights over you. Their duty is not to sully your couch by an adulterous intercourse: if they fail therein, God permits you to no longer cohabit with them, and to beat them, but not so far as to deprive them of life. If they conduct themselves well, you ought to nourish and clothe them suitably. Treat them with kindness and affection. They have delivered up their persons to you, trusting in God, and that is a trust which God has confided to you."†

* Caussin de Perceval, "Histoire des Arabes," t. iii. Œlsner, "Des Effets de la Religion de Mahomet sur l'Esprit, les Mœurs et le Gouvernement des Peuples," &c.
† Surat—Vaçoul, f. 258.

Before his time, the father of a family put his daughters to death when he found them burthensome; but, one day, one of his principal chiefs, converted to Islamism, found him holding on his knees a little girl, whom he was caressing. "What is that little lamb you are petting?" asked the Arab. "It is my child," replied the prophet. "By heaven," rejoined Cays, son of Acim, "I have had many little girls like that, but I have buried them all alive." Mahomet abolished that execrable custom. He commanded children to show love, respect, and humility to their mother, more especially still towards their father. "O, Mussulmans!" said he, "the kiss given by a child to its mother equals in sweetness that which we shall impress upon the sill of paradise. A daughter wins paradise at the feet of her mother."

The Koran having been, originally, an immutable rule, destined for a particular race, the three-fold error that we have pointed out had not at first grave consequences; the union of the religious and civil power was so conformable to the habitudes of patriarchal life, fatalism so consonant to the slothful nature of the Arab, the plurality of wives so suitable to his gross and voluptuous habits, that those prescriptions were proper to maintain order and tranquillity in a nation whose exceptional position seemed to have destined it to a perpetual immobility. Islamism, semi-Christian, semi-barbarian, was the most purified religion that it could receive, and the legislation best appropriate to its genius, its manners, to all its conditions of existence. Transported among a people of a different genius, upon whom the vicinage of Europe imposed a more active life, those principles must have produced the most fatal results. The history of the Mussulman states is, therefore, everywhere the same: a period of rapid conquests and great splendour, followed by a precocious and incurable decadence; everywhere feebleness and discord, inseparable from excess of absolute power, with a society which emits, at first, gleams of civilization; then becomes immobile, retrogrades, and descends by degrees to the semi-savage state. After having re-awakened the old struggle of the East and the West, after having precipitated the peoples into that struggle with an irresistible vigour, Islamism, "the religion of the sword," as soon as it had ceased to conquer, ceased to propagate itself; it did not subjugate the peoples in order to convert and render them better, but to ransom and dominate them. It founded nothing durable; it has everywhere shown itself impotent in face of the peaceful propaganda and progressive principles of Christianity. All the empires that Islam has successively raised up have disappeared, with the exception of three—Turkey, Persia, and Morocco—all three struck with decrepitude, and without hope, life, or future, save on condition of transforming themselves radically by the abandonment of the triple error contained in the code of Mahomet.

Let us return to history.

4. *Death of Mahomet.—Arab Conquests.*

Mahomet preached at first his doctrine at Mecca: he was persecuted there; condemned to death by the Sheik Abou-Sophian, he took refuge in Medina with his disciples (622). From that event dates the era of the Mahometans, called *hegira* or flight. Medina acknowledged the proscribed as prophet and sovereign. Then he declared that God ordered him to propagate his religion by the sword, "the sword," said he, "which opens heaven and hell." "Be humane and just among yourselves," said he to his followers; "all Mussulmans are brothers; but let not two religions subsist in Arabia: idolatry is worse than murder. The sacred months expired, slay the infidels everywhere that you may find them." At the end of ten years "the prophet, who was at once a torch to light the world, and a sword to strike the impious," had subjected all Arabia to his doctrines and his arms.

He did not stop there. "I have a mission," said he, "to fight the infidels until they cry: *There are none other Gods but God.* When they have pronounced those words, they have safeguarded their blood and their possessions from all injury on my part; as to their belief, they shall render account of it to God." He then divided the earth into two parts, *Dar-ul-Islam*, the house of Islam, and *Dar-ul-Harb*, the house of the war or country of the infidels, and he said to his followers: " Achieve my works, extend on all sides the house of Islam ; the house of war is for God, God gives it to you." That was a proclamation of the *jehad*, or state of permanent war, a state which might be suspended by treaties, but which subsists by law so long as there remains a single infidel unconverted to Islamism, or who has not consented to pay the tribute.* He traced even the plan of the conquest, regulated beforehand the condition of the conquered nations, and promised to the believers the possession of Constantinople. But at the moment when he was preparing to enter Syria at the head of an army, he died (632), leaving of his seventeen women only a daughter, named Fatima, married to the first of his disciples, Ali. His work accomplished itself after him : he had caused to pass into the souls of all his followers his warlike fanaticism. " The Mussulman," says the Koran, " is a soldier in the service of God; he enrols himself by conscience; the handling of arms is for him a religious act." Once under the standard, he cannot refuse to fight, even in a duel, when his chief commands. Desertion or refusal to contribute to the costs of the war are placed in the rank of the most odious of crimes. Children, fools and maniacs, are alone exempted from fighting; and, as war is a holy work, it ought only to be waged by holy men ; no games, no debauches, not even idle words in the camp of the faithful ; prayer must alone be a distraction from fighting.† " Fight," said Mahomet, " even to extermination. Some few among you will fall in the struggle ; for those who perish, paradise ; for the survivors, victory." *Paradise is in front of you—hell behind;* with those words alone, the successors of Mahomet hurried away the believers to the conquest of the East and the West.

The Arab chiefs elected to succeed Mahomet, his father-

* Ubicini, "Letters upon Turkey."
† Surat iv. v. 75, 79 ; ix. 38, 39, &c.

in-law, Abu-Bekr, who took the title of *Khalife y reçoul Allah*, vicar of the prophet of God; but Ali, son-in-law of Mahomet, protested against that election, and commenced the first schism of Islam. However, the holy war opened against the empire of the Greeks and that of the Persians, empires enfeebled by factions, defended by mercenary troops, divided by religious sects whose minds were favourable to Islamism. Mahomet had only been intolerant in Arabia, where he desired that his religion should reign undivided; but, in order to favour exterior conquests, he had recommended indulgence towards the *Kitabi*, or the peoples who had received *books*, that is to say, the Christians and Jews. "The nations," he had said, " who shall embrace your faith will be assimilated to yourselves; they will enjoy the same advantages, and will be subjected to the same duties; to those who shall desire to preserve their beliefs, impose only the obligation of declaring themselves your subjects and paying you tribute, in exchange for which you will cover them with your protection; but those who shall refuse to accept Islamism or the condition of tributaries, fight them even to extermination." Everywhere the disciples of Moses and of Jesus were therefore exhorted to admit "the more perfect revelation of Mahomet; everywhere the Christian heretics manifested a sincere and cordial attachment for the Mahometans."* Nestorians, Arians, Eutycheans, at the first summons, welcomed them as deliverers, hastened to embrace the new religion and stifle their discords in a new apostasy. As for those who were unwilling to renounce their faith, they adapted themselves readily to the conditions which the conquerors offered them.

Jerusalem was the first city rendered tributary (637), and the act which consecrated the submission of the Holy City served as a model for all the transactions of the Mussulmans with the peoples who, become *rayahs*, desired to preserve their religion by means of a tribute. The following were the principal clauses of the capitulation: The Christians shall pay an annual rent; they shall

* Gibbon, "Fall of the Roman Empire," vol. x. p. 335.

neither mount on horseback, nor carry arms, nor change garments; they shall not place the Cross upon their churches and shall not ring their bells; they shall not build new churches, neither in the city nor in its territory; they shall not hinder the Mussulmans from entering their churches, either day or night; they shall open to all passers and all travellers. If any Mussulman, being *en route*, passes by their city and sojourns therein, they shall be compelled to defray his expenses during the three first days of his arrival. *They shall not speak openly of their religion ;* they shall not engage any one to embrace it, and shall not hinder their relatives from becoming Mussulmans.*

These concessions, it is true, were often rendered illusory by the transports of a fanatical multitude; the Christians had to undergo a thousand insults, a thousand persecutions, the inevitable result of religious hatreds; they became, in fact, in spite of the law, the prey and sport of the conquerors; but it may be conceived that, in the origin, that spirit of tolerance with which the conquerors appeared animated must have singularly facilitated their progress.

Under Abu-Bekir (632–634), Chaldea was conquered, Syria invaded, the army of the Emperor of the East overcome; Damascus opened its gates to the victor. Three years after (637), Omar, second Khalife, who took the title of *Emir ul mouminin*, Commander of the Faithful, after having received the submission of Jerusalem, conquered Egypt. Othman, third Khalife, made the conquest of Persia (651), and the race of the Sassanides disappeared with the religion of the Magi; he began also the conquest of Africa. The fourth Khalife was Ali (655).

The Mahometans then divided themselves into two great sects, which still exist, hating each other as strongly as ever. The *shiites* regard the three first Khalifes as usurpers, and Ali as the true vicar of the Prophet; the *sunnites* pretend that sanctity has regulated the order of

* Cæsar Famin, "Histoire de la Rivalité et du Protectorat des Eglises Chrétiennes en Orient."

succession, and that Ali is inferior to his predecessors. Moreover, the first are less attached than the second to predestination, and, in admitting that the Koran has been *created*, believe that it is perfectible. The Turks of the present day are sunnites and the Persians shiites.

Notwithstanding the schism, the conquests continued, and the Koran propagated itself with a marvellous rapidity. Mesopotamia, Cilicia, the best part of Asia Minor, were subjected. In the year 32 of the hegira (654), the Arabs appeared under the walls of Constantinople. They returned thither in 668, guided by an old companion of the prophet, Eyoub, an octogenarian, who died during the siege, and whose tomb the Turks discovered later on in one of the suburbs.* The city, assaulted with fury, was only saved by the Greek fire invented for its defence. But the Mussulmans fell furiously upon that prey which was promised them. Before the end of the first century of the hegira, the capital of the Greek Empire had already been four times besieged, and it was only after twelve sieges and eight centuries of efforts that they succeeded in gaining possession of it.

5. *The First Khalifes, the Ommiades, and Abassides.*

During the glorious period of the *Perfect Khalifate* (as the Mussulmans designated the reign of the four first Khalifes), the Mussulmans showed themselves worthy of the cause to which they had consecrated their arms: they brought to the service of the God of Mahomet an indomitable courage and warlike virtues. That was the palmy time of Islamism. The Khalifes, elected by the whole of the faithful, subjected to the common law, having only the authority which they derived from the Koran, appear to us like the popular magistrates of ancient Rome. "You behold me charged with the care of governing you," said Abou-Bekr on assuming the possession of power; "if I

* The Mósque of Eyoub, wherein the Sultans now gird on the sword of Osman, was erected over his tomb.

do well, assist me; if I do ill, set me up again in the right way. To speak the truth to a depository of public authority is an act of zeal and of devotion; to conceal it from him is a treason. Before me the weak man and the powerful man are equal; I would render impartial justice to all. If I ever should deviate from the laws of God and his prophet, I shall cease to have the right to your obedience."

The first chiefs of Islamism, faithful to the example of Mahomet, lived with the greatest simplicity. The believers loved to see the prophet shear his sheep, or seated on the ground, mending with his own hand his woollen vestments and his shoes, lighting his fire, sweeping out his chamber, in order to be entirely his own help-mate.* Abou-Bekr, who was a merchant, continued, during the six first months of his Khalifate, to support his family with the produce of his commerce. Afterwards, he applied himself exclusively to State affairs, and drew daily from the public treasury that which was necessary for his wants. Before his death, he ordered a calculation to be made of the sums thus placed at his disposal. They amounted to eight thousand drachmas. "I bequeath to the Mussulmans," said he, "the land that I possess, as an indemnity for the expenses that I have occasioned them."† Omar, on quitting Medina, in order to receive the submission of Jerusalem, set forth in the most modest guise. Clad in a coarse garment, attended by one slave only, he mounted a camel laden with two sacks, the one containing barley, the other dates; before him was a leather-bottle filled with water, behind him a large wooden platter

In 661 the *Perfect Khalifate* ceased, as well as the patriarchal simplicity and the elective rule which characterized it. Moaviah, whose father, Abou-Sophian, had persecuted Mahomet, revolted against Ali, caused him to be assassinated, took the title of Khalife, which he rendered hereditary in his family, and commenced the dynasty of the *Beni-Ummahié* or *Ommiades*, which gave fourteen

* Aboulfeda, "Life of Mahomet," translated by Desvergers, p. 95.
† "Tabari," ii. 152.

Khalifes during ninety years. The empire of Islam then underwent a great change. The Ommiades placed reliance chiefly on the Syrians; Damascus became the capital of Islamism; the Arab element ceased to predominate; the Khalifes adopted the manners of the conquered peoples; the Mussulmans began to grow corrupt, to despise the too severe practices enjoined by the Koran; numerous sects were formed and sought to triumph by civil war, persecution, and assassination. Nevertheless, their conquests continued; Northern Africa was subjected; Carthage definitely destroyed; the Empire of the East parcelled out on its frontiers; the Koran overspread Khouaresm, Bokhara, Sinde, &c.; finally, before the end of the first century of the hegira, Arab domination had attained its extreme limits. It extended itself—in Africa, from the Isthmus of Suez to the Straits of Gibraltar; in Europe, in the Iberian peninsula, and in the isles of the Mediterranean; in Asia, from the Red Sea, from the coasts of Syria and the slopes of the Caucasus to the steppes of Turkestân, to the banks of the Indus and the Persian Gulf.

But the conquering march of Islam was about, for the first time, to find itself arrested by the hand of a people destined to play a great part in the history of the Mahommedan empires, and whose glorious name had already reached the ears of the Arabs.

With Islamism the struggle between the East and the West had recommenced, and the West, under the sabre of the votaries of the Koran, found itself already encroached upon. Masters of Spain, they sought to penetrate into Gaul, to pass thence into Italy, and from Italy to Constantinople. The empire of the Cæsars, thus taken in reverse, might be easily destroyed. But, if the Romans no longer existed, there was then a people who appeared to have succeeded them in the domination of the West— the Franks. Alone of all the barbarians who had invaded the Roman Empire, they had secured for themselves a future in embracing Catholicism, in defending the Latin Church, of which they called themselves the eldest sons, in preserving amidst the wreck of the ancient civilization their warlike and conquering strength. Their renown was so great that alone it had already arrested an Arab army. In fact, at the fourth siege that Constantinople underwent on the part of the Arabs, in 718, the Greeks, seeing themselves lost, had spread a report that the dominators of the West were hastening with a fleet and an army for their deliverance, and upon that rumour the siege had been raised. However, the Mussulmans entered Gaul full of pride and confidence; but they found at Tours the Frankish *hammer* (Charles Martel) who crushed them, and the Asiatic invasion was for ever arrested by that liberating victory. They kept, nevertheless, one foot in Gaul; they continued to dominate Spain; they essayed to conquer Italy; but everywhere, during a century, they encountered the sword of the Franks, which drove them out of Gaul, thrust them back into Spain, restrained them in Italy.

As a result of these events, the unity of the empire and of the religion of Mahomet was broken up. In 752 the dynasty of the Ommiades was despoiled of the Khalifate, and destroyed by the *Abassides*, descendants of the prophet's uncle. A single scion of the Ommiades escaped from the massacre of his family, sought refuge in Spain, and there founded at Cordova an independent Khalifate.

With the Abassides the empire of Islam took a new form; the domination passed to the peoples of Khorassan and Chaldea; the seat of the empire was transferred to those plains which had seen the great empires of antiquity, at first to Kouffa, then to Bagdad, and there it remained during five hundred years; the Koran, forgotten under the Ommiades, was restored to such honour that it was declared " uncreated "—that is to say, divine and immutable. Religious zeal was reborn; but, friend of the marvellous, it enveloped Islam and its founder with legends and miracles; the Khalifes became absolute sovereigns, despotic, feared, and venerated, even to adoration; the age of luxury, of light, and of Arab civilization commenced and produced, besides edifices of a perfect elegance, works in mathematics, philosophy, astronomy, and geography, which enlighted the world during centuries.

Among the Abasside Khalifes—the one who personifies for us that age so remarkable in the history of the East —is Haroun-al-Raschid, with whom we are acquainted especially, owing to his relations with Charlemagne.

The Franks, since the battle of Poitiers, had become for the Mussulmans, as they had already been for the Christians, the great people of the West. Islamism knew Europe only under the name of *Frangistan* or *Frankistan*— the country of the Franks—a name which the Orientals had not yet ceased to give it. Pacific relations commenced with the Arabs, and which had principally for object those Christians of Asia whom the Cæsars of Byzantium were henceforth incapable of defending.

Charlemagne filled the West with his glory, when the Patriarch of Jerusalem claimed his aid against the infidels who profaned the Holy Places. He warmly responded to those complaints, sent large sums of money into Palestine to be applied to the restoration of the churches; then he despatched an ambassador with presents to the Khalife Haroun, praying him to look upon the Christians indulgently. The Khalife, who had need of the alliance of the Cæsar of the West against the schismatic Mussulmans of Spain, answered his letters by sending him the keys of the Holy Sepulchre, as a testimony that he abandoned the sovereignty of the places consecrated by the death of Christ. Then, says Eginhard, Charles took openly under his protection the Christians beyond seas. He caused an hospitium to be built at Jerusalem for pilgrims, and even endowed it with a library; finally, he concluded with Haroun commercial treaties, by which tariffs of duties were fixed and places of safety assigned for the Frank merchants in Egypt and Syria. These conventions were respected for at least fifty years; for we find that in the ninth century the inhabitants of Lyons and Marseilles had, at Alexandria, factors who sent into Europe all the merchandize of Asia. A Frank bazaar was established at Jerusalem. Finally, the troops of pilgrims who turned their faces annually towards the Holy Places became veritable caravans of commerce.

The era of the Abassides marks the end of the Arab conquests. Islamism retired within its Eastern possessions, and at the same time the empire was dismembered into several independent states—independent so far as the peoples newly converted to Islamism restored to it its warlike and aggressive spirit.

It has been already said that Spain had its Khalifate at Cordova. In the ninth century, Mauritania, under the Madratites; Libya, under the Aglabites; Transoxiana, under the Samanides; the Khorassan, under the Taherides and afterwards under the Soffarides, formed separate states, scarcely acknowledging the religious sovereignty of the Khalifes of Bagdad. In the middle of the tenth century the greater part of Persia obeyed the Boujides; Georgia, Armenia, and Syria, were independent or only nominally subjected to the authority of the Prophet's vicars, and the latter had no longer any real power save at Bagdad, in Mesopotamia and in Arabia. The most considerable of these States was that of the Fatimites or descendants of Ali, who after having long sought to overthrow the Abassides, reunited all the Shiites of northern Africa, and ended by conquering Egypt; they founded (968) at Cairo an independent Khalifate, which waged against that of Bagdad a furious war; then they seized upon Syria and were acknowledged by a portion of Arabia.

In that dismemberment the history of the Abassides is merely a monstrous narrative of revolts, cruelties, battles, executions and barbarities of every kind; twenty-eight Khalifes perished by violence. Finally a new people appeared, who played a great part in the empire of the Abassides, and who was destined one day to succeed to their inheritance: these were the Turks.

CHAPTER II.

FROM THE ADVENT OF THE SELJUKIDES TO THAT OF THE OTTOMANS.

1. *Origin of the Turks.—Decadence of the Khalifate.*

THE Turks were probably the primitive inhabitants of those countries comprised between the Caspian Sea, the Altai Mountains, the Ourals and Thibet, still known at the present day by the name of Turkestân. Thence have emerged, at different epochs, the barbarian peoples who have invaded the West—those devastating hordes of Mongol-Tartars, Kirgis, and Calmucks, nations of the same origin, which we confound under the general denomination of Tartars, and of which the Turk family appears to have been a considerable fraction. Probably the name of Turk has been, at certain epochs, a generic name common to all those tribes. The Ottomans, to whom we apply it at the present time, repudiate it. They do not call themselves Turks, unless they apply the term to each other in disparagement, as denoting uncouthness or barbarism; whilst they take pride in the name of Osmanli from the bygone splendour of that line, and although the family of their princes may be perhaps that which appears with the greatest certitude to descend from the ancient inhabitants of Turkestân, they will only commence their history at Othman, the illustrious founder of their dynasty.

The Osmanli are a branch of the Turks in the larger meaning of the word. The Turks, a race distinguished from other nations by their language, customs, and physical character, are now thinly spread over an immense extent of Asia, from the Desert of Gobi to the shores of the Mediterranean, and from the northern part of Siberia to the Persian Gulf. In some parts, as in South Siberia, in Turkestân, and in the greater part of Asia Minor, they form a compact population; in others, as in Syria, Armenia, and Mesopotamia, they are much less numerous than the original inhabitants. In Europe, the Turkish population is compact in Roumelia, and in the government of Kazan, and some adjacent tracts in Eastern Russia. In Africa there are only a few Osmanli Turks.

According to an ancient legend, Oghuz Khan, the son of Kárá-Khan, a descendant of Turk, the common ancestor of all the Turks, was a mighty king in the time of Abraham. His kingdom was the country called Turkestân, known to the Persians by the name of Turán. The legend says that Oghuz had six sons. He sent them one day to the chase, as though in search of their future destiny. They brought back to him a bow and arrows which they had found. The father gave the bow to the three eldest, and the three arrows to the youngest; of the latter each took one, but the first three broke the bow, and each kept a piece of it. Oghuz called the eldest "Bosuk" (*the breakers*), and the youngest "Utschok" (*the three arrows*). He confided to the first the right wing, and to the others the left wing of his army. Under his successors the kingdom was divided. Three khans, "the three arrows," ruled over the eastern Oghuzes, and extended their dominions towards China; three other khans, "the three breakers," were masters over the western Oghuzes, around the Oxus and the Jaxartes. The first of these "three breakers" was the "Khan of the Mountains;" he is the ancestor of the younger *Oghuzes*, or that sept of the Oghuzes who preserved their name in later times, and of the Turkomans. The second was the "Khan of the Sea," the ancestor of the *Seljuks;* and the third was the "Khan of the Heaven," the ancestor of the tribe Kayi, from which are descended the *Osmanli*. These three tribes ultimately embraced Islamism, and played successively an important part in the history of the Mussulman States.*

* To each of the six heirs of Oghuz the legend gives four sons, who became the chiefs of twenty-four Turkish tribes. "Von Hammer," tom i. p. 7.

ORIGIN OF THE TURKS.

The Eastern Turks (*Oïgours*) spread themselves through the steppes, where they are still cantonned. Conquered by Zinghis-Khan, they bore, in the Middle Ages, the names of *Usbegs*, in memory of a chief of the family of the Mogul conqueror; but Usbegs or Oïgours, and although separated from their Western brothers by the whole extent of Persia, they have always remained in relations of alliance with them against their common enemies, the Persians; they speak even yet a language that is recognized as being of the same family as the dialect of the Ottomans, and which the latter call the *Old Turkish*.

The Western Turks occupy the portions of Turkestân nearest the borders of Persia and the Caspian Sea; they gave birth to three principal tribes: the *Oghuzes*, the *Seljukides*, and the *Ottomans*, whose chiefs claimed direct descent from the three eldest sons of Oghus, from the three khans of "the right wing."

All the Turkish tribes who have enacted a conspicuous part in history embraced at an early period the Mahommedan religion; their dialects have in consequence been more or less modified by an admixture of Persian and Arabic, and their historical traditions are those common to all Moslems.

Leaving, however, the other Turkish tribes to divide and diffuse themselves, some into Turkestân, to which they gave their name, others along the shore of the Caspian Sea and the valleys of Armenia, we shall restrict this history mainly to that branch of those Turks who, after having adopted Islamism and traversed Syria, conquered step by step Asia Minor and ultimately founded the Ottoman Empire.

Before tracing the rapid rise to power of that conquering race, it may be well to preface the narrative by a brief retrospect of that portion of the Christian era which preceded the birth of the rival faith of Islamism, with a glance at its early progress and gradual extension during three centuries following upon the death of the founder.

The Roman Empire at its greatest extent, during the age of the Antonines (A.D. 96—180), may be said to have taken in all the old world within the Rhine, the Danube, the Tigris, and Euphrates, and the great desert of Africa. Behind the Rhine and the Danube were the Franks, the Germans, and the Goths, and other Teutonic tribes, who were destined to overthrow the fabric of the Roman Empire in Europe; and behind the Tigris and Euphrates were the Parthians and Persians, the great rivals of Rome in Asia. Three centuries more (A.D. 476), and Odoacer, the King of the Heruli, had taken Rome, and the fall of the Western Empire was completed. But Rome still ruled the Eastern Empire from Constantinople, and Rome and Persia still contended along the border lands of the Tigris and Euphrates for the supremacy of Asia, where the memory of their rivalry lingers in the spell which the mighty names *tremendæ majestatis* of Cæsar and of Chosroes yet, after twelve centuries, exercise over the tranced nations of the East.

It was at the commencement of the seventh century that the tribe and family of Mahomet obtained the sovereignty of Mecca, and the guardianship of the Caaba, and a series of events was set in motion in the heart of Arabia which was to result in a succession of the most stupendous religious and political revolutions the world has ever witnessed. Within one hundred years from the death of Mahomet every nation and tribe of the old Roman and Persian world, from India and the confines of China to France and Spain, was almost simultaneously assailed by the Saracen Arabs. The empire of Chosroes fell at a blow. Syria, Egypt, and all the Greek possessions in Asia and Africa were subjugated almost as rapidly. For a thousand years, from the first Arab irruption in 664, until Baber founded the Mongol Empire of Delhi in 1526, and which lasted, in form at least, to 1857, the history of India is chiefly occupied with the struggles of the Hindoo races against their Mahommedan conquerors of various tribes. In the thirteenth century the Golden Horde under Baton, a grandson of Zinghis Khan, overran and barbarised Russia. And two centuries later, when the Moors were being driven out of Spain, after it had been

ARCH OF CHOSROES.

held for 700 years by the Saracens and Moors, the imperial rule of the Ottoman Turks was, on the final ruin of the Eastern Empire, permanently established in Constantinople. When the second Chosroes, at the height of his power and glory, was contemplating with pride the great Artemita which he had built, and all its fabulous treasures, he received a letter from Mahomet, then an obscure citizen of Mecca, despised and rejected of his own family and his fellow-townsmen, bidding the Persian king of kings acknowledge him as the Prophet of God. Chesroes tore the letter in pieces. "It is thus," exclaimed Mahomet, when it was told him, " that God will rend *his* kingdom, and reject *his* supplications." Eight centuries before his prophetic vision was fulfilled, he looked forward to the fall of Constantinople as the secular triumph of Islam. The faithful were never to rest until it was gained, and he promised the absolution of all their sins to the first army of his followers which should enter the city of the Cæsars and the metropolis of Christianity. For a thousand years, indeed, it was a life and death struggle between Christendom and Islam for the mastery of Europe. When the empire of the Saracens was destroyed at Bagdad by the Mongols, and at Cordova by the Moors, the hordes of Mongols, Turks, and Moors continued the Mahommedan attacks on Europe, as they continued and extended them in Asia.

We will now return for an instant to that period of Mahommedan history which is embraced by the Khalifate of Bagdad, subsequent to the rise of the Abbasside dynasty (the descendants of Abbas, Mahomet's uncle), during which the fatal policy of embodying the nucleus of a standing army of Turkish mercenaries, and their conversion to Islamism, was the signal of the overthrow of the Empire of the Arabs and the Khalifate. Long before this, however—between A.D. 499 and 678—successive hordes of those barbarians had passed from Central Asia across the Volga into Europe, where they effected a permanent settlement between the Danube and the Balkan mountains. These were the Volgarians or Bulgars. But the Turks, who took possession of the dominions of the Eastern Khalifate and Eastern Empire, came into Syria and Asia Minor across the Oxus and Jaxartes. One of these Turks was Seljuk, the founder of the second of the great Turkish dynasties of Persia, and ever since his days the Turks—first the Seljukides and then the Ottomans—have ruled in Western Asia, and the Indian Mongols traced their ancestry to the same imperial race.

The usurpation of the Ommïades and that of the Fatimites tore away from the Abbassides all the Western provinces of their empire. They were able to retain only their Asiatic possessions. Almanzor, the founder of Bagdad, Haroun-Al-Raschid, and Al-Mamoun, are the three great names of the Eastern Khalifate.

The Khalife Motassem, third son of Haroun-Al-Raschid, and twenty-seventh Khalife, who died in 842, had remarked the decline of enthusiasm, the falling off in the courage and even of the bodily strength of his subjects, from the time that all noble objects had ceased to be presented to their ambition or their activity. As mentioned above, Motassem, in order to supply the want of the military element, sent to Turkestân to purchase young slaves bred in the mountain region of the Caucasus, whom he trained to the profession of arms, and formed into a body-guard, to which he entrusted the protection of his palace. These troops soon became numerous and formidable. Their strength and courage distinguished them among a people grown effeminate by luxury; and that jealousy of disaffection among his native subjects so natural to an Eastern monarch, might be an additional motive with the Khalife Motassem to form bodies of guards out of these Turkish mercenaries. But his policy was fatally erroneous. More rude and even more ferocious than the Arabs, they despised the feebleness of the Khalifate, whilst they grasped at its riches. The rivalry which existed between them and the Syrians effectually disgusted the latter with the military career, and the Turks were soon the only soldiers of the Khalifes. The slavery in which they had been reared rendered them less faithful without being more submissive or obedient. From this time most of the revolutions of Syria were their work. They hurled from the throne, or they assassinated, those Khalifes who were not the obsequious tools of their insolence and rapacity. As early as 862 (248 of the hegira) it made a Khalife, deposed him, nominated a successor to him, and deposed him in his turn; four succeeding thus in the space of eight years. The power of this militia became such that, in 879, a Turkish chief, Ahmed, son of Tholon, rendered himself independent in Egypt, where three of his descendants reigned after him. Thus, in about one hundred years after the introduction of the Turkish soldiers, the sovereigns of Bagdad had sunk almost into oblivion. At length, an imbecile Khalife, Al Rhadi, the twentieth of the Abbassides and thirty-ninth of the successors of Mahomet, who died in 940, was the last of these that officiated in the mosque; that commanded the forces in person; that addressed the people from the pulpit; that enjoyed the pomp and splendour of royalty—the last who deserved the title of *Commander of the Faithful.** Four years previous to his death the Turkish guards elected a chief of their own body, whom they called Emir al Omara (or Chief of Chiefs, *Imperator Imperatorum*). This officer, who superseded the functions of vizier, was henceforward the true sovereign of the State. He alone disposed of the treasure, the troops, the offices of power or dignity; he kept the Khalife a prisoner in his own palace, reducing him to that life of poverty, penitence, and prayer which the early successors of Mahomet had imposed on themselves by choice. Nor did he even scruple to take his life if there was any caprice of the Chief or of the soldiers which the Commander of the Faithful found it impossible to gratify. The Emir al Omara of Bagdad has sometimes been compared to the *Maire du Palais*, who was the virtual ruler of France under the kings of the first race. The origin of the power of the two officers was, however, very different, and its abuse was more violent and more cruel on the part of

* Abulfeda, p. 261. Gibbon, chap. 52.

the Turk than on that of the Austrasian; though the
thraldom of the legitimate sovereign to his minister
presents some features of resemblance. The Turkish
Emirs governed, in fact, in the name of the Khalifes; but
their dignity became the object of so much hankering
ambition, of so many calamities, that the inhabitants of
Bagdad summoned the Boujides of Persia to their deliverance. The Turks were driven out, and the dignity of
Emir al Omara passed to the Boujides, who kept it during
a century : the Khalifes had only changed their masters.

In the early years of the following century other Turkish
hordes made their appearance; some seized upon Bokhara
at the expense of the Persian dynasty of the Samanides;
others possessed themselves of Persia and India, and
founded the dynasty of the Ghiznevides, which lasted from
960 to 1189.

Of the three great Tartar peoples, the Huns, the Mongols,
and the Turks, who have spread their devastations and
dominion over the largest and most populous portion of
the civilized world, the last alone have retained existence
as an independent people. Their first appearance in Persian
history in the early part of the eleventh century exhibits
them as one of the most numerous and formidable of the
pastoral nations. When that mighty destroyer, Mahmud
of Ghizni, had, by his twelve fanatical expeditions to
Hindostan, exhausted the energies of his people, the reported bravery and numbers of the Turks who roved over
the wastes of Bokhara alarmed the caution of his declining
years. Under the guise of friendship he asked a Turkish
envoy what assistance his tribe could afford him in case of
attack. "Send this," said the Turk, holding forth an
arrow, " and fifty thousand horsemen will repair to your
standard; add another from my quiver, and the number
will be doubled; if you need further aid, despatch my
bow through our tribes, and two hundred thousand mounted
warriors will obey the summons." Mahmud listened to
the answer with deep alarm, but the storm of invasion was
averted until his death; after which his son Massoud was
utterly defeated at Zendecan, in Khorassan, by Togrul

Beg, the Turkish chief, and this decisive action shattered into fragments the colossal empire of the Ghiznevides. The descendants of Buyah, the Boujides or Bowides as they are named, had put an end to the capricious and brutal tyranny then exercised over the Khalifs by the Turkish guards,* and under the title of Emir al Omara, which they retained during a century, ruled Persia until they themselves sank beneath the power of the Ghiznevides. The Turkish prince, as a consequence of his victory, enjoyed the high consideration resulting from the custody of the Khalife, and the possession of Bagdad. Togrul Beg, the grandson of Seljuk, Emir of Turkestân, commenced the prosperity of the Seljukides, who were about to absorb the other tribes, and dominate all the East. After having conquered the Ghiznevides and driven them into India, he entered Khorassan, which belonged to the Boujides, overthrew and took prisoner the chief of that family, who commanded the army of the Khalife. That victory opened to the grandson of Seljuk the way to Bagdad; he entered therein without opposition, compelled the Abbasside prince to confer upon him the title of *Sultan*, and wrested him from the guardianship of the Boujides to impose his own. Besasiri, the head of the fallen family, revolted, and summoned to Bagdad the Fatimite Khalife of Egypt, but he was overthrown and put to death. Togrul Beg received the title of Emir al Omara, and reigned from Bokhara to Syria, from the vicinity of the Indus to the Black Sea, in the name of the monarch whom he had reinstated; and at his death, in his seventieth year, bequeathed the vast empire which he had conquered to his nephew Alp Arslan (*the robust lion*). That great prince reigned without a rival among the Mahommedans, as the Fatimite Khalifes of Egypt, happy to maintain their independence, sought by obsequious missions the friendship of the warlike potentate whose double sway, as ruler of the East and West, was denoted by the formidable symbol of a scimitar girt on each thigh. From this epoch the Khalifes were mere nonentities; they possessed only the honorary pontifical authority; the

* Price, ii. 155; Malcolm, i. 167; D'Herbelot.

true masters of the empire were the Seljukian sultans. Recent converts to Islamism, they exhibited the ferocious ardour of the first disciples of Mahomet, and dreamed only of wars and conquests.

Alp Arslan had, in his victorious career, crossed the Euphrates, seized upon Cæsarea and Cappadocia, subjugated Armenia and Georgia, and advanced into the heart of Phrygia. The Byzantine Emperor, Cæsar Romanus Diogenes, encouraged by the success of three campaigns, in which he slaughtered or dispersed the numerous armies led against him by the feudatories or generals of Alp Arslan, advanced adventurously at the head of 100,000 men to the confines of Media. Alp Arslan, leading 40,000 cavalry, hastened to chastise the invader; but a near view of the strength of his enemy suggested moderation. When his overtures of peace were met by an insulting demand that he should surrender his capital as the pledge of his sincerity, the Turkish Sultan arrayed his squadrons on the plain of Konogo, with his own hands equipped his charger, clothed himself in his shroud, and having perfumed his body with musk according to the custom of Mahommedan burial, declared his determination if defeated to find a grave on the field of battle. The event was such as had been usual whenever infantry met on open ground the cavalry of the Asiatic plains. The rapid evolutions of the Turkish horsemen evaded the onset of the Greeks, whose dense columns were exposed, without hope of retaliation, to the carnage inflicted by the skilful archery of their enemies. Romanus, at the close of a long and hard-fought day, in which he had exhibited admirable valour and presence of mind, found himself left almost alone amidst his enemies by the fall or flight of his troops. He was disarmed and led to the presence of Alp Arslan, who, in the first ungenerous exultation of triumph, is related to have set his foot on the neck of the Emperor. This was but a momentary impulse; he afterwards treated Romanus with considerable kindness, released him on promise of a ransom of a million pieces of gold, and was preparing to assist him in the recovery of his throne, when he received information that the unfortunate monarch had been put to death by his subjects.

The attention of the Seljukian sultans was so much engrossed by the conquest of the regions of the south, that Bokhara, their original country, had escaped from their dominion, and Alp Arslan was on his march to invade it with 200,000 men, when he fell by the hand of an assassin. A Karismian chief had opposed his advance, and being made prisoner, was sentenced to a lingering death. On hearing that he was to be fastened to four stakes and left to perish, the desperate victim, drawing a dagger, rushed headlong towards the throne; and the Sultan, disdaining to let his guards interfere, bent his bow, but his foot slipping, the arrow glanced harmlessly, and he received in his breast the dagger of the Karismian, who was immediately cut to pieces. The monarch, mortally wounded, had time to utter this dying admonition: " In my youth," he said, "I was advised by a sage to humble myself before God; to distrust my own strength; and never to despise the most contemptible foe. I have neglected these lessons, and my neglect has been deservedly punished. Yesterday, as from an eminence, I beheld the numbers, the discipline, and the spirit of my armies; the earth seemed to tremble under my feet; and I said in my heart, 'surely thou art the king of the world, the greatest and most invincible of warriors.' These armies are no longer mine, and in the confidence of my personal strength I now fall by the hand of an assassin." On his tomb was placed an inscription conceived in a similar spirit : " O! ye who have seen the glory of Alp Arslan exalted to the skies, repair to Maru, and you will behold it buried in the dust!"

The empire of the Seljukian Turks attained its greatest splendour and power in the reign of his son and successor, Malek Shah (1072-1092). That empire then extended from the Caspian Sea to the Mediterranean: it comprehended the Khorassan, Persian Irak, the possessions of the Khalifes, Syria and Palestine, wrested from the Fatimites, and the greatest part of Asia Minor; it touched on the Bosphorus. Aided by his vizier, Nisamul-Mulk, the

Sultan fostered letters and arts, and founded a great number of schools. His alliance was sought by the Khan of the Oghouses, who equally advanced the prosperity of Mussulman civilization beyond the Oxus; the two chiefs were linked together by marriages and the two races combined.

After that brilliant reign, the Empire of the Seljukian Turks fell to pieces as rapidly as it had risen. The three sons of Malek Shah disputed amongst themselves and divided his inheritance, and thus several independent sultanries were formed, of which the principal were: that of Iran or Persia, that of Aleppo or Syria, and that of Asia Minor, besides a host of principalities in which the emirs and the *atabeks* (governors) ignored the authority of the sons of Seljuk. Thus it was a kinsman of Malek Shah, Soliman, who achieved the conquest of Asia Minor over the Greeks, leaving to the Emperor of Byzantium only Trebizonde and some other ports. Two Greek competitors for the Byzantine throne sought the assistance of their common foe. Soliman formed an alliance with one of them, helped to set him on the throne of Constantinople, and then rewarded himself by taking possession of the Greek provinces of Asia. By the choice of the Sultan, Nice, in Bithynia, was prepared for his palace and fortress. On the hard conditions of tribute and servitude, the Greek Christians might retain the exercise of their religion; but their churches were profaned, their priests insulted, and every means adopted to stamp the profession of Christianity with marks of ignominy. Soliman, by his Mahommedan zeal, earned the title of *Gazi*, the *Holy Champion*.

Attempting to free himself from the suzerainty of the Seljukides, Soliman was conquered and slain (1085). His sons, David and Kilidje-Arslan ultimately established themselves in Asia Minor, and there founded (1095) at Koniah (Iconium), in Cappadocia, an independent state, the sultanry of Roum or of Iconium, which became so celebrated in the history of the Crusades. The Sultanry of Syria was divided into two others: that of Aleppo and that of Damascus. In the sequel, the Fatimites profited by all these troubles to renew their attacks upon Palestine.

Such was the situation of Western Asia when the struggle between the East and the West was recommenced by the Crusades. But it does not belong to our subject to follow in detail the course of those famous wars. It will be sufficient to add that, after the annexation of Asia Minor, the Turks directed their arms against the Holy Land, at that time in the hands of Saracen emirs, appointed by the Khalife of Egypt. The fierce Turks proved irresistible, and in 1076 Jerusalem fell into their savage hands. Under the Khalifes, the Christians of Jerusalem had been allowed to meet for religious worship. Crowds of pilgrims, even from remote parts of Europe, had been accustomed to visit the Holy Sepulchre and other places sacred to Christians. But now they were abandoned to the cruel treatment of a host of barbarian Turkomans. The Patriarch of Jerusalem was dragged by the hair along the pavement, and cast into a dungeon, to extort a ransom from his Christian flock. Outrages such as these were of frequent occurrence, and provoked that spirit of religious fervour which burst forth into the flame of those holy wars known as the Crusades.

Three years before the Crusaders reached Jerusalem, the Turks in that city were overthrown by the Saracens of Egypt (1096), and then the Khalif of Cairo resumed the sovereignty of the Holy Land.

2. *Invasion of the Mongols.*

At the commencement of the thirteenth century, Islamism was master, almost without division, of all Western Asia; but, seeing that the Fatimites were no longer looked upon save as conquered heretics and reduced to impotence, it was, without assault, delivered up to anarchy, divided into a multitude of sects, shared by several hostile states. The Khalifate of Bagdad was nothing more than a name. The Sultanry of Iconium, composed of innumerable small principalities, was about to be carried away in the first tempest. The Sultanry of Cairo had fallen into the hands of an energetic man, Malek-Adhel, who had reunited under his domination the inheritances of the sons of Saladin, the valorous Sultan of Egypt and chivalrous foe of Richard *Cœur de Lion*. But, after his death, his empire was divided amongst his sons. Malek-Kamel, who had Egypt in his possession, repulsed a new crusade—the fifth—led by French and German nobles (1221); he had for successor Malek-Sahel, of whom we shall speak hereafter. Finally, he formed in Turkestân, the Khorassan, and Persian Irak, a new empire, which dates from 1227, that of the Kharismians, who renewed the domination of the Ghiznevides and threatened with destruction the Khalifate of Bagdad.

Such was the situation of Western Asia, when it was destined to be overthrown by new invaders, in whose shadow were about to appear the restorers of Islamism— the OTTOMAN TURKS.

From the same localities whence had set out, in the fourth century, that Hunnish invasion which threw barbarian Europe upon Roman Europe, rushed forth in the thirteenth century a like invasion, that of the Mongols. Of the great Tartar family, they had retained all their primitive barbarity, the ardour for pillage, their savage thirst for blood and war. Scattered over the Steppes of Northern Asia, the Mongolian hordes had lived there lazily, some even tributaries to the Chinese empire, until Zinghis Khan, chief of one of them, united all of them under his authority (1203), and resolved to lead them to the conquest of the world. After having subdued Tartary, the north of China and India, he directed his march towards the west, and encountered the empire of the Karismians. That empire was overthrown. Zinghis died in 1227. Under his son, Octaï-Khan, the Karismians, conquered and driven back by the Mongols, threw themselves upon Syria, ravaged it, seized upon Jerusalem, and massacred all the inhabitants (1244). The Sultan of Cairo, Malek-el-Sahel, made an alliance with them. The Christians, uniting with the Sultan of Damascus, gave battle to the Karismians, and were completely defeated.

The Christian colonies seemed lost, when the Karismians engaged in a struggle with the Sultan of Cairo, and were destroyed in two battles. Syria fell again under the domination of the Sultan of Egypt.

It was under these circumstances that Louis IX., King of France, attempted to restore French power in the East by a new crusade. That crusade of Saint Louis brought about a fresh revolution in the Sultanry of Cairo, the consequences of which have made themselves felt even down to our own times.

The Sultan, Nedj-Eddyn, had formed a formidable force of cavalry, with slaves purchased in Circassia, and who were called *Mamelukes*. This militia, resembling that which the Khalifes had already embodied, speedily succeeded in dominating its masters. Nedj-Eddyn having died during the battles fought with the Crusaders, the chief of the Mamelukes, Bibars, seized upon power, massacred the last Ayoubite (descendant of Ayoub), and thus founded a domination (1268) destined to last until the commencement of the nineteenth century.

3. *Sequel of the Mongol Conquests—Destruction of the Khalifate of Bagdad—Summary of the Six Preceding Centuries.*

Meanwhile the Mongols continued their conquests, and their empire, at the end of the thirteenth century, extended from the eastern extremities of Asia to the shores of the Euphrates and the Caspian. Under Gaïouk, grandson of Zinghis, they passed into the vast steppes which stretch to the north of the Caspian, subdued the Kaptschak (between the Oural, the Volga, and the Don), effected the conquest of Russia, devastated Poland, Silesia, Moravia, and penetrated as far as Hungary. They burned the towns, massacred the populations, and ruined everything in their devastating march. They seemed to have assumed the task, not of making for themselves a great empire, but of annihilating all civilization, all settled institutions, even the human race itself. Several millions of men perished in these gigantic invasions.

However, as the Mongols seemed chiefly enraged against the Mahommedan peoples—as they had passed near to the Holy Land without assailing it—as it was known that there existed in the centre of Africa, since the sixth century, certain Christian colonies, and, amongst others, those said to be governed by the fabulous Prester-John, with whom the Mongols had amicable relations—it was thought in Europe that it would be possible to convert those idolatrous conquerors to the Christian religion, and to turn their arms to the entire destruction of Islamism. This was the object of several embassies which were sent by the Popes to the Mongol Khans, and especially of that despatched by Saint Louis in 1253, under the charge of the Franciscan Rubruquis, with several other monks. It was asserted that the great Khan Mangon, fourth successor of Zinghis, had just been converted to Christianity by the prayers and entreaties of the King of Armenia. Mangon accorded a friendly welcome to the envoys of the French king; but that embassy, say the learned authors of *l'Art de Verifier les Dates*, was a perpetual misunderstanding, through the ambassadors speaking Latin, and the Tartars replying in their own language.

At that epoch Mangon was occupied with destroying the sect of the *Batheniens* or *Assassins*. This was a fanatical and mysterious association, sprung out of Islamism, and which had taken birth a short time before the Crusades. Its prophet Hassan, alike an enemy of the Mussulmans and of the Christians, had assumed the mission of redressing all wrongs and every species of crime, by sending his followers to assassinate him whom he marked out to perish by their daggers. This association made the western princes tremble during two centuries. Its chief, known by Europeans under the name of the *Old Man of the Mountain*, dwelt in the mountains of Persian Irak: his adherents, scattered throughout Western Asia, executed blindly his sanguinary commands, and immolated all those of whom the association had to complain. Three

BAGDAD. [page 41.

Khalifes were slain in this manner, as well as several heroes of the Crusades; finally, they possessed, all over Syria, fortified posts, whence they pillaged the roads and caravans. The Mongols tracked them to their retreats, and their last chief came to surrender himself into the hands of Mangon.

The latter had required for that expedition the aid of the Khalife of Bagdad; he avenged himself for his refusal by sending his brother Houlagon against the capital of Islamism. Houlagon took the city by assault, sacked it during seven days, and obtained from it a prodigious treasure. As for the Khalife, Mostasem, the fifty-sixth since Abou-Bekr, and the thirty-seventh Abbasside, he was put to death with all his family (1258), and it was thus that the race and the empire of the Abbassides terminated.

At the same time, another lieutenant of the Khan had advanced into Asia Minor, and had subjected all as far as the Bosphorus. The Seljukides of Iconium retained, nevertheless, during three generations the vain title of Sultans, under the domination of the Mongols; the last, as we shall see, was overthrown in 1307. After Mangon-Khan, the gigantic empire of the Mongols was divided: whilst one dynasty established itself in China, another branch of the family of Zinghis reigned over Persia and Western Asia; but this latter empire obtained no consistency: all its strength was employed in disputing unfortunately enough with the Sultans of Egypt for the possession of Syria. Little remains to record of them, save that these Tartars reigned only over ruins; they had remained at the end of a century as ignorant and as barbarous as in the time of Zinghis-Khan. Their chiefs protected alterately Mahommedanism, Christianity, and Judaism; they wavered always between those rival religions, and adopted none of them definitively. Rather encamped than established in the provinces which they had rendered almost deserts, they did not attempt to govern them. All their action was speedily concentrated on Persia, where they dwelt, and upon the neighbouring provinces; the furthest away from the centre of their domination were abandoned to the ravages of wandering hordes; on all sides the Governors became independent, old Mussulman emirs attempted to form there regular states; and it was thus that amidst that anarchy grew up imperceptibly the Ottoman power.

Before entering into the history properly so-called of the Ottomans, it is necessary to cast a retrospective glance over the six centuries which have been just cursorily traversed. At the outset, the first sentiment experienced is one of terror mingled with disgust at the course of those empires that are formed, that succeed and overthrow one another with such startling facility; those wars, those battles, those massacres innumerable; that frightful waste of human life, in which mankind seems entirely the sport of the genius of evil; that violent confusion of events without profit, without sequence or result, might give rise to the belief that Islamism has only produced ruins and only reigned over corpses. But if to that religion of the sword, of war, and of conquest, must be attributed a large portion of those great calamities, it must not be forgotten that the countries which were the theatre of them are those in which revolutions were the most frequent, empires the most ephemeral, conquests the most facile; the countries in which—before the Omars, the Saladins, the Zinghis-Khans—the Sesostrises, the Cyruses, and the Alexanders, made at a rush for themselves vast dominations and a sanguinary renown. It is the country in which the peoples allowed themselves recklessly to be subjugated, in which they changed masters like so many flocks of sheep, in which they stretched forwards the neck to the headsman alike without a regret and without a murmur.

The cause of all this evil therefore is less in the institutions than in the men. The Koran has not produced it; it has only continued it; but it would be absolutely unjust to forget that it has done other than evil, that the history of civilization owes to it one of its fairest pages, that Arab genius has opened new paths to the human mind, and continued the intellectual work of the Greeks and Romans. It has produced a vast and marvellous literature, works in mathematics and philosophy which have made their benevolent action felt over the whole of Europe, of precious inventions in the arts, of profitable industries, of edifices that are the placid, elegant, voluptuous translation of the doctrines happily interpreted of Islamism; a special architecture that has emanated from the Koran, as Gothic architecture has from the Gospel.

After this rapid mention of empires sprung from Islamism, we proceed to narrate the history of the last heir of those empires, of that one which, after having so long menaced Christian Europe, has lately been making vain efforts to regenerate itself by Western civilization.

CHAPTER III.

THE OTTOMAN TURKS TO THE REIGN OF AMURATH I. (1231-1360).

1. *Origin of the Ottomans.—Orthoguel.*

NOTHING could seem a more dead survival than the long succession of Abbasside Khalifes; but when their claims were passed on to the Ottoman Sultans, the successor of the Prophet became a terrible reality.

At the epoch when Zinghis, by overthrowing the Empire of the Karismians, opened Western Asia to the invasion of the peoples of the East, Soliman-Shah, son of Kaialp, chief of a tribe of Oghuz Turks scattered through the Korassan, swept by the tide of Mongol invasion, quitted that land with 50,000 of his countrymen, and established himself in Armenia, in the environs of Erz-Inghian, upon the Euphrates. Some years afterwards, regretting its native soil, the horde retraced its steps thither; but in attempting to cross the Euphrates, near the stronghold of Djaber, its chief was drowned (1231). His tomb is still to be seen on the river's bank, and is known by the name of *Turk-Mezari* (the Turk's tomb). The families that had been under his leadership dispersed; one portion, with his two eldest sons, returned into Khorassan; the rest, with his two younger sons, Dundar and Orthoguel (or Erthogrul), and who were to the number of 400 families, wandered for some time in the valley of the Upper Araxes and upon the plains of Erzeroum, towards the sources of the Euphrates, sojourning during summer upon the heights, and descending in winter to the plains, according to the custom of nomad races. Orthoguel soon advanced further to the West; and whilst journeying with his tribe upon the frontiers of the Seljukians of Roum, he came upon two armies contending for the mastery in the plain. Without knowing whom the combatants were, he resolved to aid the weakest against the strongest party, and his valour decided the fortune of the day. The conquered were the Mongols, and the conqueror, Alaeddin, the Seljukide Sultan, who, in recognition of the timely succour he had received from the nomad chief, gave him a residence in his states, and assigned him for summer quarters the eastern slopes of the Toumanidsch mountains, of which Mount Olympus in Bithynia forms a part, and for winter quarters the plains of Sægud on the Sangarius.

Vassal of the Sultan, Orthoguel served him in his wars against the Greeks, who still occupied some cities in that extreme region of the peninsula. After a battle in which his *akindschis* (pioneers, scouts, or foragers) placed in front of the army, had rendered signal service, he received in recompense a small territory in the district of Bosœni, not far from Eskischehr, the ancient Dorylea. At the same time the name of the district of Bosœni was changed, Alaeddin calling it Sultan-œni (*forehead of the Sultan*), in honour of the brave advanced guard. The name has long remained that of one of the seventeen sandjaks of present provinces of Turkey in Asia; the narrow canton which first bore it was the cradle of the Ottoman power.

All nations, and especially those of the East, delight to surround their origin with marvellous circumstances. There is scarcely any founder of a dynasty but its grandeur was miraculously announced to him. Thus we find in the Ottoman annals that Osman, or Othoman, son of Orthoguel, whom the Sultans look upon as the founder of their dynasty, had, like the Patriarch Jacob, a dream, in which the brilliant destinies of his race were revealed to him. Othoman was enamoured of the beautiful Malkatoun (*treasure of the eyes*), daughter of a learned Arab sheik, Edebali. He asked her in marriage of her father. The sheik, fearing for the happiness of his daughter from the disdain of the family of Othoman, far superior to his obscurity, refused him Malkatoun. Other neighbouring princes, attracted by the girl's beauty, proposed for her, all of them in vain. Othoman battled during two years in a contest for her with his rivals. His constancy in the meantime touched the heart of Edebali. Patience, according to the Arabs, is the price that God sets on all felicity.

One day, Othoman, more dejected, but more persevering than ordinary, had come to ask hospitality from Edebali for a night, hoping always to get a glance at least of Malkatoun. He had a dream, in which he saw the crescent of the moon issuing from the breast of Malkatoun, come to repose on his bosom; then, an immense tree began to vegetate before him, which, increasing in strength and beauty, covered with its shade earth and sea, to the extremity of the horizon of the three continents, Europe, Asia, and Africa. Four huge mountain ranges—the Caucasus, the Atlas, the Taurus, the Hæmus—supported like four pillars the overladen branches of the tree. From the sides of these mountains ran respectively four rivers—the Tigris, the Euphrates, the Nile, and the Danube. Their beds, in widening, watered countries verdant with pastures, yellow with harvests, dark with forests, and wafted vessels to the four seas. Towers, fortified cities, domes, cupolas, minarets, obelisks, pyramids crowned with the symbol of the crescent moon, arose along the verge of valleys amid rose groves and cypresses. Harmonious invitations to prayer, like to the melodies of the celestial bulbuls, were poured from the summits of those graceful monuments upon the air. All of a sudden, the branches and leaves of the trees gleamed like lance points and sabre blades, and were turned by a puff of wind towards Constantinople. Then that capital, situated between two seas, sparkled like the sapphire of a ring between two emeralds. It was the nuptial ring of the marriage of Othoman with the capital of the world. He was just about to wear it on his finger when he awoke.

After having heard the recital of this wonderful dream, the sheik gave his daughter to Othoman; and the beauteous Malkatoun became the mother of Orchan, his successor. Orthoguel lived to a very advanced age; but his son took his place long before his death at the head of the Seljukian armies.

Before relating the exploits of Othoman and the further conquests of Islamism from the Byzantine Empire, let us cast a glance over the caducity of that empire.

Since Constantine had changed the capital, the Roman Empire, too unwieldy to be managed by a single hand, began speedily to fall into dissolution. Divided between the sons of Theodosius into two empires, the Byzantine Empire, to which its capital, Byzantium, gave its name, preserved for some time, against the barbarians of the East, something of that superstitious terror that Rome had retained against the barbarians of the West. Its limits, long respected, extended from the Tigris along to the Adriatic, and from the confines of Scythia, now Russia, along to Ethiopia, where lie concealed the fountains of the Nile. Amongst the numerous heterogeneous populations subjected to the laws of this empire, the Greeks predominated by numbers, by nobility of origin, by the Christian religion primitively adopted, organized, propagated, interpreted in the East—in fine, by arts, by eloquence, by wealth, by policy. In transplanting the Empire of Rome to Byzantium, Constantine made a change, not only of capital and religion, but also of race. All was become Greek in Greece, and Asiatic in Asia. The emperors and Romans of the East had retained of the Romans in Italy but their pride and their despotism. The same vices flowed, but in another blood. Byzantium might have been taken for a Persian colony. The surnames of Cæsar or Augustus, retained to the possessor, to the heirs or to the colleagues in the empire, affected in vain, with the Roman acceptations, a resemblance which no longer existed in the manners. Theological disputes upon the mysteries of religion were become the sole texts of conversation and discussion. The petty factions of the circus were substituted for the great factions of the forum. Luxury, licentiousness of morals, effeminacy, the domination of eunuchs and women in the government, had from reign to reign emasculated the national arm and character. The palaces of Constantinople surpassed in magnificence those of Nero at Rome, and those of the kings at Persepolis. The pomp of public ceremonies took the place of the pomp of triumphs. The very costume of the later emperors, described by St. Chrysostom, reminded less of the descendants of Romulus than of the successors of Xerxes.

"The Emperor," says St. Chrysostom, "wears on his head either a diadem or a crown of gold, enriched with jewels of inestimable price. These ornaments, together with garments dyed in purple, are reserved exclusively for his sacred person. His robes of silk are ornamented with embroidery in gold, representing dragons. His throne is of massive gold. He appears in public, but surrounded by his courtiers, his guards, and attendants. Their lances, their bucklers, the cuirasses, the bridles and harnesses of their horses, are of gold, at least to appearance. The large plate of gold that shines in the centre of their shield is encircled with smaller ones, which represent the form of the eye. The two mules harnessed to the chariot of the Emperor are perfectly white and all covered with gold. The chariot of pure and massive gold excites the admiration of the spectators; they contemplate the purple curtains, the whiteness of the cushions, the value of the diamonds and plates of gold that shed their most dazzling splendour when they scintillate from agitation by the motion of the chariot. The portraits of the Emperor are painted white on a ground of azure. The monarch is represented seated upon a throne, arrayed in armour; his horses and his guards are at his side, and his enemies vanquished in chains at his feet."

The people had lost under this discipline all remembrance of their antique liberty. Servility was become the glory of the subjects, only tempered now and then by revolt and assassination. The tone of Asiatic slavery had passed into the public manners. The princes measured their elevation only by the abasement of their subjects. Such a nation, enslaved to all the caprices of a master, of eunuchs, of favourites, of wives or courtesans, was equally incapable of respecting itself, and of defending itself against the insolence of the barbarians who bordered it. Eunuchs—slaves bred in the most abject offices of the palace—received the command of armies and the titles of patrician, of consul, of father of the country. They had statues raised to them of marble and bronze in the Senate —that vain shadow of the Roman Senate preserved at Constantinople as a sort of mock palladium of liberty.

"One man," says the historian, indignant at these turpitudes, "auctions, cuts up, retails, vends the Roman provinces from the Euphrates along to Mount Hæmus; another obtains the proconsulate of Asia in exchange for a delicious country residence; a third buys off entire Syria with the diamonds of his wife; a fourth complains of having sacrificed all his patrimony to obtain the government of Bithynia. The tariff of all the provinces to be sold to the highest bidder may be seen placarded upon the walls of the palace; and as the eunuch has been sold himself, he would like to sell entire humanity. Such are," adds the writer, "the fruits of the valour of the Romans, of the defeat of Antiochus, and of the triumphs of Pompey."

A government so venal and so corrupt, encouraged, for the period of two centuries, the barbarians. The Huns ravaged Persia, Attila subjugated Sarmatia and Germany. His hordes advanced to the walls of Constantinople. The Emperors purchased their safety with gold instead of purchasing it with blood. They enrolled the Bulgarians, the Goths, the Turks, in the imperial guard, to the end of co-interesting the enemies of the Empire in defence of what remained of the Empire, by participation of its dignities and treasures. The sea was not more secure to them than the land. Adventurers, Norman and Slavic, sometimes rivals, sometimes allies, of the savage tribes of the Lake of Ladoga, founded subsequently at Kief the Russian monarchy, descended the Borysthenes to the south, and made their entrance into the Black Sea. Novogorod and Moscow, those Samarcands of the north, sprang up from the pine forests; the fleets of these

Cossacks being formed of a cloud of canoes hollowed from the trunks of immense trees. These canoes, bordered with raised planks, but without decks, carried from forty to sixty warriors with the necessary arms and provisions for the expedition. Two thousand of these canoes, coasting along the Black Sea, used to force sometimes the entrance of the Bosphorus, and come up to the very harbour of Constantinople to hurl menaces and impose ransoms upon the Emperors. The Greek fire—that last weapon of the Greeks, of which the secret is lost with them—used to burn in vain their fleets. They sprang up again with the ensuing spring like marine vegetations. The Greeks purchased peace by tributes. "Let us be content," the Russian old men used to say to the young ones who complained of their consenting to the treaties and tributes of the Byzantines. "Is it not better to obtain, without fighting, the gold, the silver, the silk, the precious stones, of these people? Are we always sure of victory? Can we sign a pact with the billows and the winds of the Euxine?"

It is not known what prophetic presentiment announced already to the Greeks that these mysterious populations, concealed as yet behind the marshes of the Borysthenes, and that those fleets which seemed to descend from the Polar Circle, were the menacing usurpers of their Oriental patrimony. An obscure inscription graven on the pedestal of an ancient equestrian statue at Byzantium, signified, it is said, that the Russians would one day reign over the Greek Empire of Byzantium, of which this bronze horseman took possession long in advance.

However, the barbarian and the Greek frontiers were in contact at Nicomedia. The Christian Emperors leagued secretly with the Mussulman Sultan against the Crusaders come to avenge Christianity. The Crusaders, impelled against nature, manners, climate, but by a pious folly, towards Palestine, bestrewed with their bones the lands and seas of the East. They conquered only the sepulchre of Christ. The tide of Islamism, a moment rolled back, returned overwhelmingly upon them. The Greek race, too old and too exhausted to bear a new and severe religion like Christianity, dissolved it into theological quibbling which was obliged to borrow substance from idolatry. Christianity, vitiated by the Greeks, flourished, on the contrary, in the West, and was doomed to vivify the Empire of the successors of Charlemagne.

The faith of the East had found its prophet in Arabia. The Roman race was exhausted at Constantinople; the race of the conquerors was young. It needed but a hero to conduct it from one bank of the Bosphorus to the other in Europe. Othoman was about to appear. Let us resume the history of the patriarch of the Ottomans or Osmanli.

2. *Reign of Othoman.*

Orthoguel lived to an advanced age; but, long before his death, his son Othoman filled his place in the command of the Seljukian armies. Scattered over the country were many Greek fortresses, the chiefs of which, entirely independent, kept up with their Mussulman neighbours relations sometimes friendly, sometimes hostile. One of these chiefs, Kæse Michal, lord of Chermenkia, swore strict amity with Othoman; later on he embraced Islamism, and his descendants, under the name of Michalogli, occupied during several centuries an eminent position among the first families of the Empire. Othoman had also for ally the lord of Belokoma or Biledchik. It was in his stronghold that he deposited his treasures, when, annually, at the approach of summer, his nomad troops regained the mountains; on the contrary, he was in perpetual hostility with the chief of Angelokoma, or Ainægel, who harassed his people by raids on their flocks whilst passing near his borders. Towards 1285 he resolved to avenge himself. With seventy followers he attempted to surprise the fortress of Ainægel, which commanded the defile of Ermeni. A combat took place in that defile between Koutahieh and Broussa, and Othoman won his first victory; but he did not succeed in making himself master of

E 2

Ainægel. A second battle gave him Karahissar, an important town situate on the Battis or Bathys. That same year Orthoguel died (1288), and Orchan was born. The year following Othoman received from the Seljukide Sultan, in recompense for his services, as well as for his conquests, the territory of Karahissar, with the title of *Bey*, and its accompanying insignia—a banner, a drum, and a horse-tail.

However, the increasing prosperity of the new Bey gave umbrage to his neighbours; his ally even, the lord of Belokoma, entered into a conspiracy formed against him. He invited him to a festival on the occasion of his marriage, with the intention of getting rid of him. Warned by his friend Kæse Michal, Othoman dissembled : he sent as usual his treasures to be deposited in the stronghold of his faithless ally ; but he had them carried by forty of his adherents disguised as old women. Having thus seized upon the place, he rushed in front of the nuptial cortége, slew the traitor, carried off his bride, the lovely Niloufer (lotos flower), and kept her as a wife for his son ; then he attacked suddenly the fortresses of Jarhissar and Ainægel, the possessors of which had organized the plot, and became master of them after an obstinate resistance.

At that period, Aladdin III., the last of the Seljukides, after a reign which had reflected some lustre upon him, was dethroned (1307) by Ghazan, khan of the Mongols. Upon the ruins of his empire arose numerous independent principalities, which took the names of their founders, and which played a great part in Ottoman history. Thus were formed the States of *Karaman*, in Cappadocia and part of Cilicia, with Iconium as the capital; of *Kermian*, in Phrygia; of *Karasi*, in Mysia; of *Sarou-Khan*, in Lydia; of Aïdin, in Ionia ; of Mentesche, in Caria ; of Tekieh, in Lycia and Pamphylia ; of *Hamid*, in Pisidia and Lycaonia ; and of *Kastamouni*, in Paphlagonia, &c. The possessors of these principalities all usurped sovereign rights, coined money, and caused their names to be pronounced in the public prayers. Othoman was not the least powerful amongst them : master of almost all Bithynia, he possessed, with Eskischehr, Karahissar, and the other strongholds he had conquered, a part of Phrygia, of Galatia, and the upper basin of the Sangarius. He fixed his residence at Jenishehr (*new town*), upon the northern frontier of his States, between Nicæa and Broussa, two cities already coveted by the Ottomans.

Everything prospered, besides, with the son of Orthoguel. Protector of learned and of holy men, he had, from the time of his earliest conquests, founded communities, schools, attracted towards him pious and instructed men, stirred up amongst his followers religious zeal; thus had he inspired his people with boldness and confidence. According to a belief accredited amongst the Mussulmans, at the commencement of each century of the hegira, there should appear a man destined to regenerate Islamism. In the eyes of his companions, Othoman must be the glory of the eighth century, which was about to commence. His name even was of happy presage. "Names come from Heaven," says the Korân; Othoman's signified "legbreaker;" and that image amongst Orientals attaches itself to ideas of strength and grandeur. That name, moreover, had not been borne with glory by any Mussulman prince since the second Khalife, the collector of the Korân, the conqueror of Persia and of a part of Asia. The fanatical soldiers of Othoman believed him, therefore, destined to renew the grandeur of the Khalifes; they thought it an honour to bear his name, and he himself took the title of *Padischah* or sovereign of the *Osmanlis.**

His first enterprise, as sovereign prince, was directed against the fortress of Keuprihissar, neighbour of Jenishehr. On this occasion, his uncle Deindar, who must have been at that time upwards of ninety years of age, attempting to moderate his love of conquest, ventured to oppose the undertaking as a source of needless difficulty and danger. Othoman, irritated at such opposition, answered, we are told, the shafts of his uncle's words by an arrow from his bow, and the old man sank down a corpse

* *Othman, Ottoman* and *Osman* are the same name; and it is the same with *Ottomans* and *Osmanlis*.

at the feet of the nephew. This may be regarded as an early introduction to the subsequent system of fratricide among the Ottoman princes, and it is remarkable that the Turkish historian, Edris, who professes to relate nothing which can reflect disgrace upon the memory of Othoman, records this event without any extenuation or comment. Keuprihissar and various other fortresses were speedily captured, and repeated advantages were obtained over the Greeks. Next, an advance was made in the direction of Nicæa. A Greek army, commanded by the heteriarch or chief of the body guard, was defeated in the environs of Nicomedia, and in that combat a nephew of Othoman perished; his tomb, which has been preserved, is to this day a place of pilgrimage. As the walls of Nicæa forbade all surprise, further progress against the city was arrested; but a fort was erected on the slope of the mountain, to keep the garrison in check. Six years later (1307), the governors of several Greek places united together to attack Othoman; they were vanquished, and the Ottomans marched on as far as the shores of the Propontis (Sea of Marmora); all the borders of the Gulf of Mondania were devastated.

At the same epoch the other Turkish princes of Asia Minor desolated the Archipelago, drenching with blood and enveloping in fire Chios, Samos, Lemnos, the Cyclades, Rhodes, Candia, Malta, and, thence, carrying terror everywhere about the Mediterranean. At the same time they tore from the Greeks upon the coasts of Asia Minor, the last places that remained to them: Ephesus, Tripolis upon the Meander, and Cenchrea yielded to that revival of the spirit of conquest of the Mussulmans. The tribe of Othoman took part in that general movement: all the strongholds in the vicinity of Nicæa were subjected; their defenders compelled, under pain of death, to embrace Islamism, Kœse Michal voluntarily giving them the example. The Greek Emperor, terrified, had implored the aid of the khan of the Mongols and had sent him his daughter in marriage; a Tartar horde invaded thereupon the States of Othoman, but it was repulsed by his son

Orchan, to whom he had given charge of Karahissar. In recompense of that exploit, Orchan was entrusted with a command to follow up the conquests of his father. Very soon all was subjected as far as the mouth of the Sangarius; Nicæa and Nicomedia were invested, and two forts were built at the gates of Broussa (Prusa). During ten years this latter city was kept nearly blockaded; at length, in 1327, it was resolved to assault it. Othoman, enfeebled by age, gave to his son the command of the enterprise. The fortress of Edrenos, situate on Olympus, and which dominated the whole country, was first assailed, carried by main force and destroyed. Then, on the Osmanlis presenting themselves before Broussa, they met with no resistance: its governor obtained, at the price of 30,000 ducats, permission to retire with all his belongings, and the city opened its gates. Thus fell without striking a stroke the strongest place in Asia Minor, the ancient capital of the kingdom of Bithynia; already taken in the middle of the tenth century by the Mussulmans, then again occupied by the Greeks, it escaped from them definitively to become the first capital of the Osmanlis. It is now considered as the third city of their Empire.

When Othoman learned that important conquest, he was at the point of death. He expressed a wish that his body might be transferred to the new capital where his son was about to reside. Austere and without ostentation, like the first soldiers of the Prophet he left neither gold, silver nor precious stones; all had been liberally distributed amongst his companions. In his dwelling at Jenishehr no treasure whatsoever was found—only a cafetan embroidered with coloured thread, a linen turban, a wooden spoon and a salt-cellar; a few thorough-bred Arabian coursers, a few yoke of oxen for the plough, some flocks of sheep, and that comprised his whole estate. The breed of sheep has been piously perpetuated, and the sultans of the present time cause to be fed on the mountains round Broussa and the grassy sides of Mount Olympus, sheep which, it is affirmed, are the descendants of those of the founder of the empire. There was to be seen also at Broussa, a few years back, before the conflagration that reduced his tomb to ruins, the simple wooden chaplet of beads of the father of the Ottomans, and the drum which he had received from the Seljukide sultan in token of investiture. The double-pointed sabre and the banner that at the same time were sent him by the Sultan, are still preserved in the Imperial Treasury at Constantinople.

3. *Reign of Orchan.*

At the period of Othoman's death, the Byzantine Empire had sustained considerable losses in other parts of Asia Minor as well as in Bithynia and part of Paphlagonia, which he had subdued. Ephesus, as has been said, had fallen under the power of the Turks; and so also had Lydia, as far as Smyrna; Magnesia, as far as Pergamus; and Phrygia, both Greater and Lesser.

Othoman had designated Orchan as his successor, to the prejudice of Aladdin, his eldest son. The latter, far from revolting against the parental will, would not even accept the moiety of the flocks and herds; he consented, however, to share with his brother the duties and responsibilities of government under the title of Wezir or Vizier, an office which he discharged in a most efficient manner, assisting the growth of the empire by his internal regulations, while Orchan was adding to his territories by foreign conquests. The title of *Vizier* signifies properly "the carrier of a load," an expressive term reminding the all-powerful ministers of oriental princes of their obligations, and pointing out the sovereign authority to be only a burden. Aladdin was his brother's vizier in the fullest acceptation of the word; he was the first legislator of the Ottomans, and his memory is equally venerated amongst them as that of their first sovereigns.

Prusa (Broussa) having been captured at the close of the preceding reign, the seat of government was transferred to that city, and a series of successes ensued.

Among the Mussulman nations, for which the Korân is the supreme or rather the only law, the part of human legislation is sufficiently restricted: it must only be the commentary of the divine law; it can only bear upon details of forms; but those details are not wanting in gravity, since they must be observed with the same feeling of respect as the things of religion. It is that which explains the formal spirit of the Osmanlis, the importance which they attach to exterior usages and to costume. Those objects, elsewhere so indifferent, are regulated amongst them by laws, and by laws based upon the Korân. Three points especially attracted Aladdin's attention: the coinage, the costume, and the army. Othoman, after his investiture, or at least after the extinction of the Seljukide Sultans, had enjoyed the sovereign rights of *sikke* and of *khoutbe* (right of coining money and the privilege of being named in the public prayers); but he had only availed himself of the latter, and the Seljukian coins were those only current in Asia Minor: new money was issued in the name of Orchan.* As for costume, it was regulated in all its details, but especially the head-covering, which is, in the East, the distinctive sign of peoples and castes. For the different classes of the nation, therefore, the form and colour of the turban. For the prince was reserved the cap of red felt wound round with white muslin in puffed folds; for the military head-dress, the soldiers and functionaries wore a cap of white felt of elongated shape. These regulations were modified later on at different times: the white felt was reserved for persons of the sultan's suite; the soldiers assumed the red felt; and then it was ornamented with gold lace and embroidery.

The most important of the institutions of Orchan's reign was the creation of a standing army, and one which mainly contributed to the support of the Ottoman Empire; and it took place, it may be remarked, about a century before the time of Charles VII. of France, who is usually regarded by historians of the Middle Ages as the inventor of that policy. The Turkish horsemen were now subjected

* It should be remarked that the money bore only the name and not the effigy of the sovereign; any representation of man or beast being regarded by Mussulmans as an idolatry. The name and titles of the prince were alone traced in elegant characters upon his seal and coins.

to stricter discipline than hitherto, and to this period may be referred the establishment of the *sipahis* or regular cavalry. The *akindschis*, light-armed horsemen, had formed the strength of Othoman's armies and were never regularly organized; they had been enlisted for each expedition and disbanded after the campaign. But, by the exertions of Aladdin, the most remarkable of the military arrangements now made was the formation of a regular body of infantry, called *piadés* (foot soldiers), paid and kept up permanently, composed of the children of Christian parents who were forced to embrace Mahometanism, and of renegades who voluntarily embraced the religion of the Prophet, and abandoned at once their faith and their country. This was the odious origin and nucleus of the Janissaries, a select corps which did not disappoint the expectation of its founder, and which, from a mere body-guard at first, becoming gradually augmented by Amurath I. and his successors during several centuries, long constituted the chief strength of the Ottoman armies.

Whilst Aladdin was strengthening the empire by his institutions, Orchan aggrandized it by fresh conquests. His companions in arms were Konour Alp, Adjé-Hodja, Abdurraman-Ghazi, Mursal the Black, Ali the Black, and others whose names have remained dear to the Ottomans. They succeeded in driving the Greeks from the banks of the Sangarius and the shores of the Propontis. All the strongholds with which those countries bristled were successively captured. At length, Nicomedia and Nicæa alone remained, invested on all sides. The first was taken in 1330, by Adjé-Hodja. The Greek Emperor, Andronicus the Younger, alarmed at the progress of the Ottoman arms, passed over into Asia at the head of an army and made an effort to save the second. A battle was fought near Philocrene (now Tawschandschil), upon the shores of the Gulf of Nicomedia, and the Turks, victors, had only to present themselves at the gates; the town capitulated. Nicomedia, which had flourished so conspicuously in the time of Diocletian and Constantine, had long since lost its importance; at the present day, under the name of Ismid, it is nothing more than a mean township. Nicæa (Isnik), in passing into the hands of the Turks, remained a considerable city; it was the second capital of Orchan and the rival of Broussa. The Church of Saint Synode, in which the famous creed of the Catholic faith had been drawn up, was converted into a mosque, and near that mosque was founded the first *medressé*, or upper school, and the first *imaret*, or public kitchen for the poor; but Nicæa waned rapidly, and now it is a mere village.

Hitherto the Ottomans had aggrandized themselves at the expense only of the Greeks. The capture of Nicæa was followed by a new line of conquests. Orchan now commenced an attack upon the emirs or chiefs who shared among themselves the remnant of the Seljukian dominions. In 1335 he had, for the first time, occasion to intervene in the affairs of one of the neighbouring Mussulman States. Adjlan Bey, prince of Khorasi,* had left two sons; the youngest, who had been brought up under the care of Orchan, proposed to aid him in overthrowing his brother, promising to give up, as a reward of such service, four of the principal towns of his States. Orchan consented thereto, and invaded Khorasi. The menaced prince took refuge in the citadel of Pergamus, thought to be impregnable. He entered upon negotiations, and appeared disposed to come to terms; but, having made himself master of his brother's person, he caused him to be assassinated. Orchan marched immediately against Pergamus. The inhabitants opened their gates and delivered up the fratricide. His life was spared, and an abode assigned him in Broussa; and the principality of Khorasi was, without striking a blow, annexed to the Ottoman States. This conquest was followed by other successes in the western regions of Karamania, or the ancient Phrygia; and the long period of profound tranquillity that followed, and touching which the Ottoman historians maintain a disdainful silence, appears to have

* These small Turkish states, the names of which will frequently recur in the course of this history, had no very distinctly marked boundaries. The *Khorasi* occupied the southern slopes of the Toumandsch Mountains and the basin of the Caïcus, that is to say, a great portion of Mysia.

been not unprofitably occupied by Orchan in adjusting the internal regulations of his increasing dominions, and in making pious foundations. Mosques, cloisters, schools, and *imarets* arose on all sides. Broussa was favoured in this respect, not only by the care of the prince, but also by the liberality of his companions, whom war had enriched. The umbrageous slopes and the cool valleys of Olympus became peopled with dervishes and santons.

Under those names are indicated all those Mussulmans who devote themselves to an ascetic life, whether in community, like monks, or in solitude, like hermits. Their number became considerable under the first Ottoman princes. Mahomet had said, "There are no monks in Islam;" words which seemed to interdict all imitation of Christian asceticism; but the inclination of the Orientals for a contemplative life prevailed over the will of the Prophet; and another maxim: "Poverty is my glory," helped to legitimate that infraction of his law. Thirty-seven years after the death of Mahomet, Oweis, an Arab of Yemen, founded the first order of dervishes. At the present time as many as seventy may be reckoned in the different Mussulman countries. Under Othoman the order of *nakschbendis* arose, which is still one of the most famous. Under Orchan the *saadis* were instituted, who have degenerated into jugglers. Hadji-Begtasch, the patron of the Janissaries, was founder of the order of the *begtaschis*, an order—semi-religious, semi-military—to which the Janissaries themselves were affiliated.

The members of the greater part of these religious orders live in community in cloisters. They are called *dervishes*—a word that signifies "threshold of a door." The highest in dignity are called *sheiks* or elders. As for the *santons* or *sahids*, those are veritable hermits; hidden in their cells amongst the most secluded sites, they enjoy, for the most part, a great reputation for sanctity. Those among them of the most renown receive the names of *abdals* or *babas*—fathers. "There are always," say the Mussulmans, "forty abdals upon earth"—that is to say, forty persons of an eminent sanctity, destined to occupy a distinguished place in heaven; but there are always more than forty hermits on whom popular opinion bestows that title; they are often those who make themselves remarkable by the strangest extravagancies. Several of these saints were in high favour with Orchan, who built cloisters for their disciples. The most famous among them were Gheilik-Baba, " father of the stags," so called because that, mounted on a stag, he had sought out Orchan to predict to him his victories; Dogli-Baba, the father potter, who fed himself solely on curds of milk; Abdal-Mourad and Abdal-Musa, who both accompanied the son of Othoman to the conquest of Broussa—the first armed with a wooden sabre, with which he carried terror amongst the enemy's ranks; the second, holding burning coals upon cotton. Abdal-Mourad's wooden sabre is still shown to pilgrims. Solyman the Great took a bit from it, which he had preserved in the treasury of the seraglio.

Protector of science as well as of religion, Orchan attached to himself by his liberality the most famous among the learned men; he placed them at the head of the newly founded schools and admitted them to his councils. Such were the *Mollahs* or legists David of Cesarea and Tadscheddin the Kurd, who fulfilled one after the other the functions of first *Mouderris* or professor in the Upper School of Nicæa; and Sinan the Persian, who was called from his importance, Sinan Pacha.* Moreover the city of Broussa, long after it had ceased to be the residence of the Ottoman sovereigns, preserved the privilege of attracting the learned, the ascetic, and men of letters. It was in those delightful environs that the first Turkish poets sought their inspiration, that the most famous legists pondered their works. Their tombs, mingled with those of the Sheiks and abdals, have made the vicinity of Broussa a district doubly sacred; it is for the Ottomans, the land of

* This title of Pacha, under which are designated the Governors of provinces, marks no special function; it is an honorary qualification which, especially in the early time of the Ottoman Empire, was given to every considerable personage. Aladdin, Orchan's brother, and Solyman, his son, bore the title of Pacha; under Othoman, two learned men had already borne it.

saints and poets, the sanctuary of the arts and at the same time the rendezvous of the elect.* In the mosques of the city were erected the mausoleums of the six first sovereigns who were the founders of them; around them are ranged those of their brothers, sons, wives and daughters, twenty-six princes of their blood, their most illustrious viziers and beylerbeys, and about five hundred tombs of pachas, sheiks, professors, rhetors, poets, physicians, and even celebrated musicians. Full of memorials of the first age of the Ottoman dynasty, Broussa is not only one of the most flourishing towns of the empire; but it is above all, the holy city.

4. *Early contests of the Turks and Greeks in Europe.*

Meanwhile Orchan, though anxiously occupied with the internal prosperity of his States, did not neglect opportunities of extending abroad his power and influence. Those twenty years unmarked by any military enterprise, served to prepare the most important of all by its results —the first establishment of the Ottomans in Europe.

Towards the end of the thirteenth century, shortly after the restoration of the Greek Empire by Michael Palæologus, a large Turkish horde, in number from 10,000 to 20,000, crossed the Bosphorus and made a settlement upon the European continent: these were the Turcomans, subjects of the Seljoukides. They had at first planted themselves on the coast of Bulgaria, in the Dobrudscha; but they did not remain long there and emigrated to the Crimea. It has been said that, after the fall of the Seljoukides, the Turks of the principalities of Aïdin, Khorasi, &c., began to ravage the Archipelago and the coasts of Greece. Not long after we find the Tartars, who had espoused the quarrel of a Seljukian prince, advancing to the very walls of Constantinople. In 1307 a band of Turks from Aïdin (the ancient Ionia) assisted the Catalans in their hostilities against the Emperor; these, after hav-

* It is well-known that very lately Abd-el-Kader chose Broussa as the place of his retreat or of his exile.

ing ravaged the Chersonesus, and rendered themselves more or less formidable during seven years, were at length either destroyed or compelled to return to Asia. The Ottomans, in turn, landed for the first time in Europe in 1321, but that was only a piratical expedition which ravaged the coasts of Thrace and Macedonia; and it is only in the reign of Orchan that the first relations took place between the Ottomans and the Byzantines. Andronicus the Elder had succeeded, in 1282, to Michael Palæologus. After having long struggled against the Ottomans in Asia, he was threatened by the revolt of his grandson, Andronicus the Younger, and sought aid from Orchan. That aid did not prevent him from being beaten and constrained to share his crown with the rebel. The Byzantine Empire, fallen to the lowest degree of abasement, was cankered with the same vices, the same anarchy, the same corruption, the same theological disputes, which had begun its ruin. The few enlightened men it yet contained, among others Michael Palæologus, knew that there was no other salvation for it save in the sincere and complete reunion with the Latin Church, a union that would interest all the West in their dangers and would revive the crusades. This they essayed by sending to the council of Lyons, presided over by Pope Gregory X., an act of union signed by the Emperor and thirty-five bishops, but their efforts failed through the fanaticism, blind hatred, and folly of the people and clergy. Never had nation better prepared and deserved its ruin.

In this situation, Andronicus the Younger become sole Emperor, no longer calculated upon shielding himself from the invasions of the Turks, save by seeking their alliance; he treated, therefore, in 1330 with the princes of Aidin and of Sarou-Khan; in 1333 with Orchan; but these alliances proved altogether abortive. Orchan, during his peace with the Emperor, suddenly passed over to Constantinople in 1337, with thirty-six ships, with a view to effect a permanent conquest. A vigorous resistance was made by the Emperor and his great courtier, John Cantacuzene, and the invader was repulsed with the loss of nearly all his armament. In 1340 a body of 8,000

Ottomans crossed the Hellespont, ravaged Thrace and Mæsia, and returned laden with booty. Andronicus the Younger died in 1341; and the discord that followed upon his death tended to deliver up the empire to the barbarians. Profiting by the minority of John Palæologus, "the great courtier," Cantacuzene, who exercised the regency, assumed the purple and declared himself the colleague of the young Emperor. Seeking to lay the foundation of absolute sovereignty and undivided power in the internal dissensions of the Empire, Cantacuzene, in order to carry on the civil war, summoned to his aid the Prince of Aïdin, Umer-Bey, who was his firm friend. The partisans of Palæologus purchased the assistance of the Prince of Sarou-Khan, and 30,000 Turks marched to ravage the empire in the names of the two Emperors. In 1347 the Prince of Aïdin, recalled to Asia by an attack of the Venetians,* abandoned his ally. Orchan then intervened. He demanded of Cantacuzene his daughter's hand, which was immediately accorded him. The nuptials were celebrated with great pomp at Selymbria, and, the year following, the aged husband went to visit his father-in-law at Scutari. Strengthened by this new alliance, Cantacuzene imposed upon his rival an apparent reconciliation, and returned to Constantinople. But shortly after, in spite of the alliance and the ties of relationship, a band of Ottomans ravaged afresh the coasts of Thrace. Umer-Bey died in defending his States, and Orchan found himself sole arbiter of the Greek Empire. Solicited by both parties, he profited by that fortunate position, which allowed him to perpetuate their discords that he might gather the fruit of them; without breaking with his father-in-law, he sent reinforcements to the Genoese, his enemies,† fought the Venetians, his allies, and gave hopes to John Palæologus.

* The principality of Aïdin comprehended Ionia and had Smyrna and Ephesus for chief cities. The Venetians, already masters of so many maritime points in the Mediterranean, coveted the possession of Smyrna and had united in a kind of crusade with the Pope and the King of Cyprus.
† The Genoese had remained, since the Latin Empire, masters of Pera and Galata, and they kept them until the capture of Constantinople by the Turks.

Such was the state of things, when a *coup-de-main* caused the fortress of Tzympe, situate upon the European coast, at a league and a half from Gallipoli, to fall into the power of the Ottomans. Solyman Pacha, Orchan's son, was encamped on the Asiatic shore of the Hellespont facing that city, not far from the ruins of Cyzicus. Favoured by a stormy night, he crossed the strait upon rafts with sixty of his companions, surprised the fortress, and captured it (1356). This gave the Turks their first permanent footing in Europe; and it is remarkable that the record of this event is the first mention which the Ottoman historians make of the passage of the Turks into Europe, disdaining, perhaps, to notice those earlier expeditions which left no lasting trace of victory behind them. Cantacuzene protested loudly against this violation of engagements; and during his negotiation for the restitution of Tzympe, a violent earthquake desolated the coast of Thrace, and destroyed in part several towns. Gallipoli, the key of the Hellespont, and the great emporium of the trade of the East, the walls of which having been shattered by the convulsion had left it exposed to the attack of an invader, fell into the hands of the Ottomans. Whilst the inhabitants had fled in terror, the Turks entered by the breaches the scourge had made, and in this manner was Gallipoli taken (1357), and thus was the foundation of the Ottoman Empire in Europe permanently laid.

Besides that place, the possession of which sufficed to assure them a free entrance into Europe, they made themselves masters of Boulaïr, Ipsala, and Rodosto; they were not more than thirty leagues from Constantinople. Thenceforth, there was no longer any question of restitution; in vain Cantacuzene offered 40,000 ducats; Orchan delayed the negotiation interminably; then he appointed an interview at a certain place, to which the Greek Emperor alone repaired. Finally, to every complaint Orchan replied that it was not force of arms, but the divine will which had opened to the Turks the walls of Gallipoli. That important acquisition was announced to all the Mussulman princes of Asia by official letters, the original model of the emphatic circulars which have remained in use in the Ottoman Chancery.

From that time the Turks made annual inroads into the Greek territories, until they had extended their dominions from the shores of the Propontis to the banks of the Danube. Solyman Pacha fixed his residence at Gallipoli, but he did not long enjoy his triumph; he died, in 1359, of a fall from his horse. His body was deposited in a mosque which he had caused to be built at Boulaïr; and of all the tombs mentioned as places of pilgrimage, none is more revered than that of the founder of the Ottoman power in Europe; none attracts a greater affluence of visitors. Orchan survived his son scarcely a year; he died in the seventy-fifth year of his age and thirty-fifth of his reign (1359). The annals of this prince are not stained with an account of the murder of his kinsmen, or of other sanguinary deeds; meanwhile the discipline and tactics of the army were materially improved, learning was encouraged, and as a lawgiver and author of the constitution, Orchan is usually regarded as the Numa of the Ottomans. Hereditary claim to the throne was now firmly established; and by the policy of Orchan, who had founded a great number of mosques, colleges, and hospitals the Ottoman prince was universally respected as the head of the Moslem faith. Born under the tent of an obscure chief of a horde, he died master of both shores of the Hellespont, and the Turks, who quitted with his father the steppes of Tartary, now dominated Asia Minor and threatened the relics of the Byzantine Empire.

5.—*History of Servia, Bosnia, Albania, &c.*

The authority of the Emperors no longer extended beyond the Strymon, in the west, or further than the chain of the Hæmus, to the north. Besides the south, which still belonged to the French and the Venetians, the western and northern provinces, for a long period occupied by Slav or Tartar nations that had frequently rendered themselves formidable to the Cæsars of Byzantium, came to be, by the means of the discords which weakened John Palæologus and his rival, torn away definitively from the Greek domination, and *Servia, Bosnia, Albania, Bulgaria*, and *Wallachia* formed distinct and independent States.

1. The Serbs belong to that one of the four branches of the Slav race* commonly called *Illyrian*, and which at the present time peoples Bosnia, Servia, Croatia, Dalmatia, Slavonia, &c. Towards the middle of the seventh century they occupied the country of the ancient Triballi, in the Upper Mæsia. Their conversion to Christianity dates from the reign of Heraclius, who sent priests to them; but it was not complete until that of the Emperor Basil, whose suzerainty they acknowledged by receiving a second baptism. Twice subjected by the Bulgarians, they re-entered with them under the domination of the Greeks in 1018, but ere long they emancipated themselves. In 1085, under Bodin and Voulkan, Servia and Bosnia rose in insurrection and took the national title of *Schoupans*. Beli-Ourosch, son of Voulkan, entitled himself Grand Duke of Servia, and had for successor (1143) Stephen Nemania, his grandson, who caused himself to be recognized by the Greek Emperors as the independent Prince of Servia, and was the founder of a dynasty which lasted three hundred years. Nemania had three sons: Stephen II., who succeeded him (1197); Volkan, Duke of Zeuta and Choulm, that is to say, of a portion of Dalmatia and Herzegovina; lastly, Sava, founder of the patriarchate of Servia. Stephen obtained from the Court of Rome the title of King. Emeric, King of Hungaria, took offence at it, drove him out of Servia, and immediately took the title of King of Rascie; but the dynasty of Nemania was speedily re-established, and took fresh lustre under Stephen Ourosch III. Finally came the glorious reign of Stephen Douschan

* The three others are the Zechs or Tchekes, who inhabit Bohemia, Russia, and Poland. The country of which Novi-Bazar is the chief town is so-called. It was celebrated in antiquity and in the Middle Ages by the valour of its inhabitants, and by its position hemmed in between Bosnia, Servia, Albania and Macedonia.

(1333), who was very near replacing the Greek by a Serb Empire, rendering abortive the Ottoman power, and thereby changing the destinies of Europe.

A conqueror and a legislator, Stephen Douschan was in some sort the Charlemagne of the Serbs. He possessed by himself, or by his vassals, almost the whole of what was actually Turkey in Europe, that is to say, Servia, Bosnia, Bulgaria, Macedonia, Dalmatia, Herzegovina, Albania, Etolia, &c. He caused himself to be crowned in 1340, at Uskioup, *Emperor of the Romans and of the Triballi*, and conceived the project of destroying the Empire of the East. After having for the first time besieged Constantinople and compelled the Emperor Andronicus to sue for peace, he marched anew against that city at the head of 80,000 men, when he died on his way thither (1356).

He had for successor Ourosch V., who did not inherit his sterling qualities, and under the attacks of its vassals, who sought to render themselves independent, the Serb empire was dismembered. We shall see what it became during the reign of Amurath II., and how the Turks profited by the conquests of the Serbs, who had cleared the way for them towards Constantinople.

2. Bosnia, as has been said, inhabited by a people of Slav race, had followed the destinies of Servia until the period (1085) at which Voulkan made of it a State, sometimes independent, sometimes vassal to the King of Hungary. It was comprised in the Empire of Stephen Douschan, separated itself after his death, formed an independent kingdom in 1376, under the Ban Stephen Tvarko, and finally fell, as will be seen, under the domination of the Turks.

3. The Albanians were of a very ancient race. Feebly attached to the Greek Empire, they had reconquered, in the decadence of that Empire, their independence, when they were subjugated temporarily by Stephen Douschan; after his death they resumed their isolation, divided themselves into several small principalities which took part in all the wars of the Serbs against the Turks.

4. The Bulgarians, of Tartar origin, established them-

selves, towards the end of the seventh century, in Mæsia, and were for three centuries the terror of the Byzantine Emperors. Subdued by John Zimisces (971), and converted to Christianity, they rendered themselves once more independent in 980, and formed a kingdom which was in continual war with the Serbs and Greeks. Basil II. annexed them afresh to his own empire. When Constantinople had fallen into the power of the Latins, the Bulgarians regained their independence, and waged a fierce warfare with the Frank Emperors. They fell subsequently under the domination of the Serb Kings, who accorded them nevertheless their national chiefs. On the death of Stephen Douschan, they again formed a separate State under the Prince or *Kral* Sisman, and followed the Serbs in all their wars against the Turks.

5. It only remains to speak of Wallachia. The origin of the people who call themselves *Roumains*, and who are scattered in the Hellenic peninsula, Hungary, &c., has already been mentioned. These people, in the tenth century, became tributaries to the Hungarians, &c. They regained their independence under Radoul, *the Black* (1290-1314), but they soon fell back again under the Hungarian domination. Their princes or Hospodars had numerous friendly relations with the Krals of Servia, and struggled with them against the Ottomans until the end of the fifteenth century.

Thus it will be seen that of all these peoples the most important, without contradiction, is the Serb race; in fact, it had absorbed so large a portion of the Hellenic race that the population which at the present time bears the name of Greek is only composed in reality of Hellenised Serbs. It had mixed itself up with the Albanians; it had given its language to the Bulgarians, who are now blended with it; and it spread almost throughout the Hellenic peninsula. Such a people appeared destined to achieve a great future, but the Slav race founded nothing during the Middle Ages, and the Illyrian branch, brave, poetic, light-hearted, unambitious, without thought for the future, has never lived save for the hour, preserving its primitive instincts, its vagabond habits, not caring to assimilate itself with the remains of the ancient civilization; in short, being tainted with the defect which has ruined all the Christian peoples of the East—its isolation from Latin unity. It will be shortly seen how this interesting people, to whom the heritage of Constantine seemed predestined, were about to leave it an easy prey to the victorious Osmanli.

CHAPTER IV.

REIGNS OF AMURATH I. AND BAJAZET I. (1360-1402).

1. *Amurath I.—Organization of the Janissaries.*

MOURAD or Amurath, second son of Orchan, destined by his birth to serve under his brother, had been kept aloof from State affairs until the moment when the death of Solyman summoned him to share the sovereign power. He showed himself worthy to wield it, and his reign, of prodigious activity, was only one long series of wars and conquests.

The early part of Amurath's administration is rendered remarkable by the organization of the celebrated body of infantry called Janissaries. A great number of Christian captives having been taken by the Turks, Kara Halil Pacha, the prime vizier, recommended the Sultan to appropriate a portion of them to the service of the Court and the army. An edict was accordingly issued, by which every fifth captive was claimed for this purpose; officers were stationed at Gallipoli to select and seize the most robust and handsome of the Christian youth; and great numbers of these were secured, who were to be educated in the Moslem faith, and trained as a regular militia to form the strength of the Ottoman army. The corps thus raised was next to be named and consecrated; and for this purpose it was sent to Hadji Bektash, a celebrated Dervish, in the environs of Amasia, who, standing in front of the prostrate ranks, and stretching his sleeve over the head of the foremost soldier, pronounced his benediction in the following manner:—" Let them be called *Jengi cheri* ;* may their

---

* *i.e.*—New soldiers or recruits, hence, by corruption, *Janissaries.*

countenance ever be bright, their hand victorious, and their sword keen! May their spear ever hang over the heads of the enemy! and whithersoever they go may they always return with a white face!"* Such was the singular formation of a body of men of desperate character; strangers, at first, to every tie except that of obedience to the Ottoman Prince, and contributing, by the introduction of military subordination and veteran experience, to the constitution of a vigorous and irresistible army. The sleeve of the Dervish was represented by a tassel hanging down from the back of the cap, in which respect only the dress of the new recruits differed from that of the other infantry; and the name which they had received was speedily conveyed on the wings of victory throughout the wide regions of Asia and Europe. The original number of the corps appears to have been 1,000, which was augmented yearly, and subsequently fixed by Amurath at 10,000. It afterwards rose under Mahomet II. to 12,000, under Solyman *the Great* to 20,000, and under Mahomet IV. to 40,000. When the extension of dominion had put an end to personal captivity, this body was supplied by a tax on every fifth male child levied on the Christian population of the Empire; and at last the children of the Janissaries themselves were enlisted into the service, a regulation which materially contributed to the relaxation of their discipline and their tumultuary spirit in later times. Up to the reign of Mahomet IV., that is to say at the period when the decadence of that celebrated corps began, it was not otherwise recruited, so that the number of Christian children has been estimated to have been not less than 5,000,000, who, in the space of three centuries, were thus converted by force and sacrificed to the barbarous policy of the Sultans. It was the most frightful tribute of human flesh that has ever been levied by a victorious religion over a vanquished faith. It gives the measure of the profound imbecility and subjection into which the Christian populations had fallen under the unmitigated despotism of the Moslem conquerors. It may

* *i.e.*—With praise and honour, as a black face is a term of disgrace.

ORGANIZATION OF THE JANISSARIES.

be observed, that by this strange mode of recruiting, the Ottomans found at one and the same time a method of carrying off the most virile portion from the Christian populations, and of doubling the strength of their forces without putting arms into the hands of the conquered. This it is which explains how they were able to set on foot armies of 300,000 to 600,000 men, whilst at the present day, when the Janissaries are no longer in existence, and when the rayahs are unfitted to enter the ranks of the Turkish armies, they have found it so difficult to raise 300,000 men. It will be seen what organization the Janissary militia received under Solyman *the Great*.

As the new militia was raised and maintained by the Sultan, it took for its rallying sign the flesh-pot (*Kasan*) which served to distribute their food; the flesh-pot was to the Janissary as sacred an object as his flag to the Christian soldier. Following out the same idea, the officers bore culinary titles; the commander-in-chief was called *tchorbadgi-bachi*, "first soup-maker;" after him came the *achtchi-bachi*, "first cook," and the *sakka-bachi*, "first water carrier;" and instead of a tuft the soldier's cap was ornamented with a wooden spoon. These eccentric customs lasted as long as the Janissary militia.

The *piadés* (foot-soldiers) were retained, but remodelled. The conquered lands were given them, on condition of defending them and keeping the roads in good order: this was a territorial militia. All those who fought on foot besides those privileged corps, without pay or fiefs, were ranked under the name of *azabs* (free); these were irregular infantry. A paid cavalry corps was also embodied, divided into four sorts: the *sipahis* or horsemen; the *silihdars* (vassal horsemen); the *ouloufedjis* (mercenaries); the *ghourebas* (strangers). These four picked corps, which, under the name of *sipahis*, made themselves, in the wars of Europe, as famous as the Janissaries, composed the Sultan's bodyguard when he joined his army; and to them was confided the sacred standard of the Prophet. An auxiliary corps of cavalry was also organized from the possessors of lands, in imitation of the piadés; they were called *mossellimans* (exempt from tax). Finally the *akindschis* were retained as irregular cavalry; they were, during several centuries, commanded by the Michaellogli, descendants of Kæse-Michael, who led the first skirmishers of Othoman.

Aladdin, Emir of Karamania, who had long been jealous of the conquests of Amurath, encouraged by the death of the celebrated vizier, Chaireddin Pacha, whose wisdom and valour had materially contributed to the success of the Ottoman arms, commenced open hostilities. This prince was at the head of a branch of the ancient Seljukian empire, inferior in importance only to the Ottoman itself; and he was aided in his enterprise by several other Moslem chiefs, who, like himself, were impatient of the advancing and encroaching power of their neighbour. Amurath marched in person against the enemy, and, after a decisive victory on the plains of Iconium, followed by the recapture of the city of Angora, granted peace to Aladdin. The Prince of Karamania then made an alliance with Amurath, and received from him his daughter in marriage. By this signal success the Ottoman power was established in Asia on a firmer footing than ever.

After that rapid and brilliant expedition everything was prepared for a campaign in Europe. Amurath gave the command in chief of the troops, with the title of *beylerbey* (prince of princes), to Lalaschanin, one of the companions-in-arms of his father, and who had accompanied Solyman at the taking of Tzympe. The office of judge of the army, until then only temporary, was made permanent, and conferred on Kara Halil-Djendereli, he to whom the institution of the Janissaries was owing, then upwards of seventy years old, and destined to play an important part in the events of the new reign. Besides those two veterans, the army counted amongst its chiefs Ewrenos-Bey, a renegade, Hadji-Ilbek, Timour-Tasch, who, all three, had distinguished themselves by their successes.

Aided by his lieutenants, Amurath, early in 1361, advanced into Thrace. Cantacuzene had abdicated (1355) after the loss of Gallipoli, and John Palæologus reigned alone; but, reduced to impotence, he did not attempt to oppose the slightest resistance to that threatening invasion. After capturing Dimotika and some secondary places, the Ottomans marched straight upon Adrianople. That city, built by Adrian at the confluence of three rivers, the Maritza, the Arda, and the Toundja, had promptly become, thanks to its admirable position, rich, populous, and flourishing; it was, under the Byzantines, as under the Ottomans, the second city of the Empire. The Greek commander advanced to meet the Turkish army, was defeated and fled; the garrison, discouraged, surrendered almost without resistance (1361). Ewrenos and Lalaschanin were then ordered, the one to descend, the other to ascend the banks of the Maritza, and to subdue the circumjacent towns: the first-named advanced as far as the mouth of the Vardar; the second took Philippopolis and the two Sagras, strong towns at the foot of the Hæmus. Consequent upon these expeditions the law was established which fixed the share of booty. By virtue of a precept of the Korân, which allots a fifth part to the poor and to the Prophet, the exchequer levied previously a fifth upon the price of every prisoner.

After the capture of Philippopolis, Amurath made peace with the Greek Emperor, and returned to Broussa; but whence he was soon recalled by an unexpected attack. The Christian princes on the other side of the Hæmus, who had been startled at the sight of the Mussulmans approaching their frontiers, had given the alarm to Europe. Pope Urban V. preached a crusade against the Turks. Without awaiting aid from the West, Ourosch V. King or *Kral* of Servia, the voïvodes of Bosnia and Wallachia, leagued together; King Louis of Hungary joined them, and 20,000 Christians descended from the banks of the Maritza to within two days' march of Adrianople. The Turks were not strong enough to risk an engagement with open force; but, under cover of a dark night, Hadji-Ilbek, with a body of 10,000 men, surprised the carelessly guarded camp; the Christians, unarmed, heard with terror the war-cry of the Mussulmans, *Allah! Allah!* resounding.

They fled in disorder, and perished, for the most part, in the waters of the Maritza (1363). The plain bears to this day the name of *Sirh-Zinddughi* (defeat of the Serbs).

Amurath employed the leisure which that victory left him to construct mosques, cloisters, schools, and baths at Biledschik, at Jenitschehr, and Broussa. At this time also he concluded the first treaty ever made by the Ottomans with a Christian power: he granted to the small republic of Ragusa commercial privileges in his States. When it became necessary to sign the act, the barbarous sovereign dipped his five fingers in the ink and thus made his mark upon the parchment, to which a scribe added his name and titles. The *toughra* or seal of the Sultans still recalls by its form that primitive impression.

On his return to Europe in 1365 his presence was the signal for new conquests, which gave for delimitation to his possessions the chain of the Hæmus from the source of the Maritza as far as the sea. Whilst his lieutenants captured Islivné (Selivno) and Jamboli, upon the Toundja, Ichtiman and Samakov, in the Balkans, he himself seized upon Aïdos and Karnabat, places which command two of the principal defiles of the Hæmus. Visa, Kirk-Kilissia, Binar-Hissar (Castle of the Springs), Sizeboli, &c., fell successively into his power. Five years were employed in these expeditions. At the same time, from Dimotika, in which he had at first established himself, he hastened the erection of the seraglio of Adrianople, which became his chief residence. At the same period the office of vizier, vacant for ten years past, was given to Khalil-Djendereli, who filled it during some eighteen years, under the new name of Chaireddin-Pacha. That dignity remained hereditary in his family until the epoch of the capture of Constantinople.

The following year was passed in chastising certain Byzantine towns, the governors of which had disquieted the Ottoman territory, or in making conquests at the expense of petty Serbian or Bulgarian princes. Next, he renewed his attacks against Palæologus and wrested from him Tschatal-Borgas, Indschigis, &c., upon the road from

Adrianople to Constantinople. He accorded him a fresh truce, in order that he might turn his arms against the Slav or Wallachian princes established in ancient Macedonia, to the west of the Rhodope. That branch of the Hæmus, which had until then served as a barrier to the incursions of the Ottomans, was overleaped : to the south, all was conquered as far as the town of Seres, and the two Serb princes of the country, Drages and Bogdan, were made prisoners. Then, Amurath himself marched against the *Kral* of Servia, Lazarus Brankovich, illegitimate grandson of the great Douschan; crossed the Balkans and vanquished him near Samakov, seized upon the important town of Nissa, and compelled him to pay tribute and to furnish him auxiliary troops. The Kral of Bulgaria, Simans, who had taken part in the war, underwent the same treatment, and was forced to send his daughter into the harem of Amurath.

2 *Acquisitions in Asia Minor.—Feudal Organization of the Sipahis.*

Six years of peace having followed the capture of Nissa, Amurath employed them first with the marriage of his eldest son, Bajazet, to the daughter of the Emir of Kermian, which gave him Koutaieh and five other towns of Phrygia; next, in the acquisition by purchase of the six chief towns in the principality of Hamid, in ancient Pisidia : a compulsory bargain with which the sovereign of that small territory was forced to comply in order to avoid a contest that had become too unequal. Finally, during that interval of rest, an important modification in the military organization was introduced.

"There were erected," says D'Ohsson, "fiefs in all the provinces of the empire, with the object of providing for their defence and for the reward of military services. The *sipahi* (horseman) invested with such a grant collected to his profit the product of public imposts levied upon the lands of his fief, cultivated by peasants, whether Mahometans or Christians, over whom he exercised at the same time a seignorial jurisdiction. The latter possessed the proprietorship; but when they transmitted it to individuals of their family, other than their sons, the heirs could not enter into possession of it without having obtained the consent of the *sipahi* and paid him a fine. If the possessor left no heir, his land property was to be given by the *sipahi* to one of the neighbours of the defunct. On his part, the *sipahi*, obliged to reside in his fief, under pain of incurring disherison, received in concession (*ihtaá*) the revenue of the land, that is to say, a part of the total of the tax due from it, but in nowise the capital, which remained in the hands of the State." *

The fiefs thus constituted were divided into three classes, according to their extent : the *timars*, the *ziämets*, and the *beyliks*. Each fief was bound to furnish a horseman, armed with a cuirass, for every 3,000 aspres † of his income. In the sixteenth century there were reckoned 50,000 fiefs of the third class, 300 of the second, and 200 of the first. The *timariots* marched under the orders of the *zaïms;* the latter obeyed the *beys;* the beys were obliged to range themselves under the banner of the pacha of the province. The fiefs could only be conferred on the sons of the *sipahis*, and, on each vacancy, the candidates were bound to prove their descent by the testimony of two zaïms and two timariots. The advancement of the feudatories was regulated according to their services on the field of battle : he who brought in the head of an enemy received an increase of an aspre of revenue for each dozen of aspres that his fief yielded; fifteen heads gave a right to a more considerable fief. That powerful organization subsisted until the reign of Solyman *the Great*, when the fiefs furnished not less than 200,000 horsemen.‡

Amurath, on reorganizing his powerful squadrons of

* "Tableau Générale de L'Empire Ottoman," tom. vii. p. 372.
† The aspre was then worth a little more than the piastre of the present day, it is now worth only the 120th of a piastre.
‡ Ubicini, "Lettres sur la Turquie."

sipahis, gave them a particular standard, the red banner; the white had been the colour of the Ommiades; the black that of the Abassides, the green that of the Fatimites; the yellow, the hue of the sun, had been that of the Prophet; the red, the colour of blood, became that of the Ottomans.

3. *New Conquests in Europe and Asia.—Battle of Iconium.*

In 1381 war was recommenced against the Serbs. Timour-Tasch, become *beylerbey* after the death of Lalaschanin, having succeeded in driving them out of Macedonia, pressed forward as far as the frontiers of Albania and seized upon Monastir, Pirilpa, and Istip. Another army crossed the Hæmus, on the side of Samakov, and laid siege to Sophia, the ancient Sardica; after a resistance of two years, the governor was taken by treason, and the city opened its gates. After Sophia, Monastir, and Nissa, the Ottomans found themselves masters of military positions which dominated the Hellenic peninsula.

Meanwhile, the Greek empire, reduced almost to the suburbs of Constantinople, and placed in absolute dependence upon the Ottomans, no longer existed save at their pleasure. Palæologus tried to stir up the Western nations in his favour; he went himself to Rome, acknowledged the supremacy of the Pope, and subscribed to the reunion of the two Churches. Urbain V. promised him as a recompense a fleet and an army, but those promises remained without fulfilment. The West stirred not a step; and the Greek Emperor, on returning from Rome, found himself detained at Venice by his creditors, and one of his sons was compelled to dispose of his effects in order to release him. This attempt served only to aggravate his position: trembling at having irritated his formidable neighbour, he made a solemn declaration of submission, and sent Theodore, his youngest son, to serve in the Ottoman army.

Shortly afterwards, Andronicus, son of Palæologus, and Sandschi-Bey, son of Amurath, dared to conspire against their fathers. At the first rumour of the revolt, Amurath, who was in Asia, summoned the Emperor before him, and made him promise to put out his son's eyes; then he passed into Europe where his presence alone sufficed to scatter the rebels. The Greek prince was rendered blind; Sandschi-Bey was put to death; all the nobles who had taken part in the conspiracy were, in Amurath's presence, flung from the walls of Dimotica into the river. Unterrified at the fate of his brother, another son of Palæologus Manuel, governor of Thessalonica, attempted to surprise Seres. That fool-hardy enterprise miscarried; Chaireddin Pacha marched upon Thessalonica and took it. Manuel had taken flight; his father dare not receive him at Constantinople; and after having wandered up and down the Archipelago, repulsed everywhere by the dread which his terrible enemy inspired, he was reduced to go and implore his clemency. Amurath pardoned him, but kept Thessalonica.

The Ottoman empire became more and more formidable to its neighbours. Of the numerous principalities that were formed after the fall of the Seljoukides, three already were absorbed; Karasi by conquest, Kermian by marriage, Hamid by purchase. The princes of Karaman, who had been long the most powerful heirs of the Sultans of Roum, saw themselves dominated and menaced; thus, in 1386, one of them, Aladdin, emboldened by some symptoms of internal troubles, and especially by the death of the wise Chaireddin Pacha, thought the occasion favourable to assume the offensive. He joined to his troops the Turkoman hordes, scattered throughout Asia Minor, and invaded the province of Hamid. Suddenly, he learned that Amurath, whom he thought to take unawares, was collecting together in the plain of Koutaieh all his military forces; that the *beylerbey* had arrived from Europe with an army in which were marching 2,000 auxiliary Serbs and the inhabitants of all the countries recently conquered. Instantly he sent an ambassador to implore peace, but it was too late; the young vizier, Ali Pacha, rejected all his proposals. The two armies encountered each other under the walls of Iconium, the capital of the princes of Karaman. It was there that Bajazet, who was destined to succeed Amurath, first bore arms and merited by his fiery valour the surname of *Ilderim* (the Lightning). The Karamanians were vanquished; the town, immediately besieged, could not offer a long resistance; Aladdin submitted. Thanks to the intercession of his wife, who was Amurath's daughter, he preserved his capital and States on condition of paying tribute.

The Sultan next found himself upon the frontiers of the small principality of Tekieh, formed from the ancient Pamphylia and a part of Lycia. He was urged to make himself master of it. " The Lion makes not war upon flies," was his disdainful reply. Then he added:—" Know you not that the lord of Tekieh reigns only over Istinos and Attalia?" The latter took the hint and offered him the rest of his domains in order to keep the two towns indicated.

4. *Battle of Kassova.—Death of Amurath.*

Scarcely was the war ended in Asia, ere it broke out in Europe. Lazarus, Kral of Servia, and Sisman, Kral of the Bulgarians, leagued together, attacked a body of 20,000 Turks who were pillaging Bosnia and destroyed it almost entirely (1387). The Vizir Ali Pacha advanced immediately towards Bulgaria, and penetrated therein by the defile of Nadir-Derbend: Pravadi was taken by force; Shumla surrendered, Sisman, besieged in Nicopolis, was compelled to submit; Amurath, from consideration for his daughter, demanded only from him payment of tribute in arrears and the giving up of Silistria. Ali Pacha then directed his march towards Servia. Scarcely had he set out, than Sisman, instead of surrendering Silistria, increased its fortifications. The vizir immediately retraced his steps, and the war recommenced: it terminated by the almost entire submission of Bulgaria.

During this interval, Amurath marched in person against the Serbs. Lazarus had called to his aid the princes of Bosnia, Wallachia, Albania, and Herzegovina; he was joined even by contingents from Hungary and Poland. All these allied forces awaited the Turkish army in the plain of Kassova, the military importance of which has been already noted; it was there that was about to be decided to whom should belong that Empire of the East which was no more than a name (1389). The Turks were so inferior in numbers that they hesitated to give battle. The vizir opened haphazard the Korân to seek therein, according to Mussulman custom, a sign of the celestial will; he fell upon that passage: "O Prophet, subdue the infidels and the hypocrites, for often a weaker force overthrows a greater." Thereupon, he insisted upon giving battle; the ardent Bajazet supported his opinion; but, as a violent wind was raising clouds of dust that blinded the Ottomans, night came on ere a decision was arrived at. Towards morning a slight rain fell, and battle was resolved upon. On the side of the Christians none doubted of victory, and when it was proposed to attack the enemy during the night, Castriot the Albanian opposed it, because the darkness, he said, would hinder pursuit of the runaways. As soon as the rain had ceased, the two armies formed their battle array; a few Janissaries placed in front of the Ottoman army, handled awkwardly some large cannons, a recent invention derived from the West, and upon which they calculated little more than wherewith to frighten the enemy. The battle had already begun and the *mêlée* was raging furiously, especially on the left wing, when, rushing into the midst of the Sultan's guards, a noble Serb, Milosch Kabilovitch, cried out that he wished to confide a secret to him. Upon a sign from Amurath, he was allowed to approach him, whereupon he stooped down as if he would kiss his feet, and then plunged his dagger into his stomach. Then, freeing himself violently from the attendant guards, he sprang forward and ran as far as the bank of the river Ibar. Overtaken at the moment he was about to plunge into the stream, he was cut to pieces.

Such is the narrative of the Ottoman historians; the following is the Servian tradition as related by the Byzantine historian Jean Ducas: "On the evening before the battle, the King Lazarus whilst drinking with his nobles out of cups called *Stravizas:* 'Empty this cup to my health,' said Lazarus to Milosch, 'although you are accused of betraying us.' 'Thanks,' replied Milosch, 'the course of to-morrow will prove my fidelity.' The next morning, Milosch, mounted upon a powerful courser, rode into the enemy's camp, and requested as a deserter to kiss the feet of the Sultan, which was granted him. Then he stooped down . . ." &c. However that might be, Amurath had time to give orders that assured the victory; Lazarus, taken prisoner, was brought before him and beheaded, he himself expiring in the course of a few hours. A Turkish chapel marks the spot where he died; three large stones, placed at fifty ells apart, mark, as it is asserted, the three bounds made by the assassin in his attempt to escape. The name of Milosch Kabilovitch has remained popular amongst the Serbs and is no less remembered by the Turks; in the arsenal of the seraglio they have preserved his armour and the trappings of his horse; finally, it is said, that after that event was introduced the custom of holding by both arms every one who was presented to the Sultan.

The battle of Kassova was the ruin of the Serbs. It decided the abasement or the subjection of all the Slav peoples, and was calculated to give definitively to the Osmanlis the domination of the country which had formed the Byzantine Empire.

5. *Bajazet I. (Bajezid Ilderim).—Abasement of the Greek Emperors.—Acquisitions in Asia Minor.—Conquest of Wallachia and Bulgaria.*

Bajazet was proclaimed Sultan upon the battle-field of Kassova. His first act was to order the death of his brother Yacoub, whose valour and popularity gave him umbrage. "Sedition," says the Korân, "is worse than murder." That maxim of the Prophet has served to justify the political atrocities which have inaugurated the reigns of the majority of the Sultans.

After having accorded magnificent funerals to his father and brother, Bajazet vigorously pushed on the war against Servia; whilst his lieutenants penetrated into Bosnia and Bulgaria, he compelled Prince Stephen, son of Lazarus, to acknowledge himself his tributary, and to give him his sister in marriage. At the same time, he made and unmade emperors, much more the master at Constantinople than the phantom sovereigns whom he allowed to reside there. Andronicus, son of the Emperor John Palæologus, condemned by the order of Amurath to lose his sight, had not been wholly blinded; from the depth of his dungeon he solicited Bajazet's protection, promising, if he gave him the empire, to pay an enormous tribute. The Sultan went to Constantinople with 6,000 horsemen and 4,000 foot soldiers, seized the Emperor John and his son Manuel, and placed them in the hands of Andronicus, advising him to make away with them. The latter contented himself with incarcerating them; but shortly afterwards the prisoners escaped, and went to seek succour from him who had overthrown them. They had no trouble in deciding him in their favour. The old Emperor promised to continue the tribute and to contribute annually a body of 12,000 men to the Ottoman army. However, Andronicus was not sent back to prison, but received from Bajazet, as his vassal, Selymbria, Heraclea, Rodosto, and Thessalonica. Manuel was crowned as co-regent with his father. There only remained to the one and the other Constantinople and its suburbs.

However, they had not reached the last degree of abasement. There was reserved for them a last, unique, and incredible humiliation. One town only in Asia was still occupied by the Greeks—Philadelphia (now Alaschehr), upon the confines of the principality of Aïdin, and of the Ottoman States; Bajazet resolved to make himself master of it in order to devote the revenues to the construction of his mosque at Adrianople. The governor having refused to open the gates, Philadelphia was invested by an army, in the ranks of which figured Byzantine troops, commanded by the Emperor himself and his son; both themselves mounted to the assault of their own city, and took possession of it in the name of the Ottomans! Manuel remained at the Sultan's Court among his valets and guards.

Master of Alaschehr, Bajazet appeared disposed to invade the principality of Aïdin. The Turkish prince went to make his submission, acknowledged himself as vassal, renounced his sovereign rights, and delivered up his chief towns. The princes of Sarou-Khan and Mentesché, who reigned in Lydia and Caria, imitated his example, and speedily all three, renouncing the vain shadow of authority, fled into the principality of Kastemouni. Thus disappeared without resistance those three States to be transformed into Ottoman provinces. At the same blow was confiscated what remained of the principalities of Tekieh and Kermian. The princes of Karaman and Kastemouni alone remained standing. The first was attacked and Iconium invested. To avoid being entirely stripped, he abandoned the greater portion of his possessions.

After these easy conquests Bajazet commenced his march towards Europe, and found himself at Broussa, when he learned that the Emperor had caused two new towers to be built at Constantinople at the Gilded Gate. He ordered him to raze those structures, if he did not wish to see his son Manuel's eyes put out. The Emperor obeyed. At the commencement of the year following (1391) he died. On learning this, Manuel escaped furtively from Broussa, where he was performing his service at the door of the Sultan. Scarcely had he arrived in Constantinople when he received an order to instal there a cadi to judge the affairs of the Moslims; and upon his refusal the surrounding country was invaded by a Turkish army, which kept the city besieged. Manuel resisted during seven years, and was during the whole of that time a prisoner within the walls of his capital.

Then Bajazet, already master of a portion of Bulgaria, crossed the Danube and attacked Wallachia. The duke, or voïvode, Marcea, who had figured at the battle of Kassova, was defeated and constrained to accept a treaty (1393), by which the Sultan compels "the principality, subjected to his invincible laws, to pay tribute, and consents that it may continue to govern itself by its own laws." The King of Hungary, Sigismond, who advanced pretensions to the suzerainty of the Danubian principalities, advanced into Bulgaria, but was compelled to retire precipitately. The year following, the vizir, Ali Pacha, achieved the conquest of the province. Finally, the Prince of Bulgaria, long shut up in Nicopolis, capitulated with his son, who embraced Islamism (1394).

6. *Submission of Asia Minor.—Battle of Nicopolis.—Conquest of Greece.*

War was resumed in Asia. Aladdin, Prince of Karaman, attempted a final effort. He threw himself suddenly upon the Ottoman provinces, penetrated as far as Broussa, and seized upon the beylerbey Timour-Tasch. At these tidings Bajazet recrossed the strait. In vain Aladdin again tried to negotiate. A great battle was fought in the plain of Aktschaï, in Kermian; the Prince of Karaman was taken and put to death; the whole country was conquered and incorporated in the empire (1392). It was destined to resume its independence, and for a long while yet embarrass the development of the empire of the Osmanlis.

That conquest brought about the submission of the last of the Turkish States, Kastemouni, which comprehended, as has been said, the ancient Paphlagonia, with a part of Pontus. Amisus (now Samsoun), Amasia, Sinope, ancient Milesian colonies, had been considerable towns in the

BAYAZID.

flourishing times of the Roman Empire, and had not yet lost their importance; rich in mines, industrious and populous, that country prospered under the government of the Isfendiars, who had there established their domination at the commencement of the fourteenth century. The last representative of that dynasty, Bajazet the Perclus, had given an asylum to the dispossessed princes of Aïdin, Mentesché and Sarou-Khan; this was the pretext for war. The attack was so sudden that the strongest places offered little resistance. Bajazet Isfendiar shut himself up in Sinope, and treated with the conqueror, who left him that town and its territory; but, not thinking himself in safety, he fled, and went to seek a protector in Timour, whose conquests were beginning to resound throughout the East. Leaving to his beylerbey the care of securing his domination in those remote provinces, Bajazet returned to Europe to watch more closely over Constantinople, which his forces were then besieging. He snatched away Thessalonica from the Greeks, which he had restored to them, and defeated a Christian fleet despatched from Italy to succour the place.

The Greek Empire was now at his mercy; the least effort would deliver it up to him; his domination extended in Europe as far as the Danube, in Asia to the Taurus; he appeared to have reached the apogee of his power. It was then that, dissatisfied with the title of Emir borne by his predecessors, he sent an embassy to the Khalife of Egypt, that shadowy phantom which the Mamelukes presented to the Mussulmans as the descendant of the Abassides, asking his authorisation to assume the title of *Sultan:* he obtained it readily.

Never had Christianity sustained such terrible losses, nor seemed so near to entire destruction; never was a crusade so necessary. King Sigismond of Hungary, after having uselessly attempted to defend Bulgaria, seeing his frontiers menaced, made an appeal to Europe, and a band of knights from the West hastened to the banks of the Danube. The French gave the example; in 1395, the Count d'Eu, Constable of France, led forth some five to six hundred knights with whom Sigismond entered Bulgaria and retook several fortresses upon the Danube. In the following year arrived a small army of a thousand lances, among which figured the Count de Nevers (John *Sans-Peur*), son of the Duke of Burgundy, the Sire de Bourbon, Henri and Philip de Bar, cousins of the King of France, the Constable, the Admiral Jean de Vienne, the Marshal Boucicaut, Guy de la Tremouille, the Sire de Coucy, and the flower of the French nobility. In crossing Germany they brought with them the Teutonic knights and their Grand Prior, a troop of Bavarian nobles commanded by the Elector Palatine, and the young nobility of Styria under Hermann, Count of Cilly. The Grand Master of St. John of Jerusalem came from Rhodes with his chevaliers; and finally, the Voïvode of Wallachia refused tribute to the Turks, and made alliance with the King of Hungary.

Towards Pentecost of the year 1396 about 60,000 Christians were assembled at Vienna; they divided themselves into two corps, and directed their march towards Bulgaria: the Hungarians went by way of Servia, which they ravaged; their allies by Wallachia. Widdin and Orsova were taken, and they reunited their forces to attack Nicopolis. It was then that the Christians encountered the army of Bajazet, 200,000 strong, and which was composed, to the shame of the schismatics of the East, of as many Serbs, Greeks, and Bosnians as of Osmanlis. Here, as at Kassova, a foolish confidence, a blind presumption, preluded a disaster of the Christian army; to those fatal tendencies was further added that fiery insubordination which caused the loss of so many battles to the French armies of the Middle Ages. When the approach of the Turks was announced, the greater part of the Crusaders refused to believe it; then the French, in spite of the representations of the prudent De Coucy, insisted upon being placed in the first line, and to begin the combat; finally, on the eve of the battle, they massacred their prisoners, thus justifying beforehand the sanguinary reprisals which were destined to render that day one of sorrowful memory. On the 22nd September the vanguard of Bajazet began the action. Nothing could resist at first the *furia Francese*: the *Azabs* were dispersed in an instant, the Janissaries broken; the sipahis, behind whom they rallied to reform their ranks, left 5,000 of their number upon the field of battle, and were put to the rout. The French thought themselves the victors, and they pursued in a disorderly way the fugitives; when, on reaching the heights, they found themselves in presence of the veritable Turkish army: 40,000 men in good order awaited them. At the first moment, seized with a panic terror, some took to flight; the greater part launched themselves in desperation upon those huge masses, resolved to sell dearly their lives, and to save at least the honour of chivalry. At a thousand paces in the rear stood drawn up the Hungarian army; at the moment it saw disorder spread amongst the French ranks the whole of the right wing, commanded by the traitor Lazkovitz, Voïvode of Transylvania, fled; Marcea, who formed the left wing with his Wallachians, immediately ordered a retreat. The centre remained, consisting of faithful Hungarians, under the orders of King Sigismond, and some German auxiliaries, in all 12,000 men: they marched resolutely forwards. Notwithstanding the inequality of numbers, the fight was renewed; and the victory would have perhaps remained with the Christians, had it not been for the savage fury of the Serbs, who served as auxiliaries in the Turkish army; it was they who decided the fortunes of the day, more fatal for their country than the battle of Kassova! The King of Hungary and the principal German chiefs extricated themselves from the *mêlée*, found two barks on the river's bank, and descended as far as its mouth, where a Venetian fleet received them. All the remainder were slain or made prisoners after a terrible struggle. Sixty thousand Turks had, it is said, perished. Bajazet, frenzied with rage, rode over in the evening the field of battle covered with the dead bodies of his soldiers; never had a victory cost him so dearly, and he determined to take a fearful revenge for it. The next morning at daybreak he caused all the prisoners to be mustered; they numbered 10,000, bound hand and foot, and half naked: the massacre began. The Count de Nevers obtained his own life and that of twenty-four of his companions, but he was compelled to be present at the slaughter of all the Christians; at length, at four o'clock in the afternoon, yielding to the entreaties of his lieutenants, the Sultan consented to spare those who remained. Among the survivors was Schiltberger, a young Bavarian equerry, who, later, after thirty-four years of captivity, returned to his native country to give details of that terrible day. The kings of Hungary, France, and Cyprus joined together to pay the ransom of the unfortunate captives: it amounted to 200,000 ducats.

This brilliant success raising to its highest point the power of Bajazet, the moment seemed arrived for taking Constantinople, which continued to be blockaded by the Ottoman troops. However, the Sultan feared lest that enterprise might drive the Greeks to despair and draw upon him a league of the Christian princes; he therefore contented himself with imposing a truce on Manuel, with the following conditions: an annual tribute of 30,000 gold crowns, the introduction of the public worship of Islam into Constantinople, the foundation of a mosque, and the establishment of a cadi.

That truce lasted but for a very short time: Bajazet made alliance with the Prince of Selymbria, John, nephew of Michael, and who had pretensions to the throne; then he blockaded Constantinople again. Manuel implored aid of the King of France, who sent him a small body of troops commanded by the Marshal de Boucicaut, one of the conquered at Nicopolis. The latter, with four ships of war, forced the entrance of the Hellespont, defended by seventeen Turkish galleys, and entered into Constantinople with 600 men-at-arms and 1,000 archers. That succour drove away the Ottomans at first, and allowed of their retaking several fortresses; but shortly they returned in greater numbers. Boucicaut, despairing of success, offered Manuel to conduct him into France, and advised him to share the throne with his nephew. In fact, Manuel left Constantinople to John, and withdrew to the Morea.

Bajazet lost no time in pursuing him thither: he invaded Thessaly, passed through Thermopylæ, penetrated as far as Attica without meeting with any resistance; all the towns opened their gates to him. As for Manuel he had taken ship to go and solicit the succour of the West. It was only under the walls of Athens that the Ottomans had to fight. There still subsisted the French establishments of the preceding century, a principality tributary to the Kings of Sicily and Aragon. The town, defended with courage, was taken by assault; Argos had the same fate; all the Peloponnesus was sacked, and colonies of Turkomans were brought from the centre of Asia to replace the Hellenic populations transported into Anatolia (1397). At length Bajazet reappeared under the walls of Constantinople and summoned it to open its gates. The Byzantines, who were supplied with provisions for a long siege, made this thoroughly Christian answer:—" Go and tell your master that, weak as we are, we know of no power to which we can have recourse, if not to God, who sustains the feeble and abases the strong. Let the Sultan do that which pleaseth him." The siege was about to commence, when the invasion of Tamerlane saved Constantinople.

7. *Conquests of Tamerlane.*

The Empire of the Zingiskhanides had entirely fallen into dissolution within less than a century after the death of its founder. In one of the innumerable little States that had been formed out of its fragments, was born, in 1335, Timour, commonly called Timour-Lenk (Timour *the Lame*), and by Europeans Tamerlane. Sovereign by his birth of a small canton of Transoxiana, he commenced at thirty his warrior life by rising in arms against the Sultan of Balkh, of whom he was the vassal or ally. The capital was taken and destroyed; the prince, slain by his emirs; in him ended the family of Dschagatï, who descended from one of the sons of Zingis Khan. Timour seized upon his States. Fifteen years passed away in obscure struggles against the Dgetes, semi-barbarous tribes of Turkestân, and against the Shah of Karisme, whose capital was destroyed and the empire conquered in 1379. From that time, Timour, master of the country beyond the Oxus, conceived vast projects of conquest, and began to accomplish them with an astonishing rapidity. The Khorassan was subjugated in three years. Of the two families who shared Persia, one, the Mozaffer, became vassal of the victor; the other, the Ilkhans, was compelled to flee. Soon, in consequence of a revolt, which was punished by massacres, the whole of Persia became reunited under the domination of Timour; yet it required five years of wars and torrents of blood before he could consolidate his conquest. The Princes of Georgia and of Kirvan had hastened to make submission; the Prince of Diarbekir, who dared resist, was punished by the devastation of his States and the capture of his fortresses. The Khan of Kaptschak, or of Great Tartary, was defeated in a great battle; his possessions aggrandised the new empire; in a second campaign, Timour pursued him beyond the Caucasus and devastated Russia as far as Moscow. In 1393, he seized upon Bagdad, upon all Mesopotamia and Armenia; at length, five years afterwards, he made an expedition into India, took Delhi, with the principal towns, and penetrated as far as the Ganges, collecting an immense booty.

All these conquests were marked by frightful cruelties: in Persia, 70,000 inhabitants of Ispahan were massacred in one day; in the Khorassan, 2,000 men were buried alive and covered over with lime to form the courses of a tower, a monument of vengeance reserved for rebels; upon the banks of the Ganges more than 100,000 captives were slaughtered in cold blood. Timour, however, was not solely a savage slaughterer, he did not confine himself merely to destroying, and he ought to be distinguished from amongst all those man-slayers who have scourged the world, and whose names posterity so stupidly glorifies. Zingis Khan and his sons had not had any well-established religion: alike the enemies of Mussulmans and Christians, they had even seemed to lean by preference towards the religion of Europe. Under their successors, the Mongols were converted to Islamism, but they embraced the doctrines of the Shiites, and, in the time of Timour, they were in all the fervour of proselytism. The latter developed that religious spirit, and showed himself a zealous Mussulman. He employed the spoils of India to construct at Samarcand a magnificent mosque; he made Kesch, his native country, "the dome of sciences and civilization;" everywhere upon his way he visited, endowed or embellished the tombs of the Saints, the monuments of Islamism, and marched onwards accompanied by a train of learned men. The Shiite doctrine more liberal, more pliant than the blind faith of the Sunnites, left greater latitude to human legislation; Timour was a legislator, and, as such, he showed a remarkable talent for government. His *Toufoukat*, or code of laws, presents a great number of wise precepts concerning finance, justice, hierarchical administration, organization of the army. In his immense armies composed of a hundred different barbarous peoples, he maintained a wonderful discipline; and it was amongst the Tartars of Timour that the first example of wearing a uniform is found. He knew, moreover, how to inspire his soldiers with a boundless enthusiasm and devotion; and they were often seen to sacrifice to his wish even their booty. Special agents traversed his vast States, like the *missi* of Charlemagne, and rendered him an exact account of their observations; others visited foreign countries, and the information they reported was carefully registered. Head of a numerous family, Timour was aided by it both in his conquests and the administration of his empire: his sons and grandsons commanded his armies, or governed the provinces; he made them conclude marriages with reigning families; and all the States of Central Asia found themselves bound to him by links of relationship. He was, however, badly seconded by his own kin, and that was the cause of the ruin of his dynasty. This conqueror, so ferocious towards his enemies, manifested a singular gentleness for his children: he pardoned all their revolts, he redeemed all their faults; but, after his death, his immense empire fell into anarchy and was dismembered.

8. *War between Timour and Bajazet.—Battle of Angora.— Death of Bajazet.*

The Turkish Princes, dispossessed by Bajazet, had gone, as has been said, to seek an asylum with Timour; a little later, two enemies of the conquering Tartar sought refuge in the States of Bajazet; these were Ahmed-Djelaïr, Prince of Bagdad, of the dynasty of Ilkhan, and the Prince of Diarbekir, Kara-Yusuf, of the Turcoman dynasty of the "Black Sheep." Finally, in the last conquests of the Ottomans was found comprised the territory of Erz-Inghian upon the Euphrates, which belonged to a faithful vassal of Timour. An embassy was sent to Bajazet to demand in menacing terms redress for that wrong; but the Sultan, far from satisfying the requirement of his terrible neighbour, ordered instantly, in the first outburst of his wrath, the massacre of the ambassadors; then growing calmer, he dismissed them with an insulting letter. Timour immediately entered upon a campaign, and on the 22nd of August, 1400, he invaded the Ottoman territory, directing his march towards Sivas. That city, one of the richest and most populous of Asia, had given itself up to Bajazet in order to escape from the domination of Kara-Youlouk, a Turcoman Prince of the dynasty of the "White Sheep," the ally and vassal of Timour. Defended by Erthogrul, son of the Sultan, it offered at first an obstinate resistance; then, after a siege of eighteen days, it surrendered. Timour put to death Erthogrul with a portion of the garrison and the principal Mussulman inhabitants; as for the Christian population, which comprised more than the half of the city, he caused the whole of them to perish under the most excruciating tortures.

Bajazet received the news of this disaster at the moment when he was about to attack Constantinople. He hastened immediately to the succour of his Asiatic States. Already Timour had commenced a retreat : he had a greater injury to avenge upon the Sultan of Egypt, who had put his ambassadors to death. Syria was devastated with so much the more fury, that the Shiites there met at every step the monuments of the opposite sect. After two victories obtained, one under the walls of Aleppo, the other before Damascus, those two capitals were taken: at Aleppo there was a wholesale massacre ; Damascus, after having paid a ransom of a million ducats, was, at a word of displeasure from the conqueror, delivered up to the fury of the soldiers, and completely burnt (1401). Master of Syria, Timour returned to Bagdad, where, in his absence, Ahmed-Djelaïr had re-entered and had re-established his authority, with the consent of the city: this fault was punished by the extermination of all its inhabitants.

During this sanguinary career, Timour had sent to Bajazet a fresh embassy, charged with a conciliatory message ; the latter only replied thereto by renewed insults, and the war recommenced. It was near Angora that the two armies found themselves in presence of each other (30th June, 1402). They amounted together to nearly a million of men ; all the nations scattered between the Danube and the Indus were there represented. It was the most formidable struggle that either of the two empires, that either of the two monarchs had hitherto had to sustain. But the dispositions of the two armies were not the same: whilst the Tartars were animated by a ferocious enthusiasm, and the most entire confidence in their chiefs, the avarice and rigour of Bajazet had rendered the Ottomans disaffected ; the troops from Asia Minor had been tampered with by the agents of Timour, and were ready to betray the Sultan ; finally, the haughtiness and the obstinacy of which the latter had given proof during the negotiations, made the soldiers doubt the justice of his cause, a fatal disposition in minds so deeply imbued with fatalism. At the very outset of the combat, the troops of Aïdin, Mentesché, Kermian, and Sarou-Khan passed over to the enemy. However, the struggle lasted the whole day; the Servian auxiliaries, who formed the left wing, and the 10,000 Janissaries placed in the centre, sustained with an unshakable courage the assaults of the enemy. At last, with night a rout began; Bajazet, hurried away by the fugitives, was pursued and made prisoner, together with him his son Mousa, his faithful beylerbey, the chief of the harem, the commander of the eunuchs, and the principal emirs.

All the European historians have related, on the faith of a Byzantine chronicler, how Timour humbled the pride of his prisoner, how he dragged him in the train of his army, shut up in an iron cage. Not the slightest trace of this fable is to be found in Eastern writers; it appears, on the contrary, that Bajazet was treated with great consideration, the dignity of a prince, though fallen, being carefully conceded to him; Timour even conversing familiarly with him and giving him some hope of liberty. But after the failure of an attempt, on the part of himself or his friends, to effect his escape, the Imperial captive was subjected to a more severe kind of treatment, being closely watched during the day, and even secured with chains at night. When the army was on the march, Bajazet appears to have been carried in a kind of latticed or grilled litter, suspended between two horses, such as was used in the East in conveying the harem from place to place. Hence arose the well-known but questionable story of the iron cage. The Turkish word *kafe*, which signifies a litter of the description above mentioned, does also denote a cage, and this was probably the origin of the mistake that has prevailed respecting the mode of Bajazet's confinement. But the fiery Sultan could not long resist the despair of his defeat and the weariness of his captivity: he died in the camp of Timour on his return towards the East, at Akshehr, 9th March, 1403.

The reign of Bajazet *the Lightning*, so remarkable by the Ottoman conquests and by the disaster which interrupted them, is not less so by the weakening of the religious spirit and the moral decadence of the conquerors. The first chiefs of the Ottomans had had the simplicity, the ferocious zeal, the fanatical austerity of the first successors of the Prophet; but Bajazet, although, indeed, following the example of his fathers, he protected the learned, built mosques and cloisters, yet had no scruple about violating the precepts of the Korân and of giving an example of intemperance and debauchery. His vizier, still more corrupt than himself, favoured the old vices of the East, and introduced every kind of disorder into the seraglio of the Sultan by creating the corps of *ichoglans* or pages, which was recruited like that of the Janissaries. Corruption spread on all sides—in the army, in the tribunals; and the venality of the judges became so scandalous, that Bajazet ordered in one day eighty prevaricating judges to be put to death. We will not dwell upon the cruelties that sully the conquests of the Osmanlis; they are the shame of their annals, as they are of the history of every other people of the East, and the lugubrious and disgusting recital of massacres, tortures, and barbarities of every kind is not yet ended.

CHAPTER V.

REIGNS OF MAHOMET I.—OF AMURATH II.—AND OF MAHOMET II.—TO THE CAPTURE OF CONSTANTINOPLE (1403-1453.)

1. *Interregnum.—War between the Sons of Bajazet* (1403-1413).

THE disaster of Angora plunged the Ottoman Empire into anarchy, and for a while it was thought had entailed its ruin. All the recently conquered States—Bulgaria, Servia, Wallachia, the Morea, &c., resumed their independence; Constantinople breathed again, and in Asia Minor were seen to reappear the rival dynasties of Kastemouni, Sarou-Khan, Aïdin, and of Karaman, which the Osmanlis had had so much trouble to destroy. Four sons of the Sultan had escaped from the field of battle: Solyman, the eldest, followed by the vizir, Ali Pacha, the aga of the Janissaries, and the valiant Ewrenos-Bey, fled precipitately to Broussa, and thence into Europe. Mahomet, the second son, who was destined to restore to the empire its unity and grandeur, shut himself up in Amasia, and defended himself obstinately against the enterprises of the Tartars and the malevolence of his neighbours. Mousa, the third son, hid himself in Karamania; the fourth, Mustapha, disappeared, at least for some years, for he will be seen to reappear on the historic stage. The Tartar troops spread themselves all over Asia Minor. Mirza Mahomet, Timour's grandson, being launched in pursuit of Solyman, followed at his heels with 4,000 horsemen to Broussa, traversing seventy-five leagues in five days: he seized upon the treasure and the harem of Bajazet, and gave up the city to pillage and flames.

Other bands destroyed Nicæa, placed under contribution the less important towns, and sacked all the country districts.

Meanwhile, Timour, with the bulk of the army, repaired to Koutaieh, where he temporarily fixed his residence. His first care was to reconstitute the Turkish principalities and dynasties destroyed by Bajazet. At the same time he placed himself in communication with the three Ottoman princes, encouraged their pretensions, left Solyman master of the European provinces, welcomed the envoy of Mousa, and invited Mahomet to visit him. This skilful line of conduct threatened with entire dissolution the empire so patiently constructed by the first Osmanlis: Asia Minor was about to find itself parcelled out afresh as at the commencement of the fourteenth century; but Timour did not remain there long enough to consummate his work. After having helped to ruin Smyrna, where the knights of Rhodes defended themselves with a bootless heroism, after having, during nearly a year, devastated and ensanguined the coasts of the Archipelago and the Mediterranean, the destroyer withdrew, reckoning upon the germs of discord that he left behind him to hinder the Ottoman Empire from again raising its head. He confided to the Prince of Kermian the body of Bajazet and the care of his son Mousa, who had shared his captivity; then he directed his march towards the East with the design of conquering China, but death surprised him (1405).

As soon as Timour had departed, the struggle commenced between the sons of Bajazet. Manuel Palæologus, to whom the battle of Angora had restored the throne of Constantinople, took a great part in it; he made alliance alternatively with the three brothers, and obtained from Solyman the restitution of Thessalonica, certain places on the Strymon, and on the littoral of the Black Sea. This was a sort of resurrection for the Byzantine Empire, which was destined yet to have another half century of duration. Meanwhile, Mousa appeared at Broussa, accompanied by the beylerbey, Timour-Tasch, and there established his authority, but could not maintain himself therein against his brother Mahomet. After having successively implored the support of Solyman, of the Prince of Kastemouni, of the Lords of Aïdin, of Mentesché and of Kermian, four times defeated, he disappeared from the political theatre, and lived for a while in obscurity under the protection of the Emir of Kermian.

There remained Mahomet and Solyman, who each took the title of Sultan,* the one in Europe, the other in Asia; their rivalry was destined to be longer and more desperate. Djouneïd, Solyman's Lieutenant, seized upon, in his name, the principality of Aïdin; then he rendered himself independent therein, and strengthened himself by alliance with the Princes of Kermian and Karaman. Summoned to Asia by this treason, Solyman seized upon Broussa, and thus placed himself in hostility at once with his brother and with the leagued princes. He had at first some successes; his enemies separated; Djouneïd made a prompt submission; at the same time his army seized upon Angora. But Solyman, a voluptuous and effeminate prince, had to cope with an active and indefatigable rival: his good fortune was not of long duration.

After having allied himself with the Turkish princes of Asia Minor (1406), Mahomet sent into Europe his brother Mousa, whom the Emir of Kermian had delivered up to him, and secured him the alliance of the Princes of Servia and Wallachia, who again took up arms. Solyman, thus attacked in his own States, was constrained to abandon Asia. Meanwhile, Mousa was conquered through the treason of the Kral of Servia, and sought refuge in Wallachia; but, whilst Solyman gave himself up in the seraglio of Adrianople to his sensual proclivities, Mousa appeared suddenly at the gates of that city (1410). That pressing danger could not tear Solyman from his inaction: he caused the beard of the aga of the Janissaries to be shaved off when he came to announce the arrival of the

* The Ottoman historians do not give the title of Sultan to either Solyman or Mousa, but only to Mahomet, as having eventually retained possession of the throne.

enemy. His emirs, indignant, abandoned him; constrained to flee, he was slain on the road to Constantinople by the peasants.

Mousa, who succeeded him, was active, sober, courageous, but of a tyrannical cruelty; he soon rendered himself odious to all his followers. However, he commenced war against the Greek Emperor, seized upon Thessalonica and the towns on the Strymon, then he went to besiege Constantinople. Manuel having implored the aid of Mahomet, the latter hastened to render it; but he could not overcome his brother, and returned hastily into Asia, where several revolts had broken out. Two years after he returned with more considerable forces. The increasing tyranny of Mousa had created fresh discontents; the defection became general: left with 10,000 Janissaries whom he had attached to himself by dint of gold, he was abandoned by them at the moment of giving battle; he took to flight, and the horsemen charged with the pursuit of him found in a marsh his mutilated body.

2. *Reign of Mahomet I.* (1413-1421).

Mahomet saw himself at length sole master of the empire, but of an empire diminished and abased: he found his territories reduced, his forces exhausted, the acquisitions of two reigns lost, the nations of which his father and grandfather had been sovereigns reascended to the rank of allies or rivals. To all this must be added the prestige of the Ottoman name gravely compromised, the confidence of the soldiers of Islam, until then invincible, shaken; ill-boding germs of discord and of rebellion in men's minds by twelve years of anarchy and civil war. Mahomet therefore had much to do to restore the empire to its former grandeur: it was a task that demanded a rare combination of prudence and firmness, and which he was competent to accomplish. Loyal towards his allies, moderate towards his enemies, equitable and clement in his relations with his subjects, he established order and peace interiorly, whilst abroad he preserved a defensive attitude which his successes caused to be respected. At length, in a judicious reign of some eight years, he succeeded in effacing the traces of disorder which had very nearly annihilated the Ottoman Empire.

As soon as he was delivered from his brother, the Greek Emperor, the Princes of Wallachia, Servia, Bulgaria, Epirus and Achaia addressed to him their felicitations. He gave a favourable reception to their envoys, and on dismissing them, said:—"Tell your masters that I send peace to all, and that I accept it from all; and may God punish the violaters of it!" Faithful to his word, he restored to the Emperor the places which Mousa had recently wrested from him; he renewed with the Venetians the commercial treaty made with his brother; and he released the Princes of Wallachia and Servia from all tribute, &c. Meanwhile, a twofold danger required his presence in Asia—the Prince of Karaman had marched to the attack of Broussa, and Djouneïd, the former Lieutenant of Solyman, had again seized upon Ephesus, Smyrna, and Pergamus to construct out of them an independent principality. Mahomet first confronted Djouneïd, who sued for pardon, obtained it, and was made, some few years afterwards, Governor of Nicopolis. He marched next against the Prince of Karaman, defeated him on several occasions and forced him to sue for peace (1415). During this expedition the Sultan reduced to submission the Prince of Kastemouni; he obtained from him one of his sons to serve in the Ottoman army, and made him cede the greatest portion of his State.

On his return to Europe he despatched an expedition against the Duke of Naxos, Lord of the Cyclades, who was molesting the Turkish vessels in the Archipelago. This duke was a noble Venetian, Pietro Zeno, who summoned his countrymen to his aid, and thence sprang the first hostilities between Venice and the Ottomans. On the 29th May, 1416, a Venetian squadron appeared under the walls of Gallipoli; it displayed in vain a white flag in token that it desired to negotiate. The Turks, unable to believe in an embassy accompanied by so large a fleet, opened fire upon it, but lost twenty-seven vessels burnt or captured. That war, however, caused by a misunderstanding, was promptly terminated; a treaty was concluded on the 9th July of that same year, and the solemn ratification of it was made the year following at Venice, by a Turkish ambassador, the first who had appeared in Christendom. By this treaty the Ottomans bound themselves not to sail out of the Strait of Gallipoli in armed vessels.

The following years were occupied with peaceful concerns or with hostilities of small importance. The Sultan intervened in the affairs of Wallachia, and compelled the Voïvode to pay tribute; then he invaded Bosnia and Croatia; but his troops were defeated by Nicholas Peterfy, vice-palatine of Hungary, and by King Sigismond (1419). In Asia he contracted relations with the princes who were disputing for the remnants of the Empire of Timour, and promised them his alliance whilst he awaited the opportunity to profit by their discords.

In the midst of this reviving prosperity an extraordinary sedition broke out—a sedition at once democratic and religious, which attacked not only the personal authority of the Sultan, but even the principles of Islamism and Mussulman society. In the environs of Smyrna a sect appeared, the adherents of which preached absolute equality, poverty, community of goods; and seemed moreover to adore the same God as the Christians, and to welcome them as brothers. On all sides the rajahs, the poor, the oppressed, embraced the new doctrine, and especially a great number of dervishes. The veritable promoter of these strange dogmas was Bedreddin de Siman, a learned jurisconsult and distinguished theologian, who, after having been judge of the army under Mousa, was occupied with judicial functions at Nicæa. He did not, however, place himself openly at the head of the insurrection; his instruments were a Turk of obscure birth, Berekloudje-Mustapha, who assumed the title of Dede-Sultan (*father and lord*), and gave himself out as, or fancied himself, a prophet. Associated with him was an apostate Jew, named Torlak-

Kemali, who, followed by a band of 3,000 dervishes, went about the country preaching the doctrine of equality.

The headquarters of these sectaries were at Mount Stylarios, opposite Scio, the native place and abode of Dede-Sultan. There, having mustered to the number of 10,000 strong, they exterminated the first body of troops sent to disperse them, and defeated the governor of the province, who had placed himself at the head of another expedition. It became necessary to send a considerable army against them, under command of the youthful Amurath, son of the Sultan, and Bajezid Pacha, his best general. After a sanguinary battle, Dede-Sultan was taken, with those of his adherents who had survived. All were put to the sword; men, women, and children refusing, under the extremity of torture, to abjure their doctrine. Ephesus was drenched in blood. The Jew Torlak and his dervishes were afterwards pursued and defeated near Magnesia; that chief with his principal disciple was hanged, and the others dispersed. Finally, the army returned to Europe, where the chief focus of the insurrection had next declared itself, Bedreddin having appeared in the mountains of the Hæmus, and had rapidly raised there a considerable force. Defeated near Seres, he was hanged, notwithstanding the reputation he possessed as a learned man, and the high dignity with which he had been invested. Thus ended the revolt of the dervishes, a unique episode in the Ottoman annals, unique even in the history of Islamism, and which has been but very imperfectly noticed in European history; for it cannot be doubted that it involved an attempt of the Christian races to regain their independence.

This revolt was scarcely crushed ere it produced another of a nature wholly different. A pretender to the throne appeared, giving himself out to be Mustapha, the fourth son of Bajazet, who had disappeared after the battle of Angora. The Ottoman historians affirm that this was an imposter. Supported by Marcea, Voïvode of Wallachia, and by Djouneïd, for the third time a rebel, he invaded Thessaly. Conquered near Thessalonica, he sought an asylum in that city. The Emperor Manuel, who was the friend and ally of Mahomet, detained him prisoner with his partisans, and received for that service an annual pension of 900,000 aspres.

In the spring of the following year (1421) Mahomet, after a journey of some months in Asia, halted at Gallipoli, and died there of apoplexy. He left three sons, Amurath his heir, who was then in Amasia, and two young princes, whom he had commended to the care of his friend Manuel. His courtiers kept his death secret until Amurath could be apprised of it; but a report of his malady having spread abroad, the troops mutinied, demanding to see the Sultan. The order was given them to recross the Strait and march to Broussa. The Janissaries thereupon refused obedience. With a view to appease them, the body of the deceased Sultan was placed upon a throne behind the windows of a darkened kiosk, whilst a page concealed behind the corpse, with his arms passed through the sleeves of its pelisse, saluted the soldiers with his hands, who defiled without suspecting the trick. They then set out immediately, and learned, on arriving at Broussa, the death of their master and the presence of his successor.

3. *Amurath II.* (1421-1450).—*Civil War.—Siege of Constantinople.—Submission of the Turkish States of Asia Minor.*

The reign of Amurath II. opened with civil war. The Emperor Manuel demanded of the new Sultan that the young Ottoman princes, whose education had been confided to him by Mahomet, should be sent to his Court. He received for answer that it was contrary to the law of Islam that the Sultan's brothers should be brought up amongst the *Giaours.* Whereupon Manuel released Mustapha from prison, had him brought to Constantinople, and signed a treaty with him, by which the pretender engaged to restore to the Greeks Gallipoli, Thessaly, and the northern shore of the Black Sea as far as Wallachia.

A few days afterwards Mustapha presented himself before Gallipoli at the head of a Greek army. The city opened its gates; from thence, and accompanied by Djouneïd, whom he had named his vizier, he marched to Adrianople, where the sons of Ewrenos and several beys came to join him, as well as a host of irregular soldiers, out of which he formed an army. Amurath, however, had hastened to despatch Bajezid Pacha into Europe, who mustered all the troops of Roumelia,* and with them confronted the rebels. But Mustapha, at the moment the battle was about to commence, advanced alone, harangued the soldiers of the Sultan, and at his voice all passed over to his side. Bajezid was taken and massacred.

Mustapha already believed himself master of Europe. Assuming the offensive, he passed the Strait, and took up a position threatening the camp of Amurath. There he lost several days in hesitation, which brought about his ruin. All his cavalry was composed of "akindschis" (*scouts*). Amurath, to seduce them, employed their former commander, Michalogli, kept in prison since the fall of Mousa. He was set free and brought into the camp. As soon as he appeared his old soldiers hastened to rejoin him. At the same time Amurath's vizier had an understanding with Djouneïd, who secretly quitted the camp of Mustapha. As soon as his absence was perceived, all the rest, seized with a panic terror, dispersed, Mustapha himself fleeing precipitately to Lampsacus, and thence to Gallipoli. Amurath followed him closely; he passed the Strait by the aid of some Genoese vessels, and cast anchor near the latter city. A combat ensued, and Mustapha, defeated, fled towards Adrianople; halting there only to carry off the jewels from the treasury, and then continued his flight in the direction of Wallachia. He had scarcely accomplished a day's march, when his followers seized upon him, and brought him back to Adrianople, where Amurath had just arrived. The pretender was hanged upon one of the towers of that city.

* *Roumelia* signifies the country of the Romans, it being the name given by the Ottomans to their possessions in Europe.

The Greek Emperor, on learning this sudden catastrophe, essayed to disarm the resentment of Amurath; but the time for that had passed. The Sultan refused to listen to his ambassadors, and sent them back with the announcement that he would quickly follow them. In fact, 20,000 Ottomans soon appeared under the walls of Constantinople (1422). They burned the villages and harvests, destroyed the vines and olive trees, and massacred the inhabitants. Then they dug a trench round the city which closed every issue to the besieged on the land side. The promise of a general pillage drew into the Ottoman camp a host of soldiers and adventurers of every kind. Five hundred dervishes repaired thither, led by the Grand Sheik of Broussa, Seid Bochari, who was called *Emir-Sultan;* they claimed, as their share of the booty, the nuns of the convents in Constantinople. After consulting the books of the diviners, the Sheik announced that, on Monday, August the 24th, an hour after noon, he would mount his horse, brandish his sabre, shout thrice his war-cry, and then the walls of the city would tumble down. When the day came, he gave the signal for the assault, which was terrible. The fight raged furiously along the entire extent of the ramparts from the Golden Gate to the Wooden Gate. Women, children, and old men alike laboured at the defence; still the struggle lasted until sunset with the same desperation, when suddenly the Turks burned their siege machines and retired. The Greeks attributed their deliverance to the Virgin Mary; and Emir-Sultan himself affirmed, it was said, that when the *mêlée* was at its height of fury the Holy Virgin had appeared on the walls clad in a violet vestment, the dazzling brightness of which attracted the gaze of all, and that that supernatural intervention had changed the course of destiny.

The raising of the siege may be explained otherwise than by a miracle. Amurath learned that a fresh revolt had broken out in Asia; that his youngest brother, also named Mustapha, supported by the Prince of Karaman, and solicited by the Greek Emperor, had taken up arms, and had seized upon Nicæa. He instantly despatched troops into Asia. At their approach, the accomplices of Mustapha took him prisoner, and delivered him up to the Sultan, who caused him to be strangled.

Freed from this danger, Amurath did not resume his projects against Constantinople, preferring to secure his domination in Asia. He first directed an expedition against the Prince of Kastemouni, which obtained renewed submission from him, the cession of the mines of the country, and the hand of his daughter (1423). Then, the year following, the irrepressible Djouneïd, with numerous bands of adventurers, having taken possession of the principality of Aïdin, Amurath sent an army to chastise him for his many rebellions. Djouneïd being unable to resist the forces directed against him, his brother and son were taken prisoners; whilst he himself, reduced to shut himself up in the fortress of Hypsela, was there blockaded by land and sea by the aid of Genoese ships. He surrendered, stipulating that his life should be spared; but Hamsa Bey, brother of Bajezid, caused him to be strangled in his prison with all his family. Resuming possession of the Aïdin country, Amurath next seized upon the territories of Mentesché, to the prejudice of the nephews of the last prince, who were kept in prison. At the same juncture, the Princes of Tekieh and Karaman having attacked Attalia, both perished under its walls. The territories of Tekieh were reunited to the Ottoman possessions; that of Karaman, diminished by one-half, was left to one of the sons of the deceased prince. Thus, of the Turkish States retrieved by Timour, there only remained Karaman, very much diminished, Kastemouni, reduced to impotence, and Kermian. Shortly after, the aged Prince of Kermian went to visit Amurath in his European provinces; he was received with magnificence, and, in return, he bequeathed his States to the Sultan, dying in the following year. Finally, upon the Eastern frontier on the side of Diarbekir, certain tribes of Turkomans being in commotion, Amurath stationed there, as governor of Amasia, Turked Pacha, one of his beys, who made himself master by treason of the most turbulent of the chiefs, and by their death secured the tranquillity of the frontiers. Henceforward, the Ottomans having no longer any rivals on the side of Asia, devoted all their efforts on the side of Europe.

4. *Wars in Albania, Wallachia, and Servia.—Hunyade Corvinus.—Defeat of the Ottomans.*

Amurath intervened at first in a war between the Serbs and the Hungarians, and he thus came to acquire a first station on the Danube, Cœumbatz, at the entrance of the defile of Orsova and Kruschevatz, the central position of Servia (1428). Next, he dealt such blows against the Greeks as were calculated to bring about definitively their ruin. The Ottomans had already made divers efforts to get possession of Thessalonica. John Palæologus, the new Emperor of Constantinople, finding himself incapable of defending that important city, had ceded it to the Venetians. Amurath, irritated, broke with those rulers of the Mediterranean and attacked Thessalonica (1430). The inhabitants were disposed to surrender, but they were restrained by the Venetian garrison, who made a furious defence. After a siege of fifteen days, the city was carried by assault, and sacked, the churches pillaged, and all the population massacred or reduced to slavery. The Venetians again made an unsuccessful attempt against Gallipoli, but they treated, and peace was established.

The Sultan then turned his arms against Albania, Servia, and Wallachia, desirous of becoming master of all the detached provinces of the Greek Empire, before he attacked Constantinople. That inevitably led to the Turks being brought in contact with Hungary, and a memorable struggle was about to be engaged in.

Albania was divided into two principal dominations: the south, as well as Ætolia and Acarnania, belonged to the heirs of a Florentine adventurer, one Carlo Tocci, who had made himself master of them in the preceding century, and those heirs now disputed the possession. So soon as the Ottomans entered their territory, Janina and the principal strongholds submitted, on condition that the inhabitants should preserve their laws and religion. The north was subject to John Castriot, the descendant or heir of the Balsas; he was forced to deliver up his four sons to the Sultan, who, at his death, took possession of the country, and even sent some bands as far as into Croatia.

At the same period, Wallachia changed masters. Mad Drakul, or *the Devil*, overthrew and put to death Dan, his kinsman; he defeated the Turkish troops sent against him, but he only preserved his throne on condition of paying tribute and supplying troops to the Sultan (1431).

In Servia reigned Georges Brankowich, a descendant of Lazarus. He was attacked in his turn by the Turks, obliged to submit and to give his daughter in marriage to Amurath. From thence, dragging after him the auxiliary corps of Brankowich and Drakul, the Sultan entered Transylvania, ravaged the country, and carried away 70,000 prisoners (1438). The Kral of Servia having put Semendria, on the Danube, in a state of defence, Amurath demanded from him the keys of that place, and, on his refusal, besieged it, took it, and put out the eyes of the Kral's son, who defended it. Albert, then King of Hungary, went to the assistance of the Serbs, but at sight of the Turks his soldiers fled (1439). An Ottoman army besieged Belgrade in vain during six months; then it penetrated again into Transylvania, and went to besiege Hermanstadt.

Ladislas, King of Poland, had succeeded to Albert on the throne of Hungary; the voïvode of Transylvania was John Corvinus Hunyade, whose task it was to arrest the conquering march of the Turks during twenty years. That hero, of Roumanian race, had raised himself by his merits to the command of the Hungarian armies. It was to him that Ladislas owed the throne of Hungary, and through gratitude had made him Voïvode of Transylvania. Hunyade hastened to the defence of Hermanstadt, defeated the Turks, killed 20,000, and drove the remainder beyond the Danube. He sent to the Kral of Servia a carriage laden with booty, amongst which were the heads of the conquered Turkish generals, inviting the Kral to join him. A fresh army of 80,000 Turks appearing to arrest his progress, he boldly ventured, with only 20,000 men, to give them battle at Vasag, and achieved a victory fully as complete as the first (1442).

The campaign of 1443 was still more disastrous to the Ottomans, and raised the reputation of Hunyade to the highest pitch; it was called by the Hungarians his "long campaign." Setting out from Ofen, the 22nd July, at the head of an army of all nations, he passed the Danube at Semendria, traversed Servia, ravaging it as far as Nissa, and there fought a great battle, in which the Turks left 2,000 dead and 4,000 prisoners. Then he seized upon Sophia, ventured, despite the rigour of winter, to cross the Hæmus, forced the defile of the Soulu-Derbend or "Gate of Trajan," notwithstanding the efforts of the Turks, and, on Christmas Day, entered upon Bulgarian territory, where the inhabitants received him as a liberator. Finally, he obtained at Yalovaz, at the foot of Mount Konovicza, a great victory, and retook the way to Ofen laden with an immense booty, and dragging after him a long train of captives, amongst whom was the beylerbey of Roumelia.

Amurath was constrained to humble himself. He restored Wallachia to Drakul, surrendered to Brankowich Semendria and his other strongholds, and then sued for peace at the hands of Hunyade. A truce of ten years was concluded (July, 1444), which placed Servia and Wallachia under the suzerainty of Hungary.

To so many reverses was now added the death of Aladdin, the Sultan's eldest son. Disgusted with power, Amurath could not bear up against this last blow. Entrusting authority to his son Mahomet, then fourteen years old, he sought retirement amongst the dervishes of Magnesia, in the government of Saru-Khan, with the intention of ending his days in peace.

V. Battle of Varna.—Scanderbeg.—Battle of Kassova.

Scarcely had he reached his retreat ere he was drawn from it by an unforeseen event—peace was already broken. The Turkish negotiators of it had scarcely retired when the Cardinal Cesarini, the papal legate, summoned King Ladislas to tear up the treaty to which he had sworn upon the Evangelists; the faith that he had pledged to the infidels being, he said, null and void in law. To this summons were added letters from the Greek Emperor and Cardinal Condolmieri, commandant of the pontifical fleet, who insisted that the absence of the Sultan should be taken advantage of: a great crusade, they affirmed, had been resolved upon to drive the Turks into Asia. The army of these Crusaders was merely composed of German and Italian adventurers, of whom Cardinal Cesarini had taken command, and the Hungarian forces did not exceed at most 10,000 men. With these feeble resources they proposed to destroy the Ottoman power. Perjury was never more barefaced. It was expected that the Turks would have evacuated the Servian strongholds; then, on the first September, 1444, war was declared, and the march of the Crusaders, in conjunction with Drakul and the Wallachians, was directed along the Danube. Bulgaria was devastated, and Varna besieged, Suddenly news came that Amurath had returned; the Genoese, won over by the Sultan's gold, had transported his troops from Asia to Europe, and sailing through the fleet of the Crusaders, he had encamped four miles distant from the Christian army with 40,000 men. Despite inferiority of numbers it was determined to give him battle. On the 10th of November the two armies found themselves in presence of each other. Amurath, posted in the centre with his Janissaries, caused to be carried before him at the point of a lance the original of the broken treaty. At the first shock, Hunyade drove in the left wing of the Turkish army; the Wallachians scattered the other wing, and penetrated the Sultan's camp. Already Amurath was inclined to flee; one of his beys scized his horse's bridle and implored him to stand firm.

At that moment King Ladislas rushed upon the Janissaries, pierced through their ranks until he reached the Sultan, whom he struck with his fist, and, at the same instant, his horse fell with him. A Janissary cut off his head and placing it on the point of a pike, shouted, "Giaours, behold your king!" At this spectacle, the Hungarians broke their ranks, and their remnants sought shelter behind the entrenchments, whilst John of Hunyade and the Wallachians took flight. Next day the Turks carried the Christian camp by assault, the defenders of which were massacred, and amongst the number was the legate Cesarini.

The victory of Varna permitted Amurath to resume the projects of the Ottomans against the remnants of the Byzantine empire.

The Emperor Manuel had divided those remnants between his seven sons: the eldest, John, possessed only Constantinople and its environs; two others—Constantine, who was the last Emperor of Byzantium, and Thomas— possessed the Morea, Thebes, and a part of Thessaly. Foreseeing the attack which threatened them, Constantine and Thomas caused the ancient fortifications of the Isthmus of Corinth to be restored. But after having imposed his alliance on the Duke of Athens (one Neri, a Florentine), Amurath advanced to the wall of the isthmus, besieged it with cannon, and carried it by assault. That obstacle once overthrown, Corinth was taken and burnt, and the Peloponnesus sacked without mercy. The two Palæologi obtained peace on condition of paying tribute.

That facile expedition terminated, Amurath turned his efforts against Albania, which had grown restless. There had arisen a new Hunyade, who was destined to become no less celebrated than the Hungarian hero. George Castriot was the youngest of the sons of John Castriot, despot of northern Albania, or more strictly of the canton of Mirdita. It has been already said that Castriot had been compelled to pay tribute and give his four sons as hostages. The three eldest died poisoned, it is stated; the fourth, George, obtained the Sultan's favour; and when Mirdita, after John's death, had been annexed to the Ottoman Empire, he obtained the command of 5,000 men in the army of Amurath, in which, on account of his impetuous valour, he was known by the name of "Iskender Bey" (*Lord Alexander*), a name which Europeans have transformed into *Scanderbeg*. The favours of the Sultan did not make him forget his religion and country, and in 1443, after the first battle of the "long campaign," he resolved to abandon the infidels. He presented himself before a secretary of the Sultan, forced him, with his dagger at his breast, to sign an order addressed to the commandant of Croïa, to give up that place into his hands; he then killed the secretary and fled into Albania. Collecting together a band of 600 partisans in the environs, he effected an entrance into Croïa, opened the gates, and massacred the Turkish garrison. This was the signal for a general insurrection. The Ottomans scattered through the villages were put to death, the garrisons of the towns compelled to surrender, and in thirty days Scanderbeg found himself master of Albania; all the Christian princes and nobles of the country acknowledging him as their chief, and each furnishing him with his contingent. From 1443 to 1447 three armies were sent against him and successively defeated; a fourth began its march, stronger than those preceding; it was also beaten, and the Ottoman general taken with his principal officers. Amurath then resolved to assume the direction himself of a decisive expedition, for which preparations were made in the following year (1448); but at that epoch, the war recommenced with Hungary.

Hunyade, with an army of 24,000 men, invaded Servia, ravaged the country, and directed his march towards the plain of Kassova in order to descend into Macedonia. Amurath mustered all his forces, and with more than 150,000 men, awaited his coming on that famous plain where the destinies of the Hellenic peninsula are decided. It was agreed that Hunyade should be joined by Scanderbeg and an Albanian army, but instead of waiting for them, he determined at once to fight. Thereupon a terrible and unequal struggle took place, which lasted three days. Betrayed by the Wallachians, and taken in the rear by a portion of the Turkish army, the Hungarians defended themselves during the entire day; but when night came, Hunyade, despairing of success, fled, and his soldiers dispersed. There alone remained on the field of battle the German auxiliaries with the artillery; that handful of men recommenced the fighting on the morrow until they were annihilated.

In the following spring, Amurath entered Albania with his immense army of Kassova. He took Sfetigrad and Dibra; but he lost before those two mean strongholds 20,000 men, and was compelled to put off the siege of Croïa until the year following (1450). The place made an heroic resistance; at the same time Scanderbeg, with 8,000 men, kept himself within a mile of the besiegers, and harassed them by incessant attacks. The Sultan tried to corrupt the commandant of the garrison; he attempted to negotiate with Scanderbeg; both alike repulsed his overtures. At length the siege was raised. Amurath had scarcely returned to Adrianople ere he died of apoplexy (9th February, 1451).

6. *Reign of Mahomet II.—Siege and Capture of Constantinople.*

The successor of Amurath II., scarcely in his twenty-second year, was consumed and carried away by a restless ambition. From the moment at which he had seen power escape from his hands, on his father reassuming the authority with which he had briefly invested him, he had champed the bit at Magnesia. When, therefore, news of his father's death reached him in his banishment, he sprang into the saddle shouting, "Who loves me follows me!" and in two days he reached Gallipoli. He was the stamp of man to hurl the already crumbling Empire of Byzantium in the dust.

Mahomet received at first the ambassadors of the Emperor, the representatives of that Constantine Dragozes, the defender of the Morea, who, in the year preceding, had succeeded to his father under the protection of Amurath. He testified to him his pacific intentions, and even engaged to pay a pension of 300,000 aspres for the maintenance of Solyman's grandson, who was kept captive at Constantinople. He then renewed the treaties existing with all his Christian allies, concluded with the envoys of Hunyade a truce of three years, and crossed over into Asia to make war upon the Prince of Karaman. Whilst he was occupied in that direction, Constantine, who had not received the promised pension, had the imprudence to claim it, adding that, if it were not paid, he would set his prisoner at liberty. Irritated at that menace, Mahomet thenceforward thought only of making an end of Constantinople. He returned to Europe, and to starve out the city and cut it off from the Black Sea, he ordered to be built upon the European shore of the Bosphorus, in the narrowest part, facing the fortress constructed by Mahomet I. in Asia, a formidable stronghold, to which he gave the significant name of Boghazkesen (*cut-throat*), now called the "Castle of Europe." Three thousand workmen, protected by an army, were employed in its construction, which was finished in three months under the eyes and direction of the Sultan. Every ship passing within reach of the battery of this castle was compelled to pay tribute, and a Venetian vessel which refused was fired upon and sent to the bottom (August 1452).

The Emperor, terrified at these tidings of the Sultan's preparations, sent an humble embassy to Mahomet, offering to pay him tribute, and entreating him to spare the country round about, upon which Constantinople depended for its supplies of food. The only answer the Sultan gave was to order his sipahis to feed their horses upon the crops of the Greeks; and some few days after, a quarrel arose between the soldiers and the peasantry, which proved the commencement of the war. The Emperor sent a last message to Mahomet:—" Since neither oaths, nor treaties, nor submissions can secure peace, proceed with hostilities."

And he ordered the gates of the city to be shut, and thought only of taking the best means for its defence.

The situation of the magnificent city of Constantinople, so long the favourite abode of the Emperors of Rome, was at the period of the foundation of the Ottoman Empire, when the powers of artillery were only partially developed, such as rendered it all but impregnable. Seated on a promontory, it was accessible on one side only by land, and everywhere surrounded by lofty massive walls. If completely garrisoned and provisioned, it was capable indeed of holding out against the most overwhelming force for a great length of time. Bajazet had long determined on the reduction of this all-important capital; but it did not fall to his lot to achieve it.

Mahomet, on his part, returned to Adrianople in order to make preparations for the siege. His ardour and restlessness were so great that he was unable to sleep, and his days were wholly occupied in discussing with his lieutenants the means of taking the city. During the erection of the castle on the Bosphorus, an Hungarian iron-founder, named Orban, constructed the most enormous cannon of which history makes mention. This gigantic machine projected granite balls twelve palms in circumference, and weighing twelve quintals. It required 700 men to move and serve it. A trial of it was made at Adrianople. The smoke from its charge of powder covered the entire city; the report was heard at many leagues off, and the ball, at the distance of a mile, embedded itself a fathom deep in the ground. Other pieces of smaller calibre were afterwards cast, and troops were mustered from every point of the Empire. A fleet of 400 sail was equipped and placed under the orders of the Bulgarian renegade Baltaoghli.

Meanwhile the greatest confusion prevailed in Constantinople. On an estimate being taken of the entire military force, it was found that only 4,973 men were efficient. To these were added 2,000 foreigners and 500 Genoese who arrived in two galleys, commanded by John Longus Justiniani. As there were no ships, the Christian vessels which arrived from the Archipelago were retained for the defence of the city; but there were only fourteen of these in port. The walls, unrepaired for centuries, having crumbled into ruins, were hastily renovated. The Emperor sent all over Europe to solicit reinforcements; and, in the hope of interesting the West in his cause, he announced his firm resolution of terminating the schism existing between the two Churches. "But," says Æneas Sylvius, "Christianity was a head without a body, a republic without magistrates; the Pope nothing more than a dazzling phantom." Instead of sending an army to "the last heir of the last spark of the Roman name," a papal legate was despatched to accomplish the reunion of the Churches. A solemn assembly took place in the church of St. Sophia on the 12th December, 1452. The legate celebrated mass, the Emperor and all the Court being present. But the monks, the clergy, and all the people revolted against that act, which they looked upon as sacrilege. At the head of the most fiery among the *orthodox* stood the Greek Patriarch Gennadius and the Grand Admiral Notaras, who declared that they would rather see in Constantinople "the Sultan's turban than the cardinal's hat." All the energy of that degraded people seemed reserved for those miserable discords. No efficacious succour came from the West. The princes of the Morea and the isles of Greece kept themselves aloof, and the Genoese of Galata entered into a treaty of neutrality with the Sultan. It is true that, in spite of this treaty, they assisted the besieged in various ways, which made Mahomet swear that "he would crush the serpent after he had slain the dragon." The defence was despaired of on all hands. All were convinced that the fatal hour had come. Among other sinister predictions there were found, it is said, in the convent of Mount Athos, two prophetic tablets attributed to Leo *the Wise*, containing a list of emperors and patriarchs; the names of the existing emperor and patriarch being wanting. It was related also that an old woman had told John of Hunyade, after the defeat of Kassova, that the reverses of the Christians would end when Constantinople should have been destroyed by the Turks. All these predictions passing from mouth to mouth had the effect of depressing men's minds.

Such was the state of the city when, in the month of April, 1453, 200,000 Osmanlis invested it on the land side. It was the twelfth time that it had been besieged by the Mussulmans; firmly convinced, as they had ever been, that the city was destined to belong to them—for Mahomet had promised it to them, sheikhs and dervishes in numbers traversed the ranks of the Ottoman army, and animated it by their predictions. The most famous among them, the Grand Sheikh Akjemseddin, discovered the bier of the standard-bearer Eyoub, killed during the third siege. A tomb had been erected to his memory, over which, later on, a mosque had been built. This incident, which appeared miraculous, contributed powerfully to exalt the fanaticism of the besiegers. The great cannon arrived, drawn by fifty pair of oxen, supported in equilibrium by 400 men, and preceded by 250 carpenters and pioneers. It was pointed at first against the Caligaria Gate (now called *Egri Kapouci*); afterwards it was moved to the St. Romain Gate, which still retains the name of the "Gate of the Cannon" (*Top Kapouci*). On either side of it were planted two pieces which discharged balls weighing six quintals. Fourteen other batteries shook the rest of the walls. The monster gun, however, did not render all the service expected from it. It took two hours to load and an enormous quantity of oil to lubricate it after each discharge to prevent it bursting. It could only be fired eight times in the course of a day. At the end of a few days it burst and killed its inventor.

However, animated by the example of the Emperor, who fought in person on the ramparts, and by the indefatigable activity of Justiniani, the defenders of the city performed prodigies: they filled up every night the breaches made during the day, raised new ramparts, and dug deeper ditches. The Turks made little progress; they were not yet skilled in the handling of artillery. It was the renegades who taught them how to promptly open a breach by aiming alternately to the right and left, and then in the centre of the wall-space already shaken. They had constructed a wooden tower covered with a triple casing of skins, and provided with draw-bridges to approach the battlements on a level, but this huge machine was burnt.

At the end of April five ships, one Greek and four Genoese, appearing in sight of the harbour, the entire Ottoman Fleet sailed out to meet them, and a sea-fight took place near the shore. Notwithstanding the disproportion of their force, the Christians threw themselves resolutely into the midst of the Turks. From their lofty decks they rained upon the low vessels of their foes such a hail of projectiles and torrents of Greek fire, that the Turkish Fleet was thrown into disorder, several vessels fouled one another and sank to the bottom. Mahomet, who witnessed this disgraceful defeat from the shore, wished in his furious rage to have urged his steed into the sea, in order to chastise the unskilfulness of his sailors. At length he saw the five ships sail right through his whole fleet and enter the harbour, the chains across which were fastened behind them. He avenged this affront upon his admiral. He caused him to be loaded with chains, inflicted a hundred blows of the bastinado with his own hand, and then deprived him of his possessions and sent him into exile.

This check made the Turks aware that they could make no progress so long as the city should be at liberty seaward, the Greek ships being masters of the Golden Horn, and even of the Propontis (Sea of Marmora). It was then that Mahomet, despairing of forcing an entrance to the harbour, conceived the singular project of conveying his vessels therein by land. The Turkish Fleet closed the Bosphorus at Beschiktasch. A road was made for it behind the hills of Pera, to a distance of two leagues, by St. Dimitri and Khalskoei. This road was covered with planks plentifully greased, and, during a single night, seventy galleys, of two, three, and five benches of rowers, were dragged by thousands of men and horses across the hills and valleys in the Golden Horn, in front of the gates now called Balat and Haïwan. On each galley the captain " stood at the fore, the pilot abaft; the sails were loosed to the wind, the trumpets sounded, the drums beat, and, at daybreak, the besieged beheld with as much surprise as terror more than seventy vessels cast anchor in the centre of their harbour." They made, it appears, no attempt to hinder or trouble the strange manœuvre of the Turks.

As soon as night came, Justiniani attempted to burn the Turkish Fleet; but he was betrayed by the Genoese of Galata, who, during the entire siege, played a double part: the vessel on board of which he was sank to the bottom; his companions were taken or drowned, he alone saving himself with much difficulty. The Turks then constructed a pontoon in the harbour, from which they cannonaded the walls.* The Greeks attempted to set fire to this pontoon and the enemy's vessels, but that enterprise failed like the preceding; forty picked Genoese to whom it was entrusted were put to death next morning in sight of the besieged; whilst the latter, by way of reprisals, placed upon their battlements the heads of 200 Turkish prisoners.

Pressed by land and sea, the city was in a desperate strait. Its slender garrison was weakened, decimated by six weeks of previous struggle, and, further, it was forced to divide itself to offer resistance at two points simultaneously. An enormous breach had been opened at the St. Romain Gate; the wall on the side of the harbour could not offer a long resistance. Mahomet sent a message to the besieged, promising, if the city capitulated, life and liberty to the inhabitants, to the Emperor peaceful possession of the Morea. Constantine preferred rather to bury himself beneath the ruins of his capital.

On the 24th of May the Sultan announced a general assault for the 29th. The Ottoman camp immediately presented the aspect of a fête; the soldiers of the fleet, who had been thrown into prison after their defeat, were

* " Von Hammer," vol. ii. p. 409.

set at liberty; the Janissaries were promised the pillage of the city, *timars* and *sandjaks* to those first to scale the ramparts; the dervishes visited the tents to reawaken the fanatical ardour of the Moslems. When evening came, the whole of the fleet and camp were illuminated; Constantinople saw itself surrounded by a belt of fire; on all sides the noisy clamours of the foe were heard, and the cry a thousand times repeated:—" God is great, and Mahomet is His Prophet!" From the heart of the mourning city the only reply to that cry were groans and prayers: " *Kyrie eleison!* Lord, have mercy upon us!"

However, the last days were employed in repairing the breaches, in reconstructing the ramparts, in digging ditches behind those which had disappeared. In the night between the 28th and 29th the Emperor took the sacrament in great pomp at St. Sophia, and then went to his post at the gate of St. Romain, attended by his staff. At daybreak the attack began. The Sultan, in order to tire out his adversaries, sent forward at first his worst troops; their bodies soon choked the ditches. Towards ten o'clock, the besieged still sustained the struggle without disadvantage, when Justiniani, wounded in the hand, retired in spite of the supplications of the Emperor, and his retreat caused discouragement among those around him. However, the example of Constantine reanimated them, and the fighting was renewed; when suddenly a cry of alarm arose:—" The Turks are in the city! The city is taken!" The Wooden, or Circus Gate, walled up for two centuries past on account of an ancient prophecy, had been reopened the previous evening for the purpose of a sortie, and by that fifty Turks had gained an entrance and took the defenders of the breach in the rear. All were dispersed immediately, and every one fled towards the harbour. The Emperor ran to the Caligaria Gate, and reached it at the moment when the assailants broke their way through it; the unfortunate Constantine rushed in desperation among their ranks and fell beneath the sabre of a Janissary.

Meanwhile crowds rushed precipitately towards the harbour, seeking refuge in the Greek and Genoese vessels.

Some succeeded in thus saving themselves, but the guards shut the gates towards the sea and threw away the keys. The torrent of fugitives then flowed back towards the centre of the city, and the greater number hastened to shut themselves up in St. Sophia and the other churches. The Turks soon followed them, and broke open the doors with axes. Then commenced scenes of pillage, profanations and excesses of every kind. There was, however, very little bloodshed, except during the first flush of victory. Men, women, and children were tied together in couples, and driven towards the ships. The pillagers then spread themselves through the streets, entered the houses and palaces, carrying off enormous booty. The Sultan had said to his soldiers on the previous evening:—"The city and its public edifices belong to me; but I give up to you the captives and the booty—the precious metals and the beautiful women; be rich and happy."

Thus fell Constantinople, after eleven centuries of existence. Its fall, after the Empire of the East had been divided into a multitude of hostile States, was inevitable; that it had not taken place sooner was probably owing to the respect with which it still inspired the barbarians, who threatened for ages that last remnant of the Roman Empire. In reality that event only put an end to a name, to a title of Empire; it even renewed the existence of the city of Constantine. It was, however, through its consequences an entire revolution. It swept away the last obstacle in the path of Islam, inimical to that faith establishing itself in Christendom. It gave definitively the triumph to the East in its struggle against the West; it seemed to menace Europe with the fate from which it had escaped eighteen hundred years back by the victories of Salamis and Marathon; it gave up the Mediterranean, that sea of civilization, to Oriental barbarism. Europe was struck with consternation at it; she felt herself sullied by a great disgrace, and at the same time menaced with a great danger. She dreaded the intrusion of a people foreign to her religion, to her manners, to her mind; who, until that dark day, had been only encamped upon her soil, but who now appeared to be definitively settled upon it. What would have been her alarm if she could have foreseen the interminable embarrassments which that barbaric domination should one day raise up in her bosom, and the infinite dangers with which even now (1880) it threatens the future?

BOOK II.

FROM THE CAPTURE OF CONSTANTINOPLE TO THE PEACE OF CARLOWITZ
(1453-1699).

CHAPTER I.

REIGN OF MAHOMET II. FROM THE CAPTURE OF CONSTANTINOPLE
(1453-1481).

1. *Condition of the Greeks after the Conquest.*

MAHOMET *Ghazi*, who had well earned that title, entered Constantinople towards noon by the breach of the St. Romain Gate. Surrounded by his body guards and viziers, he went direct to St. Sophia, on the ancient and magnificent architecture of which he long gazed with admiration. Seeing a soldier break off some mosaics from the walls, he stretched him at his feet by a blow of his sabre. By his orders, a muezzin, from the summit of the blood-stained steps of the sanctuary, summoned the Mussulmans to prayer; and thus was inaugurated the reign of Islam in his new capital.

The victorious Sultan then caused a search to be made for the Emperor's body, which was recognized from amongst a heap of slain by his purple buskins ornamented with eagles of gold. Although Constantine Palæologus had fallen while bravely fighting in defence of his crown and capital, his head was exposed upon the square of the Augusteon, at the foot of the equestrian statue of Justinian; and thence it was sent into the provinces. About 2,000 of the inhabitants were put to the sword; many thousands more were sold into slavery, or sought a refuge in other lands; and the vacancy thus created was supplied by a Turkish population. The former metropolis of the Christian world thus assumed the aspect of an Eastern city, and the desire of Sultan Bajazet I. was at length accomplished—to obtain possession of Constantinople, and "to convert the great workshop of unbelief into the seat of the true faith."

On quitting St. Sophia the Sultan had entered the Blaquernes palace, the latter residence of the Emperors, and, whilst traversing its deserted halls, he recited, in a sorrowful voice, that distich of a Persian poem:—"The spider establishes itself as custodian in the palace of emperors, and the owl makes its imperial halls echo with her lugubrious hooting." Next day he celebrated his triumph by orgies, followed by sanguinary executions. The Grand Duke Notaras, honoured at first with marked favour, was put to death with all his family; his crime being the refusal to deliver up his youngest son to the harem of the Sultan. A great number of distinguished Greeks, whom Mahomet had pardoned on the evening previous, were also given over to the executioner—the Venetian *bayle*, an envoy from the king of Aragon, being included in the massacre.

At length, at the end of three days, those scenes of violence and disorder ceased; the fleet and army withdrew laden with an immense booty; the Sultan thought about rebuilding, repeopling, and reorganizing that which he had devoted to destruction. The capture of Constantinople had spread consternation amongst the ancient portions of the Byzantine Empire. "All Greece felt itself struck by that disaster. In the Morea and in the isles men fled without knowing whither to go. The sea was covered with vessels and barks bearing away the families and the wealth of the Greeks. The mountains, the monasteries, the islands occupied by the Genoese and the Venetians, served for refuge." "It was," says the chroniclers, "a dispersion like that of the Hebrews after the capture of Jerusalem."*

Mahomet, however, in consolidating his new empire,

---

* Villemain, "Essay upon the condition of the Greeks after the Mussulman Conquest."

was guided by politic and enlightened counsels. To entice back the fugitive Constantinopolitans, the free exercise of their religion, the preservation of their possessions and the customs of their ancestors were proclaimed by a firman. The Greek clergy and learned men were treated with indulgence; the patriarchate was permitted to subsist; and Gennadius, the head of the party which had opposed a union with the Latin Church, having been elected to that dignity by an assembly of the chief citizens, was confirmed in it by the approbation of the Sultan. He himself assisted at the ceremony, and conferred on the newly-elected functionary a pastoral staff, studded with diamonds, emblems of the double authority, civil and religious, which he was called up to exercise over his countrymen. The renewal of the patriarchate gave rise to that remarkable population of Greek nobles called Phanariots, who attained a considerable share of wealth and independence. In spite, however, of these measures, a void was still left within the walls of Constantinople, which Mahomet was employed several years in filling. As his conquests proceeded, he drafted to the metropolis families from Servia and the Morea; the Genoese colonies on the Black Sea, as well as Trebizonde, Sinope, and other places, were with the same view deprived of a considerable portion of their inhabitants, and even Adrianople was compelled to contribute its reluctant quota of citizens to the new seat of Turkish empire.

Although the Greeks preserved their churches, with the exception of St. Sophia, the free exercise of their religion, the right of administering themselves, and thus formed a large community entirely distinct from the conquering nation, they were subjected to a double capitation tax, whether for their persons or their lands, and which was called the *Kharadj*. At the head of the nation or Greek community was the patriarch assisted by a synod. This patriarch had the rank of vizier, and he had a guard of Janissaries. All civil and correctional causes of the Greek rayahs in the diocese of Constantinople, marriage contracts, legacies, wills, divorces, thefts, and other offences were under the jurisdiction of his tribunal. That tribunal, composed of the principal dignitaries of the clergy, could pronounce the punishment of imprisonment, the bastinado, the galleys, &c. All the military authorities were bound to carry into execution the sentences of the patriarchs concerning Greek Christians in the same way as those of the bishops in their respective dioceses.

The synod formed the great council of the nation; it took cognisance of appeals from the sentences passed by the bishops in their dioceses, administered the revenues of the Church and of the nation, &c. The patriarch and the members of the synod were exempt from the *Kharadj*.

Every bishop exercised in his diocese the same attributes and enjoyed the same privileges as the patriarch at Constantinople; they were also exempt from the Kharadj. Finally the *papas*, or inferior members of the clergy, exercised over their flocks a civil jurisdiction analogous to that of the bishop.

The lands of the great Greek families were confiscated and transformed into *limars*; but those of the rayahs remained in their possession, and, apart from the numerous extortions to which the conquerors subjected them, they were liable also to the impost of the *Kharadj*. Each commune was governed by its *primats*, magistrates elected, whose principal function was to apportion the *Kharadj* amongst all the inhabitants, as well as the other taxes.

2. *The Conquest of Servia.*

After having secured the existence and the condition of the conquered, Mahomet caused to be transferred from Sinope, Trebizonde, and a dozen other towns, Mussulman families to repeople the capital; he ordered the fortifications of Galata to be rased, at the same time leaving to the Genoese their commercial privileges; he collected a vast number of workmen to rebuild the ruined walls; then he returned to Adrianople.

"The conquest of Constantinople," says a Turkish historian, "was the key which opened the lock of many

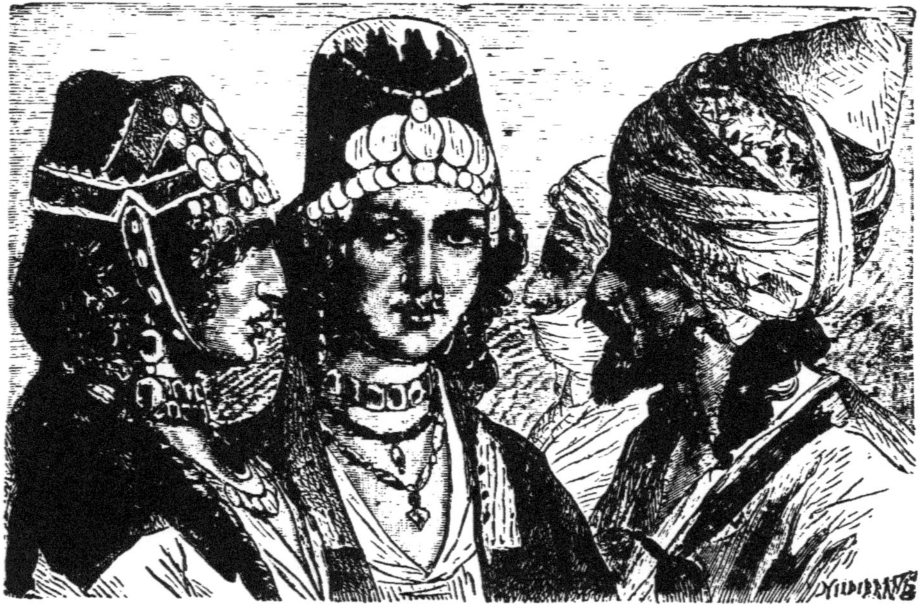

I. SERVIAN COUNTRY PEOPLE. *page* 128.

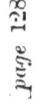

difficult things." In fact, it will be seen that all the conquests marked out under the preceding reigns were accomplished with an astonishing facility under Mahomet; that Greece, Wallachia, Servia, Bosnia, Albania, the Crimea, and the principal islands of the Archipelago were completely subjected, and that the Turkish Empire attained very nearly its definitive limits in Europe. This rapid development of the Ottoman power was the work of less than thirty years. It was certainly by the highest methods of statesmanship and military organization that a small tribe of Turkomans extended their dominion from the Danube to the Euphrates, from the Caspian Sea to the Indian Ocean.

The return of the Sultan from Adrianople was marked by the punishment of his Vizier, Khalil Pacha, the great grandson of Khalil Djendereli, Vizier of Amurath I. Convicted of connivance with the Greeks during the siege of Constantinople, he was flung into prison, and afterwards put to death. The post of Vizier remained vacant for more than a year, a solitary fact in the sequel of Ottoman history; it was conferred the year following upon Mahmoud Pacha, the son of a Greek father and of a Serb mother, and it was the first instance of those Hellenes becoming Mussulmans, who have, almost without interruption, governed the Empire of the Osmanlis.

Mahomet received the felicitations and the tributes of the Asiatic Princes, of the Genoese of the Archipelago, of the Greeks of Trebizonde, and of the Republic of Ragusa. Then he carried his arms against the most powerful of the dismembered States of the East—Servia (1454); he seized upon Ostrowitz, miscarried before the fortress of Semendria, and left an army of 30,000 men to occupy the country. The Kral Georges, assisted by Hunyade, defeated that army and obtained a truce by means of a tribute of 30,000 ducats. The year following the war recommenced, and the Turks took possession of Novoberda.

At length, in June, 1456, an army of more than 150,000 men, commanded by the Sultan, traversed Servia and laid siege to Belgrade. Three hundred pieces of artillery, many of which were of monstrous calibre, thundered against the ramparts; a flotilla of 200 small vessels intercepted the navigation of the Danube, above and below the city. Unmindful that his father had failed before Belgrade after a six months' siege, Mahomet vaunted that he would reduce that place in fifteen days; but a crusade was preparing in Hungary by the preaching of the Franciscan John Capistrano, of Roumanian race. Hunyade, with an army, threw himself into the place; he destroyed the Turkish flotilla, and successfully repulsed the assaults. At last a vigorous sortie, commanded by Capistrano, threw the Ottoman camp into disorder, and determined the raising of the siege; the Sultan withdrew, himself wounded, and taking along with him a hundred carts filled with wounded, leaving under the walls of Belgrade 24,000 dead and all his artillery. The two saviours of the city did not long survive their triumph. Hunyade succumbed at the end of fifteen days; Capistrano three months after.

In spite of this great success, Servia remained occupied in part by the Ottomans; the succour brought by the Hungarians was repugnant to her, on account of the hatred she bore the people of the Latin Church. Meanwhile, Prince Georges died; his youngest son Lazarus seized upon his power, but kept it only two months. He left two brothers, both blind, and a sister, the widow of Amurath, who disputed the heritage for three months, and then took refuge with the Sultan. Whereupon the Grand Vizier, Mahmoud Pacha, invaded Servia, seized upon the strongholds on the Danube, carried his devastation as far as Hungary, returned to besiege Semendria, and took it on the 8th November, 1459. In two years the conquest of Servia was completed, and that country, which had had so glorious an existence, which seemed called to such high destinies, was reduced to a province of the Ottoman Empire.

3. *Subjection of the Morea.—War against Scanderbeg.— Conquests in Asia.*

At the same period the subjection of Greece was consummated. Demetrius and Thomas Palæologus, brothers of the last Greek Emperor, disputed for possession of the Morea, and each had to struggle against his own subjects and the attacks of the Albanians. They were only maintained in the country by the protection of the Sultan, to whom they paid tribute.

Mahomet, early in 1458, himself sailed into the Peloponnesus, at the head of an armament; he seized upon Corinth; intimidated, by his cruelties, the other cities, which surrendered without resistance; dispossessed Thomas, and left nearly the rest of the Morea to his brother on condition of an enormous tribute. He had scarcely retired, when Thomas took up arms at once against the Turks and against his brother; and that unfortunate country was delivered up by all parties to the most frightful devastation. Demetrius ended by throwing himself into the arms of the Turks; he even accompanied the Sultan, who in person returned to terminate that terrible war. Mahomet caused to be pitilessly massacred the inhabitants of every city that attempted to resist him, inflicting upon the chief men of such places the most refined torments; and when he at length retired, he left nothing behind him but ruins. Modon, Pylos, and a few strongholds which belonged to the Venetians, alone escaped the Turkish barbarities. Thomas fled into Italy; Demetrius was banished to Enos; finally, the last Duke of Athens, Franco Accajuoli, having been strangled, the Turks ruled undividedly all the Greek peninsula (1460). During this time, an Ottoman fleet of 184 sail traversed the Archipelago. It put to ransom Lesbos and Chios, occupied by the Genoese, and subjected Imbros, Thasos, Samothrace, &c.

Another war in Europe occupied the Ottoman armies— the war in Albania, the success of which was destined to be neither so prompt nor so easy. Since the accession of Mahomet II., Scanderbeg had sustained, with an indefatigable perseverance, the continual attacks of the Ottomans. In spite of the treason of two of his companions, he defeated successively three armies. That long series of exploits won for him the admiration even of his enemies. Mahomet, on his return from the Peloponnesus, preferred

SCANDERBEG.

peace, and left him in tranquil possession of Epirus and Albania (1460).

The Sultan next turned his eyes on the side of Asia. Upon the coast of the Black Sea still subsisted three independent States wedged in among the Ottoman possessions: the Greek Empire of Trebizonde, founded by the Comnenes after the capture of Constantinople by the Latins; the colony of Amastris (*Amaszrah*), the depôt of all the Genoese commerce in these regions; finally, between those two cities, and upon the road which led to either, Sinope, where an Isfendiar still reigned. When, at the commencement of 1461, the Ottoman army set out on its march, no one knew against which of these places the expedition was directed. One of the judges of the army having ventured to ask the Sultan, the latter angrily replied, "If I thought that a hair of my beard knew my designs, I would pluck it out and cast it into the fire." The Genoese were the first attacked; Amastris opened its gates; two-thirds of its inhabitants were transferred to Constantinople. Next, the Prince of Sinope was summoned to deliver up his city, and the Grand Vizier, with a fleet of 150 sail, blockaded the port. Isfendiar yielded, and received in indemnification domains in Bithynia. Lastly, Mahomet, after an expedition into Armenia against a Turkoman prince, who had been allied with the Emperors of Trebizonde, presented himself before that city. No resistance was attempted; the Comnenes were embarked for Constantinople, and on his return thither, the Sultan ordered their execution. The youngest alone was spared, because he had embraced Islamism; the Princess Anne, daughter of the last Emperor, became a slave in the harem; and the Empress Helena, after having witnessed the massacre of her children, buried them with her own hands, in spite of the prohibition of the Sultan, and expired from grief and misery.

4. *Conquest of Wallachia.—Cruelties of Wlad the Devil.*

These expeditions were followed by a war in Wallachia. That country had been for some thirty years under the sway of the most sanguinary tyrant of whom history makes mention. This was Bladus, or Wlad, called by his subjects Drakul (*the Devil*); by the Hungarians, Wlad *the Executioner;* by the Turks, Wlad the *Empaler*. The atrocities related of him surpass all that imagination can conceive of the most horrible: executions in mass—400 young Transylvanians who had come into Wallachia to preach a crusade, 600 merchants who had returned rich from Bohemia, 500 nobles and magistrates who had complained of the cruelties of Wlad were burnt or empaled at the same time. Next all the beggars of the country were summoned to a great feast and burnt alive whilst at table; women mutilated and children compelled to eat the flesh of their mothers. His favourite amusement was to dine with his court in the centre of a circle of empaled victims. He caused the feet of his Turkish prisoners to be scorched, and the muscles laid bare rubbed with salt. The number of his victims was estimated to exceed 30,000. Mahomet made preparations to attack this ferocious beast, not on account of his crimes, but to bring Wallachia under Ottoman domination. Disturbances in Germany, then torn by domestic wars, as well as the contest between the Emperor and Matthias, favoured the progress of Mahomet II., who often stroked his beard and vowed to take vengeance for his defeat at Belgrade. After converting Servia into a Turkish province, he next turned his views towards Bosnia. Stephen Thomas, King of Bosnia, was already a tributary of the Porte; but disgusted with Turkish tyranny, he had appealed to an Hungarian Diet held at Segedin in 1458, which agreed to protect him, and invested his son with a portion of Servia that still remained unconquered. For the next three or four years Mahomet left Bosnia without much molestation, and in 1462 occupied himself in reducing Wallachia. The Voïvodes or Hospodars of Wallachia had been vassals of Poland, but after the fall of Constantinople became, like other neighbouring princes, tributary to the Porte. Here had reigned since 1456 the cold-blooded tyrant Bladus, or Wlad, already mentioned. On the entrance of Mahomet into Wallachia Wlad hastened to make his submission, and obtained from the Sultan a treaty, which is still regarded at the present day as the charter of the rights of Wallachia with respect to the Ottoman Empire. This treaty, which confirmed that of 1393 concluded between

Bajazet and the Voïvode Marcea, declared that the Sultan engaged for himself and his successors to protect Wallachia, and defend it against all enemies, without exacting anything else than the suzerainty of that principality; that he should not interfere in any way with the internal administration; that the nation should continue to enjoy the exercise of its own laws; that the Duke or Voïvode should be elected by the bishops and the boyards; that it should preserve the right of peace or war, of life and death over its subjects; that it should never be subjected by its acts to any responsibility towards the Porte; that the Wallachians should be exempt from the *kharadj* when they should find themselves upon the soil of the Empire; that the Turks should not establish themselves in Wallachia; that the tribute should be 10,000 ducats.*

Scarcely had the treaty been signed between the Sultan and Wlad, than the latter signed another with Matthias Corvinus, King of Hungary, and bound himself to attack the Ottomans. Mahomet tried to get rid of his enemy by stratagem, and despatched Hamsa, Pacha of Widdin, with his secretary, to draw him into a conference. Wlad divined its object, and seizing the two envoys, had them empaled with all their followers, "the Pacha on a stake higher than the others as a mark of honour." Then he entered Bulgaria, destroyed or massacred all along his route, and carried away 25,000 captives. The Sultan sent other ambassadors to him; Wlad admitted them to his presence; but as they refused to take off their turbans to salute him, he caused them to be nailed to their heads. On hearing this Mahomet, wrought to a pitch of fury, ordered his army to march by land, whilst he himself with 175 vessels reascended the Danube, took Kilia and Braïla, and then pursued his enemy, who devastated all before him as he retreated. The Sultan's forces numbered, it is said, 150,000 men. Wlad had no more than 10,000 soldiers; but he not the less surprised one night the Ottoman camp, made a great carnage, and was very nearly taking or slaying the Sultan himself. Some days

* Vaillant, "La Roumanie," &c., tom i. p. 228.

after Mahomet directed his march upon Bucharest; but when he reached the plain of Prœlatu, at some distance from that town, he stood horror-stricken: for half a league in length and a quarter in breadth arose a most frightful forest—20,000 Turks and Bulgarians, men, women, and children, were empaled! The body of Hamsa Pacha was seen in the midst of all these victims. After having contemplated for a while this terrible spectacle, Mahomet exclaimed, almost with admiration,—" How can I despoil of his States a man who does such things to save them?" He himself, it may be added, mercilessly caused his prisoners to be decapitated, beaten to death, mutilated, and sawn in two. This abominable war desolated the whole country during several months. At length Wlad fled into Hungary, where Matthias Corvinus flung him into prison. The Sultan established his brother Radul in his stead, who had been brought up in his seraglio, but he reduced him to the rank and condition of a Pacha, and Wallachia thus found itself definitively reunited to the Ottoman Empire. Fifteen years after Wlad reappeared, again terrified the country by his cruelties, and at last came to his end by assassination.

5. *Conquest of Bosnia.—War with the Venetians and in Albania.*

The year 1463 saw commence simultaneously three wars: against Bosnia, against the Princes of Karaman, against the Venetians; the two last embraced Asia, Europe, and the isles, and lasted to the last years of Mahomet's reign; as to the war with Bosnia, it was promptly terminated.

After the death of Stephen Douschan, who had annexed Bosnia to the Serb Empire, Tvartko (Stephen), Ban of Bosnia (1376), took the title of King; but he and his successors had to struggle continually against the Hungarians and Turks, and became alternately tributaries to one and the other. King Stephen having refused to pay tribute, Mahomet entered upon a campaign at the head of an army of 150,000 men, seized upon the Castle of Babicza, reputed as being the strongest place in Bosnia, and received the submission of the greater number of the towns. He thus separated its population: the lower classes were left in the country; those of the middle class were given as slaves to the troops; the wealthy were sent to Constantinople. The King and his son had shut themselves up in the Castle of Kliacza, upon the Sanna; besieged by the Grand Vizier, Mahmoud, they surrendered, after obtaining a treaty which guaranteed their lives. The Sultan, dissatisfied with that treaty, caused to be issued by the Sheik Ali-Bistami, as famous by his science as by his fanaticism, a *fetwa*, which declared the treaty null; the Bosnian Prince was executed with all his family by the hand of the same learned barbarian who had pronounced the sentence.

These movements of the Turks were a principal reason with King Matthias Corvinus for concluding with Frederick III., in 1463, the peace already mentioned. In September of that year, having assembled his vassals at Peterwardein, Matthias crossed the Save into Bosnia, drove the Turks before him, and, after a siege of three months, recovered the important Fortress of Jaicza. At Christmas, having been forced to retire through a want of provisions, he entered Buda in triumph, followed by a long train of Osmanli prisoners in purple dresses. In the following year, however, Jaicza, after a memorable defence, and in spite of the attempts of Matthias to relieve it, was captured by Mahomet after great loss. Bosnia was then reduced to the condition of a province of the Ottoman Empire: 30,000 of its inhabitants were incorporated with the Janissaries, and the majority of the remainder constrained to embrace Islamism.

The war against the Venetians broke out on account of a slave having taken refuge at Coron, and whom they refused to give up because he had become a Christian. The Ottomans devastated the territory of Lepanto; but a Venetian fleet having disembarked some troops in the Morea, all Greece revolted. Argos was taken, the rampart of the isthmus repaired and put into a state of defence, and Corinth besieged; but, on learning the arrival of 80,000 Turks, the defenders of the isthmus dispersed: the Ottomans entered freely into the Morea, retook Argos, and ravaged the Venetian territory; 500 prisoners were sent to the Sultan, who had them all sawn in two. The year following (1464), the Venetian admiral attempted to make himself master of Lesbos; but he could only transfer a part of the Christian population to Negropont. His successor, more fortunate, seized upon Imbros, Thasos, Samothrace, and found himself for an instant master of Athens; but on land the Venetians experienced only reverses; three successive defeats decimated their army.

Pope Pius II., however, strove to reawaken the zeal of the Crusades; he desired even to put himself at the head of the Christian army, when his death broke off the enterprise. The sole result of his efforts was a fresh rising in Albania. Scanderbeg, released by the Pope from the treaty to which he had sworn, took up arms again, and defeated, blow after blow, five Mussulman armies. After having tried to negotiate anew, after having attempted to compass the assassination of this formidable enemy, Mahomet went himself with 100,000 men to besiege Croïa; he failed, and the army which he left before that place was, after his departure, destroyed by Scanderbeg in two battles. The Ottomans confined themselves to ruining Tchorli, founded by the Christian hero, and fortifying Elbassan. Such was the state of things when *the Dragon of Albania* died at Alessio (1467), from the effects of a fever, after being for five-and-twenty years the terror of the Moslems. When Mahomet, some years afterwards, obtained possession of Alessio, he caused Scanderbeg's tomb to be opened, and his remains to be exhibited to the wondering Osmanli. Pieces of his bones were sought for with avidity, to be converted into talismans, which were deemed capable of inspiring the wearers with some portion of the valour of that unconquered hero.

After a year of truce, hostilities recommenced between the Turks and the Venetians. The latter seized upon the Isle of Lemnos, took Enos in Europe, and Phocæa in Asia; but those slight successes were promptly effaced by the loss of Negropont, the ancient Eubœa. That island was the centre of the Venetian possessions of the Archipelago; Mahomet attacked it with a fleet of 300 sail, and an army of 70,000 men who crossed the Euripus on a bridge of galleys. A Venetian fleet, stationed at the mouth of that stream was present, without stirring, at the passage of the Turkish troops, during the siege, which continued seventeen days, and which cost the Sultan 50,000 men; lastly, during the capture of the town, the defenders of which were delivered over to the most atrocious tortures (1470).

At the same time, an important war broke out in Asia.

6. *Conquest of Karamania.*

The Princes of Karaman, for a hundred and fifty years, did not cease to make war against the Sultans so soon as they saw them occupied in Europe: Mahomet seized the opportunity of making an end of that small State, the distant situation of which constituted its sole strength. Ibrahim, Prince of Karaman, at his death, had left his throne, not to his legitimate sons, but to Ishak, whom he had had by a slave. Mahomet took the former under his protection, defeated Ishak, and set up one of the sons of Ibrahim as Pacha of Konieh; then, Ishak having again taken up arms, he vanquished him anew, reunited all Karamania to his empire, and gave the government of it to his son Mustapha. In the sequel of this war, the Grand Vizier Mahmoud, who displeased the Sultan by his moderation, was disgraced.

The conquest, however, was far from being definitive; risings took place in favour of the fallen family. Three viziers who succeeded to Mahmoud, were successively sent into the country, seized upon some few places, but could not wholly subdue it. Further, the Karamanian princes found a protector in Ouzoun-Hassan, the most powerful of the Turkoman princes, who invaded the Ottoman provinces. He was the grandson of that Kara-Youlouk, of the dynasty of the *Black Sheep*, who was an ally of Timour, and aggrandized himself under the protection of the conquering Tartar. He had, in 1466, put an end to the rival monarchy of the *Black Sheep*, which was the ally of the Sultan, conquered Khorassan, which a descendant of Timour possessed, and extended his domination from the Oxus as far as the Euphrates. He believed himself to be in a condition to make head against the Ottoman power. After the fall of the dynasty of the *Black Sheep*, he had sent to the Sultan the head of the conquered prince; then he had given an asylum to the last Isfendiar and to the dispossessed Princes of Karaman; lastly, he had addressed to Mahomet an insulting letter, in which he called him simply Mahomet-Bey. He assumed the offensive, appeared before Tokat, carried the town by assault, delivered it up to the horrors of pillage, and caused all the inhabitants to perish. In that peril, Mahomet restored the dignity of vizier to the conqueror of Servia and Bosnia; then he made preparations for a great expedition, and ordered his son Mustapha, Governor of Karaman, to go in search of the enemy. The latter came up with him at Koraïli, on the frontiers of Hamid, and inflicted upon him a sanguinary defeat.

Then (1472) the Sultan advanced with an army of 100,000 men. Ouzoun-Hassan awaited him a short distance beyond Sivas; he at first put to the rout the Ottoman vanguard; but a few days after he was conquered at Outloukbeli, near Erz-Inghian, not far from the Euphrates; several thousands of Turkomans were made prisoners, then massacred in detail. The Sultan returned into Europe, and left to his lieutenants the care of finishing the war in Cilicia.

Scarcely had he returned to Constantinople when he deposed Mahmoud Pacha, and caused him to be put to death. Mahomet had no liking for that descendant of a conquered race, converted even from childhood and by force to Islamism, who contributed by his talents and courage to the aggrandizement of the Empire of the Osmanlis. The humane and generous disposition of the Vizier contrasted with the cruelty and vices of the Sultan. He had not forgiven him the treaty formerly accorded the King of Bosnia; his moderation in that transaction and during the war of Karamania had been the cause of his first disgrace; this time the Sultan made a crime of the too prudent counsel he had given him in his march against Ouzoun-Hassan. Lastly, Prince Mustapha having died in Cilicia, he reproached him with having rejoiced at it, and ordered him to be executed. "I arrived at the Porte," said Mahmoud in his will, "with my sabre, my horse, and five hundred aspres; all the rest is the property of the Padischah." Conqueror of Servia, of Bosnia and Negropont, protector of learned men, founder of useful edifices, benefactor of the poor, his death incensed the people, and his memory was venerated as that of a martyr.

Meanwhile the war against the Venetians continued. Ouzoun-Hassan and the Karamanian princes sent to ask succour from the West. All the enemies of the Ottomans leagued together. A Venetian and pontifical fleet brought cannons and reinforcements to the Karamanians, attacked Attalia, ran along the coast and made war as the Turks did, ravaged the country, and seizing upon the inhabitants to sell them as slaves. Selefkeh was reconquered, as well as some fortresses; but speedily the Ottomans regained the upperhand. Keduk-Ahmed, who become Vizier in place of Mahmoud, and was also of Christian origin, achieved the entire submission of the province; and Prince Djem succeeded his brother Mustapha in the quality of governor.

7. *War in Moldavia.—Conquest of the Crimea.*

The warlike ardour of the Ottomans did not confine itself to the expeditions just related; Servia and Bosnia opening to them the Balkans and the basin of the Danube, they rushed towards the West, not in regular armies, but in savage bands, that sought only the pillage and massacre of Christians. They invaded thus, during those four years (1470 to 1473), Croatia, Carniola, Carinthia, and Styria. Germany began to tremble; but the peril that menaced Europe failed to unite the Christian kings in a common defence, and the Ottomans were able, without hindrance, to continue their conquests or their ravages.

The possession of Wallachia had only given to the Turkish Empire a portion of ancient Dacia; Moldavia, inhabited in the same way by Roumanian peoples, was independent, or, to speak more correctly, the suzerainty of it was disputed by Hungary and Poland. At that time reigned in Moldavia Stephen IV., the prince who, by his victories and his talents, has embellished the history of that country with its noblest pages. He had already defeated successively the Hungarians, the Poles, and the Tartars, when Mahomet sought to compel him to pay tribute. He refused, and an Ottoman army of more than 100,000 men invaded the country, but was put to a thorough rout by 40,000 Moldavians near Racovitza, upon the Berlatu (1475). Following the example of his neighbour, Wlad *the Devil*—for these Christian princes were as ferocious as the Turks—Stephen caused his prisoners to be empaled. Mahomet became infuriated at the news of this defeat; but, the better to assure his vengeance, he determined to attack Moldavia on two sides, and make the Tartars of the Kaptschak or the Crimea march against her.

The Crimea had been included in the great Empire of Zinghis Khan, and after the partition of that Empire, in the Khanate of the *Kaptschak*, which comprehended all the country north of the Caspian and of the Black Sea, with Russia. The invasion of Tamerlane having overthrown the Kaptschak, the race of Zinghis entirely perished, with the exception of a prince, Devlet Sheraï, who was the founder of the Khans of the Crimea. But that country already belonged only nominally to the Tartars. A small Christian republic had comprehended the importance of that peninsula, which commanded the Black Sea and the Bosphorus. Already mistress of Pera, and of twenty other maritime points in the Mediterranean, it had seized upon the coasts of the Crimea, had established there commercial depôts, and founded a very flourishing town, Kaffa. Mahomet could not leave to his vassals of Pera a possession which menaced Constantinople, and the Moldavian war having furnished him the opportunity, he directed a fleet of 300 sail upon the Crimea. Kaffa held out for only six days, when it was delivered up by treason to the Ottomans, who carried off almost all the inhabitants. The other Genoese places surrendered without resistance; and the peninsula thus finding itself for the greater part in the power of the Turks, Mahomet installed there as his vassal and tributary the son of Devlet, Mengli Sheraï. It thus formed a barrier against the Russians, which he thought impassable; for "he feared," says a Turkish historian, "lest the Muscovites, whose power was beginning to increase, might profit by the perpetual divisions of the Tartar tribes."

The war in Moldavia was then resumed. The victorious fleet sailed back to Akerman, which was carried by assault, whilst the Sultan himself passed up the Danube at the head of 100,000 men. Stephen IV. had acquired, like Hunyade and Scanderbeg, the renown of champion of Christianity, or, as the Pope called him, "the athlete of Christ"; but he asked in vain for aid from Hungary and Poland. He then retreated before the formidable army that menaced him, drew it into a forest near Robœni, and there thoroughly routed it. Mahomet lost 30,000 men (1476).

That reverse only slightly weakened the Turkish Empire, and the Sultan found amongst the unfortunate Christian populations wherewith to renew the ranks of his armies.

8. *Capture of Croïa.—Siege of Scutari.—Peace with the Venetians.*

After the capture of Negropont by the Osmanlis, the Turkish and Venetian war, for the next two or three years, offers little of importance. In 1476, the Turks had approached the Salzburg Alps, and the very borders of Italy; and in the summer of 1477, having invaded Croatia and Dalmatia, crossed the Julian Alps, they arrived upon the Isonzo, defeated a Venetian army, sacked the Frioul, and extended their ravages in a still more dreadful manner as far as the banks of the Piave. Crossing the Isonzo, they menaced even Venice herself, and the Sea-queen might have beheld from her towers the columns of fire that rose in the plains between the Tagliamento and the Piave. After the enemy had retired, the Venetians attempted to secure themselves from a repetition of this insult, by throwing up a lofty rampart on the banks of the lower Isonzo, from Gortz to the marshes of Aquileia, protected at each end by a fortified camp. But scarcely was it completed, when a fresh swarm of Osmanlis, under Omar-Bey, broke through in several places, and a hundred villages became at once a prey to the flames. The historian Sabellico, who beheld this fearful spectacle from a town near Udine, likened the whole plain between Isonzo and the Tagliamento to a sea of fire. In other respects, the arms of the Turks had not been successful. An attempt on Croïa in 1477 had been repulsed, and in Greece, Lepanto had been delivered by Loredano and his fleet. But the war had now lasted thirteen years, and the resources of Venice were nearly exhausted. Discouraged by the late reverses, the Republic decided to make peace by abandoning Croïa. The defenders of that place were the

SCUTARI. [page 145.

last companions of Scanderbeg: reduced to all the horrors of famine, they surrendered on condition of a promise, signed by the Sultan, that their lives would be secured. On quitting the fortress, they were arrested and conducted before Mahomet, who had them beheaded.

Croïa being taken, the exactions of the Sultan increased; he demanded from the Venetians the cession of Scutari, and, upon their refusal, he went himself to besiege it. The place offered a desperate resistance; the walls, reduced to ruins by the Turkish artillery, which discharged balls weighing thirteen quintals, were defended with frightful slaughter. After six weeks of continual assaults, in which he lost the moiety of his army, the Sultan found himself compelled to renounce his enterprise, and the siege was converted into a blockade.

The Ottomans, however, took their revenge upon less important places, which surrendered one after another; then the Venetians treated (January 26th, 1479), and the principal condition of the peace was the giving up of Scutari. The inhabitants, reduced to 450 men and 150 women, preferred rather to expatriate themselves than support the Mussulman yoke. The peace concluded at Constantinople by Giovanni Dario, the Secretary of State, was ratified by an Ottoman ambassador despatched to Venice, who was received with the greatest honour. It was even reported that a secret alliance was then concluded between the Republic and the Porte. We are approaching a period at which the Ottoman Empire is about to play a great part in the affairs of Western Europe.

9. *Expeditions into Hungary and Italy.—Siege of Rhodes.*

Forced to respect the Venetian frontiers, the Turkish ravagers threw themselves with renewed fury upon Transylvania; the Voïvode, Stephen Bathori and Paul Kinis, Count of Temesvar, strove to repel them. A great battle was fought on the 13th October, 1479, at Kenger-Mesæ, near Karlsbourg. At the moment when the Hungarians began to waver, and when Bathori, mortally wounded, thought the battle lost, Kinis of Temesvar came up with reinforcements and decided the victory: 30,000 Turks perished. In the evening, the conquerors celebrated their triumph by an orgie : the tables were laid over heaps of corpses; blood was mingled with the wine, and Kinis himself, holding a Turk between his teeth, performed a warlike dance. That memorable defeat did not hinder the Turks from reappearing early in the year following, and from penetrating as far as Styria.

Two important expeditions signalized the year 1480. Keduk-Pacha, with twenty-nine vessels, attacked the Ionian Isles, and wrested St. Maura, Zante, and Cephalonia from the despot of Arta. This conquest gave the Sultan an opportunity to display one of those singular caprices in which despotic power alone can indulge. He caused some of the inhabitants to be conveyed to the islands in the Sea of Marmora, where he compelled them to intermarry with Africans, in order that he might have a race of coloured slaves. He next set sail with a fair wind towards Italy, and appeared suddenly before Otranto. It was a signal that Mahomet had entered upon new projects: to his conquest of Greece, he was desirous of adding that of Italy. It was said that he had promised himself to make his horse eat oats upon the high altar of St. Peter's at Rome. Otranto was taken (11th August); that unfortunate city saw itself delivered up to the customary barbarities of the Ottomans, and of which Italy had lost the remembrance since the first incursions of the Saracens.

Another fleet had set sail at the same time from Constantinople. It was composed of more than sixty galleys, under the command of Mesih Pacha, and was directed against Rhodes. The Knights of St. John of Jerusalem, who had occupied that isle since the end of the thirteenth century, were, by the very spirit of their institution, in perpetual war with the Mussulmans. However, having to struggle already against the Sultans of Egypt and the Tunisians, they had avoided offending the too formidable power of the Ottomans, and had maintained a good understanding with the predecessors of Mahomet II. With the consent of even Mahomet I., they had fortified Halicarnassus, Cos, and the less important isles that cover the approaches to Rhodes. The Grand Master, Pierre d'Aubusson, foresaw the peril with which he was menaced; he hastened to conclude peace with the Sultan of Egypt and the Bey of Tunis, and made his preparations for defence. On the 23rd of May, 1480, the Turkish fleet and an army drafted from Asia appeared under the walls of Rhodes, and the town was battered in breach by land and sea. All the population flocked to its defence: men, women, children, old men laboured to repair the walls ruined by the artillery, to raise fresh ramparts, to remove, by means of subterranean passages, the fascines and stones by the aid of which the Mussulmans tried to fill up the ditches. Three assaults were directed against the St. Nicholas Tower, which formed the principal defence of the harbour; they were valiantly repulsed. Upon the ruined walls the besieged had erected an enormous catapult, which hurled back upon the Turks the fragments of their stone cannon-balls, and which was derisively called by the knights *the tribute*.

At length, on the 28th of July, the same day on which the squadron of the vizier appeared before Otranto, a general assault was delivered against Rhodes. The Turks rushed in mass upon the breach, and it was already carried, when Mesih Pacha restrained the ardour of his soldiers by forbidding them to pillage the town. The assailants, in turn, were repulsed in disorder, having lost 9,000 dead and 15,000 wounded, which compelled them to reimbark. The Admiral, on his return to Constantinople, was ignominiously deposed.

The year following these expeditions, the Sultan Mahomet Ghazi died, August 3rd, 1481.

10. *Character of Mahomet II.—His Institutions.*

Mahomet II. is, of all the Ottoman sovereigns, the one of whom Europeans have most spoken. His contemporaries, the Byzantines especially, have painted him in the darkest colours; to his actual cruelties they have added imaginary ones; thus, when his death became known at Rome, the Pope ordered prayers and rejoicings for three days. Christianity believed itself delivered from its most formidable enemy. Later, however, fanciful writers indulged in his praise, in panegyrics that pompously enumerated the cities and kingdoms he had conquered, that vaunted his tolerance and intelligence. The truth is that he had all the vices of a corrupt barbarian, and though he might love letters and protect them, he was not the less a dissolute, perfidious, and sanguinary tyrant—one of the most detestable man slayers recorded in history. But he did not solely occupy himself in wholesale massacres of peoples and the destruction of their cities, he was desirous of founding, administering, governing. Thus we have seen that by his care Constantinople acquired a new existence; he therein constructed four mosques, amongst which was conspicuous the great mosque of the conqueror (*Fethiyé*). He caused, moreover to be built a multitude of schools, imarets, baths, two palaces, the old and new Seraglios.* Artists and workmen from all countries were sought for to embellish these edifices; and he knew well how to recompense them; thus the architect of the Fethiyé received as a gift an entire street of the city.

As a warrior, Mahomet, in spite of the extent of his conquests, was not an extraordinary man; he owed his chief

---

* Upon the site of the Acropolis of the ancient Byzantium, there, where arose in antiquity the temples of Pallas, Bacchus and Jupiter; under the Christian Emperors, the Churches of SS. Demetrius and Minas, of Theodore Sergius and of the Holy Virgin, there might the following inscription be read: " May God eternize the honour of its possessor! May God consolidate its construction! May God strengthen its foundations!" (" Constantinople and the Bosphorus," tom. 1.)

successes to the number of his soldiers and the weakness of
his enemies; but as a legislator he was favourably distinguished from his predecessors. Before his reign the Ottomans were rather an army than a nation; their institutions
were those of a semi-nomad and adventurous people. It
was Mahomet II. who regulated those institutions and
gave them a character of stability. His code of laws,

MAHOMET II.

called the *Kanoun-Namé* (fundamental law), was divided into
three parts; the first treats of the hierarchy and the
grandees of the Empire, the second of ceremonies, and the
third of the penalties for crime and the financial and municipal administration.

The number four is taken as the basis of the hierarchical
government, in honour of the four angels who support the

Korân, and of the four Khalifes disciples of Mahomet. The State is compared to a tent; the government of it is the door or most conspicuous part of it. The *Sublime Porte* (*Babi-Dwelet*), it is well known, has served from the origin and still serves to designate the government of the Sultan. The four supports of the Sublime Porte, the four columns of the tent, are the four first dignitaries of the Empire; the *vizier*, the *Kadi-asker*, or judge of the army, the *defterdar*, or secretary of the treasury, and the *nischandji*, secretary for the signature of the Sultan.

At first there was only one vizier, then two, then three; under Mahomet II. their number was increased to four; but the grand vizier was much above the others, both by his prerogatives and by the importance of his functions: he was the keeper of the Seal of State, that was the symbol of his dignity; he bore it always suspended round his neck; he had the right of holding under his roof a particular divan, which was called the High Porte, in which was debated affairs of detail; he received the official visits of all the other great dignitaries.

The highest dignity, after that of vizier, was that of *Kadi-asker*. There was only one at first; in the last year only of Mahomet's reign, two were created, one for Europe and one for Asia. They were, each in his department, the supreme heads of the judiciary order; they nominated to all the posts of judges and professors (*Kadis and mouderris*), with the exception of some privileged places of which the grand vizier reserved the disposal.

The *defterdar* came next, who kept the registers of the finances. There was only one in Mahomet's time; later on there were four. The *nischandji* affixed the *toughra* upon the diplomas, and further prepared and revised them. That function became later almost entirely honorary, its most important attributes having passed to the *reis-effendi*, secretary of State.

After those four categories of dignitaries, who alone had entrance to the divan, ranked the exterior *agas* or heads of the army; those were the aga of the Janissaries, charged, besides the command of that militia, with the safe-guard of Constantinople; the agas of the sipahis and other corps of regular cavalry; the *topdschi-baschi*, the general of the artillery, the general of munitions, and the general of transports; the twelve officers of the imperial stirrup, the standard-bearer, the equerries, chamberlains, masters of the hunt, &c. Under the name of interior agas were designated the great officers of the Seraglio; the principal were the *Kapou-aga* (aga of the Sublime Porte), or chief of the white eunuchs; the treasurer, the superintendent of the table, the commander of the *Kapidjis* or guard of the Courts; of the *bostandjis* or gardeners; the *tschauch-bachi*, chief of the messengers of State, who were also called beys of the divan, because they watched over the maintenance of order in the hall of council; lastly, the chief of the black eunuchs (*Kislaragaci*, aga of the girls), who frequently found himself the most powerful of all by his secret influence.

The provinces were governed by beys, pachas of one tail, beylerbeys, pachas of two tails, who levied the taxes and assembled under their banner (*sandjak*) the feudatory horsemen. The names of possessors of fiefs were inscribed upon the registrars of the defterdar; Mahomet ordered to be added thereto a statement of the value of their domains, which served to regulate proportionally their ground-rents: a notable amelioration in the system of finance. The other sources of revenue of the empire were the customs duties, fines, the mines, and the tributes, a part of which the Sultan gave over to the viziers and defterdars.

The most remarkable monument of the legislation of Mahomet was the hierarchy of the judicial and religious functionaries which was called the *chain of the ulemas.*

The ulemas are not priests, but legists and theologians; it is a learned body* from which are exclusively recruited

* The priests properly so-called, that is to say, the clergy of the mosques, the callers to prayer, the imans, and the preachers, do not enjoy, probably, in any State less influence than in the Ottoman Empire; the teaching corps, on the contrary, has an importance and an authority of which an example is nowhere else seen, China excepted. Von Hammer, liv. xviii. p. 342.

the judges, doctors, professors, and the highest civil functionaries of the empire. The organization of that singular body was especially the work of Vizier Mahmoud, learned himself and the friend of the learned. The chain of the ulemas comprehends those who teach, and those who study, the functionaries and the candidates. The first all come out of the higher schools or *medressés*, wherein they learn grammar, logic, metaphysics, rhetoric, geometry, astronomy, then civil law, dogmatic doctrine, the traditions of the Prophet, the interpretation of the Korân, in short, jurisprudence and theology; for those two sciences make one only amongst the Mussulmans; the Korân, the traditions of the Prophet, those of the Khalifes, the *kaouns* or decrees of the Sultans, are at once the sources of law and of religious doctrine. In the course of their studies, the candidates take successively the names of *thalebs*, students, or more commonly of *souktès* (inflamed with zeal), of *danischmends* (gifted with science), and of *moulasims* (prepared). The grade of *danischmend* suffices to obtain the posts of *imans*, of *naïbs* (inferior judges), or of masters of elementary schools; that of *moulasim* gives access to the functions of *mouderris* (professors of medressés), of superior judges and of *mollahs*. All these posts, as has been said, depend upon the Kadiaskers; but since Mahomet II. the nominations, to the lowest as well as to the highest, must be confirmed by a diploma from the Sultan. The mouderris are divided into several categories according to the importance of their posts and the nature of their teaching. They are distinguished by the number affixed to their emolument; and they are called the twentieth, the thirtieth, the fortieth, fiftieth, sixtieth, according as they receive 20, 30, 40 aspres *per diem*. The title of *mollah* is reserved for the highest functionaries of the judicial order. The first of all, in the time of Mahomet, were the Kadiaskers; next came the *chodja* (preceptor of the princes), the judge of Constantinople, then the grand *mufti*. This title of mufti (interpreter of laws) designated the learned whose decision (fetwa) constituted authority in matters of religion and jurisprudence; such was the sheik who authorized the execution of the King of Bosnia.* Later, the authority of the grand muftis, supported by religion, became omnipotent; they acquired the supreme rank in the body of the ulemas, and their fetwas often balanced the revered power of the Sultans.

This corporation of the ulemas, so strongly constituted, embracing all the degrees of the administration, is the most important of the institutions of the Ottoman Empire. It has powerfully contributed to maintain, amongst the Ottomans, in spite of the contact with Europe, the immovable spirit of Islam in all its primitive rigidity; it still nourishes that religious fanaticism, that servile attachment to the letter of the law, that blind respect for tradition, which repulses all attempt at change and which rises like an insurmountable barrier between the Mussulman and the European world; finally, it has become one of the most threatening causes of ruin for the Ottoman Empire.

The second portion of the *Kanoun-Namé* presents less of interest. It may however be remarked upon the prescriptions relative to the ceremonial of the Seraglio, for the fêtes of the Beïram,† that disposition which characterizes the despotism of the East and the person of Mahomet: "It is my will that no one should eat with My Imperial Majesty. My illustrious ancestors had formerly admitted their viziers to their table; that custom I have abolished." That notorious law of fratricide may be specially instanced as a lasting testimony to the ferocity of the Ottoman usages: " The ulemas have declared this permitted: whosoever of my illustrious sons or grandsons shall arrive at supreme power may cause his brothers to be put to death to assure the repose of the world." Let us add that that barbarous custom has been faithfully observed; that it was practised indeed before they had the brutal audacity to erect it into a law. The proscription is extended not only to brothers, but to nephews and great-nephews of the Sultans, and the sons of their

* See p. 137. † The Easter of the Mussulmans.

daughters; it was only to the second generation of the descendants of the Sultanas that it was permitted to live.

As for the third portion of the code of Mahomet, it regulates the penalty, that is to say, *the price of blood:* " The price of blood must be levied by the agents of the police; it shall be, for a murder, 3,000 aspres; for an eye destroyed, 1,500; for a wound on the head, 50, &c." It was thus one of the principal resources of the treasury.

The *Kanoun-Namé* is, with the ordinances of Solyman the Magnificent, all the civil legislation of the Ottomans. It will be seen by that in what a narrow circle the Korân confines the societies that it forms; but it must be added that the Turks, on establishing themselves in the Byzantine empire, permitted to subsist almost all the laws, customs, forms, ceremonies, pompous etiquette, the administrative, financial, and municipal systems, in short it may be said nearly all the social state of the Lower Empire and of the provinces that were for a long time separated from it. Too simple, too ignorant, too proud to distinguish between the useful or the injurious, the just or the unjust, the oppressive or the salutary in the subtle, confused, despotic, venal, corrupting legislation of that empire, which had only retained of Greece and Rome their vices; seduced by those traditions so convenient to the arbitrary, for oppression, for the anarchy which they found everywhere existing, they accepted all and employed it to their profit, without calculation, thought or reflection for the future, anxious only to enjoy the present, as those barbarous conquerors have always done. "At the same time that they adopted, in its spirit if not in its details, the mode of administration and of impost in vigour amongst the Hellenes, they recognized the privileges of the great feudatories of Bosnia, Albania, and Servia; lastly, they instituted themselves by degrees, under the name of *beylouks*, vast fiefs founded upon the bondage of the peasants and which encouraged the sipahis possessors of *ziamets* and *timars* to change their right of tithe into proprietary right over land and persons."*

* Hipp. Desprez, "Les Peuples de l'Autriche and de la Turquie," i. 201.

THE TURKISH FEUDAL SYSTEM. 155

In all Ottoman conquests there was a distribution of forfeited lands into fiefs. It was Mahomet II. who introduced the old feudal usages of the Seljukian empire. This was called the Timariot system, and in some respects it is singularly parallel with the English feudal system. Large tracts of the richest land having reverted to Government by confiscation, a considerable proportion was divided into fiefs, and conferred on distinguished warriors. The Timariot held his fief on the condition of serving the Sultan in compact with a certain number of followers proportioned to its value. It was the Timariot system, in conjunction with the tributes of Christian chiefdom, which mainly consolidated Turkish power in Europe. Lord Byron has an allusion to the feudal system of Turkey :

"We Moslems reck not much of blood;
But yet the line of Karasman
Unchanged, unchangeable hath stood,
First of the bold Timariot bands,
That won and well can keep their lands."

The word *sipahi* originally denoted the lowest class of Timariot. It was only by means of their feudatories that a small minority of conquerors, like the English in India, were enabled to retain their authority over a vast population, with a large subject element of farmers and landed proprietors. The Christian cultivators, in a large proportion of cases, retained their lands, paying revenues to the Timariot, who, in turn, rendered service to the Sultan. Unfortunately, as differences of creed were added to those of race, there was never the same fusion which took place in Western Europe. The system might be defective, and it manifested growing defects, but at the same time there were some points on which it favourably contrasted with the Western system. The condition of the Ottoman rayah would be one of greater comfort and security than that of the Russian serf or French *villein*. Like the old condition of baron and knight, the feudal military organization of Turkey has now passed away, but it survived nearly to our own times, and traces of it still remain.

A feudal system has two sides, the military and the territorial. The feudal militia, in conjunction with the Janissaries, for generations constituted the strength of the Ottoman power. The Turkish feudal system has to be studied both in Asia and Europe. In Asia Minor we find the same decay and depopulation as in European Turkey —the fallen bridge, the ruined caravanserai, the thinned population, the deserted district. Mahomet II. swept away Othoman's feudal system in Asia Minor; it is a common criticism, however, that he would have done better had he tried to reinvigorate and restore it. The ruins of the feudal castle are found in many a sequestered valley of the Asiatic provinces. In Europe other causes have been at work; not only lust and cruelty, the fundamental vices of Islamism, but the denial of justice and fair play to Christians, and the blundering finance which has been injurious to all creeds and classes. The decline of cultivation, credit, and population is not essentially due to the feudal system consequent upon the Turkish conquest, except that the fief not passing from father to son constituted a further great barrier to improvement. The laws affecting land have always been of the most iniquitous and suicidal description, and have fallen with equal harshness on the "infidel" and the "true believer." For two months annually all agricultural industry is paralyzed. The tax is paid in kind—a certain proportion of the annual crop. The harvest waits the leisure of the tax-gatherer; and the most primitive, cumbrous operations are retained because they best suit the convenience and the precedents of government. It is calculated that the Christian provinces could sustain fourteen times the present population. The magnificent resources of Turkey have been an immense lure to speculators in loans, but these resources can never be developed under an intensified system of misgovernment. The old feudal system has passed away without the substitution of anything better, but with the aggravation of its worst elements. When the soil is owned by the Mussulman, but cultivated by the Christian, the landlord farms the taxes or combines with the tax-collector.

Even the feudal system has been ill-exchanged for the abnormal monstrosities that have succeeded it.

This result ought not to surprise, if it be considered that there was no great moral difference between the conquerors and the conquered; the one and the other had been intermingled for two centuries in war, peace, commerce and transactions of every kind: that they had very nearly the same manners, the same cupidity, the same corruption and moreover the same cruelty; lastly, that if we regard the fundamental difference, that of religion, we find that the corrupt, degenerate, deteriorated Christianity of the eastern peoples had very nearly approached to Islamism.

To these considerations if we add that the Ottoman armies were in great part composed, either of Christians converted by force to Islamism, like the Janissaries,; or of Christian auxiliaries, like the Serbs, Bulgarians, Albanians, whom we have seen so frequently figuring in the ranks of the Osmanlis; that the majority of the Grand Viziers,* statesmen, generals, were of Christian race; that almost all administrators, collectors of imposts, scribes, diplomatic envoys, were Hellenes or Slavs; finally, that "it was a maxim of state among the Osmanlis," says Hammer, "that he must be the son of a Christian in order to succed to the highest dignities of the empire." The following conclusions, therefore, may be drawn by which a clear understanding of the history of the Ottomans and the prescience of their destinies may be arrived at:—"That the Turkish people has been formed, as originally was formed the militia of the Janissaries, which was in one respect the image of Turkey, by recruiting itself from the Greek, Slav, Albanian, and Bulgarian populations, on which violence imposed apostacy. That if the Ottoman power trod under foot so many nations, that result ought not to be attributed to the indolent and stolid character of the Turkish race, but to the spirit of finesse and address which distinguishes

* Under Mahomet II., of five Grand Viziers, four were of Christian origin, two Greeks, and two Illyrians; under Solyman the Great, of nine Viziers, eight were of Christian origin, &c. The five Krupuli were Macedonians.

the Greek and Slav peoples, to the intrepidity of the Albanians and Dalmatians, to the perseverance of the Bosnians and Croats; in short, to the valour and talent of the inhabitants even of the conquered countries;"* lastly, that the Ottoman empire has been, from the reasons just given as well as from the evils and embarrassments which it has caused Europe, only the restoration, transformation, and continuation of the Lower Empire.

* Ranke, "Hist. de la Revolution Serbe;" Hammer, "Hist. of the Ottoman Empire."

CHAPTER II.

REIGN OF BAJAZET II. AND OF SELIM I. (1481-1520).

1. *Revolt and Adventures of Djem.*

MAHOMET II. left two sons, Bajazet, Governor of Amasia, and Djem, Governor of Karamania. This Prince Djem, or Zizim, as European historians have called him, was the youngest of the two brothers. He was then in his twenty-second year. Of lively and cultivated mind, an expert wrestler, and no mean poet, he had succeeded in winning the affections of the indocile people whom he governed, and had created for himself a party from amongst the grandees of the empire. The vizier, Mahomet Karamani, who had an understanding with him, agreed to conceal the death of the Sultan until his successor was declared. He sent messengers to the two princes, and, as Mahomet had died at Scutari, he had his body carried to Constantinople in a shut-up bark, giving out that the Sultan was going to take the baths there for the recovery of his health. But the people already suspected the truth—*the adjem-oghlans* (recruiters of the Janissaries) enlightened the army. The Janissaries immediately rose in arms, pillaged several quarters of the city, and put the vizier to death. That militia, during the continual wars of the latter reigns, had acquired an immoderate importance, and began to render itself formidable. Already, at the beginning of the reign of Mahomet II., it had demanded tumultuously additional pay, and the Sultan, whilst punishing the ringleaders, had been forced to yield to the exactions of the soldiers. That fatal example was about to be renewed; it passed into a custom, and the bounty on their accession was paid by all the Sultans down to 1774.

The messengers despatched to Djem, however, had been arrested by the Beylerbey of Anatolia, but Bajazet was warned in time; he quitted his government, arrived in nine days at Scutari, and caused himself to be proclaimed Sultan. The Janissaries went tumultuously to meet him. They demanded an amnesty for the disorders they had committed, the accession bounty, the banishment of Mustapha Pacha the favourite of the new prince, and the elevation of Ishak Bey, Governor of Constantinople, to the dignity of Grand Vizier. All was granted, and thus the tyranny of these new pretorians was consecrated.

The new Sultan was of a pacific character. In his government of Amasia he had lived surrounded by poets and writers, himself cultivating letters. The Ottoman historians call him Bajazet *the Sofi*, a name which they give to learned men who devote themselves to a contemplative existence. He was thrown, however, by the necessities of his position, and, so to speak, by the destinies of the Ottoman Empire, into almost perpetual war. Djem had taken up arms, marched upon Broussa, defeated a corps of 2,000 Janissaries, and entered the city. Whilst he there installed his Court, and was making the environs recognize his sovereignty, Bajazet raised an army and advanced to maintain his rights. The Sultana Seldjukchatoun, great-aunt of the two brothers, endeavoured in vain to reconcile them. "There is no relationship between princes," was the reply of Bajazet. Djem divided his already insufficient forces, was defeated near Jenischehr (20th June, 1482), and compelled to flee towards Karamania. Thence he sought refuge in the States of the Sultan of Egypt. Bajazet, after having pursued him for several days, regained his capital. In passing before Broussa, the Janissaries demanded that the city should be given up to pillage as a punishment for having acknowledged Djem; the Sultan, after having harangued them, was constrained to treat with the mutineers, and distributed 1,000 aspres per man in order to ransom the city.

The following year, Djem returned from Cairo to Aleppo, and allied himself with Kasim Bey, the last of the Karaman princes. Several Ottoman governors took part with him, and Konieh was besieged. But fortune was again favourable to Bajazet, thanks to the ability of Keduk Ahmed, the conqueror of Kaffa and Otranto, and Djem found himself compelled to raise the siege of Konieh. The Governor of Angora was defeated and slain; desertion spread itself throughout the army of the rebel prince, and he was forced to flee a second time. He sent ambassadors to Bajazet, proposing an equal share of territory; the Sultan replied,—"The bride of the empire cannot be shared. Let my brother cease to plunge his horse's hoofs in Mussulman blood; let him content himself with his legitimate revenues, and expend them at Jerusalem." Djem refused, and preferred rather to throw himself into the arms of the enemies of the empire. As for Kasim Bey, he made his submission, and all Karamania was pacified; but Keduk Ahmed, who had conducted that war, having rendered himself odious to Bajazet alike by his pride and popularity, was put to death. He was son-in-law of the Grand Vizier, Ishak Bey : the latter was deposed and replaced by Daoud, beylerbey of Anatolia.

Djem, however, had undertaken to raise the Ottoman provinces in Europe with the aid of the Christian Powers, and with that intention, one of his secret agents was despatched to the Grand Master of Rhodes. The surprise of the knights was extreme; they, however, promised the Prince an honourable reception and a secure retreat. On the 23rd of July, 1482, a galley of the Order brought him to Rhodes, where he was received with great pomp. Soon after agents from the Sultan arrived charged to make magnificent offers, and negotiations were also entered upon with them. But first, a treaty was concluded with the fugitive Prince which secured great advantages to the Order, should Djem be one day established; then, under pretext that he was not in safety at Rhodes, they made him take his departure for France. Some days after he had set out the knights signed a treaty with the Sultan, by which the latter engaged to remain at peace with the Order during his life, and to pay to it an annual pension of 45,000 ducats for keeping his brother in custody. That treaty was a manifest violation of that made with Djem, a perfidy so much the more odious, that it was stipendiary. The Pope, the King of Hungary, and the Emperor of Germany, in vain demanded that the Prince should be set at liberty, hoping to make him assist in the weakening of the Ottoman power; but the Grand Master, won over by the fresh promises or flatteries of the Sultan, eluded all their entreaties.

Arrived at Nice, the Ottoman Prince could no longer dissemble with himself that he was not a captive; the greater part of his suite was taken from him and sent back to Rhodes. From Nice he was transferred successively to Chambéry, to Puy, and to Bourganeuf. During seven years he was dragged from one stronghold to another, guarded with increased rigour. At length, in 1489, the Grand Master delivered him up to Pope Innocent VIII. On the death of the latter, his successor, the infamous Alexander Borgia, proposed to the Sultan to keep his brother captive for an annual payment of 40,000 ducats, or to get rid of him by murder for 300,000 ducats promptly paid down. Whilst that bargain was under debate, Italy was invaded by the King of France, and the Ottoman Empire threatened with serious troubles.

The Quixotic Charles VIII. had dreamed of the conquest of Constantinople and Jerusalem: the submission of the Kingdom of Naples was destined to be only the prelude to that gigantic expedition, for which the French chivalry had been convoked as for the ancient crusades. A son of Thomas Palæologus had sold to the young French King his rights to the throne of the East. The Grand Master of Rhodes was to command the army when it should arrive in Greece; several sovereigns of Europe had promised to contribute to the expedition either their money or their soldiers. Agents had been sent to rouse up Macedonia, Greece, and Albania; arms and money had been distributed among those countries; the Archbishop of Durazzo and the Mirdites were at the head of the conspiracy; the route of the French was marked out from Otranto to Avlona, from Avlona to Byzantium, through the Albanian and Greek populations, whose concurrence was hoped for. Finally, they reckoned upon Djem in person, whom Charles VIII. claimed, to disquiet Bajazet and effect a diversion, by rekindling civil war in the Turkish provinces.

At the news of Charles's march into Italy, where the people hailed him with the titles of Defender of the Church and Liberator of the Faith, terror and hope spread through the East; the Greeks took up arms; the Turks evacuated their positions in Albania. "Bajazet," says an historian, who blindly repeats a popular rumour, "Bajazet took such a fright that he collected all his fleet to escape into Asia." But the Pope, the Republic of Venice, and Ferdinand of Naples, in order to oppose the French conquest, solicited the Sultan to make a descent upon Italy. Alexander VI., besieged by the French in the Castle of St. Angelo, and constrained to deliver up his captive, gave him up, but poisoned; lastly, the Venetians arrested the deputies whom the Greeks and Albanians sent to the King of France, and forwarded their papers to the Sultan, who, instructed in all the details of the conspiracy, extinguished it in the blood of 40,000 Christians. Djem died at Naples, whither he had followed the French army (24th February, 1495). His body, deposited first at Gaeta, was some years after transported to Gallipoli, and thence to Broussa, to the burial-place of the first Sultans. The remembrance of his misfortunes, of his long captivity, and of his romantic love for the beautiful Hellene, daughter of the Castellan of Sassenage, was long afterwards preserved in France.

2. Expeditions in Hungary, Moldavia, and Asia Minor.

The captivity of Djem, and the events consequent upon it, contributed to multiply the relations of the Ottomans with Western Europe. That fact constitutes the most important feature of Bajazet's reign; for that long reign is only occupied with expeditions on the frontiers, of no great brilliance or interest. In Hungary and Bosnia the war was very nearly permanent—a war of pillage and atrocities, in which Kinis, Jaxich, Tekeli, and other Christian chiefs rivalled the Turkish pachas in ferocity; every year both shores of the Danube were devastated far and wide.

In 1483, the Sultan had directed personally an expedition upon the Hungarian frontiers; but that was a mere military promenade, in the sequel of which he renewed for five years the truce concluded with the King of Hungary. At the same time, one of his lieutenants attacked Herzegovina. That province, which was only a dependence of Bosnia, was subjected without resistance and incorporated in the Ottoman Empire. In 1484, Bajazet turned his arms against Moldavia, and seized upon Kilia and Akerman; at the siege of this latter place appeared as auxiliaries 50,000 Tartars from the Crimea, led by the Khan Mengli Gheraï.

The year 1486 saw the commencement of a more serious war. Since the latter years of Mahomet the Second's reign, misunderstandings had arisen between the Ottomans and the Sultan of Egypt; they were renewed on the subject of certain Turkoman tribes located in Cilicia, towards Tarsus and Adana. Those tribes being in strife with the inhabitants of the country, their chiefs at length sought the aid of the Sultan of Egypt, and aided him to render himself master of the strongest fortresses of the country. The Governor of Karamania received orders to oppose those usurpations; but his army being thrice defeated, the Grand Vizier took command of it himself (1487). The Egyptians not the less obtained a great victory between Adana and Tarsus, and pillaged the Ottoman camp. Bajazet was meditating taking himself the direction of that war, when the Bey of Tunis proposed to mediate between the two Mussulman princes. An honourable peace put an end to hostilities (1491).

In 1492 the war recommenced overtly with Hungary. Taking advantage of the troubles which agitated that country after the death of Matthias Corvinus, the Sultan attempted to surprise Belgrade; he failed, but the marauding of his troops did not the less desolate Transylvania, Croatia, Dalmatia, Illyria, Carniola, and Styria. The Emperor Maximilian sent reinforcements to these unfortunate provinces, and the Turks were defeated at Villach; they took their revenge the year following (1493) at Udwine, where 25,000 Hungarians perished. In 1494, whilst they were desolating the left bank of the Danube, Kinis and the Hungarians crossed over to the right bank, burned the suburbs of Semendria and brought back from Belgrade troops of prisoners with an immense booty. Lastly, in 1495, peace was momentarily re-established, and the pillaging Turks threw themselves upon the Venetian provinces.

3. *First Relations with Russia.—War with the Venetians.*

At this epoch commenced the first relations of the Ottoman Empire with Russia. From the ninth century, and chiefly under the first successors of Rurik, the Russians had rendered themselves formidable to the Greek Empire. They had ravaged the Wallachian provinces, occupied Bulgaria, and even menaced Constantinople. It was a consequence of these expeditions that they embraced Christianity; they received it with the Greek schism, which they have retained. Divided later into a great number of principalities, Russia became almost entirely subjected to the Mongols. At length, in 1481, Ivan III., Grand Duke of Moscow, freed himself from the Tartar domination, reunited under his authority the greater part of the principalities, and became, in a word, the veritable creator of the Russian Empire. In 1492, he made friendly propositions to the Sultan through the medium of the Khan of the Crimea, his ally. In 1495, a Muscovite ambassador appeared at Constantinople, and four years after a second envoy obtained commercial privileges for the Russian merchants.

Bajazet entered into pacific relations also with Poland. In 1490 he concluded with John Albert, third Prince of the Jagellon dynasty, a treaty which was renewed in 1493.

But three years after, that good understanding was interrupted through both princes contending for the suzerainty of Moldavia. John Albert having invaded that country, the Turks drove him out, and made two irruptions into Poland, seconded by the Prince of Moldavia, Bogdan, who made his submission to the Porte. They devastated the country, burned several towns, pillaged Jaroslav, and were only arrested by famine and cold, which decimated their army.

At the same period a rupture took place between the Sultan and the Venetians. A Turkish fleet and army were sent against Lepanto; a naval combat, fought near Sapienza, opened the entrance of the gulf to the fleet; the city, menaced by sea and land, surrendered. At the same time, Iskender Pacha, Governor of Bosnia, invaded Friuli, crossed the Isonzo, and ravaged the Venetian territory; his cavalry pushed even beyond Tagliamento and appeared under the walls of Vicenza. In the following campaign the Venetians seized upon Cephalonia, and burned, at Previsa, a squadron of forty Turkish ships; but later, they lost Modon, Coron, and Navarino.

In this peril, the Venetians implored the aid of Christendom, and a kind of crusade reunited for awhile the Pope, and the Kings of Spain, France, and Hungary. Navarino was retaken, then a second time lost; the French galleys and those of the Pope crossed into the Archipelago, besieged Mitylene, and burned some Turkish vessels; another squadron seized upon St. Maure. In turn, the Turks captured Durazzo. However, the war upon the Hungarian frontier having proved disastrous, Bajazet himself made overtures for peace; and two treaties were concluded, in 1502 with Venice, in 1503 with Hungary, in which all the Christian States were comprised.

4. Revolt of the Sons of Bajazet.—His Death.

The last years of the reign of Bajazet II. were troubled by the ambitious pretensions of his sons. He had had eight, of whom three survived him—Korkud, Ahmed, and Selim. The first passionately devoted to letters and the arts, a protector of learned men, and a friend of peace, displeased the soldiers; the Sultan even was little disposed to designate him as his successor, and leaned visibly in favour of Ahmed. Ahmed reckoned, moreover, among his partisans the Grand Vizier, Ali Pacha, and the most influential personages in the divan. But the third son of Bajazet, Selim, by his martial bearing, by his decided inclination for war, and also by his marked attention to the soldiery, had won the favour of the army, and especially of the Janissaries. A struggle appeared imminent. Bajazet, to prevent it breaking out, distributed the chief governments amongst his sons; Korkud had that of Tekieh, Ahmed that of Amasia, Selim that of Trebizonde. Solyman, the young son of Selim, was also made governor of Kaffa.

This arrangement did not satisfy the ambition of Selim; he abandoned, without orders, his government to repair to Kaffa, where he brought about an understanding with the Tartars of the Crimea. He was ordered to return to his government. To this he replied by asking for a government in Europe, in order, he said, to be more within reach of conferring with his father. Upon the refusal of the Sultan, he openly revolted, and marched towards Roumelia. Bajazet hoped to intimidate the rebel by sending an army against him; but Selim stood firm, and it was the Sultan's army that was compelled to retire to avoid an engagement. The Sultan then treated with his son, and gave him the government of Semendria and of Widdin (1511).

Selim was slowly directing his steps towards his new residence, when he learned that Korkud had seized upon the government of Sarukhan, to be nearer the capital also. At this news, Selim fell back and entered Adrianople as a sovereign. Bajazet, yielding to the representations of his ministers, resolved to punish his son; a collision took place near Tchorli, and Selim, defeated, fled to the Crimea. The Janissaries then revolted, and forced the Sultan to recall his son to the government of Semendria. The Prince having set out on his way thither, they went to meet him, and conducted him as it were in triumph to Constantinople. Some days after (25th April, 1512), they carried him to the Seraglio with the sipahis and a great concourse of people. "What do you want?" asked Bajazet. "Our Padischah is old and sick!" was the reply; "We would have Selim Sultan." "I cede the empire to him," answered Bajazet; "and may God bless his reign!" He then went and shut himself up in the old Seraglio, abandoning the new to his son. Twenty days after he set out for Dimotika, his birthplace, where he wished to die. He expired on his way thither (May 26). Several historians accuse Selim of having poisoned him.

The reign of Bajazet forms a resting-place in the ascending period of the Ottoman Empire, which must be especially attributed to the character of the prince. His pacific and easy-tempered disposition was in disagreement with the spirit of the nation; the wars also which he waged against the Christians were above all inspired by religious motives. He caused the dust that had gathered on his garments during those holy expeditions to be collected, and ordered that it should be placed under his head when in his coffin in order to conform to that maxim of the Prophet:—"He whose feet are covered with dust in the paths of the Lord shall be preserved from the fire eternal."

5. *Selim I.* (1512-1520).—*War with Persia.*

Raised to the throne by the Janissaries, whose darling he was, Selim caused 3,000 aspres, or fifty ducats per man, to be distributed amongst them. A sandjak-bey, emboldened by the occasion, asked for an increase of pay—Selim struck off his head with one stroke of his sabre.

Then, leaving to Solyman, his son, the government of the capital, he hastened into Asia Minor, where two sons and seven grandsons of Bajazet menaced his power. Whilst a squadron watched the coasts, he marched against his brother Ahmed, and pursued him fruitlessly beyond Angora. On passing Broussa he found therein five of his nephews: he ordered them to be put to death. One of them, a child of tender years, threw himself in tears at the feet of the executioner; another, twenty years old, defended himself with all the energy of despair; Selim had their execution remorselessly carried out.

Korkud, his younger brother, was residing peaceably at Magnesia in his government of Sarou-Khan; Selim repaired thither secretly with the intention of surprising him, and the Prince had scarcely time to effect his escape. He wandered during several weeks in the Tekieh mountains, was discovered in his retreat, and put to death. Lastly, Ahmed, after having employed the winter in collecting troops, entered upon a campaign at the commencement of 1513. Victor at Ermeni, he gave his brother time to repair his losses, was conquered in turn near Jenischehr (24th April), captured in his flight, and put to death.

Seated firmly on the throne by those seven murders, Selim returned to Adrianople, where he received the homage of the tributary Princes, and the ambassadors of Venice, Hungary, Muscovy, and Egypt. The truces were renewed with all the European States; it was towards Asia that the new Sultan turned his gaze.

In the latter years of Bajazet's reign an important revolution had been accomplished in the East—a revolution at once political and religious, which reawakened the sleeping quarrel of the Shiites and Sunnites, and raised upon the ruins of the Tartar and Turkoman Empires the new Persian Empire of the *Ssafis*.

Towards the commencement of the fourteenth century there lived at Erdebil a shiite sheik, renowned for his sanctity, named Ssafieddin. It was from his name that his descendants took their title of *Ssafis* or *Sofis*. They inherited the religious authority which this sheik had acquired, and sought to found upon it a political domination. For more than a century their efforts were unfruitful. At length, one of them, Ismaïl, towards the year 1400, commenced the celebrity of his family. The religious authority he had acquired became perpetuated in his descendants. His great grandson, Djounéid, first attempted to make use of it to acquire political power. Protected by Ouzoun-Hassan, the conquering Prince of the *White Sheep*, he collected followers and launched himself upon a life of warlike adventure. He was defeated and slain by the Prince of Chirvan. His son Haider trod in his footsteps and perished similarly in 1488. He left a son named Ismaïl, who, about 1500, undertook to avenge his father and grandfather, and founded the fortunes of his house. Half warrior, half prophet, mingling the Shiite doctrine with some new maxims, he assembled upon the frontiers of Tekieh and of Hamid a great concourse of Shiites, hurried them away to the conquest of Chirvan, and succeeded therein. He next intervened in the quarrels of the grandsons of Ouzoun-Hassan, profited by them and established the seat of his power at Tebriz, the residence of the princes of the dynasty of the *White Sheep*. Then he subdued Irak-Arabi on the West, Khorassan on the East, Diarbekir wherein still remained a last representative of the Ouzoun-Hassan race; and one of his Emirs seized upon Bagdad. In 1510 he added to his empire Farsistan and Aderbaidjan; destroyed, the year following, the State of the Usbeks upon the Oxus, and extended his domination from the Persian Gulf to the Caspian Sea, from the sources of the Euphrates to beyond the Oxus.

This new power was just reaching its apogee, when the revolt of the sons of Bajazet II. broke out; the adherents of Ismaïl profited by it to harass the Ottoman frontiers; the *Schah* himself quarrelled with Selim; he took part with Ahmed and offered an asylum to his fugitive sons; lastly, he solicited the Sultan of Egypt to form a league against the new sovereign of the Ottomans. But already

Selim was preparing to assume the offensive. The doctrines of Ismaïl being widely spread in the conterminous provinces of the Empire, and especially in the Tekieh and the Hamid, all the votaries were sought for, an exact census of them taken with the most profound secresy, and then a general massacre was ordered: 40,000 heretics perished in one day. It was the St. Bartholomew of the Mussulmans; but massacres are such common things in the history of Eastern peoples, that this one has no more celebrity than many others, and is lost in the multiplicity of those great crimes.

After that massacre, war was announced in the divan, and the army entered upon a campaign (March 1514). It was a holy war. The grand mufti declared it even obligatory, adding that the death of a Shiite was more agreeable to God than that of sixty and ten Christians.

Selim sent his enemy a threatening message; Ismaïl replied to it by a letter in terms sufficiently measured; it ended by saying: "Your letter is unworthy of a Sultan; it is doubtless the work of some secretary intoxicated with opium." The Sultan, infuriated, caused the bearer of the message to be massacred. Meanwhile, Ismaïl himself changed into a desert all the country which the Ottoman army had to traverse; thus, when that army of 140,000 men reached the frontier, it found itself at close quarters with famine; Ismaïl retired before it, and in spite of the insults and provocations of Selim, he refused any engagement. The Turkish army murmured; a part of it was compulsorily left by the way; at length, the Janissaries loudly demanded a retreat. At the first outcry, the Sultan rushed into the midst of them and overwhelmed them with reproaches. "Let the cowards," said he, "separate themselves from the brave men who have taken up the sword and quiver!" Their enthusiasm rekindled at his voice, and the march was directed towards Tebriz. Some days after it was reported that the Schah, tired of retreating, awaited battle in the valley of Tchaldiran. It was there that a decisive action was fought (23rd August, 1514). The Ottoman army arrived fatigued; the viziers advised that some rest should be given it; the defterdar Piri-Pacha insisted that battle should be delivered without delay. That was the making of his fortune. The fight immediately began, and the Ottoman artillery gave them the victory. Ismaïl very nearly perished in the action; he fled precipitately as far as Tebriz, but dared not there await the enemy. Tebriz opened its gates without resistance; the Sultan made his entrance therein on the 4th September. He seized upon the Schah's treasures and caused the most skilful artisans of the city to be sent to Constantinople.

After a halt of eight days, he resumed the pursuit of Ismaïl; but having reached the banks of the Araxes, his soldiers refused to advance further. Winter was approaching and provisions were wanting: he was compelled to yield; but the Grand Vizier was dismissed. After reducing in his retreat several fortresses, the Sultan traversed Georgia and Armenia, and went to pass the winter in Amasia.

Hostilities recommenced in the spring; but they were confined to the capture of the castle of Koumach and the conquest of the principality of Soulkadr (1515). Selim returned to Constantinople, leaving to his lieutenants the care of continuing the war. The historiographer Idris displayed remarkable activity therein. The Kurds, zealous Sunnites, were raised; the chief towns of the Diabekir submitted almost without resistence; and when Ismaïl, who had re-entered Tebriz, entered upon a campaign, the Ottoman troops, in concert with the population of the country, successfully repulsed him. The struggle was prolonged until the following year; the capture of Mardin (1515); that of Offa (the ancient Edessa), of Raka and of Mosul, achieved the conquest of the Diarbekir. To Idris was confided the task of organising that new province; and he, well knowing how to treat with caution the jealous independence of the Kurds, left the authority in the hands of their chiefs of tribes, and, by that means, secured the Ottoman domination in those countries.

6. *Conquest of Egypt.—Death and Character of Selim.*

The war was scarcely terminated on the banks of the Tigris, ere already Selim prepared for a more important enterprise. For a long time the Sultans of the Osmanlis had borne envy and hatred to the Sultans of Egypt. The latter, who had kept the Khalifes in captivity and bore the title of "*Servants of the Holy Cities*," attributed to themselves a sort of supremacy over all the princes of Islam; they had often been irritated at the depredations of the Ottomans upon the frontiers of their States; lastly, Kansou-Ghawri, Sultan of Cairo, had made alliance with the Shah Ismaïl and was preparing to bring him aid. Selim resolved to make war upon him, and caused his aggression to be justified by a fetwa of the Grand Mufti. "If a padishah," asked Selim, "engaged in a holy war for the destruction of the impious, encounters obstacles in the succour lent to the impious by another padishah, does the law permit the former to strike down the latter?" The Mufti replied: "He who aids the impious is himself impious." Immediately war was declared, and Syria invaded. The Egyptian Sultan attempted to negotiate, and offered his mediation between Ismaïl and Selim; his ambassador had all his retinue massacred, and was ignominiously sent back. He then marched to meet the Ottomans. The two armies came to blows near Aleppo, in the plain of Dabik, where stands, according to the Mussulmans, the tomb of King David. The discord which reigned amongst the Mamelukes brought about their defeat: the *djelbans*, mamelukes of the first class, jealous of those of the third, or *korsans*, refused to take part in the action. The powerful artillery of the Ottomans in the end gave them the victory. The Sultan Ghawri, who was eighty years old, perished in the retreat.

That victory gave the whole of Syria to Selim. He entered Aleppo, the governor of which, Chair Bey, made his voluntary submission; and in the great mosque of that city he heard, for the first time, added to his titles that of

"Servant of the Two Holy Cities." Hama (Epiphania), Hems (Emesa), and Damascus opened their gates. The Sultan placed governors therein, received benevolently the learned men, visited the sheiks, enriched and repaired the mosques, particularly the great mosque of Damascus, the most magnificent edifice of Islamism.

However, the Mamelukes had elected a new prince, Touman-Bey. Selim sent him an offer of peace on condition that he would acknowledge the Ottoman suzerainty. At the moment when his envoys quitted audience of the prince, a Mameluke, indignant at their proposals, rushed upon and killed them. War was instantly declared. In the month of November, 1516, a first engagement took place upon the Syrian frontier. The Mamelukes were again defeated, and the towns of Ramla and Gaza, which had risen at their approach, were punished by the massacre of their inhabitants. The Ottoman army set out on its march in the depth of winter, and in ten days crossed the desert that separates Egypt from Syria, in spite of continual attacks from the Arabs, and on the 22nd January, 1517, found itself in presence of the enemy at some distance from Cairo. The fight was about to begin when a detachment of horsemen, all clad in steel, threw themselves upon the centre of the Ottoman army, and penetrated as far as the Sultan. This was Touman-Bey and the boldest of his followers. They had determined to lay hands on Selim, but fell into an error by mistaking him for the Grand Vizier Sinan Bey, whom the Mameluke Sultan slew with his own hand. Notwithstanding that, the Mamelukes lost the battle. Eight days after, the Ottomans entered Cairo. The vanquished defended themselves from street to street, from house to house, during three days and three nights; at last they surrendered conditionally on the promise of an amnesty. They were almost all massacred, and with them 30,000 of the inhabitants.

Touman-Bey had withdrawn beyond the Nile, and, seconded by the Arabs, he carried on a war of skirmishes to which there appeared no end. Selim tried to negotiate, but the Mamelukes slew his envoys. However, weakened by the desertion of several chiefs, Touman-Bey entrenched himself in the Delta, kept there on the defensive, and was abandoned in it by the Arabs. A few days after, a combat took place with the Ottomans. The Arabs fell upon the rear of the Mamelukes, and determined their defeat. Touman-Bey, with some hundreds of horsemen, sought refuge in the desert. Betrayed by his host, he was captured and brought into the presence of Selim. "God be praised!" exclaimed the Sultan, "now Egypt is conquered." Touched by the dignity of his language and his countenance, he at first treated his captive with consideration, but certain traitors having aroused his suspicion, the last Mameluke Sultan was hanged at the gate of Cairo (15th April, 1517).

Selim passed a month in the capital of Egypt, distributing his favours and dignities, organizing the government, visiting the mosques and public establishments. He sojourned for some days in the Isle of Randa, where the Nilometer stands, and had a vault constructed to protect it. He was present at two great Egyptian fêtes—the opening of the Cairo Canal and the departure of the annual caravan for Mecca. He received from the Sherif of the Holy City the keys of the Kaaba, and, in return, raised to 28,000 ducats the *sourré*, or annual present, which the Ottoman sovereigns, from the time of Mahomet I., had been accustomed to send to Mecca. At length, yielding to the murmurs of the army, he quitted Egypt, the government of which was confided to Chair-Bey. He carried away the treasures of the Mameluke Sultans; and took with him a colony of artizans, whom he established at Constantinople. Finally, he caused himself to be followed by Mahomet XII., the last representative of the Abasside Khalifes, nominal head of Islam, to whom the rulers of Egypt had always preserved his honorary title. Selim enforced the relinquishment by him of the rights and distinctive ensigns of the Khalifate—that is to say, the standard, the sword, and the mantle of the Prophet; and it is thus that the Sultans of Constantinople have become the representatives of the Khalifes and the religious and political chiefs of Islam. After paying pious visits to the Holy Sepulchres of Hebron and Jerusalem, after a sojourn of several months in Syria in order to organize the government of that province, Selim returned to Constantinople at the end of July 1518, and shortly after to Adrianople, where he received numerous embassies, and renewed treaties with the European Powers.

The rapidity and magnitude of his conquests naturally attracted the attention and excited the alarm of the European potentates. Venice and Hungary, the States more immediately exposed to the fury of the Turkish arms, had deemed it prudent to conciliate the friendship of the Porte; and both Wladislaus, King of Hungary, and the Republic of Venice had, at Selim's accession, renewed the peace which they had made with his father. The Venetians, ever alive to the interests of their commerce, congratulated Selim upon his conquest of Egypt—a country so important to their trade with the Indies—endeavoured to obtain from its new ruler the confirmation of their ancient privileges, and transferred to him the tribute of 8,000 ducats, which they had before paid to the Sultan of Egypt for the possession of Cyprus. On these terms the peace was confirmed (September 17th, 1518), and was not disturbed during Selim's lifetime.

After two years of repose, he made preparations for a new expedition. One hundred galleys and a hundred and fifty other vessels were fitted out; numerous troops were assembled both in Europe and Asia. A fresh attack upon the island of Rhodes was meditated. Leo X., who was alarmed, or pretended to be so, in order the better to promote his mercenary designs, decreed a war against the Infidels in the last session of the Lateran Council (March 16th), and obtained a grant of a tithe on all ecclesiastical property in Europe for the purpose of defraying the expenses; and he published a Bull enjoining all Christian princes to observe a five years' truce. But though the Pope put on every appearance of earnestness, nothing resulted from these measures save a profitable compact between himself and the French king. The scheme met with no better success in other countries. In this want of zeal among the Christian nations, it was fortunate that Selim's attention was engrossed by his Eastern provinces, and the revolts of his unruly Janissaries. His gigantic expedition against Rhodes was not destined to be accomplished. Flying from Constantinople to avoid the plague, he was seized with that malady at Ischorli, and expired September 21st, 1520.

Selim I. has received from the Ottoman historians themselves the appellation of *the Inflexible*. His fame as a great conqueror is sullied by acts of the most impious cruelty. He is even said to have contemplated the murder of his son and successor Solyman, through fear of experiencing at his hands the fate which he had himself inflicted on his own father. Never was prince more formidable to his ministers : the post of vizier became under him so perilous, that a man was wont to say proverbially to his enemy : " May you be the vizier of Sultan Selim ! " He who was highest in his favour, Piri Pacha, said to him one day in a moment of gaiety, that he hoped Selim would give him warning when he wished to get rid of him, in order that he might arrange his affairs; and the Sultan replied that he would on that very instant if he knew some one else who could replace him. One day he gave the order to one of the viziers to muster the army; the latter having asked in which direction the tents were to be pitched, he put him to death. A second vizier put the same question and perished in the same way; at last, the third bethought himself to set them up at the four cardinal points; Selim then said : " The death of two viziers has procured for me the one I wanted."

In spite of these sanguinary whims and crimes, Selim is reckoned amongst the great men of the Ottoman Empire; first, on account of his conquests; next, by reason of the care he bestowed on the administration of the provinces. Bold in his projects, of invincible obstinacy in their execution, the violence of his disposition did not hinder him from securing, by wise precautions, the success of his enterprises. The Ottomans relate that a sheik had predicted that his reign would be of short duration. He then interrogated him on the fate of his son. "He will reign for nearly half a century," replied the sheik, "and be distinguished by his warlike virtue and his great successes." "Ah!" exclaimed Selim, with a deep sigh, "if Allah had granted me so long a reign, I should have equalled King Solomon."

CHAPTER III.

REIGN OF SOLYMAN I., 1520 TO THE YEAR 1535.

1. *First Acts of Solyman.—Capture of Belgrade and of Rhodes.*

THE successor of Selim was Solyman—Solyman *the Great, the Magnificent, the Conqueror, the Legislator.* These titles, which history has confirmed, are not too pompous for the extraordinary man whose reign is the most brilliant in the Ottoman annals.

Solyman was twenty-five at the death of his father. From Magnesia, of which he was governor, he hastened to Constantinople, rendered the last duties to Selim, and ordered a mosque to be erected over his tomb, the *Selimiie*, with a school and a *medressé;* then he distributed the accession donative amongst the Janissaries. His first acts showed his love of justice and his generosity: several high functionaries were displaced or put to death for abuse of power ; the Egyptian artisans brought by Selim from Egypt to Constantinople were restored to their native country; and the Persian merchants, whom the edicts against the commerce of Persia had ruined, were indemnified.

One revolt alone troubled the commencement of the new reign: it was that of Djanberdi Ghazali, governor of Syria, who thought the moment favourable for raising that newly conquered province; and he essayed in vain to draw Chair Bey, governor of Egypt, into his enterprise. To the third vizier, Ferhad Pacha, was confided the suppression of the revolt. Ghazali, after having attempted to seize upon Aleppo, fell back at the approach of the

Sultan's army and reached Damascus, where by treason he caused 5,000 Janissaries to be massacred. A few days after he fought a battle before the gates of that city (27th Jan. 1521). Defeated and delivered up by his followers, he was put to death and his head sent to Constantinople.

Scarcely was that revolt suppressed ere hostilities were resumed with Hungary. A *tschaouch* having been sent to demand the tribute, was outraged and massacred; the Sultan made immediate preparations for war, and began his march with 150,000 men, followed by 30,000 camels laden with munitions and provisions, and 300 pieces of cannon. Whilst the Grand Vizier, Piri Pacha, was beginning to invest Belgrade, and the *akindschis* were carrying on their ravages on the other side of the Danube, the Sultan marched towards Czabacz. The garrison, numbering between 200 and 300 men, made an heroic resistance; it was exterminated, and Solyman made his entry into the town between two ranges of heads stuck upon stakes. He then returned to press operations against Belgrade, which was shattered by his artillery, and capitulated (29th Aug. 1521). The besieged were reduced to 400 men, and had repulsed more than twenty assaults. The Serb population was transferred to Constantinople; and 3,000 Janissaries formed the garrison of the conquered city, which became thenceforth the strongest bulwark of the Empire.

Solyman having regained his capital, received the ambassadors and the felicitations of the Grand Duke of Russia, and several other princes. Peace was renewed with the Venetians, and a treaty concluded which secured to them fresh commercial advantages, and fixed at 10,000 ducats the tribute paid by the Republic for possession of Cyprus and the Ionian Isles. Then the Sultan resumed the projects of his father against the Isle of Rhodes.

Since Syria and Egypt had been joined to the empire, the possession of that island became necessary to secure the communications with those provinces. The circumstances were, moreover, favourable. The one-half of

Europe, engaged in the struggle of Francis I. against the Emperor Charles V., had not time to lend aid to that advanced post of Christianity; the capture of Belgrade had terrified Hungary, which only asked for peace. Venice had just renewed her friendly relations. Solyman might, therefore, hope to efface at Rhodes, as at Belgrade,

HARBOUR OF RHODES.

the remembrance of the checks sustained by his grandfather.

At the commencement of 1522, a fleet of 300 sail was ready, and 100,000 men, commanded by the Sultan, took their way by land to second it. The fleet appeared before Rhodes on the 6th of June, the army arrived on the 28th of July, and the siege was begun. An entire month passed in digging mines, with partial combats, the advantage of which frequently remained with the Christians. The first assault took place on the 4th of September, with a loss to the Turks of 2,000 killed. It was followed by several others; the garrison, consisting for the most part of Knights of the Order, struggled with an heroic obstinacy, stimulated by the example of the Grand Master, the aged Villiers de l'Isle-Adam, whose name has been immortalised by that memorable defence. On the 24th of September the ramparts were assailed on all sides at once; a terrible *mêlée* took place in the breaches, the women even joining the struggle, carrying food and munitions, and pouring boiling oil upon the assailants. One amongst them was seen, after having slain her two children upon the breach, to rush sword in hand into the ranks of the Janissaries, and there meet her death fighting furiously to the last. The Turks retreated after sustaining a loss of 15,000 men.

Solyman redoubled his efforts, and, after two months more of continual fighting, he offered the knights a capitulation (10th of December). Powder and provisions were about to fail them; they had no hope of succour; they, however, still continued the defence and repulsed two fresh assaults. At length, on the 21st of December, the Grand Master sent two knights to negotiate the capitulation; it was agreed that the Order should evacuate the town within twelve days, leaving therein fifty hostages; whilst the Ottoman army should retire to the distance of a mile in order to secure the unmolested retreat of the besieged. But, five days after, on Christmas Day, a band of Janissaries forced one of the gates, seized upon the town, and began to pillage the houses and churches. Thus fell Rhodes, after a siege of five months, and which had cost the Turks more than 100,000 men. Solyman gave the Grand Master an honourable reception, and secured with regard to the knights the exact observance of the capitulation. "I am truly grieved," he said to those about him, "to have to drive that old man out of his palace." The knights embarked on the 1st of January, 1522; they found a refuge in Malta, which

Charles V. gave up to them, and whence they determined to wage war against the votaries of the Korân.

2. *The Grand Vizier Ibrahim.—Troubles in Egypt, in the Crimea, in Wallachia.*

On the return of the expedition from Rhodes, the grand Vizier, Piri Pacha, was deposed (1523), and his post given to Ibrahim Pacha, for a long time the Sultan's favourite, and Grand Master of his falconry. This man, celebrated amongst all the other ministers of the Ottoman Empire by the extraordinary favour which he enjoyed for more than twenty years, and by the almost sovereign influence which he exercised over the events of this reign, belonged by birth, like almost all the great men who have governed the Ottoman Empire, to the Christian race; he was the son of a sailor of Parga. Carried off by Turkish corsairs, he had passed his youth in the abode of a rich Magnesian widow, who had bestowed upon him an excellent education. Solyman having met with him when governor of the city, was charmed with his good mien, mental qualities, his skill as a player upon the violin, and made him his page and favourite, and afterwards his first vizier.

The nomination of Ibrahim was seen with chagrin by Ahmed Pacha, who had coveted that high dignity; dissembling his spite, he solicited the government of Egypt, which was granted to him. He won over the Mamelukes by distributing fiefs among their principal chiefs; then he threw himself into open rebellion, seized by surprise the Castle of Cairo, and assumed the title of Sultan of Egypt. A *tschaouch*, sent to him to signify his deposition, was put to death, as well as the governor who went to displace him; money was also coined in his name. Already an army of 30,000 Janissaries was on its march to encounter him, when the rebel, betrayed by one of his viziers, was constrained to flee from Cairo. Delivered up by the Arabs, he was put to death. Kasim Pacha replaced him (1524).

In Wallachia, an attempt was made to destroy the last

vestige of the independence of that country, and establish therein the direct domination of the Porte. After the Belgrade campaign, a detached corps of the principal army had entered that province, carried away to Constantinople the son of the last voïvode and reduced the country to a *Sandjak*. But the boyards speedily revolted and nominated a voïvode. The latter was slain; a second succeeded him, and, supported by John Zapoly, voïvode of Transylvania, he was enabled to make head against the Ottomans. It became necessary, therefore, to renounce the accomplishment of the subjection of Wallachia; thus the old order of things was re-established with an augmentation of the tribute (1524).

Three years, however, having passed away in inaction, the Janissaries began to murmur. At the close of 1525, a revolt broke out in their ranks; they sacked the houses of the viziers and the Jews' quarter. Solyman hastened to confront them, and cut down three of the most mutinous with his own hand; but the others dared to menace him with their arrows. To appease their turbulence, he distributed 100,000 ducats amongst them. But the two agas of the Janissaries, some sipahis, and several superior officers were executed. At the same time, a campaign was announced against Persia and the successor of Shah Ismaïl. But Solyman could not enter upon that war until eight years after, and, during all that time, he had to turn his eyes towards the West, where important events were passing. The moment had come when Turkey was about to enter actively into the system of the European States, and to exercise therein a preponderating influence.

3. *New Policy of France with relation to the Ottoman Empire.—Francis I. asks aid from Solyman.—The Sultan's Letter.*

At this period, France, surrounded by the States of the House of Austria, saw herself with terror isolated from the rest of Europe, and excluded from the Mediterranean.

Before that House, mistress of the Low Countries, of Germany, of Italy and of Spain, what part could she take in the affairs of the Continent? Before that House, mistress of Barcelona and of Naples, of Minorca, and of Sicily, having Genoa and Florence as vassals, allied with Venice, which gave her Corfu and Candia; lastly, possessing Oran, and threatening to subject Algiers and Tunis, what became of the legitimate action of France in the Mediterranean? It was necessary at any sacrifice to restore the equilibrium by a new counterpoise, to oppose to the Austrian power a power equally formidable both upon the Continent and upon the sea, to restore to France her liberty of action in Europe by rendering uneasy by a new enemy the Austrian frontiers; to restore the power of France in the Mediterranean, if not by her own forces, at least by an alliance; finally, to resume, by other modes than those of the Middle Ages, by pacific means, by commercial relations, her influence over the countries of the Levant.

There was only one nation in a position to fill so great and useful a part—the Ottoman Turks. Their Empire, seated at once in Europe, Asia, and Africa, appeared established upon immutable bases. Their arms menaced, by way of Hungary, the heart of the Austrian States; their ships dominated the Adriatic as far as the Bay of Tunis, the Levant to the Sea of Azof. No rivalry of position or interest could exist between the Ottoman Empire and France: both had the same enemies; both were united by the same needs of commerce; both mutually esteemed each other by reason of their warlike reputation. It was thus that France, after having been during the whole of the Middle Ages at the head of the struggle which Christian Europe sustained against the Mussulman races, was the first to be reconciled with them, in order to derive advantage from their new position That was, it must be owned, a great scandal to Christianity; such an alliance seemed shameful and unnatural; it was at first kept secret and even formally denied; later, when it was avowed, it excited throughout Europe a general clamour against *the impious union of the Lilies with the Crescent.*

The danger, however, was more apparent than real: seeing that the Ottoman power was still in its period of growth; seeing that, for a century back, it had obtained a steady footing in Europe, overthrown Byzantium and subjugated all the provinces of the Greek Empire, it seemed impossible that it could make much further progress. The West was henceforth too strongly constituted to need fear a new invasion. Islamism came too late. It had only taken firm hold upon Greece, isolated by schism from the rest of the Christian commonwealth. Already it was exhausting itself in vain efforts against Italy, Spain and Hungary, and its wrath must extinguish itself, as well as its powers, before those foremost barriers of Christendom. But the throng still terrified itself at the victories of the Turks, and clamoured for a crusade; yet the statesmen troubled themselves but very little about the turbaned enemy, and were only desirous of waging with them a political warfare. The times were no longer those of Charles Martel and of Gregory VII.; a rising in mass of Christians was no longer needed to arrest the infidels; the regular means and ordinary efforts of a few States sufficed. France might, therefore, without betraying the cause of Christianity, seek alliance with the Ottomans.

Was Francis I., in seeking to form such an alliance, moved by the political ideas above developed? It cannot be certainly affirmed; especially if it be considered that the policy of that prince was almost always of a passionate character, and ordinarily inspired by the necessities of the moment; but it is certain, although the origin of the alliance was enveloped in mystery and obscurity, that those ideas were entirely conformable to the opinion of his council, and that they inspired the policy of France during three centuries. As for her chivalrous king, he probably only saw in the Turkish alliance a momentary weapon, an arm snatched at in despair, for the first demand of that alliance issued from his prison at Madrid.

The sensation produced in all the European States by the battle of Pavia is well known. That captivity of Francis I. showed the allies of Charles V. what an impolitic path they had entered, in contributing to overthrow the sole barrier which protected Europe against the ambition of the House of Austria. The regent-mother, Louise of Savoy, turned that sensation to profitable account, and succeeded in forming against the Emperor a league composed of the King of England, the Pope, the Venetians, and the Swiss. It was then that, to alarm Charles in his Austrian States, and to hinder him from marching troops into Italy, she determined, whether by orders of Francis I., who would have, he said, invoked the Devil himself to free him from the hands of his enemy, or whether by the advice of the Chancellor Duprat, who played the greatest part in this daring proceeding, she resolved to seek the aid of the Turks. Almost immediately after the battle of Pavia, a first agent was despatched with presents, and, it is said, even the signet ring of Francis; he was arrested by the Pacha of Bosnia and murdered, with twelve men who accompanied him.* This ring, a ruby of great price, was subsequently recovered, and was in the possession of Ibrahim in 1533. There is a lurking suspicion that this deed of violence was committed with the privity of Ferdinand of Austria, who appears to have known that negotiations were being carried on between Francis and the Sultan; and the Turks have indeed often expressed their horror at the assassinations committed by the House of Austria. After this failure, Francis, whilst still a prisoner at Madrid, contrived at the close of 1525 to send a second envoy, who safely reached Constantinople. This was John Frangipani, an Hungarian gentleman, a kinsman, doubtless, of that Christopher Frangipani who was, at the same period, one of the most intrepid defenders of Hungary. He was the bearer of a " very humble " letter from the King of France, which, according to the Turkish historian Solakzadé, ran substantially thus:—" Let the great Padishah attack the King of Hungary and give him a check; we will attack the King of Spain and take our revenge upon him. We beg and pray that the great

* " Mémoire sur les Premières Relations Diplomatiques entre la France et la Porte," par M. de Hammer. *Journal Asiatique,* tom. x.

Emperor of the World may do us the favour of repulsing that haughty personage, and we shall be henceforth the obliged servant of the great Emperor, the Master of the Age."

It was not the first time that the King of France entered into communication with the Ottomans. For some years past, and under pretext of acquiring Oriental manuscripts, he had sent agents into the Levant, who were charged to collect exact information as to the condition of the Turks, and by them he had entered upon secret negotiations with the Sultan for the protection of French commerce. These first relations being established, the secret embassy of the vanquished at Pavia caused Solyman no surprise, who was, moreover, informed upon the political position of Europe; it is even thought that he had received at that time propositions of alliance on the part of Charles the Fifth.

He had not responded to the advances of a prince who was his natural enemy, and with whom no alliance was possible, since his States touched the Ottoman States and were the first Christian countries that the Turks desired to conquer; but he welcomed eagerly the request of a king, the most formidable foe of his enemy, who was about (for this was with the Ottomans the cardinal reason for their alliance with France), by his defection from the Christian cause, to deliver up to Solyman the West denuded of its best defenders. The Sultan received (6th December, 1525) the envoy of the King of France with great honours; and—"thing unheard of!" relates a Venetian ambassador, eye-witness of that reception, "he made him rich presents." Finally, "Moved with compassion," says a Turkish historian; "he determined to make war upon the King of Spain, whose designs were so bad," and invade Hungary. Yet no treaty was concluded upon this matter. Pride and Mussulman fanaticism would have regarded a direct alliance with a Christian prince as an opprobrium and an impiety.* The Sultan

* The Turkish historians say that the relations of Solyman with France were accepted without a murmur by his subjects by reason of a tradition

contented himself with replying to the letter of the very Christian King by the following missive—an epistle of proud and protecting friendship, the pompous preamble of which we will pass over.

"To thee, Francis, who art king of the country of France. You have sent a letter to my Porte, asylum of sovereigns, by your faithful agent Frankipan; you have also commanded him to make certain verbal communications. You have made known that the enemy has seized upon your country, and that you are actually in prison, and you have asked here asylum and succour for your deliverance. All that you have said having been laid open at the foot of my throne, refuge of the world, my imperial science has embraced it in detail, and I have taken complete cognisance of it.

"It is not astonishing that emperors are defeated and become prisoners. Take, therefore, courage, and let not yourself be cast down. Our glorious ancestors and our illustrious grandfathers (may God illuminate their tombs!) have never ceased to make war to repel the enemy and conquer countries. We also, we have marched in their footsteps. We have conquered at all times provinces and strong citadels difficult of access. Night and day our steed is saddled and our sabre is girded on.

"May the very-exalted God facilitate the good! To whatsoever object your wish may attach itself, may it be granted. For the rest, after interrogating your agent about affairs and news, you shall be informed thereon. Know it to be thus.

"Written at the commencement of the moon of Rebiul-akhir, 932 (15th February, 1526), at our residence in the capital of the Empire, Constantinople, the well guarded."

Such was the first act of alliance of France with the

which made the Padischah descend from a princess of the royal family of France. In fact, if we may credit the historians Petchevi, Selaniki and Ali Effendi, Saroudj, admiral of Amurath II., had captured in 1428 a ship richly laden, on board of which was found a French princess destined to be the bride of the Emperor John IV. Amurath II., who was then reigning, placed her in his harem, espoused her after she had embraced the Mahometan religion, and had a son by her, who was the conquerer of Constantinople, Mahomet II., grandfather of Solyman.

Ottoman Porte—an alliance which is a very grave event in the history of Europe, since it was the rock upon which the power of the House of Austria struck. Begotten on both sides by the necessities of the hour and by interests of position, it was maintained still more by benevolence than by calculation, in spite of religious hatreds, difference of manners, and divergent destinies of the two States; in spite of the ignorance, the brutality, the fanaticism of Turkish policy; in spite of the want of attention, the oblivion, the defections of French policy. It has not been one of the least causes of the grandeur of France, and the Ottoman Empire is indebted to it for having taken a share in its preservation.

4. *The Battle of Mohacz.*

Early in 1526 the most alarming tidings arrived in Hungary of Solyman's vast preparations for invading that kingdom. The Hungarian magnates, at continual feud with one another, were totally unprepared to resist. The lower classes, who in great numbers had imbibed the doctrines of Luther, justified themselves for not taking up arms by appealing to one of his propositions which had been condemned by Leo X., in his Bull of excommunication, viz., " That to fight against the Turks is equivalent to struggling against God, who has prepared such rods for the chastisement for our sins." Above all, the treasury, ever since the reign of Wladislaus, had been in a state of utter exhaustion. So complete was this poverty that the capture of Belgrade, five years before, was attributed to the want of fifty florins wherewith to defray the expense of conveying to that place the ammunition which was lying ready at Buda.

In the spring of 1526, Solyman, after visiting the tombs of his forefathers and of the old Moslem martyrs, set out to invade Hungary by the route through Servia and Belgrade, with 100,000 Ottomans commanded by himself and his three viziers; they were supported by 300 pieces of cannon and by a flotilla of 800 vessels. The course of the Danube was ascended by the right bank; Peterwardein was taken by assault in fifteen days; Illok surrendered at the end of a week; Essek, upon the Drave, was pillaged and burnt. On the 28th of August, the Ottoman army reached the plain of Mohacz, and the next morning began a battle which decided the fate of Hungary.

The Ottoman army was in three lines: in the van, the troops of Europe; in second line, those of Anatolia; in rear, the Sultan with his Janissaries, his sipahis and his guns, fastened together with iron chains, so as to form a kind of rampart. The ponderous Christian cavalry, headed by King Louis, fell with its usual impetuosity, upon the first lines, broke them, overthrew them, and penetrated as far as the Sultan. A fearful *mêlée* took place around him, and several blows were dealt upon his armour. Suddenly the Turkish artillery was unmasked; its terrible fire threw the assailants into such confusion that all dispersed. The greater number of the fugitives perished in the marshes that bordered the river, and amongst them doubtless King Louis, whose body was never recovered. That sanguinary battle did not last two hours. It had a great influence upon the destinies of Europe, since therein perished the Hungarian nationality.

Solyman crossed over to the left bank of the river, and received at Fœldward the keys of Buda, but only approached the capital of Hungary by slow marches, which he entered on the 10th of September. In spite of the express prohibition of the Sultan, the soldiers burned two quarters of the city and the great church. At the same time, the *akindschis* spread themselves throughout the surrounding country, burning the villages and massacreing the inhabitants, but not without suffering at times great losses. Wissegrad and Gran successfully resisted; Moroth made an heroic defence; at Bacs, the church, converted into a fortress, was defended during an entire day; between Bacs and Peterwardein the Hungarians made an entrenched camp, the capture of which cost the Turks more men than did the battle of Mohacz. But these partial resistances only served to increase the ferocity of the conquerors, and the number of Hungarians massacred in this campaign is estimated at 200,000. At length the Sultan, after having promised the magnates to give them John Zapoly for their King, retook the way to his capital, trailing after him an immense booty. Amongst the precious things carried away from Ofen figured, with the royal treasure and the library of Matthias Corvinus, those fine antique statues which decorated the royal castle and which were set up as trophies upon the hippodrome at Constantinople.

5. *Revolts in Asia.*

Harassing news from Asia had hastened the return of the Sultan from Hungary. The Turkomans of Cilicia had revolted through the brutalities and exactions of the Turkish agents. They had massacred the cadis and the Sandjak-bey, defeated the Beylerbey of Karamania, and soon after, near Sivas, those of Roum and Anatolia. At length, Chosrew Pacha, Beylerbey of Diarbekir, succeeded, by uniting all his forces, in arresting their progress. The insurrection recommenced the year following, but under another form. A descendant of the Sheik Hadji-Bektasch, patron of the Janissaries, was at the head of the movement, with several thousands of his religious votaries— dervishes, abdals or kalendars. He defeated successively the beylerbeys of Diarbekir, Roum and Anatolia. The grand vizier was himself compelled to march against them. He negotiated with the revolted Turkomans, succeeded in detaching the rebels from them, and then quickly stamped out the remaining embers of the insurrection.

Meanwhile the war continued in Hungary and in the countries annexed to that kingdom, Croatia, Slavonia, and Dalmatia, the submission of which was effected in 1528. Solyman had set out from Buda after promising, as has been said, the Hungarians a king in John Zapoly, voïvode of Transylvania; but another pretender presented himself, Ferdinand of Austria, brother of Charles V., to whom ties of relationship gave claims to the vacant throne. The two rivals encountered each other at Tokay (1527), and Zapoly was conquered; he implored succour from the King of Poland, his father-in-law, and soon after that of the Porte. His ambassador, with the aid of the Venetian, Louis Gritti, succeeded in gaining over the Vizier Ibrahim to his interests; and met with a favourable reception from the Sultan (3rd February, 1528). Solyman made a formal promise to put Zapoly in possession of Hungary, and even signed a treaty of alliance with him. Ferdinand vainly endeavoured to bring over the Sultan to his interests; his envoys were, however, thrown into prison.

6. *New Relations of Francis I. and Solyman.*

At this juncture, the king of France sent an ambassador to the Porte. The expedition against Hungary which he had solicited had proved a fresh check to him, since it had furnished to the House of Austria the occasion of enriching itself with two kingdoms. He had more than ever need of the Ottoman alliance. On the other hand, Charles V. began to suspect his rival's relations with the Porte, and accused him openly of treason against Christianity. Francis I., becoming uneasy at the clamours to which that denunciation gave rise, denied formally his alliance with the Turks, and told Charles V. that " he lied in his throat " (*en avait menti par la gorge*). But he not the less continued his relations with Solyman, and sought to make them agreeable in the eyes of Christians and of his subjects, by employing them to protect the faithful in the East, and to restore French influence in those countries. A gentleman named Rincon was entrusted with this negotiation, and succeeded therein. The French alliance was too precious to Solyman for him not to accede liberally to the requirements of the " very Christian " king. Long since, moreover, French commerce had received protection at the hands of the Turks: at the time that they were still in Asia, the merchants of Marseilles had obtained commercial advantages. In 1507 they had procured for themselves from Bajazet II. privileges which were increased by Selim I., and which contain the elements of the capitulations concluded between France and the Ottoman Empire. In 1528, Solyman renewed those privileges in an act the text of which is lost, some few fragments only existing : it is called the *trêve marchande* by the old French historians. The factories, consuls, and pilgrims from France were placed by this *trêve* under the protection of the Sublime Porte and guaranteed from all insult. The French flag then reappeared with confidence in the Mediterranean, and it was thankfully welcomed by Christians in the East, who hoped for solace and protection from it. The pilgrimages to Jerusalem recommenced ; a French bishop went to visit the churches of Albania, which, since Scanderbeg, had been forgotten in its wild mountains, and he reawakened the name of France amongst the *Skipetars* of the Mirdita.

The religious zeal of Francis I. caused neither surprise nor discontent amongst the Ottomans: in the East men and nations are esteemed according to the fervour of their belief; the alliance became even more intimate, as may be judged by the following letter of the Sultan (Sept. 1528) to the King of France:—

"To thee who art Francis, Bey of the country of France.

"You have sent to the Palace of the Sultans and to my Porte of felicity, which is the Orient of prosperity, and the place which the lips of kings and princes come to kiss, a letter in which you have spoken of a Church appertaining formerly to the Christians at Jerusalem, which forms a part of our well-guarded States, and since become a mosque. I know in detail all that you have said on this subject. The friendship and affection which exist between my glorious Majesty and you render your wishes admissible to my person, source of happiness. But this matter resembles not any other matter of domain or property, it concerns our religion. According to the sacred command of the Most High God, creator of the world and benefactor of Adam, according to the law of our Prophet, sun of two worlds (may the divine blessing and salvation be upon him!), that Church has long been a mosque, and the Mussulmans have therein said their *namaz* (prayer). Now, it is contrary to our religion that a place which bears the name of mosque, and in which the *namaz* is made, should be now altered by a change of destination. If even our law should authorize in general that change, your demand could not be welcome to our person, source of happiness. Other places beside the mosque shall continue to remain in the hands of the Christians; no one shall molest, under our equitable reign, those who dwell therein. They shall live tranquilly under the help of our protection; it shall be allowed them to repair their doors and windows; they shall preserve in all surety the oratories and establishments which they actually occupy, without any one being allowed to oppress or torment them in any manner. Let it be known so."

Such were the official results of Rincon's mission; but it is probable that the presence of that envoy must have contributed to the ill-treatment that the agents of Ferdinand received, and that he carried away a promise of a speedy taking up of arms. Before going to Constantinople he had visited Hungary and Poland; and, at his request, an Hungarian bishop had been sent to France. The result of the negotiations, opened by him and that bishop, was a treaty of alliance concluded between Francis I. and King Zapoly, a treaty by which the latter designated as his heir one of the sons of the King of France.

7. *Second Expedition into Hungary.—Siege of Vienna.*

During the time that Francis I. was endeavouring by his diplomacy to confederate all the enemies of the House of Austria, Solyman set himself to cut short the question to his own profit by force of arms. The Austrian envoys, after nine months of captivity, were brought into his presence. "Your master," said he ironically, "has not felt sufficiently up to the present moment the effects of our friendship and of our vicinity, but he will shortly. You may tell him that I shall go in search of him myself with all my forces, and that I earnestly hope to restore with my own hand that which he claims. Tell him also that he may prepare everything for our reception."

On the 10th of May, 1529, Solyman set out from Constantinople with an army of 150,000 men. It was a pretension of the Ottoman Turks that wherever the horse of the Grand Seignior had once trod, and he himself had rested for the night, the Osmanli power was irrevocably established. Solyman had once slept in the palace at Buda, and had only refrained from burning it because he intended returning thither: all Hungary, therefore, belonged to the Sultan. As a last resource, Ferdinand, wholly unprepared to fight, despatched another ambassador, provided with letters to Solyman and his Vizier, Ibrahim, couched in the most humble terms, and with instructions to offer a considerable sum in the form of a yearly pension, for that of *tribute* was too degrading. To such a point was Ferdinand content to humble himself! But it was now too late. Before the end of August Solyman was again encamped with an innumerable host on the blood-stained plain of Mohacs. Here, where the pith of his countrymen had been destroyed, John Zapoly, at the head of a large body of Hungarian magnates, met the Sultan, and did him homage. He was received with great ceremony, and admitted to kiss the Sultan's hand, but the crown of St. Stephen, the palladium of Hungary, which had already adorned the heads of both competitors, was surrendered into Solyman's possession. Three days after the Ottoman army appeared before Buda, which Ferdinand had seized upon. The place surrendered after a resistance of six days; the Janissaries massacred the German garrison, notwithstanding the capitulation, and made a great number of the inhabitants prisoners; but pillage was interdicted. Zapoly entered the city with great pomp, and was again crowned in the regal castle by the hands of one of the Turkish generals, the lieutenant-general of the Janissaries presiding over the ceremony, and a Turkish garrison was left in the place.

From thence the army set out on its march for Vienna,

and on the 27th of September Solyman encamped before the capital of the Austrian States, whilst Ferdinand was anxiously waiting at Linz until the German princes should rally round him with their promised succours. Even the Protestants—for the German Reformers had now acquired that name by their famous Protest at Spires in the spring of this year (1529)—had not withheld their assistance from King Ferdinand, and the Elector John of Saxony himself had sent 2,000 men under the command of his son. The defence of Vienna with only 16,000 men, 72 guns, and ramparts of six feet thickness, against an army of 300,000 Turks with 300 cannon, besides a strong flotilla on the Danube, is one of the most brilliant feats in the military history of Germany during the sixteenth century. A small number of Hungarians accompanied the Turkish army, but King John, who is said to have possessed neither military talents nor even personal courage, remained at Buda with a garrison of 3,000 Osmanlis. From the top of St. Stephen's tower the Turkish tents might be discerned scattered over hill and dale for miles, the white sails of their fleet gleaming on the distant Danube. Ibrahim Pacha, recently appointed Seraskier, conducted the operations of the siege. The walls of Vienna were weak and out of repair, and had no bastions on which guns could be planted. The garrison, commanded by Philip of Bavaria, as the representative of the Count Palatine Frederick, the Imperial commander-in-chief, consisted of picked troops from various parts of Germany, including a few Spaniards. The citizens vied with the troops in valour. The heads of most of the noble Austrian families took part in the sallies: among them the veteran Nicholas von Salm particularly distinguished himself. Solyman sent in a message, that if the garrison would surrender, he would not even enter the town, but press on in search of Ferdinand; if they resisted he would dine in Vienna on the third day, and then he would not spare even the child in the womb. No answer was made; but the preparations for defence were urged on with dogged resolution, though without much hope of success. The

Osmanlis, however, had no well-concerted plan of operations. Their army, according to traditional custom was divided into sixteen different bodies, to each of which a separate place and a definite object were assigned; and although they had made several breaches and mined a portion of the walls, all their assaults were repulsed. A breach having been opened in the Corinthian Gate, and the explosion of a mine having given a breadth of forty toises, the Ottomans renewed the attack with great fury during an entire day (14th of October). They were again repulsed, and the Sultan, discouraged, gave the signal for retreat that night. Robertson and several other historians have attributed the raising of the siege to the treason of the vizier Ibrahim; but that is very little probable. The season was advanced, provisions were failing, and the soldiers had begun to murmur. So large an army could not be provided for during any long-continued siege or blockade, although their flour was conveyed to them by 22,000 camels; already at Michaelmas the Janissaries had begun to complain of the cold; and the forces of the Empire and of Bohemia were beginning to arrive. These reasons, coupled with the courageous defence of the city, suffice to explain the retreat of the Turks. In this invasion they committed their usual barbarities; and wasted the country up to the very gates of Linz. They suffered much in turn during their retreat, as well from the weapons of their foes as from hunger and bad weather, and the Germans recaptured from them a considerable portion of their booty. The discomfited Ottomans did not reach Belgrade till November 10th. Solyman arrived in Constantinople December 16th.

It was the first check that the arms of Solyman had encountered. He pretended to transform it into a victory, by distributing rewards to his soldiers and in representing his retreat as an act of generosity; but he deceived no one. Terror, nevertheless, continued to spread throughout Germany: "We have not," wrote Busbek, ambassador of Ferdinand I., "we have not to combat an enemy of the same species as ourselves. We have to do with the Turk, a vigilant, adroit, sober, disciplined enemy, one inured to military labours, expert in tactics and fit for all the hardships of the service. It is by these qualities that he has made for himself a way through desolated empires, that he has subjugated all from the frontiers of Persia, and that he has threatened Vienna."*

8. *Third Expedition into Hungary.—Embassy of Francis 1.—Siege of Güns.—Peace with Austria.*

In the following spring (1531), a German army entered Hungary and went unsuccessfully to besiege Buda; at the same time, an embassy from King Ferdinand repaired to Constantinople. After enduring the disdain and insults of the Grand Vizier, he obtained a brief audience which led to nothing; the Sultan would neither acknowledge Ferdinand as King of Hungary, nor as King of Bohemia, but simply as Lieutenant of Charles V., to whom he accorded only the title of King of Spain.

In the month of April Solyman had completed his preparations for avenging the affront undergone before Vienna. His army was raised to more than 300,000 men by reinforcements drawn from Bosnia and the Crimea. Solyman began his march from Constantinople (26th of April) with all the magnificence of Oriental pomp. A long continued train of 120 cannon was followed by 8,000 picked Janissaries, and by droves of camels carrying an enormous quantity of baggage. Then came 2,000 horsemen, the sipahis of the Porte, with the Holy Banner, the Eagle of the Prophet, gorgeously adorned with pearls and precious stones. Then was borne in state the Sultan's crown, followed by his domestics, 1,000 men of gigantic stature, the handsomest that could be found, armed with bows and arrows, some of whom led coupled hounds, while others carried hawks. In the midst of them rode Solyman himself, in a crimson robe trimmed with gold embroidery, and a snow-white turban covered with precious stones, mounted on a chestnut horse,

* "De re Militari Contrà Turcam Instituenda."

and armed with a superb sword and dagger. The procession was closed by the Sultan's four viziers, amongst whom Ibrahim was conspicuous, and the rest of the Court nobles with their servants. Thus did Solyman, *the Magnificent*, inaugurate his march of vengeance.

At Nissa he was met by a new embassy from Ferdinand, and at Belgrade by the French ambassador, Rincon. Francis I. had been compelled to lay down arms and to sign the humiliating treaty of Cambrai; but a rupture with Charles V. was imminent, and Rincon's mission was to renew the alliance between the two monarchs and to require of the Sultan, in the event of war recommencing between France and Austria, the assistance of his fleets. He was received with extraordinary honours, and of which there has been no repetition given by the Sublime Porte to any Christian ambassador. A part of the army was under arms; the whole artillery of the camp fired a salute; a magnificent escort was sent to meet him; the Sultan received him upon the throne, in all his Oriental splendour, gave him his hand to kiss and enquired after the health of "his brother," the King of France. These honours contrasted strikingly with the humiliations that the envoys of Ferdinand were made to undergo, who had come to solicit a truce. "Francis," says a Turkish historian, "was master of great territories, had brave soldiers and enjoyed a great power upon the sea; as he persisted in his long-continued devotedness to the Sublime Porte, its regard for him was thereby redoubled. So the Grand Vizier spoke to his envoy as a friend, but to those of Ferdinand like a lion."
. . . . "The King of France," says another, "was sincerely attached to the Sublime Porte, which is generous as the sea, and the other King did not seek its refuge; thus the treatment that their respective envoys received was very different. The French ambassador was the object of the gracious regard and discourse of the Sultan, who humbled himself to the level of treating his master as friend, brother, and *padisha*, in the imperial letters with which he dismissed him; the others were detained prisoners." The Austrian envoys, when the Sultan had deigned to

grant them an interview, were conducted through a lane of 12,000 Janissaries to Solyman's tent, where they found him sitting on a golden throne; near him was his magnificent crown, made at Venice at the cost of 115,000 ducats; against the legs or pillars of his throne were two gorgeous sabres, in sheaths studded with pearls; also bows and quivers richly ornamented. The ambassadors estimated the value of what they saw at 1,200,000 ducats. Their errand was, of course, fruitless.

The Ottoman army, late in July, crossed the Drave at Essek on twelve bridges of boats. The march of Solyman through Hungary resembled a progress through his own dominions. No fewer than fourteen fortresses sent him their keys as he approached; and he tried and punished the magnates who had deserted Zapoly. The Turkish Fleet also ascended the Danube as far as Presburg; at which point Solyman, instead of directing his march towards Vienna, turned to the south, and leaving Neusiedler lake on his right, took the road to Styria. On the 9th of August, he arrived before the little town of Güns, a poorly fortified place, situated at the foot of the Bakony-Wald upon an affluent of the Raab. This insignificant stronghold was destined to inflict upon Solyman *the Conqueror* the most humiliating disgrace ever experienced by the overweening pride of Oriental despotism since the memorable invasion of Attica by Xerxes. All that pomp and splendour of Eastern warfare, all those formidable myriads of Turkish troops—for the army had entered Hungary with 350,000 strong—led by the Grand Seignior in person, were detained more than three weeks by a garrison of about 700 men, of which only thirty were regular troops, and those cavalry, under the command of the brave Nicholas Jurissich, who had been one of the Austrian ambassadors to the Porte. This heroic little band repulsed no fewer than eleven assaults, and the Great Sultan was at length compelled to content himself with a capitulation, by which ten Janissaries were allowed to remain an hour in the place in order to erect a Turkish standard.

This delay, and the defeat by Sebastian Schärtlin of a

body of 15,000 Turkish cavalry who were to enter Austria by the Sommering Pass, proved the saving of the country. In expectation of seeing the Sultan appear before Vienna, an army was shut up in that city, and Charles V. summoned all Germany to the defence of the Austrian States. Informed of these formidable preparations, and intimidated by the resistance of Güns, the French and Venetian ambassadors in Solyman's camp advised him not to renew the attempt of 1529 with an army thus weakened, and discouraged any general engagement with Charles's fresh and well-organized forces. Moreover, the diversion caused by Andrea Doria, the Emperor's admiral, with his fleet in the Morea, served to support this advice; who, after capturing Coron, Patras, and the two castles which defend the entrance to the Gulf of Lepanto, the Dardanelles of the Morea, had landed his troops and excited the Greeks to revolt. Perhaps even from the opening of the campaign, Solyman had not contemplated again besieging Vienna; he had only taken light field guns with him; in his reply to the messages of Ferdinand he announced his intention of seeking Charles V. to fight in a pitched battle that only rival worthy of him. However that might be, immediately after investing Grätz, which was well defended, Solyman reluctantly abandoned an enterprise for which he had made such vast preparations, and on the success of which he had so proudly relied. In spite of the rewards that were distributed on his return, in spite of the pompous letters of victory that the Sultan sent into all the provinces, that retreat, like the first, resembled a defeat.

Charles V. was prevented from pursuing the retreating Turks by the lateness of the season, the want of provisions, the sickness that had begun to prevail among his troops, and the desire of several of the princes to return to their homes; yet, on the whole, his first appearance at the head of his armies had been attended with considerable glory and success. The subsequent dispersion of the Imperial army much annoyed King Ferdinand, who had helped to recover with it the whole of Hungary, Belgrade included; but the German leaders would not listen to such a proposal. For fear of such an event, however, Solyman, at the request of Zapoly, left 60,000 men behind at Essek. Meanwhile, a war appeared on the point of breaking out in Asia. All these events inclined Solyman towards peace. Fresh negotiations were entered upon; but, during seven weeks, the envoys of Ferdinand had to struggle against the haughtiness and cunning of the Grand Vizier and of the Venetian Gritti, whom he had made his chief adviser; they had brought a letter from Charles V. to the Sultan, a friendly letter; but in which the Emperor had taken unadvisedly the title of "King of Jerusalem:" this was the occasion of interminable recriminations on the part of the vizier. " How different and truly royal," said he, " is the letter that the King of France sent us during the campaign in Hungary, in which he signs simply, ' Francis, King of France!' Also the Padisha, wishing to do honour to King Francis, did not in his reply make an enumeration of his titles, and wrote to him as a tenderly loved brother." It was on this occasion that the vizier avowed openly that the first invasion of Hungary had only been made at the demand of Francis I. "The King of France," said he, " having been conquered at Pavia, his mother wrote to my master: ' My son has been made prisoner by Charles of Spain. I thought that the latter would have the generosity to set him at liberty; but, far from doing so, he has treated him infamously. I entreat of thee, great Emperor, to show thy magnanimity by delivering my son.' The Padisha, moved by compassion at that letter, invaded Hungary." At length, by dint of patience and discretion, the envoys succeeded in obtaining a treaty by which the Sultan promised alliance and friendship to King Ferdinand, but without stipulating anything with regard to Hungary, of which he declared himself absolute master by right of conquest. Such was the first peace concluded by the House of Austria with the Porte (1533).

9. *War with Persia.—Capture of Bagdad.—Chaireddin-Barbarossa.—Capture of Tunis by Charles V.*

Since the commencement of Solyman's reign, peace had never been solidly established between Persia and the Ottomans; the reciprocal defections of certain governors of frontier towns brought about a complete rupture. Whilst the Khan of Bidlis betrayed the Ottomans, the Persian Governor of Aderbaidjan ranged himself on their side, and the Governor of Bagdad sent them the keys of the city. This latter having been assassinated, the Grand Vizier Ibrahim was ordered to reduce Bagdad and bring back to obedience the Khan of Bidlis. He set out towards the autumn of 1533, and learned by the way the defeat of the rebel. After passing the winter at Aleppo, he resumed his march, received the submission of places in the vicinity of Lake Van, and then took the road to Tebriz, the residence of the Shah, and entered therein without obstacle (13th July, 1534). The Sultan went to join him there in the month of September, and the army began its march upon Bagdad. It suffered greatly upon the way thither, not from attacks of the Persians, but from the difficult nature of the country and the rigour of the weather. The capital of the Khalifes made no resistance, and Solyman made his entry therein at the close of 1534; he there sojourned six months. He returned afterwards to Tebriz, retook the road to Constantinople, and arrived therein in January, 1536.

Whilst that triumphant expedition was aggrandizing the Empire upon its eastern frontiers, the Ottoman Fleets were at close quarters with the Marine of Charles V. Two remarkable men directed the naval forces of the two empires: these were the Genoese, Andrea Doria, Admiral of the Emperor, and, on the side of the Turks, the celebrated Chaireddin, known under the name of Barbarossa.

That adventurer was of Greek and Christian origin; he was the son of a sipahi of Mitylene; and following the too frequent custom of the inhabitants of the Archipelago,

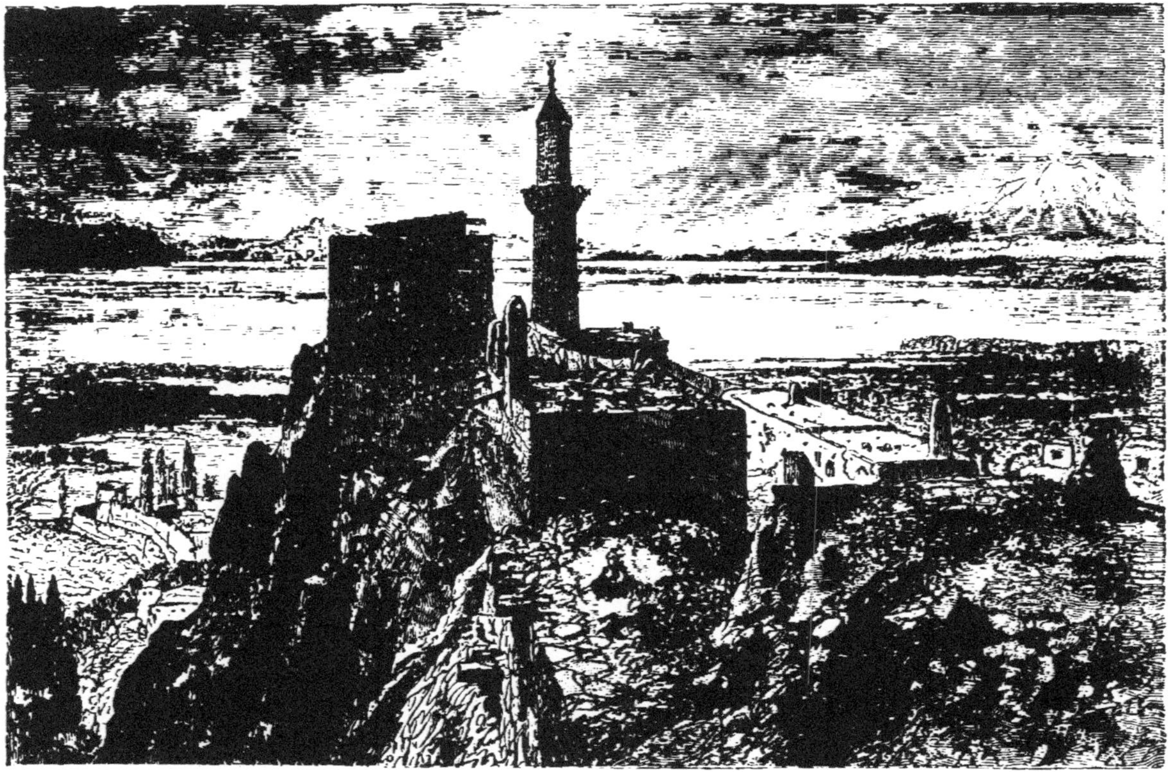

I. LAKE AND FORTRESS OF VAN. [page 204.

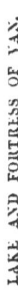

he had devoted himself, with his brother, Baba-Aroudj, to piracy during the reign of Bajazet II. The two brothers entered the service of the Sultan of Tunis, Mahommed, of the family of Beni-Hafsz. Having captured a Christian ship, they sent it to Constantinople, and received as a reward from the Sultan two galleys, and caftans of honour. They then strove to seize upon some port on the coast of Barbary, made attempts upon Cherchell, Bougia, and Algiers, where the Princes of the Beni-Hafsz reigned. At length Aroudj seized upon Cherchell, then upon Tlemcen, where he was attacked by the Spaniards, and perished in a sortie. Barbarossa made himself master of Algiers by assassinating the Moorish prince, and did homage for his conquest to the Sultan Selim, who had then just conquered Egypt, and received from him the title of Beylerbey of Algiers. The Spaniards had established themselves in the islets opposite the town, and had there built a fort; he attacked them, captured the garrison, razed the fort, defied a Spanish squadron sent to defend it, and connected the islets to the mainland by a jetty which now forms the harbour of Algiers (1520). From that port numerous corsairs began from that time to set sail, infesting the coasts of Spain and Italy and the western basin of the Mediterranean. Solyman, at the period of his alliance with Francis I., having forbidden Barbarossa to attack French vessels, the latter took his revenge upon those of Spain; he dispersed one of their squadrons, and carried away from the coast of Andalusia 70,000 persecuted Moors who helped to people Africa.

When Andrea Doria had seized upon Coron, Barbarossa was ordered to Constantinople. After having by the way burnt eighteen vessels in sight of Messina, and captured two sail of Doria's fleet, he reached the capital of the Empire at the moment of the commencement of the Persian war (1533). Coron had been already recaptured: whilst the peace with Austria was negotiating, a fleet of seventy sail was sent against that place; although beaten at the entrance of the Gulf by Doria, and weakened by the loss of at least one half, it was able nevertheless to blockade

Coron, which surrendered after a memorable siege. Barbarossa was, however, received with distinction. He was made Capudan-Pacha, and obtained investiture as Beylerbey at Algiers, and took rank before the other beylerbeys. The winter was occupied in fitting out a formidable fleet, with which he set sail in the spring; it consisted of eighty-four ships. This armament was directed at first against Italy; Reggio, Fondi, and the strongholds of the coast, were sacked; then, steering towards the coast of Africa, Barbarossa appeared before Tunis, where reigned Muley Hassan, one of those ferocious and effeminate tyrants of which the Moorish dynasties reckoned so many. He presented himself as a liberator, promising the inhabitants to give them the brother of Muley as their ruler, who had sought refuge in his fleet; then, once master of the city, he took possession of it in the name of the Sultan.

The progress of the Ottoman power upon the African coast became disquieting to the Sovereign of Spain and Italy. Charles V., therefore, determined to retake Tunis, not only in the interest of his African possessions, but also in the hope of dealing a mortal blow to the Turco-French alliance, which could only become effective by its maritime power. A powerful armament was prepared, and the Emperor took command of it himself. On the 16th of June, 1535, he disembarked before the fort of the Goulette, and carried it after a month of siege and continual fighting. Barbarossa, despairing of defending the town, in which he had to struggle with the ill-will of the inhabitants, risked an encounter in the open country. Abandoned by his African auxiliaries, he was forced to take flight. Tunis was pillaged for three days by the conquerors, 30,000 inhabitants were massacred, 50,000 Christian captives had their chains broken. The Spaniards re-established Muley Hassan, on condition that he should pay tribute, and leave to the Christians the free exercise of their religion. They kept possession of the fort Goulette.

10. *First Capitulation of the Porte with France.*

That feat of arms filled up the measure of the power and glory of Charles V. Europe looked upon him no longer save as the liberator of the Christians, the terror of the infidels, and his panegyrists took care to contrast his conduct with that of his rival, who had allied himself with the enemies of Christianity. That alliance was · no longer a secret to any one. Francis I. formed the resolution of avowing it openly, in order to acquire the right of drawing from it all the advantage possible. An official envoy, the Chevalier Jean de la Foret, was sent to the Sultan, whom he met at Tebriz (1535). He opened negotiations, ostensibly limited to the capitulations made in favour of the French merchants by the Sultans, but which were destined to have grave results. These negotiations led to a diplomatic act which was at bottom a veritable treaty, but which had not the form of one, because Ottoman pride seemed only to make concessions without granting reciprocity.* It was therefore under the form of a *hatti-cherif*, that is to say, an order emanating from the Sultan, that the first conventions which united France and the Porte appeared, and that *hatti-cherif* was the basis of all the capitulations concluded since that period between the two Powers.

The treaty was signed at Constantinople early in February, 1536, on the return from the Persian campaign. Solyman gives therein to Francis I. the title which he himself bore, that of *Padisha*,† which European

* "The Grand Seignior, by a mistaken pride, founded upon a pretext of religion, will not make *treaties* with Christian princes, pretending that they ought not to be on a par with him. That of *capitulation* is more agreeable to him, because it regards the acts which he accords, and of which he is so absolutely the master, that he revokes, extends, restrains or annuls them without ceremony when he thinks proper."—"Memoirs of the Chevalier d'Arvieux," tom. v p. 36.

† The Porte even refused that title to the Emperors of Germany, whom it recognized only as Kings of Hungary, and whom it treated as such, as vassals and tributaries; for, from 1550 until 1699, they paid it an annual tribute of 30,000 ducats. It was only in 1606 that it consented to give them the official title of *Roman Cæsar* (King of the Romans); but their Ambassadors walked all the same, like those of all the Christian States, after

diplomacy has translated by the equivalent of Emperor. That was a very great distinction, for that title was looked upon as sacred by the Osmanlis, and was only accorded afterwards to one Christian monarch, the Czar of Russia, Paul. It testified, in placing upon a footing of equality, "to the glory of the princes of the faith of Jesus Christ," with the King of Kings, the Sultan of the two earths and the two seas, the "Shadow of God," that a law of nations had commenced between Christians and Mussulmans.

The first articles were as follows :—

1. That as there is peace and concord between the Grand Seignior and the King of France, their respective subjects and tributaries may freely navigate and go into their different ports for their commerce, buy, sell, load, conduct, and transport, by water or by land, from one country to another, all kinds of merchandise not prohibited in paying the ordinary dues, without being subjected to any imposition, tribute, or other charge.

2. That when the king shall send to Constantinople or to any other part of the Ottoman Empire, a consul, in like manner as the one he keeps at Alexandria, that consul shall be accepted and sustained in his authority and shall judge according to his faith and law, without that any judge or cadi shall hear, judge, and pronounce, as well civilly as criminally upon the causes, processes, or differences which may arise, between the subjects of the king only ; and that the officers of the Grand Seignior shall lend assistance for the execution of the judgments of the consuls, any sentence passed by the cadis between French merchants to be necessarily null and void.

3. That in case of any civil contestation between the Turks and the French, the plaint of the first-named shall not be received by the cadis unless they should bring proof in writing of the hand of the adversary or that of the consul, and that in any case the subjects of the king shall not be judged without their dragoman being present.

the Ambassadors of France. Before the treaty of 1606, the greater part of the treaties made between the Porte and the Austrian monarchs were endorsed: "Graciously accorded by the ever-victorious Sultan to the ever-conquered infidel King of Vienna."

4. That in criminal matters the subjects of the king may not be brought before the cadi or ordinary judge, nor be judged at once, but be conducted before the Sublime Porte, and, in the absence of the Grand Vizier, before his substitute, in order that the testimony of the Turkish subject against the king's subject may be discussed.

5. That no use shall be made of merchants' ships belonging to the king's subjects, nor of their artillery, munitions and equipages against their will, even for the service of the Grand Seignior.

6. That if any subject of the king quits the States of the Grand Seignior without having satisfied his debts, neither the consul nor any other Frenchman shall be responsible for them; but the king shall make satisfaction to the plaintiff upon the goods or person of the debtor should it be in his kingdom.

7. That the French merchants and subjects of the king shall freely make their wills, and that the goods of those who shall die intestate shall be remitted to the heir by the care and authority of the consul.

To comprehend all the importance of these articles, it must be remembered that an insuperable barrier of hatred separated Christians and Mussulmans; that they mutually regarded one another as enemies for whom there was no law; that religious prejudices proscribed them from having communication save by war only. The establishment, therefore, of relations of justice, peace, and even benevolence between the two peoples was a great progress; but such was not solely the extent of the articles cited: they introduced an important innovation in the law of nations, in authorizing the French to have the advantage of their nationality, their laws, their customs under a foreign domination; in giving them, in many respects, more rights and liberties than Ottoman subjects had, in placing them almost entirely under the protecting dependence of their national magistrates. Those prerogatives were such that no nation had conceded the like to a foreign nation, and they had the effect of changing the French counting-houses, so to speak, into small colonies. They were still further increased by the solicitude of the consuls, who transformed almost completely their attributes of commerce and police into a civil magistracy and into political functions, and ended by arrogating to themselves so extraordinary a right of protection in the Ottoman Empire, that the denomination of *Franks* was attributed even to certain subjects of the Sultan.

The other articles of the hatti-cheriff of 1536 have not less importance : 1. The French enjoyed in all the Ottoman States the free exercise of their worship; they had the right of safe-guarding the Holy Places of Palestine by religious functionaries, who could not be disturbed, neither in respect to the edifices they inhabited, nor the churches that were in their hands. The bishops dependents of France, and other priests of the *Frank* religion, of whatsoever nation they were, could not be disturbed in the exercise of their functions, wherever they dwelt, provided they kept themselves within the bounds of their condition. This article, by the extension which was given it and the favourable interpretations of which it was susceptible consecrated the right of protection of France over all Catholics in the East. 2. European merchants, whose governments were not allied with the Porte by friendly treaties, might navigate under the French flag in all the seas, and traffic, under the protection of France, in all countries of the Ottoman domination. Venice alone had, at this epoch, commercial treaties with the Porte :* consequently, all the other Christian nations were obliged to have recourse to the protecting flag of France to trade with Turkey. 3. The liberation of slaves made on either side was stipulated for, and the Sultan engaged to renounce the right of

---

* These treaties dated from the arrival of the Turks in Europe, and placed Venice upon the footing of vassal and tributary of the Sultan. As early as 1408, it paid a tribute of 1,600 ducats, a tribute which was afterwards raised to 10,000. When Mahomet II. had made himself master of Constantinople, it purchased peace of him and a continuation of its commerce; it was then obliged to pay for the establishments it had in the new Empire an annual tribute of 36,000 ducats, and it was stipulated that it should send, as in the past, to Constantinople, a *Chargé d'Affaires* having the title of *bayle*, and whom the Turks should regard and treat as a hostage. Every peace or truce that it made with the Turks was purchased with gold.

making slaves of French subjects, on condition that the King of France should do the same with regard to the Ottomans.

Such were the principal articles of the hatti-cherif of 1536, an act the power of which could not have been understood by the contracting parties; for in making the Mussulman nations enter into pacific relations with the Christian nations, it weakened forcibly the spirit of conquest and propagation of the former, and was thus a kind of limitation for the Ottoman Empire. It was an obscure but efficacious victory of European civilization over Asiatic barbarity, of tolerance over fanaticism, of the spirit of expansion of the West over the spirit of isolation of the East, an easy victory in its origin, but which was afterwards disputed, for the treaty had to submit to many violations and was compelled to have numerous renewals.

The conclusion of this Treaty was the last political act of the Grand Vizier Ibrahim. That haughty Minister abused more and more his favour. During the negotiations with Austria he had made a display of his authority, which had offended the Sultan. During the Persian campaign he desired to lodge alone with his master in the palaces of Tebriz and Bagdad; he wrung from him first the deposition, then the condemnation to death of the Defterdar Iskender Tchelebi, whose wealth and fame gave him umbrage; finally, on his return, he assumed in his "orders of the day," and even in the treaty with the King of France, the significant title of *Seraskier Sultan*. This last effrontery filled up the measure of his presumption. On the 5th of March, 1536, Ibrahim repaired to the Seraglio, as was his custom; the next day he was found strangled therein. In the middle of the seventeenth century traces of his blood were still shown upon the walls. He had for successor the Albanian, Ayas Pacha.

CHAPTER IV.

REIGN OF SOLYMAN FROM THE CAPITULATIONS WITH FRANCE TO HIS DEATH
(1536–1566).

1. *Sequel of the Franco-Turkish Alliance.—War with Venice.*

THE capitulations of 1536 announced to Europe that a close alliance existed between France and Turkey, but they did not make known the political conditions: they were kept secret; they must be revealed only by facts; but they were as formally settled at the time as the commercial stipulations. The French ambassador was commissioned to demand from Solyman a subsidy of a million of golden crowns, "the which will not be inconvenient to the Grand Seignior, seeing that his affairs are constituted in all felicity, and ought not to cause him grievance."* He demanded, moreover, that the Ottoman fleet, under the command of Barbarossa, should attack Sicily and Sardinia whilst the king was reducing Genoa; and he had already, on that subject, conferred directly at Tunis with the "King of Algiers," as Barbarossa was called. Lastly, he was charged to concert with the Sultan the conduct of the war, and to engage him to direct his efforts, not towards Hungary and Germany, where his presence would only reunite the divided parties, but against Naples, Sicily, and Spain. That was, in fact, what was resolved upon; Francis I. should invade Piedmont, and Solyman the kingdom of Naples. As to the subsidy, it is not known whether it was accorded. Preparations were made on both sides for war; but the alliance had not the results that might have been expected from it, on account of the rupture which broke out between the Porte and Venice.

* "Instruction au Sieur de la Forêt pour son Ambassade à la Porte."

Thirty-five years had passed during which peace had existed between the two Powers. Under the administration of Ibrahim, the relations had even assumed a certain character of intimacy; the new vizier appeared disposed to maintain them on the same terms; besides, when Solyman and Francis concluded their alliance, they comprised the Venetians in it, and despatched deputies to them to obtain their formal adhesion. The Republic replied that it preferred to remain neutral; but the intrigues of Andrea Doria, who laboured to throw Venice into alliance with the Emperor, and those of Barbarossa, who saw in a maritime war only the occasion of obtaining booty, succeeded in changing the neutrality into open hostility. Already the Ottoman Fleet, with the strength of a hundred sail, had landed troops in Italy, who were ravaging the coasts of Apulia, when it was recalled to attack the Venetian island of Corfu (Sept. 1537). The Sultan went in person to assist at the siege, and encamped on the shore opposite the island; but at the end of eight days, disheartened by the resistance of the place, he renounced the enterprise. The Grand Vizier was ordered to seek retaliation upon Napoli di Romania and Malvasia, the chief towns held by the Venetians in the Morea, and whence they sallied forth to attack the Turkish territories. He besieged those places during five months without success (from June to the end of November, 1538). As to the Capudan-Pacha, he went to reduce and ravage the islands of the Archipelago—an easy conquest that brought him more booty than glory. He afterwards carried desolation into Candia; then, with a hundred and twenty-two vessels, he obtained off Prevesa a brilliant but sterile victory over a Christian fleet of one hundred and sixty-seven sail, commanded by Andrea Doria (25th Sept. 1538).

The year following, Solyman, who was accompanied by the ambassador La Forêt, assembled in Albania 100,000 men for a descent upon Italy; at the same time Barbarossa landed a force from 70 galleys near Otranto. Both awaited the operations of Francis I. who proposed to enter Piedmont with an army and send his galleys to Apulia.

But the union of the Lilies and the Crescent had raised an outcry throughout Europe: Francis, alarmed by it, left his galleys at Marseilles, and waited until the Turks had evacuated Italy before entering Piedmont; then becoming more and more uneasy at the clamours of Christendom, and seeing that the object of the Franco-Turkish alliance had failed, he signed with Charles V. the truce of Nice (1538). Solyman was dissatisfied, but did not break off the alliance; he confirmed even at that juncture the hatti-cherif of 1536, and soon showed that he had, better than the King of France, a knowledge of his perils and of the situation of Europe.

2. *Affairs of Hungary.—Capture of Buda.*

The war continued by land and sea with Venice and the House of Austria. In Dalmatia, successes were balanced: the Venetians seized upon Ostrovitz, Obrovatz and Scardona; the Turks stormed the fortress of Nadin and took Doubicza; the Christian fleet took possession of Castelnuova (27 Oct., 1538); that of Barbarossa retook the place on the 10th of August of the following year. At length the Venetians solicited peace and obtained it on onerous conditions, surrendering Malvasia and Napoli de Romania (1539).

In Hungary hostilities had recommenced early in 1537; a German army of 24,000 men, commanded by Ferdinand's General, Katzianer, was surrounded and destroyed at Essek by the Ottoman cavalry; its commander fled and carried the news of his disgrace to Vienna, where he was thrown into prison. Some time after he made his escape, essayed to sell himself to the Turks, and perished by assassination before he could consummate his treason. In the following year (1538), the Voïvode of Moldavia, Raresch, who had an understanding with Ferdinand, whilst meditating an insurrection, was driven out of his province and compelled to take refuge in Transylvania; his brother Stephen was put in his place; the fortifications of Akerman and Kilia were further strengthened and all attempts at rising prevented.

At this time Zapoly and Ferdinand, who had during twelve years disputed for the crown of Hungary, entered into an arrangement; a secret treaty was concluded at Grosswardein, by which the two rivals shared the country between them. Ferdinand hastened to reveal this treaty to the Sultan, in the hope of detaching him from the interests of his rival; but Zapoly died (1540), leaving a son, born fifteen days previous to his death, under the safe keeping of his mother Isabella. The Austrian troops immediately entered Hungary, besieged Isabella in Buda, then seized upon Pesth, Waizen, Wissegrad and Stuhlweissemburg. Solyman, however, on the news of the death of his *protégé*, had sent a diploma by which the son of Zapoly was declared King of Hungary, vassal and tributary of the Porte. A new suppliant embassy from Ferdinand having been sent to him, he maltreated his agents, declared war against him and placed himself at the head of his army (June, 1541). On the march he learned that the troops of Queen Isabella had defeated and dispersed the Austrian army, and that Pesth was evacuated; he arrived thus before Buda (August 29th). Zapoly's son having been presented to him in his camp, the Janissaries profited by the confusion incident upon that ceremony to obtain entrance within the city, of which they took possession. It was intimated to the Queen that she must quit her capital, and the next day Solyman entered therein with great pomp; he converted the great church into a mosque, made Buda the seat of a pachalic and established therein a garrison of 5,000 men. At the same time, he gave the Queen a diploma by which he engaged to keep Buda only during the minority of the young King, and to put him, as soon as he attained his majority, in possession of the throne.

On the day after the occupation of Buda, other Austrian ambassadors arrived at the Ottoman camp. They brought rich presents, among which a clock that marked the months and the course of the stars excited much admiration; they offered a tribute of 100,000 florins provided that the whole of Hungary should be given up to Ferdinand, or 40,000 ducats for peaceable possession of the portion they occupied. They were well received, but were told that peace would be accorded if Ferdinand should deliver up the places he had seized upon and pay tribute for the rest.

3. *New Alliance between Turkey and France.*

Some days afterwards, a French ambassador arrived who came to announce that war was recommencing in the West, and to renew the alliance with the Ottomans. Francis I. after the truce of Nice had changed his policy: whether he did not comprehend the whole bearing of his alliance with the Porte, or whether he was desirous of coming to terms with his rival by a show of generosity, he suddenly exhibited a warm friendship for Charles V. and ceased correspondence with Solyman. Charles V. had need at that moment of peace or of a truce (it was just after the defeat of Katzianer); he profited by the foolish confidence of Francis, and had recourse to his mediation to obtain one or the other. The King of France wrote, in fact, a sanguine letter in favour of his enemy (1539). Solyman had but slightly heeded the sudden coolness of his ally: Rincon, who had remained at Constantinople,* had skilfully kept him favourably disposed towards France; he replied therefore to Francis: "Charles, King of Spain, desires and seeks, by your mediation, a truce with my Sublime Porte. Constant in the fraternity which has existed thus far between you and me, and which I confirm by my imperial faith, I declare that, if the King of Spain wishes to obtain a truce and that it is your desire

---

* It is not known under what title and for what business Rincon had remained at Constantinople. The series of first French envoys to the Ottoman Empire is very obscure. It appears that La Forêt died in 1537, and had for successor Marillac. To Marillac succeeded, in 1539, the Neapolitan Cantelmo, who made two voyages to Constantinople. Rincon must have succeeded him.

that he may obtain it, I will that he commence by replacing in your hands all the provinces, lands and fortresses that he has forcibly taken from you. When he shall have fulfilled that condition, you will apprise my Sublime Porte to that effect, and I will do all that may be agreeable to you: it shall be open to whomsoever shall present himself there on your part, either that I accord peace, or that I declare war to our common enemy."

Charles refused to make peace upon the conditions imposed by the Sultan, and shortly Francis I., whom he had shamefully deceived, broke with him (1541). The struggle between the two rivals became more furious than ever: the King of France resolved to crush his enemy by the help of the Ottoman forces, should it expose Christendom to the ravages of the barbarians. "If the wolves come to attack me at home," said he, "it is allowable surely for me to call upon the dogs to drive them away." The King of Spain hoped to break up the Franco-Turkish alliance by raising Europe against it, and he did not recoil from an assassination in order to obtain proof of the treason of his enemy against the cause of Christianity. Rincon had been the bearer of Solyman's letter: he was ordered by Francis I. to return to Constantinople and demand of the Sultan that he should immediately place all his vessels at his disposition and that he should continue the war in Hungary. He took his way by Venice, where he proposed to embark, but he was assassinated in Lombardy by order of the Governor of Milan, who thought to find upon him the instructions of the King of France. The murderer was foiled in his expectation; Dubellay, the French Governor of Piedmont, who suspected the designs of Charles V., had retained these instructions when Rincon passed through Turin, and the Emperor was reduced to publish documents which he had caused to be fabricated. Francis I. denounced his enemy's crime to all Europe, and he replaced Rincon by a soldier of fortune, a Captain Paulin, subsequently Baron de la Garde, and General of the galleys. It was this new agent who went in search of the Sultan, then in Hungary, and whom he found at Buda and announced to him the murder of Rincon. Solyman was so chagrined and irritated at the news, that he wished to avenge the death of the French envoy by that of the imperial ambassadors. Paulin dissuaded him from it; and took advantage of his anger to explain the object of his mission.

This time the Sultan hesitated to satisfy his inconstant ally. The ambassador followed him to Constantinople, and obtained at first that the Republic of Venice should be solicited to enter into the French alliance; but that overture met with no success; then he contrived to win over to his interests the Ministers of the Porte, and found especially a zealous auxiliary in Barbarossa, who was only seeking for a fresh opportunity of marauding the Mediterranean.* The Capudan-Pacha was then in the enjoyment of the highest favour, for he went, favoured it is true by storms, to inflict a great disaster upon Charles V.

The latter was desirous of recommencing the war by a *coup d'éclat*, by another Tunis expedition. He sailed to attack Algiers with 74 galleys, 200 vessels, large and small, and an army of 24,000 men. Several ladies of the Court of Spain had accompanied the army to witness its triumph. Scarcely had a landing been effected at four leagues from Algiers, when a frightful storm assailed the fleet and troops; 130 vessels, of which 14 were galleys, were sunk. Pelted by a driving rain, harassed by swarms of Arabs, the Spaniards advanced nevertheless to the foot of the walls, where they were received by a terrible cannonade. On the fourth day they beat a retreat, and re-embarked on board the relics of their fleet, having lost one half of their numbers and a portion of their artillery (31st October, 1541). Contrary winds prevented their regaining Europe for the space of a month.

* This interested view rendered Barbarossa so favourable to France, that he passed as the head of the French party in the Divan. The Grand Vizier inquired of Ferdinand's envoy what was the object of the friendly treaty concluded between the King of France and the King of the Romans. "Interrogate thereon the grand Admiral," replied the envoy, pointing to Barbarossa. "Do I," said the latter, laughingly, "represent here the Ambassador of the King of France?"

A.D. 1543.]   NEW FRANCO-TURKISH ALLIANCE.   219

Paulin being warmly supported by the defender of Algiers, by the aga of the Janissaries, by the favourite Vizier Rustem, decided the Sultan to place his fleet and its admiral under the orders of the king. He was himself the bearer of that news to Fontainebleau; performed the voyage and journey in twenty-one days, and returned with the same promptitude to Constantinople, to hasten the departure of the Turkish vessels. During his absence Ferdinand had again made an attempt at negotiation, but his ambassador could not even obtain an audience. Paulin, however, had still to struggle against the hesitation of the Sultan, and the expedition after all was put off to the year ensuing (1543). It was then that Solyman wrote to his ally the following letter:—

"Glory of the Princes of the religion of Jesus, thou shalt know that, at the prayer of thy minister Paulin, I have granted my formidable fleet, equipped with everything that is necessary. I have ordered Chaireddin, my Capudan-Pacha, to listen to thy intentions, and to form his enterprises to the ruin of thy enemies. Thou shalt so arrange that after having happily executed them, my army may return before the bad season. Take care that thy enemy deceive thee not. He will never force himself to make peace with thee until he shall recognize that thou art determined to wage continued war against him. May God bless those who esteem my friendship, and who are protected by my victorious arms!"

In the spring of 1543, whilst Solyman was again entering Hungary, the Ottoman fleet, with a force of 110 galleys and carrying 14,000 men, set sail. Paulin was aboard the admiral's ship, and Barbarossa had formal command to follow his advice and the orders of the King of France in everything. This fleet pillaged the coasts of Sicily, respected the Pontifical States, and arrived at Marseilles, where it was received with great honours, and joined the French fleet of 40 galleys and 7,000 men, commanded by the Count d'Enghien. Francis I., who seemed always embarrassed by the Turkish alliance, knew not how to profit by such a combination of forces; by his orders the two fleets appeared before Nice, the only city which remained to the Duke of Savoy, the ally of Charles V. They made themselves masters of the place; but the French having hindered the Turks from pillaging, discord arose between the two armies, which, after assaulting unsuccessfully the castle, separated. The capture of Nice was the sole result achieved by a naval armament which ought to have annihilated the Spanish fleet, and which cost France dearly. Barbarossa, however, had permission to winter at Toulon. During their stay there, his followers acted as though they were in an enemy's country, and filled the benches of their galleys by carrying off all the men they could seize on the adjacent coasts, while the women served to supply their harems. Barbarossa even took the crews out of the royal galleys, and left them totally useless. To induce so dangerous an ally to quit France, Francis made him a subsidy of 800,000 crowns. At length, in April, Barbarossa set sail for Constantinople, and again spread terror and desolation along the coasts of Italy, whence he carried off 14,000 Christians as slaves. That expedition raised such a chorus of imprecations against the French king throughout Europe, that the following year (1544), France refused the assistance Barbarossa offered him in his master's name, and concluded the peace of Crespy. This was the Corsair-captain's last notable exploit. He died two years after at a very advanced age (4th July, 1546). His tomb may be seen at Beschiklasch, on the shore of the Bosphorus, at the point where the Ottoman fleets usually muster.

The Hungarian campaign, opened by Solyman, was marked by great successes, but did not prove decisive. Before the Sultan's arrival his lieutenants had seized upon the fortress of Valpo, in Sclavonia. He himself besieged and took Siklos, Gran, and Stuhlweissembourg, which were transformed into Sandjaks (1543). The year following, Wissegrad, Neograd, Welika, and several other fortresses, fell also into the power of the Ottomans. Two Turkish corps defeated at Louska an army of Croats,

Styrians, and Carinthians, commanded by the Palatine Zriny; on the other hand, they sustained a severe check near Salla.

In 1546 negotiations were opened with the view of putting an end to this war, which dragged on its course so tediously. They were prolonged till 1547. Ferdinand and Charles V., desirous of peace, which had become necessary for both, consented to pay an annual subsidy, the Ottoman ministers stipulating for the evacuation of several places. These difficulties were taken advantage of by the French ambassador, Gabriel d'Aramon.* He announced that his master had decided to take up arms again. He represented to the Sultan the fresh embarrassments that the revolt of the Lutheran Princes of Germany had caused the Emperor, and solicited a new and effective alliance. The death of Francis I., which happened in March 1547, put an end to those projects, and hastened the conclusion of the treaty. On the 19th of June following, a truce of five years was concluded between the Sultan, the Emperor, and King Ferdinand, on condition of an annual present of 30,000 ducats, which the latter agreed to pay for the portion of Hungary that remained in his power.

4. *War in Asia.*

Free in Europe, Solyman profited by it to extend his domination in the direction of Asia. During the ten years, the main incidents of which have been just narrated, the affairs of Europe had assumed sufficient importance to absorb his entire attention. We have, how-

* The agents of France played at this juncture a singular part, quite calculated to discredit them: at the time when the negotiations began, the Treaty of Crespy had just been concluded; Francis I. was once more reconciled with Charles; Jean de Montluc accompanied to Constantinople, in quality of Envoy Extraordinary of the King, the Imperial Ambassador, and supported his overtures with a warmth which shocked the Divan, which compromised himself and embroiled him with d'Aramon, his colleague. The latter set ont on his return to France. Shortly after a misunderstanding having again begun to show itself between the two rival monarchs, d'Aramon went back with fresh instructions, and set himself to hinder the negotiations with as much zeal as Montluc had shown in seconding them.

ever, to revert to a distant expedition accomplished during the height of his struggle against the House of Austria, and which shows with what activity he directed his attention simultaneously upon the most divergent points. In 1537, he received two Indian ambassadors sent, one by the sovereign of Delhi, who was sustaining an unequal struggle with the Mongol Emperor, the other by the Prince of Guzerat who implored his aid against the Portuguese. Already, in 1525, an Ottoman squadron had appeared in the Red Sea in order to chastise the Arab pirates; in June, 1538, Solyman Pacha, governor of Egypt, with a fleet of 70 sail carrying 20,000 soldiers, cruised along the coast of Arabia, subjected in passing Aden, and landed in Guzerat. After capturing two strong forts, he failed in besieging Diû; but, on his return, he achieved the conquest of Yemen, which became an Ottoman province.

In 1547, at the moment he was about to conclude the treaty with Austria, there arrived a Persian Prince, Elkazib Mirza, the rebel son of the Shah, who came to place himself under the protection of the Porte. War against Persia was instantly resolved upon. In the spring of 1548, Solyman passed into Asia. He conquered a portion of Persian Kurdistan, entered for the second time as victor into Tebriz, and seized upon the fortress of Van. Prince Elkazib Mirza, with an army of Kurds and volunteers, advanced nearly to Ispahan, and sent the Sultan a portion of his booty; but soon after, distrusting the Ottomans, he strove to sustain himself by his own forces alone, was taken by his brother and imprisoned. After having effected, by his lieutenants, the conquest of a part of Georgia, Solyman returned to Constantinople in December, 1549.

5. *Affairs of Hungary.—Siege of Erlau.—Sequel of the Franco-Turkish Alliance.*

Ere long the flames of war were rekindled in Hungary. Queen Isabella, relict of King John, had placed her confidence in the monk Georges Martinuzzi, whom Zapoly, when on his death-bed, had recommended to her. That ambitious and intriguing monk had an understanding with Ferdinand, and induced the Queen to cede Transylvania and the Banat of Temesvar to him. At the same time he protested his zeal for Solyman, and kept him in a fatal security by false reports. Already the treaty was concluded and signed, already a German army was on its march, a national insurrection was organized, and Martinuzzi still wrote to Constantinople to contradict what he called the calumnious reports. At length, Solyman declared that, in the incertitude, he was about to send his troops into Hungary, and the act quickly followed the menace. Ferdinand, after the conclusion of the peace, had left at Constantinople a *chargé d'affaires*, whom the Sultan had accepted under the title of a hostage. He was thrown into prison, and then an army of 80,000 men crossed the Danube, September, 1551. The greater number of the strongholds occupied by the Germans surrendered without striking a blow; but Transyvlania rose at the call of Martinuzzi, on whom Ferdinand had just bestowed a Cardinal's hat. Lippa was carried by assault 7th November, the Cardinal monk being himself at the head of the assailants, and was one of the first to mount to the assault. Soon after he meditated a fresh treason; aspiring, probably, to make himself Prince of Transylvania, he made overtures with the view of regaining the favour of Solyman. Ferdinand, informed of his new intrigues, caused him to be assassinated 18th December, 1551.

The following year was opened by a defeat of the Imperialists. After capturing Szegedin, they were surprised before the town and cut in pieces. The second vizier,

Ahmed Pacha, took Temesvar, and all the Banat returned under Ottoman domination. The governor of Buda siezed upon Wesprim and several fortresses, and defeated near Fulek an Imperial army commanded by Erasmus Teufel; the Austrian General was himself made prisoner; lastly, Szolnok was carried without a blow struck, thanks to the cowardice of the governor. But Erlau, where Dobo and Stephen Metzkey were in command, immortalised itself by an heroic defence : the women fought upon the breach as valiantly as the men. After a siege of five months and many murderous assaults, the Turks were compelled to retire (1552).

The struggle had also recommenced at sea. A follower of Barbarossa, the corsair Torghud, called by the Europeans Dragut, sustained the reputation of the Ottoman navy, and rendered himself almost as formidable to the Christians as his predecessor.

The alliance with France, however, was not broken; Henry II., foreseeing a speedy resumption of arms, had taken care to keep up friendly relations with the Porte. D'Aramon, his ambassador, on his return to France, after having accompanied the Sultan in his Persian expedition went, with a brilliant escort, to visit the Holy Places, which, since the Crusades, had not received a public envoy from the Kings of France. He was welcomed with much honour by the Ottoman authorities, with acclamations by the Christians; and that journey was in some sort a taking possession of the protectorate of the faithful of the East. On his return to France, d'Aramon found the war rekindled with Austria; he set out again immediately for the Levant. On the voyage, he stopped at Tripoli in Africa, which had fallen into the hands of the Knights of Malta, and which had just been retaken by the Turks : he compelled the conquerors, by threatening them with the Sultan's wrath, to respect the capitulation and to set at liberty the French Knights, 1551. Arrived in Turkey, he opposed steadfastly the violence exercised by the Capudan-Pacha upon the Isle of Scio ; and looking, as he said, upon all Christians as his compatriots, he procured for the inhabitants the privileges that they have in part preserved down to our own time. Lastly, he obtained the Sultan's consent that the Ottoman fleet, commanded by Dragut, should join the French fleet under the command of Paulin, 1553.

These two sea captains, after ravaging Calabria and Sicily, landed on the Island of Corsica, which the king was desirous of wresting from the Genoese, allies of Charles V.: it was needed wherewith to make a *place d'armes* at which the two fleets could make appointed meeting and then harass Italy and Spain. The French and the Turks seized upon several towns; but dissension broke out between them : the latter wished to pillage the conquered places, the former were desirous that religion, the people and property, should be respected; the two fleets separated, and the conquest of Corsica was abandoned.

That was the last occasion, until the present century, that Frenchmen and Turks were seen fighting in the same ranks. The alliance continued to subsist, but it ceased to be that which it had been since 1536, effective, direct, offensive. Such a result was inevitable. France had entered into the alliance in order to limit the House of Austria; Turkey to invade more easily the countries of Christendom. The first partly attained her object by the Treaty of Cateau-Cambresis, which suspended her struggle with Austria for seventy-six years; the second saw itself cheated of its hopes, since Hungary, Italy, and Spain had opposed invincible barriers to it. The alliance was therefore less useful to both parties; it became naturally less close, more restrained, and was directed almost solely by the Kings of France to the interests of commerce and the protection of the Christians in the East. Moreover, the political ideas of Solyman—ideas so replete with grandeur and dignity, which alone could give the Ottomans a European existence—became enfeebled by degrees, and ended by disappearing almost entirely amongst his successors. As for the sons of Henry II. of France, guided by their astute mother, Catherine de Medici, they followed, notwithstanding their stormy reigns, the policy of their grandfather with much activity and intelligence; but if, amidst the religious fury which drenched their kingdom in blood, they had been desirous of perpetuating the scandal that Francis I. had given to Christendom by uniting his arms with those of the infidels, they would have been infallibly driven from the throne.

6. *War with Persia.—The Sultana Roxalana.—Death of Mustapha.*

Whilst war was being waged in Europe to the advantage of the Turks, the Shah of Persia having resumed the offensive in Asia, and obtained divers successes upon the frontiers, the Grand Vizier was ordered to oppose him.

The post of Grand Vizier was then filled by Rustem Pacha, the most favoured of Solyman's ministers since the fall of Ibrahim. He was sustained by the patronage of the favourite Sultana, the celebrated Khourum-Sultana, whom Solyman, by pre-eminent distinction, acknowledged as his legitimate wife. This seductive woman, stated by several writers to have been a French woman named Roxalana, was, in fact, a Russian slave. She obtained an ascendancy altogether extraordinary over her master, and contributed powerfully to ruin the favourite, who, during sixteen years, had shared the Sultan's authority. She had a son, Selim, for whose accession to the throne she successfully strove, and who became the unworthy successor of Solyman. She had also a daughter, who had been given in marriage to Rustem, then third vizier. Speedily the fortunate son-in-law of the Sultan was raised from favour to favour, even to the highest dignity of the empire. The Persian campaign of 1548 had been undertaken at the instigation of the Sultana, in order to give Rustem an opportunity of displaying his military talents, and he was therefore made Commander-in-Chief. He set out, furnished with instructions from his benefactress, and soon after rendered her a repulsive service. Scarcely had he entered upon the campaign than he wrote to the Sultan that seditious movements had broken out in the army in favour of Prince Mustapha, Solyman's eldest son. In reality, Mustapha must have seen with secret discontent his young brother, Selim, made Governor of Magnesia; for it was in that government of Magnesia, the nearest to the capital, that the heirs designated by the Sultan ordinarily awaited the moment for ascending the throne. Mustapha, by his brilliant qualities, by his valour and generosity, had won the affection of the Janissaries; and the protection he afforded to letters rendered him equally dear to poets and learned men. The Vizier asserted that the soldiers already spoke of deposing the decrepid Padishah, and proclaiming Mustapha his successor. At this news, Solyman hastened to pass over into Asia, and take command of the army. Prince Mustapha went to join the camp near Ercyli (5th October, 1553); on the day after his arrival, when he presented himself in the Sultan's tent, he was there received by the mutes, bearing the fatal bowstring; and the unfortunate prince perished whilst vainly calling for his father, who, concealed behind a curtain, was present during that horrible scene. A son of Mustapha, left at Broussa, was snatched by craft from his mother's arms and put to death; and his brother, Dschihangir, linked with him in the closest ties of love, followed him speedily to the grave. The Janissaries, in their first burst of indignation, mutinied, but they were appeased by the deposition of the Grand Vizier, to whom public opinion attributed these murders; and the army began its march towards the Persian frontier.

That war presented no remarkable events: after a year passed in devastating the countries of Kerman, both sides began to wish for peace; a treaty, concluded 29th May, 1555, brought intermission to the enmity which divided the two peoples ever since the foundation of the dynasty of the Ssafis and revival of the schism: the followers of Ali were permitted to make the pilgrimage to Mecca, and the Sultan promised to protect them.

7. Affairs of Hungary.—Revolt and Death of Bajazet.

The Hungarian war continued almost without interruption. In 1554, at the moment when Solyman was about to pass into Asia, an embassy had arrived from Vienna, and negotiations were recommenced but without result; however, some advantages obtained by the Turks determined the dispatch of fresh agents, who sought for the Sultan in Amasia, and obtained an armistice of six months (1555). That armistice was badly observed on both sides: the Turkish marauders and Hungarian heydukes did not the less carry on their depredations; the animosity of the two peoples manifested itself by single combats, by partial rencontres; and, the year following, hostilities were resumed with increased fury. The Turks forced their way into Szigeth, but could not reduce the fortress; constrained to abandon the town, they were defeated upon the banks of the Rinya by Thomas Nadasdy, who seized upon Babocsa, Korothna, and several other places. The Turks, on the other hand, took Kostainicza, and devastated all the country between the Unna and the Kulpa; they again surprised the Fortress of Tata (1558) and seized upon Szikszo, which was burnt. In spite of the savage fury of the war, the negotiations were continued; but the zeal and efforts of Ferdinand's agents only ended in a truce of six months, which was rather due to fresh embarrassments caused the Sultan by the revolt of his son Bajazet.

That revolt was the work of Lala Mustapha, the former preceptor of Bajazet, become the confidant of Selim and grand master of his Court. That intriguer, having a perfect understanding with his new master, undertook craftily to put arms into Bajazet's hands; exasperated him against his brother by representing that Selim had rendered himself odious by his debaucheries, that the nation would prefer him to Selim, and was ready to support him. Swayed by this advice, Bajazet sent his brother an insulting letter, together with a distaff and female vestments, all of which Selim sent to the Sultan. Solyman, irritated, threatened Bajazet with disgrace, and ordered him to exchange his government of Konieh for that of Amasia. The Prince, instead of obeying, burned his father's letters, put the messengers to death, and took up arms. The vizier, Mahomet Sokolli, was sent to reduce him. After a fight which lasted two days (30th and 31st May, 1561), the rebel Prince was conquered; he fled to Amasia, whence he sent a humble and penitent letter to his father; Lala Mustapha intercepted the missive, and Bajazet, receiving no answer, and finding himself actively pursued, fled into Persia. He was received by the Shah with great pomp and demonstrations of friendship; but care was taken to disarm or disperse the troops he had brought with him. Messengers speedily arrived from Solyman and Selim, demanding the extradition of the rebel. After a long and secret negotiation the Persian monarch consented to surrender his guest; but to keep unbroken his promise not to deliver him up to his father, he remitted him to the agents of his brother Selim, who murdered him with his five sons (25th Sept., 1561). The throne was thus secured to Selim, who remained the sole heir to Solyman.

8. *Peace with Austria.—Naval Affairs.—Siege of Malta.*

The Austrian negotiators, however, were indefatigable: they returned unceasingly with fresh propositions scarcely different from the preceding, and struggled with a wonderful address and constancy despite the exigence and harshness of the viziers, against the claims of the agents of Queen Isabella, offering large tributes, but demanding restitutions of territories. The vizier Rustem being dead, the conciliating character of Ali Pacha, his successor, brought about a conclusion. In June, 1562, a peace was signed for eight years upon the basis of the *statu quo*. The tribute, which the Austrians disguised under the term of "annual present," was maintained.

That pacification proved again illusory: it was scarcely signed when already difficulties presented themselves; the

Divan claimed arrears of tribute; the Austrian ministers complained that the Turkish copy of the treaty was not conformable to the Latin copy. War went on upon the frontiers: whilst felicitations were being exchanged at Vienna at the re-establishment of peace, the banks of the Danube and the Drave were the theatre of furious fighting. It was not before the expiration of a year that there was any relaxation of hostilities.

Moldavia, about the same time, was troubled with internal disorders. A Candiote adventurer named John Basilicas, supported in secret by Ferdinand, dethroned the voïvode Alexander, and caused himself to be acknowledged in his place under the name of Ivan. The dispossessed Prince went to carry his plaint to Constantinople; but he had nothing to offer; the usurper, who had sent rich presents and promised to increase the tribute, was maintained (1563). A few months after, the boyards rose, besieged him in Suczava and slew him; the voïvode Alexander was restored.

The peace concluded with Austria, all precarious as it was, permitted the Sultan to give more attention to naval expeditions. On that side also the war was permanent. The Capudan-pacha, Piale, Salih Bey, beylerbey of Algiers, and Dragut, become beylerbey of Tripoli, spread terror in the Mediterranean and kept the Spanish marine incessantly in check. Masters of Tripoli, Algiers, Bougia and Oran, they had made the coast of Africa the centre of their maritime cruises. In 1560, the Spaniards had taken possession of the island of Djerbi; and had scarcely established themselves therein, ere Piale attacked them, retook the island, defeated their fleet and carried the relics of it in triumph to Constantinople.

Four years after, the Spaniards having seized upon Gomer and Pignon de Valez, the Ottomans resolved to avenge themselves by a *coup d'éclat;* a fleet of 200 sail went to besiege Malta (20th May, 1565). At the very commencement, Dragut was killed by a splinter of stone; the siege nevertheless continued; but, after a whole month of murderous struggles, the Turks only succeeded in capturing fort Saint Elmo. "If the son has cost us so dearly, what will it cost to take the father?" said the Seraskier Mustapha Pacha, on reckoning up his losses. To intimidate the garrison, he caused the prisoners to be quartered, and their limbs to be nailed upon planks in the form of a cross which were flung at the foot of the walls. The Grand Master of Valetta responded to these barbarities by causing his guns to be loaded with the heads of the Turkish prisoners, and so fired instead of balls. An old Christian slave was sent to summon him to surrender: he led him upon the ramparts, and pointing to the ditches, he said: "That is the only ground that I can yield to your master; let him fill it up with the bodies of his Janissaries." On the 11th of September, after three months and a half of siege and ten assaults, the Turkish army re-embarked.

9. Renewal of the War in Hungary.—Siege of Szigeth.— Death of Solyman.

The peace signed with Austria had already been broken. At the death of Ferdinand (1564), Maximilian, his successor, demanded the renewal of the truce. But, at that moment, Zapoly's son Stephen attacked the Austrian town of Szathmar and took it. Maximilian replied to that blow by surprising Tokay. During the course of the discussions to which this double infraction of the peace gave rise, the Vizier Ali Pacha died (1565). His successor was Mahomet Sokolli or Sokolowitch, a Bosnian slave, the greatest minister the Turkish Empire ever had. He breathed nothing but war against Austria, and it recommenced immediately. Erdœd in Transylvania, Pankotta, Kruppa, Novi in Croatia, fell into the power of the Ottomans. At length, in 1566, Solyman, ill and tormented by the gout, took the command of his army. Without waiting for his arrival, the governor of Ofen, Arslan Bey, laid siege to Palota, but an army commanded by Count Eck de Salm forced him to beat a retreat, and Tata and Wesprim were taken. When Arslan Bey made his appearance in the Sultan's camp, he paid the price of that reverse by the loss of his head. On the 29th of June, Solyman, having reached Czabacz, received in solemn audience the youthful Stephen Zapoly; he welcomed him affectionately, called him his son, and promised him that he would not quit Hungary before confirming him in possession of it; but the Hungarian Prince committed the error of quarrelling with the Grand Vizier, and the malevolence of that minister was destined to bring about his ruin.

Solyman formed the project of marching upon Erlau, in order to efface the affront inflicted upon his arms fourteen years previously; but on learning that a Turkish *corps d'armée*, together with a favourite Pacha, had been destroyed by Nicholas Zriny, Palatine of Szigeth, he resolved to go first and chastise him. The siege of Szigeth, the family seat of that noble near Fünfkirchen, was begun on the 5th of April. Determined to fight even to the death, Zriny exhibited a certain degree of pomp in the defence: he had the walls hung with red draperies and the principal tower covered with plates of brilliant tin. Solyman, on his arrival, with an army of 100,000 men and 300 guns, was courteously saluted by the cannon of the place. At the end of fourteen days, the exterior works were taken; the besieged had abandoned the town and burnt it, shutting themselves up in the citadel and there making a fierce resistance. This siege afforded another instance of the unskilfulness of the Turks in such operations. In vain the Sultan tried to shake Zriny by promises or threats; in vain was it attempted to cause division amongst the besieged or to discourage them by false news; on the 5th of September—that is to say, after more than four months—the Turks had only succeeded in destroying the principal bastion. On that day, Solyman, long ailing from the consequence of fatigue and the unwholesome air of the marshes, died. The Grand Vizier resolved to cautiously conceal that event; the secret remaining between two or three persons; pretended letters from the Sultan were read to the army in the form of orders of the day, to animate the courage of the soldiers, and the attacks were renewed. At length, on the 8th of September, Zriny found himself driven back into the great tower, which he had converted into a powder magazine. He then dressed himself in a suit of silk, took the most ancient of the sabres he had won, put in his pocket a hundred ducats and the keys of the fortress; then ordered the gates to be thrown open. At the moment when the Janissaries approached, an enormous cannon, placed under the archway, vomited upon them, almost point blank, a discharge of grape-shot; amidst the smoke, preceded by his banner-bearer and followed by an esquire, rushed forth the Palatine; he threw himself furiously into the thickest of his enemies, and laid low a considerable number. He was, however, taken alive, bound across the mouth of a cannon, and had his head struck off. The Janissaries, maddened with rage, threw themselves upon the citadel, massacred all therein, snatching hold of the women and children and tearing them in pieces. Amidst the carnage, the tower, already mined, blew up with a terrible concussion and buried three thousand of the victors in its ruins.

The death of the Sultan was still kept concealed during three weeks; letters announcing the victory were sent forth in his name; the Divan assembled as usual, and the Vizier conducted affairs until the moment when he learned that the heir to the throne had arrived in Constantinople.

Solyman had long been in bad health. Besides the gout, he was subject to attacks of melancholia, and lay sometimes totally unconscious in a swoon or trance. Navagero[*] describes him, at the age of sixty-two, as much above the middle height, but meagre, and of a yellow complexion; yet there was a wonderful grandeur in his aspect, accompanied by a gentleness that won all hearts. He was a rigid Mussulman, and insisted on a precise observance of all the precepts of the Korân. He was very temperate in his diet, ate but little meat, and amused himself chiefly with hunting. In his moments of depres-

[*] Relatione of Navagero, in Alberi's Collection.

sion he was wont to humble himself before God, and composed spiritual hymns, in which he compared his nothingness with the power of the Almighty. He was very scrupulous in keeping his word; he loved justice, and never knowingly did wrong to anybody. In short, allowance being made for his Turkish education and prejudices, he may be very advantageously compared with several Christian Princes, his contemporaries.

The long reign of Solyman, signalized externally by such vast conquests, by such a great development of power, is not less remarkable in that which concerns internal administration, institutions and legislation. It is even from this last point of view that Solyman is especially illustrious among the Ottomans: they call him *El-Kanouni*, the legislator. His attention was particularly directed to the organization of the ulemas, to the system of fiefs, to finance, justice, civil and penal law, the army, &c.

In the *chain of the ulemas*, the sub-divisions were multiplied, the advancement regulated, the hierarchy rendered more rigorous. New privileges also were granted to the members of that learned corporation: such as exemption from taxation and hereditary right in the family, in such wise that the property of the ulemas never contributed to the exchequer. It was at that epoch that the dignity of mufti became the first in the judicial and religious orders; it must be attributed especially to the extraordinary estimation which the celebrated mufti Ebon-Sooud enjoyed, who preserved under the two following reigns his title and authority.

The arrangements relative to the fiefs are one of the most important portions of the legislation of Solyman; they were for the most part supported by *fetwas* delivered by the mufti. According to the political and religious doctrine of the Mussulmans, the soil belonged to God, and, consequently, to the Sultan, his representative; the lands, however, were divided into three classes: 1. the lands occupied by Mussulmans after conquest, which were only subjected to the tithe; 2. the lands let to conquered populations, to *rayahs*, and for which they paid besides the tithe,

the *Kharadj*, that is to say, the capitation and territorial impost; 3. the domains given by the Sultans in the shape of military rewards under the names of *timars* and *ziamets*, and the institution of which dates from the reign of Amurath I. Solyman at first regulated the levy of the tithes, then that of the Kharadj, in a mode to render the one and the other less onerous and more productive; he regulated also the arbitrary imposts, levied by virtue of *Kanouns*, upon marriages, merchandize, foreigners, duties, &c. Lastly, he occupied himself with timars and ziamets, the possession of which gave place to a host of abuses. The proprietors of these domains levied upon their peasants, farm rents, a territorial tax and a tithe, which often exceeded by far the tenth of the produce; they themselves paying no ground rent to the treasury; they were only held upon oath to afford military service : thus, as already said,* for a timar of 3,000 aspres income, the tenant was bound to furnish, in time of war, a horseman fully equipped, and another horseman for every income of 5,000 aspres over and above. That system resembled Western feudalism, but differed from it in that it was exempt from the principle of hereditary right. When Amurath I., in the origin, distributed to his horsemen the conquered lands, those concessions were only for life; the fiefs were transferred ordinarily from father to son, but it was incumbent upon each new possessor to receive investiture. Amurath, had moreover, taken care to prevent those fiefs from being parcelled out, or alienated : several timars might be combined in a ziamet, but a ziamet never could be divided into timars, several individuals possessed, sometimes collectively, a fief, great or small; but they represented together only one head. The measures taken under Solyman had at first for object the regulating and moderating the taxes levied upon the rayahs by the possession of fiefs, then to preserve to those fiefs their precarious and revocable nature, to hinder the hereditary transmission, to maintain and affirm the prerogative of the sovereign. The governors of provinces

* See p. 78.

originally conferred the investiture of fiefs; but it was decided later that they could no longer confer it save for the small fiefs; when it concerned a ziamet, it was obligatory to refer to the Porte in order that proof might be obtained that the candidate was the son of a Sipahi, to ascertain his services, those of his father and the income which the latter had enjoyed; upon the favourable report of the Pacha, the *berat* or diploma of investiture was expedited. It was established as an invariable maxim that no one could receive a timar unless he were the son of a timarli. If the possessor of a ziamet of 20,000 to 50,000 aspres left several children, the latter could at first receive only one timar, it was from 4,000 to 6,000 for two sons if their father had perished in war, and if the father had died in his bed, 5,000 for two sons and 4,000 for one only. If the sons already possessed timars, there was allotted to them only a proportional augmentation.

Egypt was subjected to a particular administration. There were neither fiefs nor ziamets there, but farmers; there were also lands granted for life by the Sultan, transferred hereditarily by means of a new investiture conferred upon each new incumbent, the farmers (*moultezim*) levied likewise upon their peasants (*fellahs*), the tithe and tax, but they returned a portion of it to the treasury under the name of farm rent;* instead of military service, a contribution in money was demanded from them. That system had been established in the fourteenth century by the Mamelukes, it was maintained under the Ottoman domination; the Grand Vizier Ibrahim, in 1525, and later the governor Solyman Pacha, were charged with its reorganization, in a manner to weaken the Mameluke militia, to correct its abuses, to prevent the farmer from being illegally alienated or overburdened by mortgages.

* The *Moultezims* being only farmers, whose interest it was to squeeze their fellahs, there resulted from that state of things an oppression which necessitated continually the employment of force, and soon rendered the military chiefs alone able to hold the farms; then heirship established itself by degrees, and the French invasion found it there in full operation in 1798.—(Sacy, "Mémoires sur la Conquête de l'Egypte.")

Egypt produced to the treasury, by that financial system, at first 800,000 ducats, afterwards 1,200,000.

It will thus be seen what were the regular sources of public revenue: the Kharadj, the tithe, the farm rents, and divers duties; to these must be added the revenues of the Sultan's domains, which reached the enormous sum of 2,441 charges of aspres, that is to say about 5,000,000 ducats. These resources, however, became insufficient. At the commencement of Solyman's reign, before the campaign of Mohacz, an extraordinary contribution was laid of fifteen aspres per head, but that device was not repeated: the products of war, the tributes of Christian nations, the spoils of conquered provinces, supplemented deficiencies; Hungary, Transylvania, were subjected to a financial rule which exhausted those unhappy provinces to the profit of their masters. Finally, the venality of the fiscal burdens, the introduction of which began under the vizier Rustem, contributed to enrich the treasury, but at the expense of the future. Solyman shut his eyes to that traffic, he only kept watch, with extreme rigour, that venality should not reach the military departments.

The *Kanoun-nami* of punishments decreed under Solyman is still at the present time the criminal legislation of the Ottomans. It is divided into five parts: the first relates to offences against morals; the second to violence and injuries; the third to thefts and brigandage; the two last to the police of towns and the regulation of trades. Without entering into detail of these enacting clauses, it may be observed that corporal punishments are very sparing therein: a fine is the punishment most frequently apportioned; there is a tariff for every offence. The particular attention accorded to police regulations of markets, to all which concerns the popular welfare, reveal, in Solyman, a prince truly enlightened and of a careful spirit in all their details.

Notwithstanding all that presents itself as remarkable in the legislation of Solyman, notwithstanding the brilliancy of his reign and the glory of his name, it must be recognized, and the Ottoman historians have themselves confessed it, that he himself commenced the decadence of his empire and contributed powerfully to change its institutions. It has been seen that, since Mahomet II. the Sultans no longer ordinarily presided over the Divan; Solyman ceased entirely to appear thereat; he was never to be seen in council. That custom, borrowed from the manners of the effeminate despots of Asia, favoured sloth and indolence among his successors. He himself suffered from the consequences of it: he could not escape from the baneful influences of the harem, and was the first Sultan who allowed himself to be governed by a woman. He was also the first who made a minister of a favourite: Ibrahim passed from a domestic employment to the supreme direction of affairs; so sudden an elevation was until then without example. He showed, moreover, for that favourite, and even for the ministers who succeeded him, an excessive indulgence, made them colossal fortunes at the expense either of the treasury or the people—or, rather, at the expense of both. It has been already said that he tolerated venality in fiscal burdens, a scourge which, under the following reigns, developed itself with a frightful rapidity, and ruined the State. Finally, his example, that of his viziers, and of all his court, encouraged luxury, so formally condemned by the law of Mahomet, and carried it to such a degree that the surroundings of the Christian princes of the West paled before the pomp of Constantinople. At a solemn feast given to a Persian embassy, the court tables were served in vessels of gold and silver—an express violation of the Korân. Sensuality and love of luxury had, indeed, spread throughout that nation formed for war, and corrupted the simplicity of manners which was necessary to preserve its vigour. The use of wine, so severely interdicted, and so fatal to the Southern nations, began to be common, to the great scandal of zealous Mussulmans. Coffee was also introduced at this time into Turkey; Mahomet would probably have interdicted it; but it was not cared to interpret the law so rigorously, and the use of that exciting beverage soon became general, and was carried to excess. Several acts of his latter years seemed to testify in

Solyman to a certain access of religious zeal; but that was doubtless a result of old age : at bottom, tolerance was one of the principal traits of his character. He appeared even to sympathize with the manners of the nation : thus the native poets ventured to turn into ridicule the interdictions of the law ; Hafiz sang the praise of wine, and the Mufti Ebon Sooud, when urged to prosecute him, replied that he must not judge him with too much rigour. The progress would have been salutary could it have been completed, if a complete approach had been effected between the morals and ideas of the Mussulman nation and those of Europe ; but many Solymans would not then have sufficed to accomplish that fusion, to fill up that immense abyss which separated those two adverse societies. The little that was done only served to alter the national institutions.

The army itself began to enter on a path of decadence. At the end of Solyman's reign its strength amounted to 300,000 men, of which 50,000 only were regular troops, 300 pieces of cannon, and 280 vessels of war. His chief strength was in the Janissaries, whose power had then reached its height, at the same time that its weakness commenced. Their pay was increased, and they were divided into three categories; the recruits received from three to seven aspres per diem, the veterans from eight to twenty aspres, the invalids from thirty to a hundred aspres. Solyman had a lively affection for those turbulent warriors: he confided to them the keeping of Constantinople, which became their head-quarters and the residence of their chief, always chosen from amongst them; he distributed them in all the great towns and strongholds of the empire; they furnished the guards of honour to the ambassadors and foreign consuls. Their number soon became insufficient for all the services required of them, and it was necessary to summon recruits to their ranks, no longer only by the conscription of Christian youths, but by many privileges which attracted to the corps adventurers of every kind. They were permitted to marry, their sons were admitted into the ranks, they were allowed to follow trades, they became stationary in the garrisons they occupied, and wherein, as citizens, fathers of families, merchants, operatives, they had no longer either discipline or military virtues. Lastly, the title of Janissary being a sufficient protection against the exactions of local authorities, each desired to be inscribed upon their register; and the corps of Janissaries, which was formerly an army permanently mobilised, encamped, on the march, waging war, became a kind of national guard. Solyman took from them also the privilege they had of entering upon a campaign only when the Sultan commanded the army. That was a great political error: as the Janissaries were the nerve of the armies, it followed that, for every important expedition, the Sultans were compelled to take the command. Solyman freed his successors from that obligation, and favoured by that measure their proclivity to inertia and cowardice. Thus, in the acts of that reign, so prosperous within, so brilliant abroad, are to be found the primal causes of the degradation of the princes, of the corruption of the great men, of the enervation of the people, of the weakening of the army—in a word, all the germs of a decadence that was not tardy in revealing itself.

II.

FROM THE DEATH OF SOLYMAN TO THE PEACE OF CARLOWITZ.
(1566-1699.)

CHAPTER V.

REIGNS OF SELIM II. AND AMURATH III. (1566-1595.)

1. *Selim II. surnamed the Drunkard* (1566—1574). *Revolt of the Janissaries.—Peace with Austria.*

Selim II. arrived at Chalcedon on the 24th of September, whence he despatched a messenger to Constantinople to announce his presence; it was thus that it became known in the capital that Solyman had ceased to live. After having received at the Seraglio the homage of the principal dignitaries, the new Sultan set out for Belgrade, whither the army went to salute him. He made his appearance, clad in mourning, prayed beside the funeral car that bore the remains of his father, and withdrew, saluting to the right and left, without anything being said or done touching the accession donative. The Janissaries began to murmur: "The Ottoman princes," they said aloud, "in order to ascend the throne, ought to pass under the sabres of our militia." Nevertheless, they continued their march to Constantinople; and it was there that they broke into revolt. When Selim's retinue made its appearance at the Sublime Porte, it found the entrance obstructed by a dense crowd of Janissaries, clamouring for the accession donative, and disposed to show very little respect for their new Sultan. The second vizier, the Capudan-Pacha, the aga of the Janissaries, and several other great officers strove in vain to calm the mutineers; they found themselves insulted and maltreated; the outer court of the Seraglio was invaded; the Sultan was compelled to show himself. "Give to us!" shouted the soldiers to him, "Give to us according to ancient custom." The accession donative was at length accorded, and the distribution of numerous other gratifications amongst the officers of the Seraglio and the ulemas resulted in the exhaustion of the treasury. Thus opened the reign of Solyman's successor.

Selim is the first of the Ottoman Sultans who proved to be utterly unworthy of the throne. He commenced the series of do-nothing princes whose personal nullity has powerfully contributed to the decadence of the empire. From early youth he was wont to stupify himself by the immoderate use of wine, and when governor of Magnesia he was already designated by the appellation of *the Drunkard*. Slothful and cowardly, he had always preferred the repose of the harem to the fatigues and dangers of war. Short and obese, his flushed complexion and insignificant physiognomy, typified vividly the decadence of the nation. Happily he had sufficient good sense to leave all the cares of Government to his vizier Sokolli, who preserved the traditions of the last great reign, and maintained the dignity of the empire in its foreign relations. The decadence only became visible after his death.

Immediately after the capture of Sigeth, negotiations for peace were opened; the Austrian ambassadors were set free, and the conditions upon which it was possible to treat made known to them. Hostilities, however, did not cease: Pertew Pacha, who had taken Gyoula, in Transylvania, a few days previous to the death of Solyman, again seized upon Jenæ, Valagosvar, and several other places; the banks of the Maros were devastated. At length, peace was concluded (17th of February, 1568): Austria retained her possessions in Hungary, Dalmatia, and Croatia; she submitted to the annual tribute and recognized the Voïvodes of Transylvania, Moldavia, and Wallachia, as vassals of the Porte. To obtain these conditions, the Austrian negotiators distributed more than 40,000 ducats among the Turkish ministers.

Peace was also renewed with Poland, which obtained the restitution of several strongholds.

2. *Relations with France.*

The alliance of France was not neglected: in 1569, on the first demand of the ambassador Claude du Bourg,* the Sultan renewed the capitulations with important modifications, and sent the interpreter Ibrahim to Paris to present them to King Charles IX. Those modifications chiefly consisted in a clearer, more minute, more detailed interpretation of the first articles, an interpretation rendered necessary by the barbarism of the Turks and their hatred of the Christians. To the old privileges several new ones were also added: every Frenchman, settled in the country, was perpetually exempted from the capitation tax; the ambassadors and consuls had the right of making search after French slaves who found themselves in the power of Mussulmans and of demanding punishment of the corsairs who had captured and sold them. The Sultan engaged to make restitution for the objects carried off by the corsairs from French vessels and to punish the perpetrators; the Ottoman marine had orders to treat French ships amicably, and to lend them assistance in case of running aground on the shores of Turkey, and cause the persons and effects of the shipwrecked to be respected. Finally the French nation should enjoy, in the Ottoman States, all the privileges accorded to the Venetians, even those which they had purchased with money. Thanks to these large concessions, whilst Spain and the Venetians were exhausting themselves in warlike efforts against the Ottoman power, France was mistress of the commerce of the Mediterranean.

* To d'Aramon had succeeded, in 1554, Codignat, who betrayed France and passed into the service of Philip II. After him came Lavigne, who remained at Constantinople from 1557 to 1561; then Guillaume de l'Aube, who accompanied Solyman in his last campaign; then Gran-Campagne, who strove to bring about the failure of the treaty concluded between Austria and the Porte in 1568; lastly, Claude du Bourg.

"The Mediterranean," the Algerian corsairs complained, "is all swarming with French ships." Those vessels carried on the coasting trade upon the shores of Turkey, without paying any navigation dues. The coral fishers from Marseilles possessed several establishments on the African coast, among which was one called the Bastion of France, a sort of exchange-house situate some six miles from Bona, where a commerce in grain, wax and horses was carried on. Catholic missions were founded in the Turkish States by consent of the Sultan, and capuchin convents were seen to locate themselves even in the suburbs of Constantinople. The Christians of the East, and especially those of Syria, found in the French ambassadors and consuls protectors ever prompt to defend them against the persecutions of the Turks. Pilgrims of every nation could visit the Holy Places under the protection of the Frankish name and the letters of the ambassadors. The French flag floated over the monasteries of Syria, which appeared like oases of Christianity amidst the Mahometan domination.

Selim, after the renewal of the capitulations, sought, after the example of his father, to utilize the French alliance against his enemies. As he had formed a project of taking the island of Cyprus from the Venetians, and as the latter sought the aid of Europe, he sent an embassy to Charles IX. to invite him to declare France against them. At the same time, he suggested to him that he should give his sister Margaret of Valois in marriage to Stephen Zapoly, Voïvode of Transylvania, whom the Porte had the project of causing to be elected King of Poland. That union would, in the opinion of the Divan, bind Poland to France and Turkey, and thus give a new enemy to Austria, who would restrain her on the north, whilst Turkey confined her on the east and France to the south. Charles IX. had no fleet, and could not, amidst the troubles of his kingom, aid either the Ottomans or the Venetians; he offered, however, his mediation to the one or the other; but he rejected the proposition to marry his sister to the vassal of the Turks, France having adjourned all her projects against the House of Austria, from which Charles

IX. had himself just taken a wife; nevertheless, he conceived, from that moment, the idea of attaching Poland directly with French policy, by causing his brother, the Duke of Anjou, to ascend the throne of the Jagellons.

3. *Expedition to Arabia.*

Within the Empire, the activity of Mahomet Sokolli manifested itself by works of utility, and by the prompt repression of revolts, usual upon every accession. It was he who caused the mosque that bears the name of Selim to be constructed, and which is considered the masterpiece of the architect Sinan. He had conceived the project of uniting the Don with the Volga by a canal, and, by that means, securing the domination of the Muscovite countries; to effect that it was necessary to be master of Astrakhan; but the *corps d'armée* that ought to have taken that city was defeated and dispersed by the Russians. The Ottoman troops had shown very little goodwill on this occasion; they were persuaded that the north was closed to the Mussulmans. "The nights," they said, "were too short in summer; it was necessary to break one's rest in order to offer up sunset prayer and that of daybreak." Hunger, cold, and tempestuous weather destroyed a portion of the army, the renewal of peace was therefore hastened with the Muscovite Czar, and the enterprise was abandoned. Another enterprise of the same kind, the piercing of the Isthmus of Suez, entered also into the projects of the vizier; but the continual insurrections in Arabia adjourned the execution of it indefinitely.

Since a portion of that country had been conquered by Solyman and reduced into a sandjak, Arabia was almost perpetually in a state of revolt. Already, on the accession of Selim, Oulian Oglou, chief of the Beni-Omer, had tried to throw off the yoke; deprived of the support of the Persians, upon which he reckoned, he was easily overcome. The country, however, was not subdued. Mouthahher, chief of the sect of the Seïdijes,* seized upon Ssaana, Taas, Aden, and several other places in Yemen; assuming the titles of Khalife and Emir-al-Moumenim. An army destined to reduce him was placed under the command of Lala Mustapha, become one of the principal favourites of the Sultan. The vizier, who detested him and dreaded his influence, contributed himself to get him nominated Seraskier, in the hope of involving him in some disgrace. These manœuvres, and the jealousy of Sinan Pacha, Governor of Egypt, caused the expedition to miscarry, and Mustapha to be recalled to Constantinople, but they did not succeed in depriving him of his master's favour. Osman Pacha, nominated Beylerbey of Yemen, and the Governor of Egypt, were charged with the enterprise (1569); the first seized upon Taas and Kahirije; the second remained alone at the head of the troops, and completed the expedition successfully. Aden and Ssaana fell again into the power of the Ottomans, as well as the greater number of the adjacent strongholds; the fortress of Kewkeban detained them during nine months. Finally, in 1570, the Iman Mouthahher was reduced to submission and to recognize the suzerainty of the Porte.

4. *Conquest of Cyprus.*

The pacification of Yemen was immediately followed by the conquest of Cyprus. Selim had long meditated that expedition; it was that one of all his reign in which his personal will had the most part. He had conceived the idea of it when he was yet only Governor of Magnesia, and that conviction had been confirmed, it is said, by his taste for the wine which that island produced. A Portuguese Jew, named Joseph Nassy—so the story runs— incited the wine-bibbing Sultan to undertake the expedition against Cyprus by representing in glowing terms the excellence of its wine. This man, by ministering to his crapulous tastes, had acquired a marvellous ascendancy

* This sect took its name from Seïd, great-grandson of Ali.

FAMAGOSTA. [page 247.

over him; he had received a promise of being made King of Cyprus, and, meanwhile, had been named Duke of Naxos and the Cyclades. The Grand Vizier would have done better to have turned the Ottoman forces against Spain in favour of the Moors, who had sought the Sultan's protection; he made representations to that effect, but they could not prevail against the influence of the Jew, of Lala Mustapha, of Sinan Pacha, and of Selim's own inclination. The Grand Mufti Ebou-Sooud issued a *fetwa* declaring that the treaties concluded with the infidels were not binding, and that it was the duty of the Sultans to reconquer all countries which had belonged to the Moslems. The Venetians were indisposed for war: their great arsenal had just been destroyed by fire, burnt, perhaps, by agents of Joseph Nassy; they made some efforts to conjure the storm, but as the cession of Cyprus was demanded as a condition of peace, hostilities commenced.

On the 1st of July, 1570, the Turkish Fleet appeared before Limasol, near the ancient Amathonte; it consisted of 136 galleys and more than 100 transports, under the command of Piali Pacha; the army landed, commanded by Lala Mustapha, was about 100,000 strong. The Venetian Governor did not attempt to hinder the disembarkation; the Turks established themselves, without encountering any resistance, at Leftari, and determined to besiege Nicosia, the capital of the island. That town, finely situated, was protected by strong entrenchments of recent construction, and defended by a garrison of 10,000 men; but the unskilfulness of the governor paralyzed the defence. The siege lasted for more than a month; three assaults were bravely repulsed; at length, on the 9th of September, the place was carried and delivered up during eight hours to all the horrors of pillage. Twenty thousand inhabitants were massacred; 2,000 were crammed into the vessels holding booty; but a woman set fire to them, and all perished in the flames or in the waves.

The other towns were afterwards rapidly subdued; Famagousta alone opposed an energetic resistance; the siege of it was deferred until the following year, and the

Seraskier wintered under its walls. The operations commenced on the 16th of April, and were pushed forwards with great activity; a vast fosse was dug round the town, and behind it ten batteries were erected which thundered against the ramparts. Marc Antonio Bragadino, who commanded the place, showed no less stubbornness in its defence. With a garrison of but 7,000 men and the fortifications in ruins, he held out during two months and a half and repulsed six assaults. The want of munitions compelled him at length to capitulate (2nd of August, 1571); it was agreed that the besieged should retire freely with five cannons and fifteen horses, and should be conveyed in Turkish galleys to Candia. The capitulation was already in part executed, when it was shamefully violated. Bragadino, having refused to deliver up as a hostage a young Venetian noble, was arrested and loaded with chains, as were those who accompanied him; the Christians already embarked were despoiled, maltreated, massacred, or reduced to slavery. Then, at the expiration of twelve days, the brave Bragadino was drawn from his prison to be delivered over to the most atrocious torments. He was suspended from a yard-arm, from the height of which he was several times plunged into the sea; he was afterwards compelled to carry earth for the construction of bastions; he was put in the pillory; lastly, he was flayed alive; his body was quartered, and his skin, stuffed with hay, carried through the camp and town, and then, with his head, sent to Constantinople.

These atrocities aroused the anger of the fiery and enthusiastic Pius V., one of whose darling projects had always been to curb the power and insolence of the Turk.

By his exertions an alliance against the Sultan, called the Holy League, was at length concluded between himself, Philip II., the Venetians, and one or two other minor Powers. The French tendered nothing save their good offices. Before the end of September, 1571, the Allied Fleet, consisting of seventy-seven Spanish, six Maltese, and three Savoyard galleys, under Don John of Austria, twelve Papal galleys under Marc Colonna, and 108 Venetian galleys and six galeazzi under Sebastian Ventero, Captain-General at sea, assembled at Messina.

5. *The Battle of Lepanto.*

The war had begun in Dalmatia at the same time as it had in Cyprus; its successes on either side were balanced: the Venetians surprised Sopoto in Albania; the Capudan-Pacha ravaged Candia, Cerigo, Zante, Cephalonia, Navarino, and seized upon Dulcigno and Antivari. At the commencement of hostilities, the Venetians made several attempts at negotiation, encouraged by the vizier, who desired peace; but, at the news of the ravages committed in Candia, the negotiations were broken off, and the formidable league of the Christian Powers above described was formed to avenge the cruelties inflicted in Cyprus upon the Christians. The Porte became uneasy at it, and, by the intervention of the French Ambassador, who returned to Paris, it requested the mediation of France. François de Noailles, Bishop of d'Acqs, was appointed Ambassador to Constantinople, and charged with negotiating that affair; he passed by way of Venice, and took part with the Senate in its preparations against the Ottomans, having failed in his pacific mission. The Christian Fleet set sail for Corfu, then towards Cephalonia; thence it directed its course to the Archipelago. The Ottoman Fleet, of 300 sail, under Musinsade Ali, was posted at the entrance of the Gulf of Lepanto. The Christians determined to attack it; the Turks came out to meet them. The two naval armaments were ranged up facing each other, within sight of Cape Villa di Marmo, which stands at the entrance of the gulf. A cannon shot, fired from the Ottoman Admiral's vessel, gave the signal for the fray; Don John replied to it by a ball of large size, and the battle began.

The thickest of the fight took place at the centre of the Christian Fleet, round the vessel having on board Don John; the Capudan-Pacha vigorously attacking the Christian line, found himself engaged between the Spanish admiral and the Venetian admiral. On one side, four Ottoman galleys, commanded by the Seraskier and three Sandjak Beys; on the other, the Christian rear-guard hastened to sustain the struggle. After an hour of fierce fighting, the Capudan-Pacha fell, struck by a ball; whereupon the Spaniards rushed aboard his ship, cut off his head, and carried it to Don John, who rejected the sanguinary trophy with horror. The victory was from that moment decided. One hundred and thirty galleys fell into the hands of the allies; ninety-four were burnt; 360 pieces of cannon and 15,000 Christian slaves were brought back in triumph. The Beylerbey of Algiers alone escaped with forty galleys, the sole remains of the Ottoman Fleet.

That brilliant victory only cost the combined fleets fifteen galleys, 8,000 men, and some few prisoners. In this battle, which, though really won by the power of Venice, created the reputation of Don John of Austria, were also present two men who, like him, were afterwards to be governors of the Netherlands: Don Louis de Requesens, Grand Commander of Castile, and Alexander Farnese, the nephew of Don John. A fourth name may be added, subsequently immortalised in literature—that of Cervantes, the author of "Don Quixote," who was wounded and lost his left arm in the combat with the Turk.

Such was the memorable battle of Lepanto, from which the Ottomans may date the decline of their power. The tidings of it were received throughout Europe with transport. Mark Antony Colonna ascended the capitol like the triumphers of old, and vowed upon the altar of the Virgin a column of silver to call to mind his name and his victory. At Venice, a commemorative fête was instituted, and a chapel was consecrated, on the walls of which was depicted the triumph of the Christians; at Padua, the great church then being constructed was dedicated to St. Justine, in remembrance of the day on which the battle was fought. Lastly, the Sovereign

Pontiff, in St. Peter's Chair at Rome, celebrated that great success with enthusiasm, and applied to the Victor of Lepanto that text of the Evangelist: "There was a man sent from God, whose name was John."

The consternation was not less great at Constantinople than the joy among the Christians. It was the most terrible disaster that had yet befallen the Ottoman arms; for fifty years, the Turks had been the terror of the Mediterranean; masters of the African littoral, accustomed to carry devastation along the coasts of Christian countries and to put to flight the feeble squadrons of Spain, they suddenly saw annihilated that formidable marine collected so laboriously by Selim I. and Solyman. Their unworthy successor, on learning the catastrophe, was so cast down, that he remained for three days shut up without taking any nourishment. "The battle of Lepanto cost the Ottomans more than men and ships, the loss of which can be repaired; for they lost that influence of prestige which constitutes the chief power of conquering peoples, a power that is once acquired but never found again."*

6. *Embassy from France.—Peace with Venice.*

Meanwhile, arrived the French Ambassador François de Noailles; he entered Constantinople amidst the general consternation, through the furious shouts of the populace, who clamoured for the massacre of all the Christians. The Sultan had even already caused the Frankish monks to be imprisoned, and grievous affliction was expected, when the ambassador, by his entreaties to the Grand Vizier, by the threat of compelling France to enter the Catholic league, obtained the deliverance of the prisoners. The principal mission of the Bishop d'Acqs was to bring about a peace between the Ottomans and the Venetians. When he solicited an audience of the Sultan, he experienced a refusal, because it was known that he intended, contrary to custom, to carry thither no presents; it was even

* Bonald, " Legislation Primitive."

offered, to keep up appearances, to provide him with them. To this offer, he replied "that it was not through avarice that the King of France refused to make the Grand Seignior presents, but that his master, who was the first and greatest king in Christendom, having known that the Sultan demanded them as tribute, had forbidden him to present any." The circumstances warranted that boldness; there was need of the French alliance; its mediation might become necessary: the audience was granted. " The ambassador having presented himself at the Turkish Porte," says the historian Baudier, " as two capidjis offered to lead him by his wrists towards Selim to make his obeisance, according to the custom that no stranger should approach the Turkish Emperor without two men holding him by the arms, he would not suffer himself to be thus led, remarking that the freedom of a Frenchman and the dignity of a bishop would not endure that he should be conducted like a slave; and, repulsing the capidjis, he went free and alone towards Selim, saluting him only by kissing his robe and his hand, without throwing himself at his feet as every one else does."* Those irregularities were tolerated, and an extraordinary complaisance for the demands of the bishop was shown. His conduct even earned for him a certain personal consideration, which was not unserviceable to the success of his mission.

The victory of Lepanto, however, had been sterile for Christianity: the allied fleets dispersed without undertaking anything on account of the advanced period of the year. During that time the activity of Sokolli repaired the losses of the Ottoman marine with a marvellous promptitude; and that great reverse only served to show more clearly what were the resources of Turkey. The Venetian *bayle*, who had remained at Constantinople notwithstanding the war, repaired to the Vizier to sound his intentions with regard to peace. "Have you come to see," said Sokolli, " with what courage we bear this last misadventure? We have lost less than you have; in

* "Inventaire de l'Histoire des Turcs," p. 413.

capturing Cyprus we have cut off one of your arms; in fighting our fleet you have only shaved off our beard: the lopped arm will not grow again, but the shaven beard will return thicker than before." The dockyards were enriched at the expense of the Seraglio gardens; in the space of a single winter 150 galleys were built therein. The new Capudan-Pacha, Ouloudj Ali, representing that it was not possible to procure enough anchors and rigging for so many vessels at once: "Seignior Pacha," replied the Vizier, "the riches and power of the Sublime Porte are so infinite, that it could, if that were necessary, provide ropes of silk and sails of satin." In the month of June, 1572, the Capudan-Pacha went to sea with a fleet of 250 sail. The Christian fleet was numerically stronger; but the misunderstanding amongst its commanders hindered its action, and both sides confined themselves to observing each other. The war in Dalmatia, however, was languidly waged; and shortly the Venetians, wholly at loggerheads with the Spaniards, made propositions of peace which were zealously supported in the Divan by the French Ambassador; and on the 7th of March, 1573, a treaty was concluded as favourable for the Ottomans as though the war had been entirely to their advantage: Venice paid an indemnity of 300,000 ducats, and the tribute which she paid annually was augmented.

7. Capture of Tunis.—Affairs of Poland and Moldavia.— Death of Selim.

During the Cyprus expedition, Tunis had been retaken by the Ottomans; they had driven out the Moorish prince whom Charles V. had reinstated there, and fort Goulette was the only one remaining in the possession of the Spaniards. On the 7th of October, 1572, Don John of Austria set out from Sicily to retake Tunis; at his approach the Turks evacuated the city; he entered therein without resistance, again reinstated the Moorish prince with a Spanish garrison, and erected new fortifications.

But that conquest was of short duration. Eighteen months after, in May 1574, a fleet of nearly 300 sail left Constantinople to snatch Tunis from the grasp of the Spaniards. The town was badly defended, but fort Goulette resisted during thirty-three days; it was at length taken by assault on the 4th of August, and the garrison made prisoners or put to the sword. Two small forts still held out, that on the island and that called the bastion of Tunis: after a vigorous resistance they were carried.

About the same time important events were taking place in Poland and Moldavia. The relations established between Boghdan and King Sigismund were regarded unfavourably by the Porte; an adventurer named Iwonia, a former renegade returned to the Christian faith, solicited and obtained the investiture of Moldavia with a body of Turkish troops to enable him to hold it. Boghdan was at first sustained by the Poles; but the death of Sigismund (7th of July, 1572) having left him without support he fled to Russia, where the Czar had him put to death. Iwonia left master of Moldavia, refused to submit to an increase of tribute and raised the province (1574); sustained by the Hetman of the Cossacks, he thrice defeated the Turks and seized upon Braïla which was sacked, upon Bender, Akerman and Bielogrod. On the 9th of June, he encountered at Obloutsch, in Bulgaria, an Ottoman army. After three days of sanguinary fighting, he began to parley and surrendered, on condition that his life should be spared; but, during the interview he had with the Turkish commander, the latter flew into a rage and struck him with his sabre; he was quartered and his head nailed to the palace gate of Jassy. The country submitted and a new prince was installed in the name of the Porte.

In Poland the royal race had become extinct in the person of Sigismund; but for a long time the event had been foreseen; everything had been concerted between France and Turkey, and it was one of the chief objects of the Bishop of Acqs' mission. The united influence of the two Powers caused Henri of Anjou to be elected, an election which might have had immense results if the prince upon whom it fell had been less incapable.

Pacific relations continued with Austria, notwithstanding several infractions of the peace; the truce was renewed for eight years, and the ambassadors were even able to free themselves from certain humiliating obligations. With the Muscovites, friendly relations were also kept up, but at the same time, preserving towards them a protective and dominating attitude. Transylvania was vassal and tributary very nearly on the same conditions as Moldavia; on the death of John-Sigismond Zapoly, in 1571, the investiture was given by a tchaouch to Stephen Bathory, his successor. The Wallachian Bekes tried to supplant him by winning over the Grand Vizier with presents; Bathory outbid him, and preserved at that price his principality.

The Tunis expedition was the last salient event of Selim's reign. In the course of the year 1574 several natural scourges had afflicted the Empire: torrent-like rains, inundations, an earthquake at Constantinople, a fire which destroyed a portion of the Seraglio. In these events the superstitious Selim saw the presage of his approaching end. Some time after, having gone to inspect a bath recently constructed, he experienced a chill from the coldness of the place, and to warm himself he drank off a flask of Cyprus wine and immediately fell down insensible: he expired eleven days afterwards (12th of December, 1574).

8. *Amurath III.* (1574–1595).—*First acts of his Reign.*

Notwithstanding the nullity of Selim, his death was a misfortune for the Empire, inasmuch as it put an end to the omnipotence of Mohamet Sokolli, who reigned under his name. His successor restrained the Vizier's authority, and gave up everything to the influence of women and favourites. Amurath was brave, humane, and a friend to letters, and held out bright hopes for his future career; but soon two passions developed themselves in him even to frenzy—lust and avarice, by which he was reduced to imbecility. He passed his life in the Seraglio, surrounded by eunuchs, women and buffoons, occupied with the contemplation of his treasures and only intervening in affairs of state in order to allow the caprices of the slaves who governed him to dominate. He arrived in Constantinople on the 21st December, and during the night caused his five brothers to be strangled. Next day, he received the homage of the grandees. Ranged round him, the officers of the Seraglio awaited in silence the first word which should fall from his lips; for the orientals have preserved that superstition of the ancients, which regarded as a presage the first words uttered. "I am hungry," said he; "let them give me something to eat." Those words were considered as a bad omen, of which a famine that occurred during that year seemed to be the fulfilment.

One of the first acts of the new Sultan was a decree against the use of wine. Under the reign of Selim II., drunkenness, encouraged by his example, had scandalously increased; the public functionaries even sold wine openly; the soldiers were heard to say to one another, "Where shall we get our wine to-day, from the mufti or the cadi?" One day that Amurath was passing the door of a tavern, some Janissaries held up their glasses, shouting aloud that they drank to his health; this induced him to issue the decree. Some days after, a mutiny broke out among the Sipahis and Janissaries, and the Grand Vizier himself was both insulted and maltreated. Thereupon it was announced that the soldiers would be allowed to drink wine, provided they abstained from committing violence.

Early in 1575, it became known that Henry of Valois had deserted his throne of Poland to return to France. Thus miscarried the sole chance of securing the accession of Poland to the Turco-French alliance, an accession which would not only have checked the aggrandisement of Austria, but hindered the rise of Russia. Amurath was so dissatisfied with the flight of Henry III. that he did not notify his own accession to the Court of France. The Polish magnates having sent a deputation to compliment the new Sultan, he recommended for their suffrages the Voïvode of Transylvania, Stephen Bathory, who was elected at the end of 1575.

9. *War with Hungary.—Relations with France.*

The commencement of the new reign was marked, as usual, by hostilities in Hungary. Villages were burned on different points of the frontier, attempts were made against several fortresses, and a battle fought in the environs of Kruppa, in which the Imperialists were defeated; their chiefs perished in the action, and their heads were sent to Constantinople, where the Austrian ambassador was compelled to redeem them from the hands of the executioner. The Emperor Rodolph, who succeeded Maximilian II. in 1576, made certain protests, the result of which was, that peace was formally renewed for eight years from the 1st January, 1577; but perpetual aggressions on one part or the other continued to disturb the peace without breaking it, until the last years of Amurath's reign.

The attitude of the Porte was very nearly the same towards Poland: a nominal peace and actual hostilities. Bathory protested on several occasions against the aggressions of the Tartars; a treaty was concluded, 30th July, 1577, a treaty by which he was promised protection. However, the incursions continued; his envoys were rudely rebuffed and he was threatened with war. Poland was treated like Transylvania, as a vassal and tributary State; in the last truce with Austria it was included in the number of the countries protected by the Porte, without giving it the title of kingdom.

Venice had less cause of complaint, thanks to the dominant influence of the favourite Sultana, the Venetian Baffa. She obtained the renewal of the capitulations and greater security for her commerce. As for the alliance with France, it was respected; the Baron de Germigny, their ambassador, succeeded in acquiring great influence in the Divan. An embassy from the Sultan to the French Court had a magnificent reception, and it presented a letter to Henry III., in which Amurath offered him, with his friendship, "his naval army, comprising eighty galleys." "I have made him," says Germigny in his report, "a reciprocal offer of yours, but in general terms, to make him relish and prize the grandeur and power of your Majesty." The restriction was necessary with Henry III., who was compelled, from the want of a navy, to send his ambassadors to Constantinople on board a Venetian vessel.

Germigny succeeded in rescuing numerous Frenchmen sold into slavery, and obtained reparation for pillage committed by the Barbary corsairs; procured permission to set up and regulate the new coral fishery upon the coast of Tunis which the Marseilles adventurers had newly commenced there. He obtained the nomination of a Greek patriarch and a voïvode of Wallachia, in spite of the opposition of the favourites and even of the Sultana mother; he caused civil appointments and even military commands to be given to Turks "whom he had recognized," says he in his report, " as well-disposed to the king's service." He favoured with his protection "the affairs and subjects of the Pope, of the Emperor, of the Seigniory of Venice, of the Republic of Ragusa, of the Grand Master of Malta, to the benefit," he said, " of Christianity; so that His Holiness could send a bishop as apostolic visitor to the Churches of the Levant." He obtained the renewal of the privileges of the Holy Places of Jerusalem and Sinai, permission to establish at Pera a convent of Cordeliers, and divers favours to the profit of the Catholic bishops of the Archipelago, &c. Lastly, he obtained the renewal of the capitulations "accrued to certain important articles, as precedence, by public and solemn act, above all the ambassadors of Christian princes, and notably those of Spain." ." That precedence was accorded," said the treaty, " in favour of old ties of friendship between the Ottoman monarchs and the kings of France, who have in all time been attached sincerely to the Sublime Porte, and are in all respects the most illustrious princes of Christendom." The article which confirmed to France the protection of the Christian nations in the Ottoman States was worded thus: "That, the Venetians excepted, the Genoese, the English, the Portuguese, the Spaniards, the Catalans, Sicilians, and Ragusans, and entirely all those who have walked under the name and banner of France, from old time until the present day, and in the condition in which they have walked heretofore, they may walk therein in the same manner." Amurath having sworn, "these pactions to be honoured and maintained, without any of his pachas being able to give them hindrance," sent into France Ali Bey, first interpreter of the Porte, "to invite the king to be present, in the persons of his ambassadors, at the circumcision of his eldest son, and to congratulate him upon that ceremony, with commandment to the said ambassadors to present to the king the confirmation of the ancient treaties made between the Grand Seignior and France." That embassy was received with great magnificence.

In spite of all these offers, these professions of friendship, these concessions, Germigny appreciated at its due value the alliance and goodwill of the Turks; he did not allow himself to be dazzled by their power; he foresaw the decadence of that empire, which had no longer a Solyman to direct it. "I recognized," said he, "by certain conjectures and latterly by their manner of proceeding, treating and negotiating, the disposition in which the Grand Seignior and his pachas were to collect and receive from all parts indifferently the friendships and alliances they were able to find . . . in all of which it appears that they prefer a small present commodity to the forethought of a good or evil much more important to their state; so far are they blinded by ignorance combined with extreme avarice, perfidy and iniquity, which possesses them with such restless confusion, that they seem to have arrived at their last stage."

Germigny's ill-humour was justified by several acts. The capitulations with France had been renewed scarcely two years, when Queen Elizabeth of England, whose ships until then had only navigated the Ottoman waters under the flag of France, demanded from the Sultan freedom of navigation and of commerce for her subjects under their own flag. The ambassador charged with that negotiation was Harebone or Harburn. The Sultan acceded to the demand, in spite of the lively opposition of the French and Venetian ambassadors, giving as a reason that " the Sublime Porte was open to all those who came thither to seek protection."

That maxim received, at this period, very numerous applications. The overtures of the Christian agents of all nations were encouraged by the Viziers, the great officers of the Seraglio and the army, the favourites of both sexes, for whom it was a source of revenue. The venality of the grandees was never more scandalous: everything was bartered for, within and without, and the Sultan was the first to set the example. The historian Ali relates that Schemsi, one of the chief favourites, made use of every art to induce his master to adopt such a practice; he was a descendant of the sovereign race of the Isfendiars; he avenged his ancestors by accelerating amongst their conquerors the progress of corruption. On the first occasion that he induced the Sultan to accept a present of 40,000 ducats for the conclusion of an affair, he congratulated himself as though he had accomplished a triumph. The wide-spread venality invited to Constantinople agents from all the commercial states of Europe. Even the Swiss entered into negotiations through the medium of an Italian Jew. Spain, at length, in 1578, made propositions of peace, and sent an ambassador. It required five years of thorny negotiation to reconcile that haughty enemy to the Porte, and still the peace was very imperfect and often violated.

Whilst these negotiations and treaties enriched the Sultan and his Ministers, treasure was amassed in another way—the fruit of piracy, which no treaties stopped. The corsairs of Algiers, of Tunis, and Tripoli pillaged almost indiscriminately friends and foes, and the Porte compelled them to disgorge. Transforming them into regencies or pachalics, those three cities were made to pay an annual tribute. In 1578, the Pacha of Tripoli was ordered to carry succour to the Cherif of Fez, who had implored the aid of the Porte against a competitor; the latter, on his part, invoked the Portuguese, who landed with an army of 80,000 men. A great battle was fought near Alcazar Kebir; 20,000 Portuguese were left dead on the field, with their king, Sebastian, and the Moorish pretender; an immense disaster, from which dates the decadence of Portugal. That brilliant victory brought to the Ottomans rich presents from the Cherif and a dominating influence in the Mogreb.

These successes were sadly atoned for by the fall of the Grand Vizier, Mahomet Sokolli. Powerful through the Sultan's weakness, the favourites laboured at his ruin, and urged the prince to take the direction of affairs. At first, disgrace fell upon the friends of Sokolli: the Secretary of State, Feridoun, who was indebted to him for his fortune, was dismissed. Another of his *protégés* was the Greek Cantacuzene, to whom he had given the monopoly of salt at Anchiolos, upon the Black Sea. This man had, it is true, unworthily abused his favour; his exactions had rendered him the terror of the Greeks; the Turks themselves called him *Sheitanogli*, "son of Satan." So long as Sokolli's power lasted, Cantacuzene purchased impunity by allowing the Vizier to share the fruits of his plunder; he was also sustained by the Viziers Afemid and Piale; but, after the death of the latter, he was, upon the accusation of one of the enemies of Sokolli, dismissed at first, then arrested and hanged at the gate of the palace which he had erected for himself at Anchiolos. A more direct blow was dealt the Grand Vizier: his nephew, Mustapha Pacha, who since the death of Solyman, had been Governor of Ofen, was executed. The year after, Sokolli was assassinated in his palace. The murderer, put to the torture, made no confession; the crime was laid to the account of private vengeance (1579).

10. *War with Persia.*

Two years previously, war had broken out against Persia. The aged Shah Thamash had died in 1576, poisoned by his wife; the Circassian and Georgian parties, already contending during his lifetime, disputed for the sway. Haider, the fifth son of Thamash, was placed upon the throne by the Georgian khans, but his reign was limited to a few hours, being assassinated by the Circassian party. His brother Shah Ismaïl succeeded him; he was a furious maniac; after eighteen months of tyranny, he died strangled by the order of his sister. The Viziers in favour, Sinan and Mustapha, persuaded the Sultan to turn to profit these internal troubles of Persia in order to subjugate that country. Mustapha received the command of the expedition; and, without a declaration of war, hostilities began on both sides. Mustapha obtained (Aug. 8, 1578), near the stronghold of Tchildir in Georgia, a brilliant victory over the Persian army; several Georgian chiefs made their submission, and received, by the title of sandjaks, diplomas of investiture in the Sultan's name; Tiflis was occupied by the Ottomans, and its churches converted into mosques. On the 8th of September a second battle was fought on the banks of the Kansak; the Persians lost 3,000 men; the bridge of Kansak was broken down, and a great number of the fugitives perished in the waters. The town of Scheki opened its gates to the victors; Georgia, almost wholly conquered, was divided into four governments, confided to as many beylerbeys; then the army returned to take up its winter quarters at Erzeroum. Hostilities recommenced in the middle of winter: four Persian armies took the field; two directed their march towards Georgia, the two others threatened the Ottoman provinces of Bagdad and Erzeroum. Osman Pacha, beylerbey of Chirvan, obtained at first a signal victory over the Persian governor of Chamakie; but soon after, assailed by the great Persian army and besieged in Chirvan, he was constrained to retire towards Derbend. Tiflis was besieged by its former prince, Simon Louarsch, united with the Persians; the valiant resistance of the garrison gave time for the reinforcements to arrive, and the town was saved. The Ottomans then resumed the offensive and carried their ravages through the unsubdued cantons; at the express command of the Sultan, formidable fortifications were raised at Kars; and that city has remained unto the present day the strongest bulwark upon that frontier of the Ottoman Empire.

Intestine disorders which again broke out in Persia, and a change of commanders on the side of the Turks, now retarded the march of military events. On the death of Sokolli, Mustapha and Sinan Pachas, influential rivals, alike hoped to succeed him. They were both deceived; the Sultan bestowed the dignity of Grand Vizier upon Amed Pacha. But Sinan, by his influence over the new Vizier, succeeded in procuring the recall of Mustapha, and of obtaining command of the Georgian expedition. Some months after, the feeble Ahmed was dismissed, and the seals given to Sinan Pacha; which Mustapha took so much to heart that he died some few days after, either of grief or probably suicide—a crime, however, very rare among the Osmanlis. Sinan did not urge on the war vigorously. He met with several checks, and incurred the suspicion of allowing himself to be gained over by the Shah of Persia: he was replaced and sent into exile. The Hungarian Siawous Pacha was named Grand Vizier, and the beylerbey of Roumelia, Ferhad, seraskier for the Persian war. The campaigns of 1582 and 1583 were without results; Ferhad, the seraskier, having to struggle against the indiscipline and bad will of the troops, frequent mutinies, and continual pillage; the Janissaries making common cause with Georgian brigands to share the booty.

The honour of the Ottoman arms was better sustained in Daghestan by Osman Pacha, who there made a valiant defence from the commencement of the war. He was aided at first by the Khan of the Crimea, Mohammed Gheraï; but, in 1580, the latter withdrew in spite of his remonstrances, and Osman obtained no more than a few reinforcements sent, with the greatest difficulty and danger, by the Black Sea and the Caucasus. On the 9th of May, 1583, he engaged the Persians in a great battle upon the banks of the Ssamour. It was fought without cessation during a day and a night; the carnage continued by the light of torches; but the victory remained undecided. Two days after, the Turks found themselves surrounded; they resolutely attacked the enemy, cut their way through his masses and obtained a decisive victory; the Persian army was destroyed and the submission of the country secured. After having erected new fortifications at Chamakie, distributed garrisons in the fortresses, and established an Ottoman governor, Osman Pacha quitted Daghestan and traversed the Caucasus; the march was difficult and frequently harassed until he succeeded in reaching Kaffa, whither an order from the Sultan sent him. Mohammed Gheraï, by his desertion, had drawn upon himself the displeasure of the Porte; he was deposed and offered resistance with arms in hand, but he was taken and put to death; his brother, Islam Gheraï, replacing him (1584). Osman then returned to Constantinople, where he was welcomed with extraordinary honours: Amurath received him in private audience, desirous of hearing from his own mouth the narrative of his victories, and dismissed him with magnificent presents. A few days after he was named Vizier, and Seraskier of the army destined to invade Aderbaidjan.

11. *Relations with France, England, Venice, &c.—Peace with Persia.*

Neither the Viziers nor the Generals were the veritable depositaries of power; that was entirely concentrated in the harem: the mother, the Sultan's sisters, the Sultana

Baffa, and two Christian slaves, who disputed with her for their master's attachment—these were the true sovereigns of the Empire. After these came the chief of the eunuchs, the governor of the harem, the Sultan's preceptor (Kodja), and the mufti, who strove by endless intrigues to make themselves masters of the weak Sovereign. These latter influences provoked in him an excess of religious zeal, which manifested itself by persecution of the Christians. It became a question of transforming into mosques all the churches in Constantinople; but the efforts of the ambassadors, and especially the sacrifice of money made by the Greeks, hindered the execution of the project. However, three churches at Galata were closed, and the protests of the French ambassador were very badly received. Germigny had quarrelled with Sinan Pacha, who was then Vizier, and a disagreement arose between him and the Divan. A war was imminent at that period between France and Spain: Philip II. had just entered into an alliance with the League, and Henry III. welcomed the deputies of the United Provinces, who offered him the sovereignty of their country. It was the opportunity for putting to the proof the offers made with so much effusion some years before; Henry, by his ambassador, demanded the aid of an Ottoman fleet against Philip II. Catherine de Medicis wrote on this subject to the favourite Sultana; but the latter showed the letter to the bayle of Venice, who caused the King of France's demand to miscarry. Shortly after, Germigny demanded the re-establishment of a voïwode of Wallachia, protected by France; it was refused. He presented to the Sultan, secretly, a memorial in which he set forth the wrongs of his nation; and the latter sent it back with these words in his own handwriting: "All the favours that we have granted may be revoked if the King of France is wanting towards us in generosity." The closing of the churches brought the irritation of the ambassador to a climax. The Sunday following, he repaired, accompanied by eighty Frenchmen, to the principal church, who knocked at the portals whilst chanting psalms and retired amidst the insults and threats of the insurgent population. The reopening of the two churches was purchased by presents. To Germigny, in 1585, succeeded Savary de Lancosme, who was wholly devoted to the League, and who represented it at Constantinople. His conduct did not contribute to restore harmony: one Sunday, in St. George's church at Galata, he seized with the strong hand upon the place of honour occupied by the Imperial ambassador; the church was closed, and the Grand Vizier declared "that it should only be reopened when M. de Lancosme ceased to play the fool."

England gained the influence which France had lost. It had been seen that Harebone, the first ambassador sent by Elizabeth of England, obtained capitulations analogous to those of France, but limited to commerce, and in which there was no question concerning the Christians and the Eastern churches. He afterwards asked for aid from the Sultan against Spain; and, if he experienced a refusal, it was caused by the sacrifices which the Persian war demanded. When Harebone returned to England, he took with him a letter for the Queen, in which the Sultan offered to set at liberty the English who should be taken by the corsairs, on condition that such good office should be reciprocal. Harebone's successor, Edward Burton, demanded that the cruisers might be allowed in order to molest the commerce of the Spaniards in the Indian Ocean, and that succour should be given to the Portuguese pretender. His demands were eluded, but without being positively rejected, with a view to encourage the English Government to continue the war against the Spaniards. In 1589 Burton was charged to notify to the Porte the accession of Henry IV. of France; Lancosme had then absolutely ceased to be the representative of that country: he was merely the agent of Philip II.; the English ambassador was for some time the chargé d'affaires for the French King; he demanded on his part aid against Spain, but met with a refusal. Affirmed in his accession, Henry IV., demanded the dismission of De Lancosme as a spy of Spain, and replaced him by M. de Brèves.

The relations of the Porte with the Christian States continued to be pacific. In spite of several flagrant infractions of treaties, the protection of the Sultana preserved peace with the Venetians. The Czar of Russia, Feodor Ivanovitch, sent ambassadors with rich presents. In Poland Stephen Bathory having just died (1586), the Porte designated to the Magnates Prince Sigismond of Sweden, who was elected. The new King had, like his predecessor, to undergo the insults of the Tartars and the arrogance of the Ottoman Ministers.

The Persian war, however, under the command of Osman Pacha, began again with renewed activity: in spite of two partial checks, the Ottomans entered Tebriz as conquerors and pillaged it during three days and nights; after which they surrounded it with fortifications. But the ill-health of the vizier arrested his successes; a *corps d'armée*, under the command of the renegade Cicala, was defeated near Schembi-Ghazan by the Persian prince Hamsa; and 20,000 Ottomans there lost their lives. Constrained to effect his retreat, and already disabled from directing the army, Osman was attacked and suffered a second defeat; he died a few days afterwards. The son of Cicala, whom the Turks called Djighala Zadé, achieved, however, the retreat without serious losses, and obtained some advantage over the enemy. After his departure the Persians went to lay siege to Tebriz; the garrison resisted during ten months, sustained fifteen assaults, and fought forty-eight combats; it was at length relieved by the arrival of Ferhad Bey, to whom the command had been given. That general caused likewise the siege of Tiflis to be raised, and maintained a secret understanding with the Turcomans of the Persian army; shortly after, Prince Hamsa perished by assassination. The dissensions by which Persia was torn at this time decided Shah Khodabende to make proposals of peace; an armistice was signed; but it was almost immediately broken. Ferhad fought, in the plain of Grues, a great battle which lasted three days, and which ended in the defeat of the Persian army (1586). At the same time Djighala Zadé become Governor and Seraskier of the province of Bagdad, seized upon the fortress of Disfoul and several other strongholds, and defeated the Governors of Loristan and Hamadan.

In 1588 Ferhad, in concert with the Governor of Chirvan, Djafer, invaded the country of Karabagh, seized on Ghendjé, the capital, and converted it into a stronghold. Khodabende had then, for upwards of a year, ceased to reign : his son, who was the great Shah Abbas, had compelled his abdication. Pressed on the east by the Usbecks, the new Shah determined to demand peace ; it was signed at Constantinople the 21st of March, 1590 ; the Ottoman Empire was aggrandized by Georgia, Chirvan, Loristan, Tebriz, with a portion of Aderbaïdjan.

12. *Revolts of the Janissaries and troubles in the Provinces.—War renewed in Hungary.—Death of Amurath III.*

At this juncture a furious revolt among the Janissaries broke out at Constantinople. The spirit of that militia became more and more corrupt; during the Persian war it had more than once given proof of insubordination. The defterdar and the beylerbey of Roumelia having proposed to pay them with alloyed coin, they attacked the Seraglio, and demanded the heads of those two functionaries. It was necessary to satisfy them, and the Sultan dared only to avenge the insult by dismissing several high dignitaries suspected of having provoked the insurrection for his destruction. In the three following years the Janissaries twice broke into rebellion; the punishment fell upon the viziers, who were deposed. In 1593 it was the sipahis who revolted and demanded the head of the defterdar ; there was a hesitation in satisfying them, as the victim was an *emir*, that is to say, a member of the family of the Prophet. The Janissaries intervened, and partly by force, partly by conciliation, order was re-established. Some time after the Janissaries had the audacity to appoint, of their own authority, a voïvode in Moldavia, and their *protégé* was only deposéd because he did not pay the tribute.

At the same time troubles agitated several provinces. In the district of Keifé, in Asia, an adventurer who gave himself out as Ismaïl, son of Shah Thamasp, attempted to create a party; overcome and taken by the Governor of Erzeroum, he underwent the last punishment. In Egypt the militia of the country revolted. At Buda the garrison, to whom six months' pay was owing, assassinated the Pacha: thirty-five of the guilty were hanged. Lastly, at Tebriz, the troops mutinied because it was proposed to pay them with the alloyed coin of Constantinople; the Governor, Djafer Pacha, parleyed with the principal rebels, convoked them to a great festival in token of reconciliation, and caused them to be massacred to the number of 1,800. A terrible pestilence, which afflicted the capital in 1592, formed the climax of the public calamities. The insolence of the Janissaries became intolerable; it was resolved to go to war to get rid of them. Sinan Pacha, who had again become Grand Vizier, decided that it should be waged in Hungary.

Thereupon hostilities immediately commenced. Hassan Pacha, Governor of Bosnio, took Sissek, in Croatia, and obtained a signal victory over Nadasdy, who was taken prisoner; but, the year following, compelled to give battle to the Imperialists, under the same walls of Sissek, he was completely defeated, and drowned himself with many of his followers. War was then declared against Austria, and her ambassador imprisoned. The Grand Vizier seized upon Wesprim and Palota; on the other hand, the Pacha of Buda was overcome near Stuhlweissembourg, and nine fortresses fell into the power of the Imperialists. The year following (1594), the Austrians took Neograd, Chrastovitz, Gora, Petrinia, and Sissek; the Ottomans seized upon Jata, Saint Marton, Papa, and Raab. Successes, therefore, seemed balanced, when Transylvania, Moldavia, and Wallachia revolted all at once, with an unanimity which had not been witnessed for a long time, and made alliance with the Emperor; the Turks scattered through those three provinces were massacred. In the hope of rekindling the ardour of the Janissaries, Amurath sent to them their aga, who, until then, had never entered upon a campaign save with the Sultan; he caused also the holy banner of the Prophet to be brought from Syria and despatched into Hungary; but those devices wholly failed to remedy the insubordination and discouragement of the troops. Soon after a report of the Sultan's illness completed the dejection of his soldiers. It is related that the imbecile Amurath was singularly struck by an extraordinary dream related to him by one of his favourites; he thought that he saw in it a presage of his approaching death. He thereupon fell ill, had himself carried to a kiosk which commanded a view of the harbour, and ordered lugubrious music to be played before him. Two Egyptian galleys entering the Golden Horn on firing the usual salute the detonations broke the windows of the pavilion: this was another omen for the superstitious Sultan. "Formerly," said he, "the entire artillery of the fleet never broke a window-pane; I see that it is all over with me!" That same night he expired (January 6th, 1596).

CHAPTER VI.

REIGNS OF MAHOMET III. AND ACHMET I. (1596–1617).

1. *First acts and character of Mahomet III.—Revolt in Asia.—Independence of Wallachia.*

To Amurath succeeded Mahomet III., son of the Venetian Baffa. The death of the Sultan was concealed, as usual, till Mahomet could arrive from his government of Magnesia. He was the last heir of the Turkish throne who enjoyed before his accession an independent government; in future all the Sultan's children were brought up exclusively in the Seraglio. His accession was marked by the most horrible application of the fratricidal law of Mahomet II.: he ordered the mutes to strangle his nineteen brothers, whose coffins, decked with turbans and heron's plumes, were solemnly deposited near the paternal tomb. The insubordination of the Janissaries had to be soothed with a donation of 660,000 ducats, and it was also necessary to similarly appease a revolt of the discontented Sipahis. Lastly, to satisfy the ulemas and the faithful, Mahomet, renewing a ceremony neglected by his father, repaired with great pomp to the mosque, there to offer up public prayers.

Notwithstanding the sanguinary tragedy enacted upon his accession, the new Sultan, a pupil of the poet Nevi, and of the historian Seadeddin, was an enlightened prince, a protector of letters and legists. He composed verses himself, and signed them under the name of *Adli,* or *The Just.* He evinced, indeed, right intentions, and one of his first cares was to discharge the debts contracted by his father with several public funds. He followed scrupulously the laws of Islam, and claimed to make them observed:

"Know," said he to one of his ministers, "that I have sworn never to pardon a Grand Vizier, but to punish severely the slightest prevarication." Notwithstanding that, Mahomet did not know how to arrest the decadence of the Ottomans.

This prince, whose official language betokened pride and absolute power, was continually dominated by his mother and by his Ministers. The Sultana-validé maintained herself in favour with her son by presenting him with beautiful slaves. Sinan Pacha, Djighala Zadé, and Hassan the Cruel, who succeeded him, all renegades and *parvenus*, to power by violence and baseness, put up to auction the public posts, alloyed the coin, and established new taxes both in kind and money. Gold, embezzled by those official peculators, was often wanted for the most urgent needs, and even for payment of troops. Thence constantly occurring seditions, which the Sultan could not repress without the rivalry of the Sipahis and Janissaries.

Constantinople was not the only theatre of these insurrections. In 1599, a military revolt very nearly stripped the Porte of its Asian provinces. The insurgents formed a formidable army, and Dely-Hasan, victor over several viziers, said in his sovereign decrees : " I have overthrown in those countries the Ottoman power, and the domination undivided now belongs to me." That movement was not exclusively military: the Kurds, the Turkomans, and other Asiatic tribes took a very active part in it. Three years were occupied in reducing them. At length, Dely-Hasan consented to lay down arms; he obtained the government of Bosnia, and turned his savage hordes against the Christians. Fifty thousand men followed him; half-naked barbarians with long and flowing hair, and their arms and necks encircled with amulets, the bones of camels dangling from their stirrups. Before leaving Asia, Dely-Hasan sacrificed thirty sheep upon the tomb of Soliman, son of Orchan. Was it a fresh Turkish invasion of Europe? The Moslems themselves beheld not without terror those late comers, whose lances, with white banderoles attached, spared the Osmanlis no more than the rayahs. The army of Dely-Hasan traversed Roumelia like a devastating scourge; when, at length, having reached the banks of the Danube, it perished almost entirely in giving battle to the Hungarians (1603). That rising in Asia brought about, by a rebound, a revolt of Sipahis, who, finding themselves deprived of the income of their timars by the rebels, demanded compensation, and attempted to pillage the mosques of Constantinople. The Sultan's life was threatened; but the Janissaries, having returned from Asia, fell upon the Sipahis and brought them under submission.

The war, however, continued in Hungary and Transylvania: every year the Turks returned to those provinces, pillaging, ravaging, carrying off captives, by turns conquerors and conquered. We shall not weary the reader by tedious details of these expeditions, which were all of like character and only inspire disgust, but say a few words touching events in Wallachia, that had a great importance. That country had then a remarkable man as Voïvode, and who has remained the popular hero of it, Michael *the Brave*. At the close of Amurath's reign, he had stirred up the people to revolt and allied himself with the Emperor. The great Vizier Sinan hastened with an army against him; he seized upon Bucharest and fortified it (1595). But Michael drove back the Ottomans into some impracticable marshes; he took Tergovitz and caused the entire garrison to be empaled or roasted alive. The Turks retreated; but, whilst crossing the Danube near Giurgevo, he surprised them again and crushed them. Then he carried Nicopolis by assault and compelled Widdin to capitulate. "Thus," says a Wallachian historian, "in the space of a year, all the Turkish forces had been repulsed; the fortresses of the Danube belonged no longer to the Crescent, the eagle of Wallachia floated above their ramparts; the pachas, the best generals of the Porte, had failed against the efforts of a people fighting for the liberty of their country. It required, however, a prompt remedy for the evils of Wallachia, the inevitable consequences of war. Michael *the Brave* caused provisions and seed to be brought into Transylvania; he distributed them among the people, who, obedient to the summons of their Sovereign, emerged from the virgin and eternal forests that covered a great portion of the principality, and which, in time of danger, have been impenetrable strongholds and the surest asylums for the inhabitants. The Wallachians set about rebuilding their towns and villages; new dwellings speedily rose upon the ruins of the old, and the nation felt itself proud of the independence which it had so dearly purchased. However, that independence was not yet sufficiently ensured; it required fresh sacrifices, new combats. The Turks, although already several times vanquished, were unwilling to lose Wallachia without first trying every possible means to make themselves masters of it. For them that principality was a source of inexhaustible wealth, or, as they called it, the granary of Constantinople. In fact, that capital was solely nourished by the products of Wallachia: it drew thence oxen, sheep, wheat and other cereals, cheese, butter, and honey. To lose all those good things was an irreparable misfortune for the Porte.*

2. *War in Hungary.—Treatment of the Christians by the Viziers.—Michael the Brave.*

Whilst Michael was delivering Wallachia, the Imperialists seized upon Gran, in Hungary, and some other less important towns. Mahomet III. then had recourse to negotiations; he strove to break the alliance between Rodolph II. and Michael *the Brave:* repulsed on that side, he offered Sigismond Bathory to annex the Wallachian territory to Transylvania; Sigismond replied that he would never turn his arms against the Christians. The Sultan, in spite of those two checks in his diplomacy, not the less resolved upon a new expedition. At the importunities of the Janissaries, he followed the example of his

* Michel de Kogalnitchano, "History of Wallachia, and Moldavia," vol. i. p. 162. Berlin, 1837.

ancestor Solyman, and placed himself at the head of the army. He entered Hungary and took the town of Erlau, the garrison of which was massacred by the Janissaries, at the moment, when, according to the capitulation, they quitted the town (1596). The Archduke Maximilian and Sigismond Bathory arrived too late to succour the place; after some unimportant successes, their troops were put to rout in the plain of Keresztes : 50,000 Germans or Hungarians perished in that battle, which the Ottomans have compared to that of Mohacz. The Sultan returned in triumph within the walls of Constantinople.

After the capture of Erlau and the battle of Keresztes, there is nothing to record, under the reign of Mahomet III. save the deliverance of Kanischa, fruitlessly besieged by a German army (1602). The war was carried on on both sides with equal fury; the Hungarians and the Walloons in the service of the Empire frequently committed even greater excesses than the Turks; for, if the Viziers submitted at Constantinople to the yoke of the Janissaries and Sipahis, they maintained a severe discipline within their camps.

One of them, Ibrahim, knew how to win by his gentleness the inhabitants of the frontiers and the subject Christians. The Serbs and Wallacks of Semendria and Temeswar assembled in crowds about him; he loaded them with presents and presented them with banners. The Christian inhabitants of Posega having slain the Turkish judge during an insurrection, he pretended that matters had been thus arranged by his orders, and he even expedited an act to attest that the blood of the magistrate had been legally shed. To those who remonstrated with him upon such a mode of action, he replied, "Is it wise, by prosecuting them, to drive back these rayahs into the arms of the enemy?" He made use of bands of subject Christians, brought thus under his standards by flattery, indulgence, and liberalities, in order to exterminate the heydukes, who, for more than thirty years, had spread terror throughout Sclavonia.* Even in Wallachia he

* Hammer, tom. ii. p. 292.

found Christians willing to sustain the cause of the Turks; Michael *the Brave* had to repress, in 1597, a conspiracy formed by several primates in favour of the Ottoman Porte. That voïvode would have been a more dangerous enemy for Mahomet III. if ambition had not turned his arms against the Christians. By violence he united under his authority Moldavia, a portion of Transylvania, and thought even to make himself King of Hungary and Poland. Wholly occupied with his personal interests, he treated cleverly, in the latter part of his career, with the Moslems whom he had fought with so much energy and success; he solicited investiture of the Sultan, and negotiated secretly with Ibrahim a treaty of alliance. Death came to arrest his projects. He perished assassinated by the order of Basta, commander of the Imperial troops in Transylvania, and left Wallachia a prey to civil war and Mussulman invasion (1601). "Michael *the Brave*," says a German historian, "powerfully helped to turn Turkish barbarity from other portions of Europe. If that man had had a more careful education, if he had not fallen upon conjunctures so difficult, he might have been compared to John Hunyade. Had his reign proved of longer duration, it would have been decisive in procuring a better fate for the countries situate on the Lower Danube. But in the forty-third year of his age, he was torn violently from his career; his enterprises have had no sequel; but his name, at least, will live in history." *

3. *Relations of the Porte with France.*

Whilst the Imperialists disputed with him possession of Hungary, and the voïvode Michael tore away from him that of Wallachia, Mahomet succeeded in remaining at peace with the other Christian States. Poland solicited the maintenance of treaties and sent several ambassadors to Constantinople; the Republic of Venice congratulated the Sultan upon his successes over the Germans; the

* Engel, "History of Moldavia and Wallachia," p. 268.

English ambassador, Burton, followed him in person in the campaign of 1596; lastly, France reconfirmed her alliance. She was represented at the Porte by Savary de Brèves, the successor of Savary de Lancosme, one of those men who most contributed, by their zeal and intelligence, to extend French influence in the East.

He sought primarily to make the Ottoman alliance serviceable in his master's affairs. The Marseillais had embraced the party of the League and refused to recognize Henry IV.; the Sultan, by the advice of Brèves, wrote to them persuading them to submit to their legitimate king, and threatening them with a war that would ruin their commerce. Philip II. had sent an ambassador to Constantinople to solicit an alliance with the Turks: the Sultan, at the request of De Brèves, refused to receive him; moreover, he solemnly renewed his protestations of friendship for Henry IV., to whom he deputed one of his favourites to congratulate him upon his victories. " Finally," says De Brèves in his Memoirs, " I compelled him to keep, during four or five years, large forces at sea to divert the Spanish power and hinder it from carrying itself wholly to the aid of the League." The influence of the French ambassador became such, that the Turkish historian, Selaniki, spoke thus of it: " It very nearly happened that, in the house of Islam, a veritable enthusiasm was declared for France by the secret dealings of its accursed ambassador."

However, with a government so disordered as that of the Turks, with pachas independent and fanatical populations, with religious hatreds that no political consideration could weaken, the alliance of the Porte with France had always something precarious and wavering about it ; the capitulations were often violated, the Catholics found themselves exposed to numerous and obscure persecutions ; merchants and travellers had to submit to frequent extortions from the Mussulman authorities. Brèves busied himself, with an untiring perseverance, to prevent those tyrannies, those abuses, those violations of treaties ; and he caused to intervene, in the iniquities of the Turks towards the Christians, the name of France with so much wisdom, that he almost always succeeded in hindering them. Thus, the Janissaries having rushed furiously upon the churches of Galata, on account of three renegades having taken refuge therein, he stopped the infuriate soldiers by throwing himself before them, threatening them with the vengeance of his master, and declaring that he would defend at the peril of his life the exercise of the Christian religion. He turned aside the Sultan's anger from the Isle of Scio, who was desirous of visiting upon its inhabitants a surprise attempted by some Tuscan galleys. He stopped the Pacha of Damascus who wished to convert the church of the Holy Sepulchre into a mosque. Lastly, in 1600, "having been apprised," he himself relates, "that the Grand Seignior had resolved, on account of the bad success of the war in Hungary, to prevent not only the devotions of the pilgrims who flock to Jerusalem, but to retain them as slaves and have them led to Constantinople in chains together with the holy men, custodians of the Holy Sepulchre, suddenly as the notice of this unexpected resolution was given me, I made him revoke it, telling him that it would afford Pope Clement VIII. a means of uniting all the Christian Powers to avenge the injury that all Christianity would receive, esteeming that my Sovereign, as a very Christian and very pious prince, would be one among the first to band himself against his power."

"The influence that I had acquired," he says further, "with the Ministers of the Grand Seignior, and the language of the country which I possessed, gave me the means of serving advantageously the king and of aiding those who had recourse to the powerful protection of his name. Thus there is not a city in Europe that has not felt the effects of my assistance; for I have given liberty to more than from 1,000 to 1,200 men, at different times, who were slaves, to some by my industry, to others for having been captured contrary to the treaties and capitulations accorded to the king, as well in favour of his subjects as of foreigners who have liberty to traffic in the realm of the

Grand Seignior, under the standard and banner of His Majesty."

One of the principal cares of M. de Brèves was to hinder the encroachments of England upon French commerce. Queen Elizabeth having obtained from the Porte capitulations analogous to those of France, the English vessels entered into concurrence with the French; but they did not confine themselves to that. "They sought carefully," says De Brèves, " the means of depreciating the French flag, and they made the Grand Seignior allow that foreign nations that have no ambassadors at the Porte and that have liberty to traffic in its realm under the French flag may come thither under the English banner." England was then allied with France, and Henry IV. in part owed his crown to the help of Elizabeth; in spite of that, Brèves complained bitterly of the usurpation by the English of the most precious privilege that France had obtained from the friendship of the Porte; he demanded reparation for it, and, notwithstanding the opposition of Elizabeth's ambassador, the concession which had been made him was revoked.

The Sultan did not derive that advantage from his success in the Hungarian war which might have been expected. In the campaign of 1597 nothing decisive was achieved, while that of 1598 was highly adverse to the Turkish arms; Raab, Tata, Wesprim, Tschambock, besides several fortresses, were taken by the Imperialists, and the operations of the Turkish Seraskier, Saturdschi, were so unfortunate as to cost him his dismissal and his life. Both sides were now exhausted, and eager to conclude a peace if satisfactory terms could be obtained. In 1599, the Grand Vizier, Ibrahim Pacha, who commanded the Turkish forces in Hungary, made proposals to the Imperial General, Nicholas Palfy; but nothing was effected: the demands on both sides were too high, and the war was continued six years longer. It would be unprofitable, however, to enter into details of a struggle that was feebly carried on with varying success, and which gave birth to no events of decisive importance. Even the death of Mahomet III. (22nd of December, 1603) had little effect on the war, except that it served still further to exhaust the resources of the Porte by the payment of the accustomed donative to the Janissaries. Mahomet was quietly succeeded by his son, Achmet I., then hardly fifteen years of age.

The revival of the war between the Sultan and the Shah of Persia in 1603 tended still further to dispose the Porte to put an end to the struggle in Hungary; and the negotiations were facilitated by a revolution in Transylvania.

4. *Decadence of the Empire.*

The Turks, although not naturally fond of the sea, nor a commercial people—for what little trade they had was mostly in the hands of Europeans or Jews—nevertheless surpassed, during the period of their prosperity, the other nations of Europe in their maritime forces. Early in the sixteenth century, under Selim I., the Turkish Fleet numbered 400 sail of all descriptions, carrying 30,000 men. After the time of Selim, although still very formidable, it somewhat declined; and the battle of Lepanto inflicted upon it a blow from which it never thoroughly recovered. The rapidity, indeed, with which after that tremendous defeat the Turkish vessels that had been destroyed were replaced by new ones, excited the astonishment of the Bishop of Acqs, the French ambassador to the Porte; but fresh crews could not so easily be supplied, and still less experienced officers. Through mismanagement and neglect the Turkish Navy began rapidly to decline towards the end of the sixteenth century; and Sir Thomas Roe, who was at Constantinople in 1662, described the Turkish galleys as mostly so rotten and decayed, that not fifty were fit to put to sea, and those very ill-manned and equipped. The Corsair Fleets of Algiers, Tunis, and Tripoli appear, however, not to have shared this decay. It was remarked early in the seventeenth century that the Beys of those places possessed a fleet of forty large square-rigged vessels, with which they harassed the commerce of the Mediterranean; and they are related on one occasion to have blockaded Malaga, while another division of their ships cruised between the Tagus and the Guadalquiver.

The chief naval stations of the Turks, besides Constantinople and Gallipoli, were Nicomedia, Negropont, and Avlona in Albania. The Greeks formed the best sailors in the Turkish Fleet; galley slaves for the oars were supplied by the Christian prisoners, and there was also a maritime conscription throughout the Ottoman Empire. Before the battle of Lepanto, the Turkish galleys carried only from three to seven guns, one or two of which were of heavy calibre. After that disastrous defeat the number of guns was doubled, yet were still unequal to those of the Venetian ships. The Turks understood little of manœuvring in line; their tactics were to reserve their fire till they came to close quarters, and then to board the enemy. The Capudan-Pacha, or Chief Officer of the Fleet, not only commanded at sea, but had also the uncontrolled direction of the arsenal. In favour of Chaireddin Barbarossa, this office was elevated to that of Beylerbey of the Sea and the dignity of a Pacha of Two Tails; for the sea, like the land, was divided into sandjaks, fourteen in number. After the taking of Chios by Selim II. in 1566, the Capudan-Pacha was made a Vizier and Pacha of Three Tails.

Not only the Ottoman Navy, but also the empire in general, was beginning, towards the close of the sixteenth century, to feel the approach of decay. The wars of Selim II. had so exhausted the treasure, that he caused what remained of it to be removed to his private treasury. It had been previously kept in the ancient Byzantine Castle, called the "Seven Towers." In the palmy days of the Ottoman Empire each of these seven towers had had its appropriate use; one contained the gold, another the silver money; a third the gold and silver plate and jewels; valuable remains of antiquity were deposited in the fourth; in the fifth were preserved ancient coins and other objects, chiefly collected by Selim I. during his expeditions into Persia and Egypt; the sixth was a sort of arsenal; and the seventh was appropriated to the archives. After the time of Selim II., the "Seven Towers" were used as a prison for distinguished persons, and as an arsenal. Amurath III., whose avarice was prodigious, retained and improved upon the custom of his predecessor. He caused, it is said, a vault to be built, with treble locks, in which his treasure was deposited, and over which he slept every night; it was opened only four times a year to receive fresh heaps of wealth, which have been estimated at twelve million ducats annually; but two millions are perhaps nearer the truth.

More than a century of Turkish despotism had at length done its work. Ragazzoni describes the Christians in the Ottoman Empire in 1571 as so depressed and degraded, that they dared hardly look a Turk in the face; the only care of their listless existence was to raise enough for their maintenance, and to pay their *Karatsch*, or poll-tax—all beyond would be seized by the Turks. Constantinople, however, still afforded a secure place of residence, whither the Greeks flocked in great numbers; so that, towards the end of the sixteenth century, it was reckoned that there were 100,000 of them in that capital. Many of these acquired great wealth, either by trade or by farming certain branches of the Grand Seignior's revenue. Among them, one Michael Kantakuzenus was conspicuous both for his enormous wealth and his intrigues, which procured him the name of the "Devil's Son" (*Seitan Oglie*), although it was thought that he was not a true Greek, but an Englishman by birth, belonging to the family of an English ambassador. The fate of whole provinces lay in his hands; he could fit out twenty or thirty galleys at his own expense, and the splendour of his palace at Anchioli rivalled the Seraglio of the Grand Seignior. Kantakuzenus had gained his influence through the favour and friendship of Mahomet Sokolli; but even that powerful vizier could not at last save him from the wrath of Amurath III.; and he was hanged before the gate of his own palace (March, 1578). The Jews also occupied an important position in the Ottoman Empire. From the earliest period the physicians of the Sultan were of the Hebrew race; they monopolized most branches of commerce, they were the chief musical performers, and acted obscene comedies for the entertainment of the Grand Seignior.

5. *War and Treaty with Persia.—Treaty of Sitvatorok.*

The reign of Achmet I. marks the first steps towards the decided decadence of the Ottoman Empire. Having ascended the throne in his fifteenth year, Achmet only attained manhood at the close of his reign. According to the expression of a Turkish poet, "He was the first among all the sons of Osman who possessed empire before having carried the standard," that is to say before having reached his majority. His father bequeathed him a power weakened by seditions among the soldiers, and two wars to sustain, one in Hungary against the Imperialists, the other in Asia against the Shah of Persia.

In 1603, the formidable Shah Abbas, breaking through all conventions made with the Turks, seized upon Tebriz, Erivan, and Kars. He maintained his advantages until 1612, and then extorted a treaty from the Porte by which it renounced all its conquests since Selim. The revolts which broke out in Asia favoured the Persian arms. The submission of Deli Hassan had not put an end to the insurrection. Other chiefs succeeded to him, and the rebellion extended from the frontiers of Persia and Syria to the shores of the Bosphorus. The Kurds, the Druses, all the tribes of the Lebanon, figured in that league formed by Asiatic populations against the authority of the Osmanlis. The struggle was long and murderous. Murad Pacha, whose indomitable energy succeeded in terminating it, gained thereby the surname of *Restorer of the Empire.*

In Europe, the Hungarian war was pushed with little vigour; but Austria neglected to profit by so favourable a diversion as the war against Persia and the Asiatic rebels; she irritated the Hungarians, who chose as their king, Boskaï, uncle of Sigismond Bathory, and solicited the protection of the Sultan. The latter hastened to give the investiture to Boskaï (1605). Austria, enlightened by that act, concluded, in 1606, a treaty by which she recognized Boskaï as Prince of Transylvania and the districts in Hungary, which the Bathorys had possessed; it was stipulated that on the death of Boskaï all his possessions should revert to the empire. The Porte then consented to sign the treaty of Sitvatorok (11th of November, 1606), in which Ottoman pride stooped for the first time and abolished the humiliating conditions of preceding treaties. The annual tribute of 30,000 ducats, which Austria paid to the Sultan under the name of a gift of honour, was suppressed; "for this time only," it was said in the treaty, " 200,000 crowns will be paid to the Turks; but, in future, every three years, ambassadors shall bring voluntary presents, the value of which shall not be fixed on either side." "The Emperor and the Sultan," it added "shall treat on a footing of equality; the attacks, the surprises, the irruptions, must cease; the damages shall be repaired and the prisoners set at liberty. Gran, Erlau, and Kanischa remained in the power of the Turks; Austria kept Raab and Comorn. That peace was ratified by the States of Hungary and Austria, united with Presbourg (1608), and a convention signed at Vienna in 1615, confirmed it for twenty years.

That peace of Sitvatorok, says Hammer,* which has not sufficiently arrested the attention of publicists, and the remembrance of which is lost, effaced by that of the treaty of Carlowitz, signed a century later, has, however, a high signification in the history of political law and the diplomatic relations between Turkey and the rest of Europe. It fixed for the first time a limit to Ottoman conquest, which until then had threatened the West. The signs of vassalage, the annual tributes brought by ambassadors, were suppressed; diplomatic relations were established on a footing of equality; Transylvania was half emancipated

* Von Hammer, tom. ii. p. 327.

from the Turkish yoke, and Hungary although still subjected to Ottoman domination for a portion of her territory, was at least freed from tribute for the remainder. For the first time were observed, on the part of the Sultan and of the Grand Vizier, the diplomatic formalities in use among the nations of Europe. The act, written in Turkish, was not, as hitherto done, imposed upon the Imperial plenipotentiaries without allowing them to take cognizance of it; it was examined by the dragomans of both parties. The peace of Sitvatorok announced to the European Powers the decadence of the Ottoman Porte and prepared the way for the treaty of Carlowitz.

A short time after this peace, Boskaï died; but the Transylvanians refused to place themselves under the Austrian domination, and they took successively for princes, under the protection of the Porte, Sigismond Ragotzki, Gabriel Bathory, lastly Bethlem Gabor, the implacable enemy of the House of Austria, who fought in forty-two battles and was the faithful ally of the Sultans. That prince, in the firman of investiture, engaged to prevent the Voïvodes of Wallachia and Moldavia from acquiring any domain or any fortress upon his territory; and if those voïvodes, vassals of the Porte, revolted against the Sultan, he was bound to refuse them an asylum and send them prisoners to Constantinople. "Thus," says a Roumanian historian, "Turkey had comprehended that, so long as the Moldo-Wallachian princes should be attached to Hungary or Transylvania by interests of property or by the hope of finding therein a refuge, they would always adhere to those two countries, and, consequently, to Christianity. That article in the firman of investiture given to Bethlem separated the Moldo-Wallachians from the rest of the Christians, and subjected them irrevocably to Turkish authority."* Poland renewed, in 1609, the capitulations concluded under Mahomet III. She engaged to prevent the irruptions of the Cossacks into Moldavia; the Porte bound itself, on its side, to preserve Poland from the ravages of the Tartars; taxation had no rights over the

* Kogalnitchano, tom. i. p. 261.

estates of Poles who died in Turkey, and reciprocally, the Poles should always have the right of redeeming their countrymen from slavery. The capitulations were equally renewed in favour of the Republic of Venice. Lastly, in 1612, the United Provinces of the Low Countries obtained, for the first time, a treaty similar in its tenour to those which the Porte had concluded with France and England, but limited to commerce. The Dutch profited by it to introduce the use of tobacco into Turkey. In vain did the mufti endeavour to oppose that innovation; the soldiers and the common people rose against his ordinances, which he was compelled to revoke.

Of all the Christian ambassadors at Constantinople, the representative of Henry IV. remained, under Achmet as under Mahomet III., the most influential and the most zealous defender of European interests.

6. *Mission of Savary de Brèves.—Influence of France in the East.*

De Brèves, having obtained these capitulations, quitted Constantinople in 1605, and went to visit the churches and Christians of Asia, furnished with numerous firmans for redressing the abuses and repairing the iniquities of the Ottoman functionaries. He then saw for himself how insufficient the treaties were, how difficult it was to obtain justice in a State where the underlings had so many means of making tyrants, where religious hatreds excused and even prescribed iniquities. Although he was accompanied by an officer of the Sultan whose duty it was to watch over the execution of the commands of His Highness, he only obtained after much trouble redress or reparation of a multitude of abuses and injustice; he was compelled even to witness in silence much extortion, in order not to aggravate the position of the Christians after his departure. He was received with honours at Jerusalem by the Ottoman dignitaries; but his suite was frequently insulted by the populace. After having restored to the Latin Catholics the custody of the holy places, of which they had been deprived by the Greeks, he set sail for Tunis and Algiers. He had the Sultan's commands to the corsairs of those two places that they should cease from their piracy, that they should give up the Frenchmen whom they had carried into slavery, restore the booty pillaged from the French ships, and allow of French stations to be established on the coast of Barbary. He succeeded in part at Tunis, and concluded with the regency of that town only a slightly advantageous treaty, but which at least secured French commerce from piracy. From thence, De Brèves went to Algiers, but met with no reception there, the Corsairs remembering that, upon his complaint, three years previously, their viceroy had been summoned to render account of his piracies upon the French, and, by the Sultan's orders, strangled.

De Brèves, after his return to France, published a memoir upon his embassy and the condition of the Turks. The main object of that "Discourse" was to justify the alliance of France with the Porte, from the commercial and religious point of view, against the scruples of timorous Frenchmen, or against the declamations of the House of Austria, which was continually accusing the French Kings of treason towards Christianity.

"It was under Francis I.," he remarks in this "Discourse," "that we began to negotiate safely with the Turks; and our traffic was established there in such fashion that it could hardly be surpassed, and they, on the contrary, had no need of us; for it is very notorious that there are more than one thousand vessels upon the coasts of Provence and Languedoc which traffic throughout the extent of the Turkish Empire, and, by that means, enrich not only themselves, but many other parts of France receive advantage therefrom.

"And, although that advantage may be sufficiently great to compel us to make use of their friendship, the influence, however, cannot be estimated that it gives to the standard and banner of France, under which it permits Spanish, Italian, Flemish, and generally all kinds of Christian nations to traffic among them with the same freedom as the French; in which our kings have especially cherished, to testify to all the Princes of Europe that they do not keep up that friendship for their own particular interest nor that of their subjects, but also for the universal good of Christianity, which, by that means, appropriates to itself not only every sort of merchandise that may be gathered in their empire, but likewise all the products of Asia, Africa, and even the East Indies, which may be found abundantly amongst them, by the convenient route of the Red Sea, which carries to Egypt all the best things of Africa and the East Indies; and the Euphrates, on the other hand, freighted with the wealth of Asia, delivers it near Aleppo, the chief town of Syria, where the French merchants and those who desire to display our flag, load their vessels and thus distribute their contents throughout Europe.

"But, besides these pressing considerations, the preservation of the Christian name and of the Catholic religion in their country will be deemed very important, since it may be hoped that in the course of time there may be an increase of it, to the damage and the entire ruin of the Mohametan sect; for under pretext of consideration for us, and to give something for our friendship, the Grand Seignior permits of there being six or seven monasteries in the city and suburbs of Constantinople, which are filled, some with Franciscan friars, others with Jacobins; and, very lately, the Jesuit fathers have established their college; in such wise, that God is served there with the same worship and almost the same freedom that may be done in the middle of France; without taking into consideration an infinite number of Greek and Armenian Christians, which, in their most pressing necessities, have no recourse more certain, and seek no other protection, than the powerful name of our Kings, which shelters them by the ministry and its ambassadors.

"In fact, all the Turkish States are full of Christians;

even in the islands of the Archipelago, there are five or six bishoprics established, and the bishops nominated by the Holy Father, and the greater part of the inhabitants of those islands live under the authority of the Romish church, the principal of which are the archbishopric of Naxos, the bishopric of Scio, that of Andra and of Syra, all of which only subsist by the French name and maintain themselves with that protection. Egypt also abounds with a great number of Copts, who for the most part live under the discipline of a patriarch whom the King of Ethiopia recognizes for superior in spiritualities.

"But, when all these considerations are exhausted, which of themselves might urge such friendship to be sought for, if it were not already contracted, what an advantage to the French name, what glory to the very-Christian King of France, to be sole protector of the Holy Place where the Saviour of the world consented to live and die! What a satisfaction to behold in the midst of an infidel State the Christian name flourish, to behold in Holy Jerusalem the superb temple which Saint Helena there built, in which the Holy Sepulchre and the Mount Calvary are enclosed, and that it is served by thirty or forty Franciscans chosen from all nations, who pray God continually for the prosperity of Christian Princes, particularly for our King, their sole preserver, under the consent of whom they are enabled to inhabit Jerusalem, perform freely divine service there and receive pilgrims from every nation, who visit the Holy Places in safety, not without a feeling of the favour that they receive from His Majesty, who procures them that advantage."

De Brèves, in another place, again gives as a reason for the alliance of the King of France with the Turks the right of protection which he acquired by it over "so many peoples who have neither rest nor safety save under the authority of his name;" and he cites principally the Maronites and the Druses of Mount Lebanon. Finally, he terminates his memoir by saying that the political considerations which gave birth to the alliance ought to maintain it; and he invites His Majesty to preserve it, "in order to turn aside the arms of his enemies by the intervention of the Turk."

De Brèves had for his successor Gontaut Biron, baron of Solignac (1605). Nothing of importance passed under that ministry, save only the commencement of a persecution against the Catholic Priests. The Jesuits had established themselves in Constantinople; with their ambition and usual activity, they had conceived great projects for the regeneration of Catholicism in the East; they had already opened schools, commenced preaching at Pera, and they laboured successfully to reunite the Greeks with the Church of Rome, when the English denounced them as spies of Spain and alarmed the Divan as to their intentions against the safety of the Empire; they were thereupon arrested and imprisoned. On hearing this, Solignac ran to the Vizier, claimed the Jesuits as subjects of France, and obtained their deliverance; but the Ottoman Minister did not conceal his repugnance for those priests, and declared to him that he preferred to see ten ordinary priests than one Jesuit in Constantinople.

Solignac died in 1611, and under Achille de Harlay, baron de Sancy, who succeeded him, "commenced," says an historian, "the humiliations by which the authority of the European Ministers was destroyed at Constantinople, and the French alliance nearly broken off." That alliance had already undergone two distinct phases: offensive and warlike under Francis I. and Henry II., it had been limited to relations of good-will and commerce under the last Valois and under Henry IV. From the outset of Harlay de Sancy's embassy, and during sixty years the alliance changed gradually its character; it wavered, it decreased, it reached a point at which a rupture was to be feared. But it was so necessary and natural to the two States, that, in spite of enormous insults, blows, and even open hostilities, there was yet, on one side and the other, during all that period of disagreement and coolness, a tendency to reconciliation. Moreover, the influence of France in the East, its action upon the Christians dwelling there, was only moderately weakened.

Several causes brought about that change.

1. The Ottoman Empire, which formerly only had relations with the Christian States by war, which at first had but a single ally amongst the infidels, began to abandon its isolation, to admit of new alliances, to leave, as the Turks said, the Sublime Porte open to all. Its exclusive affection for France was changed; other counsels than those of France were listened to in the Divan; the powers inimical to France made use of the ignorance of the Turks to the disadvantage of their old and first allies.

2. France had originally sought for an alliance with the Ottomans to abase the House of Austria: it was again about to engage in a struggle with that House; but it now regarded the aid of the Turks as scandalous and little efficacious; she had found surer and less dangerous auxiliaries in the Protestants of Germany: also, during the Thirty Years' War, Richelieu and Mazarin made only feeble attempts to restore to the alliance between France and Turkey the character which it had under Francis I.

3. During almost the whole of the seventeenth century the Ottoman throne was only occupied by princes proudly barbaric, full of blind hatred of the Christians, who surrounded themselves only by ministers imbued with their prejudices, and often with their ignorance; they violated at pleasure, through thick and thin, against those "infidel dogs," the capitulations, the rights of nations, the laws of humanity; they made war against Christianity without political object and through mere fanatical brutality; lastly, they authorized the Barbary piracies, the hideous and last form which the spirit of Mahometan conquest assumed.

Another cause of the apathy of Turkey for France was the incapacity of the French ambassadors accredited at that period to the Sublime Porte, and especially their ignorance of the religion, the laws and customs of the Ottomans. The embassy to Constantinople was a post full of difficulty, embarrassment, and even of danger: it required as much prudence as energy; for it was necessary, in using unceasingly the greatest moderation, not to show the slightest weakness, to respect the prejudices of the Turks, especially in questions of form and etiquette, and for all that not to yield the least point of honour, the smallest prerogative; in all plaints and protests to negotiate with perseverance, without being tired of delays, refusals, and the ordinary disdain peculiar to Ottoman politics; to know how to scatter money *àpropos*, since all was venal and corrupt amongst the Turks; not to use menace save in the last extremity, since threats could not be followed up by deeds; finally, to do everything to maintain the alliance.

Let us return to Achmet for a momentary glance at his brief reign. On assuming the cares of government in adolescence, he showed himself to be good, active, full of noble designs, anxious to redress abuses, and desirous that justice should signalize his rule. But absolute power and the pleasures of the harem rendered null those good inclinations. Incapable of making proper choice of Ministers, he was continually changing his viziers. Hot-headed, capricious, eccentric, he allowed the inmates of the Seraglio to arrogate to themselves all authority, and most of all the Kizlar-aga, chief of the black eunuchs, who kept a court as pompous as that of his master. "One knows not, in truth," says an Italian contemporary, "who is the sovereign." A power was thus formed in the harem whose interests were neither those of the Empire, nor those of the Sultan, but solely of the women and eunuchs, that is to say, of slaves placed by religion and nature out of the province of politics and government. The viziers were compelled to submit thereto or renounce their dignities. The harem had yet another influence: the daughters and sisters of the Sultans, who at this epoch began to espouse the favourites and grandees of the Empire, diffused throughout the nation the luxurious habits of the Seraglio. In order to satisfy factitious needs the dignitaries sold justice, devastated the countries confided to their administration, and did not shrink from any exaction. Nacouh Pacha dared to propose to the Sultan to purchase of him the dignity of Grand Vizier, and when later he had obtained it, he pointed out to his master, in the dockyards of Constantinople, some old dismasted hulks as new naval constructions, and thereby embezzled enormous sums. The army did not escape this general demoralization: the Janissaries, devoting themselves with ardour to industry and commerce, lost their warlike character, and no longer had swift foot and sharp eye except to see when the cavalry began to waver and then to fly instantly at full speed. The sipahis saw the *timars* which had become vacant distributed amongst favourites; so that a given *sandjak*, that hitherto furnished a hundred sipahis, could scarcely bring fifteen, and frequently there was not one-tenth inscribed upon the registers.*

* Ranke, " History of the Osmanlis."

HAREM.

CHAPTER VII.

REIGNS OF MUSTAPHA I., OSMAN II., AMURATH IV., AND IBRAHIM I.
(1617–1649).

1. *Reigns of Mustapha I. and Osman II.* (1617–1622).

THE unimportant reign of Sultan Achmet I., with whom Austria had concluded the peace of Sitvatorok, was closed by his death, 22nd of November, 1617. Nothing can more strongly testify the sunken state of the Turkish power, than that it was possible to raise from a dungeon to the throne Achmet's imbecile brother, Mustapha. That prince's captivity of fourteen years had completely stultified him; but the ulemas, who hoped to govern in his name, gave out that his idiocy was a proof of sanctity. It was one of the pastimes of the unfortunate Mustapha to fling gold pieces to the fishes of the Bosphorus; but the Kizlar-aga persuaded the Divan that the precious metal would be better employed in furnishing the donatives customary on a new reign.

The commencement of his reign was marked by serious insults to the French ambassador. A Polish noble, who had been confined in the "Seven Towers," having escaped from his prison by the assistance of De Sancy's secretary, the vizier accused the whole of the French embassy of having favoured that flight; he caused the ambassador and his people to be violently arrested, put his secretaries to the torture and sent the functionary himself to the "Seven Towers." "Thou art not the first ambassador," said he to De Sancy, "who has been lodged in our prisons, but thou shalt be the first to whom the Gehenna shall be allotted." His deliverance could only be obtained at the end of four months by means of a ransom of 15,000 piastres, and leaving as hostage the people of the embassy. Moreover, the vizier became exasperated, in his wild rage, with the other ambassadors; he compelled them to remain prisoners within their houses, and caused a public proclamation to be made that any Mussulman who should find them out of Pera should conduct them to prison; lastly, he laid arbitrary taxes upon the Christian merchants. The Court of France, on learning these outrages, recalled the Baron De Sancy, and sent a gentleman, M. De Naus, to demand satisfaction, with threats of a rupture. But after three months' enjoyment of the sceptre, Mustapha had been led back to his dungeon, and the Vizier strangled before the arrival of De Naus. In fact, a revolt of the Janissaries had deposed the imbecile Sultan and replaced him by his nephew Osman, the eldest of the seven sons of Achmet, who was saluted Padischah amidst the acclamations of the venal soldiery (26th of February, 1618). The troops gained by that change a gratification of 6,000,000 ducats.

Until the age of fourteen Osman had been brought up less like a prince than as a dervish, and his religious rigour must have rendered the government of a corrupt State a difficult task to him. He, however, displayed a spirit and ambition beyond his years. Strong and active of body, he soon became inured to all military exercises, a bold rider and an unfailing marksman with the bow; but, with all his energy he lacked the perseverance without which nothing great can be accomplished, while his meanness alienated from him the hearts of the rapacious Janissaries.

Immediately upon his accession, he had hastened to despatch a *chiaoux* to Paris with letters of excuse signed by himself, by the Grand Vizier and the Capudan-Pacha, and to assure the French king that in future his ambassador should be honoured and respected as in the past. Sancy, who persisted in his recall, was charged to offer presents to Louis XIII.

The reign of Osman II. presents no other remarkable event save the unsuccessful war against Poland, between which country and the Porte bickerings had for several years prevailed; and he esteemed its conquest so easy that he divided the spoil beforehand. Desolating incursions had been made by the Tartars into Poland, and by the Cossacks into the Turkish dominions, which in 1620 ended in open war. Poland was then ruled by the Swedish prince, Sigismund III., as before mentioned. Caspar Gratiani, Voïvode of Moldavia, had courted the favour of Sigismund by sending to him the intercepted letters addressed by Bethlem Gabor to the Porte, complaining of the incursions of the Polish Cossacks and freebooters. Gratiani was deposed on the discovery of his proceedings; but he would not yield without a struggle; he called upon the Poles for assistance, who sent him a force of 50,000 men. Against these, posted in a fortified camp near Jassy, in Moldavia, Iskander Pacha, governor of Silistria, led an army of double their number, composed of Osmanli and Tartars; and on the 20th of September, 1620, a great battle was fought, in which 10,000 Poles were slain. The remainder, after a useless attempt to defend their entrenched camp, retreated towards the Dniester, in the passage of which river most of them perished. Gratiani himself had fallen in the retreat.

It was this success that incited Osman to attempt the conquest of Poland against the advice of his Ministers, and even the wishes of his army; and in the spring of 1621, clad in a suit of mail which had belonged to Solyman *the Magnificent*, he placed himself at the head of 100,000 men. But the march proved difficult and destructive; the mercenary troops were alienated by Osman's reluctance to pay the customary gratuity; and it was the end of August before the Turks arrived on the Dniester. Here Sigismund had encamped 40,000 Poles and Cossacks, and 8,000 Germans sent to him by the Emperor; while another army of reserve of 60,000 men under the Crown Prince, lay at Kaminieck. A first assault on the Polish camp was attended with some success; but the following ones were repulsed, although in the sixth and last the Sultan in person led one of the storming columns. A

Polish winter set in early; men and horses perished by thousands; a mutiny broke out; and Osman, after opening negotiations for a peace, began his retreat. On the 28th of December, 1621, he entered Constantinople in triumph; for though he had lost 80,000 men, he pretended to claim a victory. But his bad success, his unpopularity with the army, the dearness of provisions, and the strictness of his police which he superintended in person, by visiting the wine-houses and other places of resort, soon produced symptoms of revolt among the Janissaries. As these degenerate troops were averse to the warlike schemes meditated by Osman, he resolved to destroy them. The scheme he formed was bold and well-designed, and, if successful, might have revived the sinking fortunes of the Turkish Empire. Under pretence of a pilgrimage to Mecca, Osman was to raise a large army at Damascus, march with it to Constantinople and annihilate the refractory Janissaries; but his preparations, and some incautious words, prematurely betrayed his intentions.

On a report that the Sultan's tent was about to be transported to Scutari, the Janissaries (May 18, 1622), associating themselves to the Sipahis, rose in rebellion, repulsed with insults their aga and other officers, who had been sent to hear their complaints, and demanded from the mufti a categorical answer to the enquiry, "Whether it was permitted to put to death those who misled the Padischah, and devoured the substance of the Moslems?" The mufti having answered in the affirmative, the mutineers rushed to the palaces of the Grand Vizier and of the Chodsa, who were thought to be the authors of the plan for their destruction; these Ministers saved themselves by flight, but their palaces were plundered and destroyed. On the following day the insurrection assumed a still more formidable aspect. The Sultan having refused to give up the six authors of the pilgrimage, though he consented to renounce his pilgrimage itself, an attack was made on the Seraglio; and in the midst of the confusion, a cry of Mustapha Khan for Sultan, echoed by thousands of voices, became the watchword of the revolution. The wretched Mustapha, wasted to a shadow by want of air and food, and expecting death rather than a crown, was dragged from his obscure dungeon, carried to the throne-room and saluted Padischah. Osman contemplating flight, when it was too late abandoned his Grand Vizier and Kizlar-aga to the fury of the soldiers, by whom they were horribly murdered; the Janissaries who would listen to no terms, though large offers were made, occupied the Seraglio, and directed all the actions of the Sultana Validé, the mother of the idiot Mustapha; and Constantinople was abandoned to plunder and devastation. Osman, who had fled to the palace of the Aga of the Janissaries, was dragged from his hiding-place, and conducted with abuse and derision, first to the barracks of the mutineers, and then to the "Seven Towers." On the way thither his faithful adherent, Hussein Pacha, was murdered at his feet. Arrived there, the youthful Sultan made a piteous appeal to the rebels, but vainly endeavoured to soften them. "Forgive me," he implored, sobbing, "if I have offended you unwittingly. Yesterday, I was a sovereign; to-day, I am stripped bare. Let me serve you as an example: you likewise may experience the caprice of fate. My agas of Sipahis, and you, the seniors of the Janissaries, my fathers, through the imprudence of a young man, I have listened to bad advice; but wherefore humiliate me thus? Will you have nothing more to do with me?" "We will have neither your domination nor your blood," replied the rebels laying hands upon him. The unfortunate Osman defended himself for some time, till at length one of his executioners passed the bow-string round his neck and so despatched him. They sent one of his ears to the Sultana Validé, by whose orders to her Vizier, Daud Pacha, he had been put to death. Thus perished the first Ottoman Emperor whom his subjects had doomed to assassination.

2. *Restoration of Mustapha I.—Amurath IV.* (1623).

Once more set upon the throne, Mustapha was during fifteen months the plaything of the soldiery. The murderers of Osman soon repented of their crime; they were, however, the absolute masters of the State, and disposed, according to their caprice, of the most important posts. But those among them who had been opposed to the murder of the Sultan revolted, and were only appeased by making them frequent distributions of money; the Sipahis, in their turn, compelled concessions of the public farms, and imposed fresh taxes on the *timars*. At length the provinces of Asia were excited to revolt by the Pacha of Erzeroum, and an attempt at revolt by the ulemas of Constantinople increased the universal anarchy. The Janissaries themselves saw the abyss into which the Empire was descending, and nominated a Grand Vizier, who proposed to depose the Sultan, and appoint as his successor Amurath, eldest son of Achmet. This met with their approval, and, informed of the exhaustion of the treasury, they renounced the accession donative. Amurath was then proclaimed (1623).

The new Sultan was born in 1612. His youth seemed to secure impunity to the usurpations and insolence of the soldiery. In fact, during the first ten years of his reign, the Janissaries and the Sipahis continued to harass and oppress the empire. During that time, Persia extended its conquests: Shah Abbas seized upon Bagdad (1623), and the Osmanli vainly tried to retake that city. The Pacha of Erzeroum persisted in his rebellion until 1628, when he received the government of Bosnia. In the Crimea, the Tartars likewise rose; the Ottomans were defeated and taken in such numbers that a Turkish prisoner was sold for a glass of *boza* (a drink made from fermented barley). All these reverses had for their cause the spirit of faction and insubordination which reigned in the army. At length, Amurath grew weary of the yoke. When he saw the Janissaries and the Sipahis break in the gates of the Seraglio, and put to death under his own eyes his most faithful servants, he comprehended that, to escape the fate of his brother Osman, he had need to terrify the rebels by his energy and his audacity. "'Tis well," said he; "if God permits, you shall suffer the effects of a fearful vengeance—oppressors, who fear neither God nor humble yourselves before His Prophet!" He struck terror amongst them by the murder of their chief, Redgeb Pacha: the corpse of the traitor being flung forth in front of the Seraglio gate (1632).

From that moment the actual reign of Amurath IV. began. The Janissaries and the Sipahis took the oath of fidelity. The Sultan, the Grand Vizier, and the mufti, declared the reversion of the Spahis to the administrative posts suppressed, and proclaimed the promise made by both corps to maintain public order. "My Padischah," said one of the judges of Asia to the Sultan, "the only remedy against abuses is the scimitar." Amurath remembered that advice.

The termination of that military anarchy brought back victory to the banners of the Osmanli. Shah Abbas having died (1629), Amurath resolved to invade Persia, and placed himself at the head of the army. He took Erivan, Tebriz, and besieged Bagdad (1638). Enamoured of war, he put on the uniform of a Janissary and worked in the trenches like a common soldier. Such conduct inflamed the ardour of his troops, and the garrison, though numerous, was compelled to capitulate; but in the intoxication of victory it was massacred. Persia sued for peace, ceded Bagdad, and received in exchange the province of Erivan. That war brought the Sultan much glory but small profit.

"It may be said with truth," remarked a contemporary, "that the frontiers of Persia are for the Grand Seignior what Flanders is to the King of Spain, or the island of Candia to the Venetians. The expense there is immense and the revenue very little; and it has chanced to the Turks, under these circumstances, that which they have never experienced in any other conquest, the impossibility of establishing timariots and vassals whence they might draw troops to safeguard the country, and a militia wherewith to recruit the imperial armies. The want of men, the greater number of whom have fled to the woods, and the rest taken refuge in the towns of the King of Persia, having rendered the country uninhabitable, the Turkish soldiers have refused to accept the timars which they could not make available, and in which they would not have had the means of breeding horses, in order to draw from them the contingent imposed upon all the new timariots for the augmentation of the cavalry of the army. The conquered country yielded no impost, and Amurath was obliged to pay from his *gaznah* the numerous garrisons, such as were necessary to be kept up in a conquered country upon the frontier of an enemy so powerful and of a doubtful faith." *

3. *Character of Amurath IV.—State of the Army.*

Amurath was then in all the vigour of manhood, and seemed ready to renew the exploits of Solyman. An excellent horseman, he could spring easily from one horse upon another, hurl the javelin with unerring aim, and bend a bow with such strength that the arrow sped further than the ball from a fowling-piece; he thus pierced, it is said, sheets of iron four inches thick. But the lust of murder was developed in his soul. His mode of hunting indicated that that passion existed in him to the highest degree. He took no pleasure in pursuing the game, but had it run down by several hundred beaters, and delighted only in slaughtering it. In 1637, the number of men he had caused to be executed in the space of five years was estimated at 25,000, and many had perished by his own hand. The expression of his countenance was horrible; his pale brown eye gleamed menacingly, his face was half hidden by his long chestnut hair and thick beard; and he was never

* "Relazione della stato nel quale si retruova il governo dell' imperio Turchesco."

more dangerous than when he knitted his frowning brows. It was then that his dexterity in launching the javelin and arrow became most deadly. His attendants served him tremblingly, and his mutes could not be distinguished from the other slaves of the Seraglio, for every one spoke by signs. Murder had become no longer a means but a pleasure to this monster.

The extreme severity of Amurath tamed the insubordinate spirit of his rebellious soldiery; he interdicted their assemblages, in which, intoxicated with the fumes of tobacco and coffee, they passed whole days without other occupation than that of hatching plots. He re-established order in the timars, changed the uniform of the Sipahis, and no longer permitted them to indulge their noisy turbulence in the streets. He separated the Janissaries unfit for service from those who were efficient, and forced the latter to march against the enemy in spite of their exemptions. He failed, however, to restore the ancient valour to these troops. The Sipahis, to whom their pay was not sufficient, often renounced their pay and service. The Janissaries seemed only fit to inspire terror among the Western peoples by their aspect and shouts; they no longer exhibited either a knowledge of military tactics or courage. Their aga had set out from Constantinople one day with the entire corps; he brought back from Aleppo only 3,000—all the rest had deserted by the way. Warlike operations were shunned with as much ardour as they were sought for formerly. The Ottoman armies then fell back into their primitive condition, and the timariots appeared again as when the nucleus of them was first formed. Nevertheless, the best even of these timariot troops, that is to say, those who, cantoned on the frontiers of Hungary, were kept efficient by continual fighting, were still composed of bad soldiers. The Christians rejoiced that Heaven, for the happiness of the faithful, had only endowed the Turks with a slender capacity. They compared the bearing of their order of battle to that of a bull—menacing and dangerous in appearance, but which could be overcome by intelligence and address.

However powerful, however absolute he might appear, Amurath was not the less dominated by the influence of the Seraglio. He was the sport of his favourites and his mother, whom he relegated several times and uselessly to the old palace wherein to confine herself. Moreover, law and right had little power over him in the sight of gold, for which he evinced an insatiable thirst. He cared neither for magnificent tissues nor precious objects of art; he attached importance only to the number of purses. Then every one sought to appear poor. The possession of gold and silver ornaments, and the wearing of costly vestments, were avoided. Money was hidden, in the dread of at once exciting both ruling passions of the Grand Seignior—gold and blood. Thus did Amurath govern his empire. He filled his coffers, no doubt; he placed his life in safety, and died calmly in his bed (1640); but the terror which had procured him that safety paralyzed at the same time the strength of the empire; the sword which procured him riches deprived him of men who had been the terror of Christendom.*

4. *Relations with France.*

Under the reign of Amurath France lost much of her influence in the East. It was the fault of the greedy merchants, who went so far as to introduce spurious money, and adventurers who practised every kind of malversation, and commonly ended by abjuring their religion. The government of Louis XIII., warned of these abuses, gave more serious attention to the affairs of the Levant. Consulates were established in Albania, and missions in the Morea, at Athens, Scio, Constantinople, Aleppo, Seïde, &c. A celebrated traveller, Deshayes of Courmesmin, was sent to visit all the French establishments; he went through the greater portion of the Ottoman Empire, sojourned at Jerusalem, where he established a Consulate, and caused the custody of the Holy Places of Bethlehem to be restored

* Venetian narrative of 1637, cited by Ranke, pp. 101-104.

to the Catholic monks, of which they had been deprived by the Armenians.

The Count de Césy, however, had succeeded to Sancy, and under that Minister, the unfriendly proceedings towards France recommenced. Césy having failed to obtain from the Divan the deposition of a patriarch of Constantinople who had adopted Calvinism, he was obliged to admit the Republic of Venice to share in the protection of the churches of Galata; he could not hinder the Sultan, on the demand of the ambassadors of England and Holland, from closing the schools and printing offices of the Jesuits and from driving that religious body out of Constantinople (1628). In vain did he threaten to withdraw his embassy; the Vizier told him that the long-standing amity between France and Turkey could not depend upon the chastisement of a few spies. And the banishment of the Jesuits was maintained during twelve years. Lastly, Césy, in order to promote French commerce, having undertaken the farming of the customs duties upon goods, gave the management of it to an Armenian (1629), who incautiously became security for several merchants of Marseilles and was made bankrupt. Césy found himself responsible for his debts, which amounted to 100,000 francs, and he was sued thereupon.

Henri de Gournay, Count of Marcheville, was then sent as a successor to Césy (1631), with directions to arrange his affairs by paying the debts that he had contracted "for the benefit of commerce" in favour of the merchants of Marseilles. Marcheville was a presumptuous, ignorant person, and a bully to boot. As he entered the Archipelago, he encountered the fleet of the Capudan-Pacha, who, not knowing him, demanded a salute and summoned him to come on board; he replied by ordering his own ship to fire a gun loaded with ball at the Turkish commander, even shouting to the sailors to take good aim at the admiral, who was on deck. The French vessel was soon surrounded by the Ottoman Fleet, and Marcheville brought in a furious rage to the Capudan, to whom he told his name and mission, declaring that he would have

his head or France should make war upon the Porte.
The Turk answered him not a word, and only released
the ambassador on reaching Constantinople. At the first
audience he had with the Grand Vizier, Marcheville complained of the outrage of the Capudan, but with such a
transport of rage and volley of threats, that the Minister
interrupted him and dismissed him. He then threw aside
all prudence and circumspection, and showed such contempt for Oriental customs, that he passed for a madman
and found himself exposed to continual insult. Thus he
favoured the escape of certain Christian slaves; he charged
sword in hand, in the streets of Constantinople, the Janissaries who did not make way for him; he sent his interpreters before the Divan to make such preposterous threats,
that, if the somewhat suspicious report of the Austrian
resident may be believed, one of those interpreters was
hanged, another empaled, and the son of the ambassador
imprisoned. All this occurred under the reign of a prince
who wound up his commands thus: "Do as I have said,
or I will cut off your head!" Free course was then
given to the fanatical fury of the Ottomans against the
Christians; the Churches of Galata were closed; all the
Franks were disarmed, even the ambassadors; arbitrary
taxes were imposed upon European merchandise. Marcheville recriminated against all this violence with as much
haughtiness as malapertness, and found himself an object
of hatred not only of the Turks, but of all the Christians;
lastly, he consummated his extravagances by exciting
something like a mutiny against his predecessor, whose
affairs he had in no way arranged, and who, having returned to Constantinople touching his debts, caused to be
seized, by an order of the King in agreement with the
Sultan, the ships of the merchants for whom he had
become security. The Capudan-Pacha, who had not ceased
to persecute Marcheville, having become Kaïmacan, or
lieutenant of the Grand Vizier, took advantage of that
tumult to issue an order in the Sultan's name, for him to
quit the city instantly. "That order," he said, "is
addressed personally to Marcheville, and not to the am-

bassador of the King of France." He then had him thrust into a caïque that put him on board a French vessel, which was at once towed out as far as the Dardanelles (1634). Césy, his predecessor, was invited by the Divan, and almost constrained, to resume his ambassadorial functions, until it pleased the King to order otherwise. It was confirmed by the Court of France, who accepted the explanation of the Kaïmacan and demanded no reparation. He was still at Constantinople in 1639, when the King nominated M. de la Haye-Vautelay to the Turkish embassy.

Amongst all the damage done to the Franks during the embassy of Marcheville, the most serious was the usurpation by the Greeks from the Latins of the custody of the Holy Sepulchre. From time immemorial, the possession of the holy places had been assigned to the Franciscan Brothers under the protection of France, when, in 1634, the Greeks profited by the hostile feeling of the Ottomans against the Europeans to advance their claim to it. The matter was pleaded before the Divan with much solemnity, and in presence of all the Christian ambassadors; by force of money, the Greeks carried the day, and every effort which France made to obtain a reversal of that decree failed during some forty years. That usurpation of the Greeks dealt a heavy blow to French influence in the East; for the possession of the holy places by the French monks was not an empty prerogative; it was the remnant of French domination in the Levant, and testified to its power in the eyes of Christians as well as Turks. Those churches, those sanctuaries, those places consecrated by the life and death of Jesus Christ, were not protected by the kings of France solely through religious zeal, but from politic considerations. In proportion as one of them was taken out of their custody, the French name lost something of its *éclat* in the East, and the day on which the flag of France disappeared from the last Christian dome saw a marked diminution of French influence in the Levant.

5. *Depredations of the Barbary Corsairs.*

During the interval that France lost the custody of the Holy Sepulchre at Jerusalem and her ambassador was insulted at Constantinople, her commerce became abandoned to the depredations of the Barbary corsairs. Piracy had taken, in the early part of the seventeenth century, the most scandalous development; more than a hundred corsair craft struck continual terror on all sides, whence they carried off costly booty of all kinds, including cattle and their owners. Their ravages and cruelties excited the indignation of the whole of Europe, for a captivity among the Barbary pirates had become a common occurrence to travellers: a thousand Christians lay in chains at one time. The Mediterranean belonged no longer to Christianity, but entirely to Mahometanism, and to the most barbarous and hideous portion of Mahometanism; for the corsairs of Algiers, Tunis, and Tripoli were the rakings together of all the brigands and adventurers of Turkey, and their chiefs were most frequently Christian renegades.

The coasts of France had been respected by the corsairs in the early days of the alliance with the Porte: Solyman was obeyed by his African vassals, and Francis I. had a navy. But, under the successors of Solyman, and under the sons of Henry II., the Barbary pirates rendered themselves almost completely independent of the Porte, and France had scarcely a few galleys in the Mediterranean. Her southern shores there had their share of the ravages; no merchant vessel dare longer show itself at sea without being armed with cannon and soldiers; ships and sailors were carried off from the very harbours of Syria, from under range of the guns of the Dardanelles; Provence and Languedoc were daily assailed, and every port and every village soon reckoned some fifty of its sailors captives in chains. The inhabitants were compelled to fortify their dwellings, to invent day and night signals to give warning of the approach of the barbarians, to arm even the fishing-boats. Renegades, established in the towns of Africa, bought at a low price the pillaged merchandise and sold it again in Europe, chiefly in the ports of Tuscany. All the writings of the period contain complaints on that subject, and relate lamentable tales of captivity.

The Government of Louis XIII., moved by these complaints, made earnest representations to the Ottoman Porte; which ordered the Barbary corsairs to cease their brigandage upon French vessels, and to deliver up the slaves of that nation; but those orders received no attention. It was then decided to negotiate privately and directly with the pirates. A Treaty was concluded on the 21st of March, 1619, between the King of France and the Algerines, by the mediation of the Duke de Guise, Admiral of the Levant, without the Porte disturbing itself about this act of independence of its subjects. The Treaty was not executed, and, early in the following year, seven French galleys were sent in search of the corsairs; they made some prizes and continued their cruizing during two years; but that force was insufficient; commerce continued to suffer, and the assembly of French notables of 1626 supplicated the King "to maintain in his ports a sufficient number of coast-guard vessels to defend the littoral against the pirates that infested it." Richelieu had then need of the whole of his navy against the Protestants; he procured the intervention of the Sultan, who issued commands "to his slaves of the Algerine militia that they should have respect for the ships and subjects of his friend, the Emperor of France." One Simon Napolon, a merchant of Provence, was sent to Algiers, with two cannons, taken from the Barbary pirates and the Turkish slaves who were in the French galleys, and on the 19th of September, 1628, a new Treaty was obtained from the Algerians by which they engaged to respect, for the future, French ships only.

That Treaty was also violated; the barbarians could not conceive the idea that they ought to respect the life and possessions of certain infidels; and an inspection made in 1633 upon the coasts of Provence by M. de Seguiran by order of Richelieu, revealed the ravages of the corsairs and the condition into which the commerce of the Levant had fallen.

Richelieu would have gladly put an end to this piracy; but he was absorbed in the struggle in which he was about to embark against the House of Austria. However, he furnished the coasts of the Mediterranean with twelve galleys; he despatched to Morocco a squadron, commanded by the Chevalier de Rosilly, who recovered 600 slaves from the corsairs; he entered upon negotiations with the Knights of Malta to make their island a possession of France, and projected with them the destruction of the Barbary pirates. At last, in 1636, when the French Fleet, under the command of the Archbishop Sourdis, sailed from the Atlantic into the Mediterranean to retake the Hyères Islands, which had been seized upon by the Spaniards, he gave him the following instructions:—

"After taking the said islands, the armament shall proceed to sail close in to the Barbary shore, from Tunis to Algiers, and make a demand upon those said cities to deliver up the French slaves detained there to the prejudice of the Treaties of Peace which they have made with the King, offering to restore the Turks who are at Marseilles, or failing which, war will be declared against them, all the men and vessels of the said cities taken or burned."

The necessity of keeping the sea against the Spaniards prevented Sourdis "from going," as he himself wrote, "to Tunis and to Algiers, to make them recognize the flag of France by the mouths of her cannon." The Algerines continued their piracies with so much success, that in two years they captured eighty vessels carrying the French flag. In 1640 a new squadron was fitted out, but it encountered the fate of the first, being dispersed by a storm. The following year proved equally unlucky, and negotiations entered upon with Tunis led to no result.

Such was the untoward state of the relations between France and the East when Louis XIV. ascended the throne; it was reserved for him to aggravate them by errors that had a fatal influence upon the destinies alike of Turkey and of France.

6. *Ibrahim I.* (1639).—*War against Venice.*

Ibrahim I. had succeeded his brother Amurath IV. He made no expeditions into Asia, and, after the example of his brother, humoured the House of Austria; he enjoined even Rakoczy, Prince of Transylvania, to discontinue war against the Emperor and to break with Sweden. He showed himself more warlike towards the Cossacks, who had seized upon Azof during the preceding reign, and he recaptured that place from them, which was already coveted by the Muscovites. All the efforts of the Ottoman power were directed against the Republic of Venice.

In 1644, some Maltese galleys captured a Turkish vessel bound for Mecca, and in which were one of the women and a son of the Sultan. They were taken to Candia, where the Venetian commander had the imprudence to receive them. On learning this, Ibrahim gave way to such furious anger that at first he resolved to exterminate all the Christians in his States; then, upon the representation of the Mufti, the Europeans only; next, upon the remonstrances of his Ministers, the Catholic priests. The order for these massacres was even given, and its revocation was a matter of such difficulty, that the Franks dwelling in Constantinople believed themselves, during fifteen days, doomed to certain death. The Sultan then sent for the Christian Ambassadors, and declared that he held them responsible for the outrage committed, and that their masters ought themselves to avenge him upon the Knights of Malta and the Venetians; next he imprisoned them in their houses, ordered the offices of the Frank merchants to be closed, and laid an embargo upon all their ships. The ambassadors of England, Venice, and Holland represented to the Sultan that not one of their compatriots belonged to the Order of Malta, which was composed almost entirely of Frenchmen; and the wrath of Ibrahim was about to expend itself against France, when the Grand Vizier became desirous of profiting by the occurrence to attempt the conquest of Candia, the last Greek possession of the

Venetians. To this end he made great preparations, and, without declaring war, a fleet of 348 sail landed 50,000 men in that island, the acquisition of which was destined to cost the Ottomans twenty-five years' fighting.

Chania was taken almost without a blow being struck (1645). The Venetian Fleet having arrived too late to defend that place, avenged itself by devastating the coasts of Morea, the isle of Tenedos, and the plain of Troy (1646). But several towns of Crete capitulated, among others the important place of Retimo. The Turks failed before Candia, the capital (1647). At the same time they attacked Dalmatia, but had no success there.

Venice had asked aid from all the Christian Powers. The Catholic world was stirred up by the insults of the Turks; and the religious zeal that then animated France found vent in cries for war against the infidels. Mazarin beheld with complacency the peril of the Venetians, with whom the French were in rivalry for the commerce of the Levant; but he was unwilling that the Turks, whose friendship for France had so strangely cooled, should succeed in dominating the Mediterranean by the possession of Candia. Pursuing his wily policy, he resolved to maintain openly the Ottoman alliance, to allow French commerce to profit by the embarrassments of the Venetians, and at the same time to hinder the success of the Turks by underhand hostility which should make them repent of their bad conduct towards France, and should satisfy Catholic opinion. He sent to Constantinople an Ambassador Extraordinary, M. de Varennes, to offer the Divan the mediation of France; the mediation was haughtily rejected. He then offered to the Venetians the co-operation of the French Navy; but he limited that co-operation to three fire-ships, yet on such conditions that the Senate refused them. Afterwards he sent to Venice a subsidy of 10,000 crowns, but secretly and in his own name. The following year he further gave nine ships, but without crews, and which were to fight under the Venetian flag, conjointly with nine other vessels furnished by Spain. Finally, he allowed the Senate to recruit soldiers in France; and that permission was so largely used, that, during twenty-five years' strruggle, and although France was herself engaged in the Thirty Years' War, more than 50,000 Frenchmen, urged either by religious zeal or by love of adventure, accepted the pay of Venice, and perished under her flag. That number is confirmed by the registers of the Republic.

The glory of subduing Candia was not reserved for Ibrahim's reign; the vices of that prince, rather than the courage of the Christians, retarded the capture of the city. Worn out by excessive debauchery, he was incapable of directing the war and of pushing it vigorously. The favourite Sultanas devoured the revenues of the State and disposed at will of every appointment. The army grew weary of this shameful tyranny, and the spirit of revolt, suppressed under the preceding reign, re-awoke all the more terrible that the Imperial power had been so debased. The Janissaries deposed Ibrahim, and the principal dignitaries of the Empire caused him to be strangled (1648). His son Mahomet IV., scarcely seven years old, succeeded him.

CHAPTER VIII.

REIGN OF MAHOMET IV. UNTIL 1669.

1. *Insolence of the Janissaries; revolts in Asia.—War in Transylvania, Servia, and Moldavia.*

THE reign of Mahomet IV., which lasted forty years, may be divided into three periods; the first extending from the death of Ibrahim to the appointment of the Grand Vizier Kupruli Mahommed (1648-56); the second, during the administration of the two first Kupruli, from 1656 to the Treaty of Peace with Poland (1676); the third, from the death of Ahmed Kupruli, to the deposition of the Sultan (1676-87). The first period is filled with seditions and reverses; in the second, Ahmed Krupruli re-established the affairs of the Empire; then the troubles recommenced, and the Ottoman power, shaken within and without, tottered to its decline.

After the murder of Ibrahim, the Porte underwent anew the domination of the soldiery. The Janissaries, at first satisfied with their work, repressed an insurrection of Itchoglans and Sipahis; but they made the young Sultan pay dearly for their insolent guardianship. More than once, during the war against Venice, they compromised the honour of the Crescent by their revolts, in presence even of the enemy. In 1649, they refused to continue the siege of Candia, and the Seraskier Hussein was constrained to discontinue the operations. In 1651, a new sedition cost the life of the grandfather of Mahomet IV. Five years after, the Janissaries and Sipahis, irritated at the delay in the payment of their arrears, were seen to reassemble upon the hippodrome, the ordinary theatre of their insurrections, and to clamour with loud outcries for the death of the members of the Divan. The Sultan obeyed the call: the *lords of the hippodrome* (at-meidani-aghalari) handed him a list of proscriptions; he delivered into the hands of the executioner his dearest servants, and the whole administration was overthrown (1656). Encouraged by the example of the army, the incorporation of handicraftsmen rose also and caused the Grand Vizier to be deposed. Finally, revolts broke out in the Asiatic provinces: Ahmed Pacha, governor of Anatolia, was overcome, taken, and slain by the rebels (1659).

Fortunately for the Turks, Germany, exhausted by the Thirty Years' War, which the treaties of Westphalia had just brought to a close (1648), did not think about reconquering Hungary; France was troubled with the Fronde war (1649-52), and had not yet signed peace with Spain; the Sultan therefore had only to combat Venice. But, so long as anarchy prevailed within, he obtained no advantage without the realm, in spite of the isolation in which the Christian Powers left the defenders of Candia. The Admiral Moncenigo even obtained in the very Straits of the Dardanelles a complete victory over the Turkish Fleet, seized upon Tenedos, Samothracia, and Lemnos; and, by a strict blockade of the Hellespont, succeeded almost in famishing Constantinople (1656).

Such was the situation of the empire when Kupruli Mahommed was raised to the post of Grand Vizier. His first care, on his entrance into power, was to restore order and discipline. A military mutiny having broken out, he suppressed it by capital punishments: four hundred bodies were, it is said, flung into the sea. He hanged, at the same time, the Greek patriarch accused of treason.

The war against the Venetians was vigorously resumed. Moncenigo lost his life in an indecisive battle fought near the Dardanelles (1657); the isles of Tenedos and Lemnos were reconquered; but these successes were in part compensated by a victory which the squadron of the Republic obtained near Milo (1661).

A Swedish embassy having come to demand from the Porte an alliance offensive and defensive against Poland, Rakoczy, Prince of Transylvania, joined his solicitations to those of the King of Sweden. Kupruli rejected those propositions, and caused the Transylvanian deputies to be imprisoned in the Seven Towers, because their master had leagued himself, without the authorization of the Divan, with the Swedes and the Cossacks. Rakoczy persisted not the less in attacking Poland; and, with that view, he concluded a treaty with the Voïvodes of Wallachia and Moldavia. The Poles defeated him; the Porte deposed and drove him out (1657), as well as the Voïvode of Wallachia, Constantine I. The Sultan put in place of the latter the Greek Mihne, son of a locksmith, and Constantine went into Poland only to die. "With him," says a Moldavian historian, "ended the family of the Bassaraba, from which Wallachia had drawn almost all its princes during 417 years, from 1241 to 1658. The House of Bassaraba gave to that country, besides several princes of secondary talent, four great Voïvodes: Marcea the Great, the founder of the army; Rodolph the Great, the Reformer of the Clergy; Michael the Brave, the hero and conqueror, and Matthew I., the legislator of Wallachia."

Rakoczy, dethroned by the Sultan, did not abandon the government of Transylvania without a struggle; he defeated, at Lippa, the Pacha of Pesth (1658); but he was defeated in turn by Kupruli, and solicited the new Voïvode of Wallachia to ally himself with him. Mihne, in fact, meditated turning his arms against the Turks; but he was denounced by the boyards. "The sabre of the Sultan is very much longer than ours," said those degenerate Wallachians. Mihne, in order to obtain the pardon of the Porte, followed the Turks in Transylvania. Rakoczy, overcome, was replaced by Achatius Barcsay, who received investiture from the Sultan, under condition of paying a tribute of 40,000 ducats (1658). However, the fate of Transylvania was reserved for Wallachia. Mihne concealed for some time his projects of revolt. By degrees he increased his army and borrowed money from the principal banking-houses of Constantinople; at length he commenced open hostilities. After a massacre of all the boyards devoted to the Osmanlis, he attacked Tergowitz, took it by assault and put the Turkish garrison to the edge of the sword. Thence, he marched towards Giurgevo and Braïla, carried those two places by main force, slaughtered all the Mussulmans found therein and seized upon their property. He was not contented with driving the Turks beyond the Danube: renewing his alliance with Rakoczy, he sent 10,000 Transylvanians and 10,000 Wallachians against Ghika, Voïvode of Moldavia. Ghika was overcome near Jassy. There the successes of Mihne terminated. Kupruli ordered the Tartars to enter Moldavia, whilst the Turkish army invaded Wallachia. The Wallachians and Transylvanians lost a bloody battle upon the banks of the Baglui; Mihne sought safety in the mountains, and Ghika became master of the Wallachians (1659). "The Wallachians were accustomed to receive without murmuring the princes whom the first Turkish boatman, raised to the rank of Grand Vizier, was pleased to send them. They kissed the yoke that oppressed them. No complaints, no resistance! They received masters from the shores of the Bosphorus or the centre of Albania; they acknowledged them as their voïvodes, prostrated themselves in the dust at their feet and adored the hand that smote them. The nation had fallen into decadence; it had lost its nationality, and, in consequence, its independence. The Wallachians, in the days of Michael the Brave, rejected the Greeks even as simple officials in their government; the Wallachians of 1650 accepted with indifference either the outcasts of the Fanar and of Albania, or locksmiths or oyster merchants; they suffered and were silent. No strong voice was raised to remind Turkey of its want of faith, and demand the rights secured to Wallachia by the ancient treaties."*

Whilst Tartars and Turks put Wallachia to pillage, the Count de Souches, the Imperial general in Hungary,

* Kogalnitchano, "History of Wallachia," &c., tom. i. p. 299.

stripped the Ottomans of some portions of territory under pretext of protecting the frontiers of the empire against the incursions of the Tartars. Sidi-Ali, Pacha of Buda, complained of these encroachments ; upon the evasive answer of the commander of the German forces he attacked Gross-Wardein. Treason opened for him the gates of that fortress (1660).

The war continued against Venice ; it was commenced against Austria ; it was very nearly breaking out between France and Turkey, thanks to the imprudence of M. de la Haye, the French ambassador.

2. *Diplomatic Rupture with France.—Death of Kupruli I.*

At the commencement of the reign of Mahomet IV., says the traveller Chardin, the State was governed by the women and the eunuchs, who filled up the highest posts at their pleasure. Nearly every month a fresh Grand Vizier was appointed, who, after a few days' administration, was deprived not only of office but of life. The French ambassador, De la Haye, seeing these frequent changes, thought that, during the minority of the Sultan, matters would not be otherwise, and that thus the customary visit and presents made to each new Grand Vizier were thrown away. When Kupruli received the seals, the ambassador thought that the fortune of the former would not be more favourable than that of his predecessors ; but he judged erroneously, and a serious rupture resulted from his error.

As soon as Kupruli had entered upon his office, each dignitary made his visit to him with the customary presents, among others the foreign Ministers, with the exception of the French ambassador. The latter was repeatedly enjoined to do the same, and it was even pressed upon him ; but the desire of sparing his nation the cost of a present kept him back from it ; nevertheless, seeing that Kupruli was establishing himself at Court upon the ruin of several grandees, and that, according to all appearance, he would be for some continuance Grand Vizier, he at length went to see him and made his present. Truly, it was something more than a visit and a present thrown away; for the vizier, indignant at the negligence and little consideration shown towards him in that important juncture, had conceived the design of avenging himself upon him, and even upon the whole French nation. That was the true source and origin of the untoward correspondence that ensued between France and Turkey during the entire ministry of that vizier, and even afterwards under the ministry of his son, who succeeded him. So that the obduracy of the Porte and the divers insults offered to the French during some twenty years must be attributed originally to a personal slight, notwithstanding the reasons upon which they were founded in the sequel, of which the chief and most just were the enterprise against Gigeri and the succour given by the Emperor to the Venetians.

Kupruli soon found an occasion for giving vent to his resentment. It presented itself in such wise that he could not have wished for a better. From the commencement of the war against Candia, France had secretly assisted the Venetians, and De la Haye was expected to keep up a clandestine correspondence with the Venetians, and make them acquainted with the designs of the Turks. He had written to them advising that they should not yield to the demands of the Divan, giving them to understand that they ought to hope everything from the protection of Louis XIV., and that his master would not be the mediator of a peace disadvantageous to the Christians. Kupruli, having been apprised of this correspondence by a renegade who delivered up to him the despatches to the ambassador, written in cipher (1659), became greatly infuriated, being naturally passionate and sanguinary; and ordered De la Haye to repair to Adrianople, where the Court then was. The ambassador, being ill, sent his son in his stead. The Vizier received him haughtily, and ordered him to decipher the letters. The latter replied that "the secrets of the King, his master, must be kept." Kupruli flew into such a rage, that he shouted to his *chiaoux:* "Strike that dog!" And the latter rushing upon young De la Haye, maltreated him; and afterwards threw him into a dungeon in the great tower of Adrianople. "That cannot be suffered," said the Vizier, "from the ambassador's envoy, although he be his son, which would not be endured from the ambassador himself." The secretaries and the interpreters of the embassy were menaced with torments and even death.

De la Haye, the elder, hastened to Adrianople. The Vizier required of him in vain to decipher the letters, characterized his conduct as treason, and quitted the city to carry on the war in Transylvania, ordering a strict watch to be kept over the ambassador, and leaving his son in prison. It was only after his return from the war that he permitted him to return to Constantinople (1660).

At the news of this event, Mazarin, anxious to prevent a rupture, despatched a gentleman named Blondel with a letter from the King, which demanded amends and the dismissal of the Vizier. Kupruli received that envoy superciliously, complained of France, which gave succour to the enemies of the Porte, and threatened to send away De la Haye ignominiously. Blondel, unable to obtain an audience of the Sultan, returned with his letters. On his arrival, Mazarin recalled De la Haye (1661), and entrusted the care of the affairs of France at Constantinople to a merchant named Roboly, who remained in charge till 1665.

The rupture seemed complete; England, Holland and Austria urged France to make war, and their ambassadors at Constantinople exaggerated designedly the insults the French had received. But Mazarin, who had recently by the Treaty of the Pyrenees (1659) marked out for France the policy which he thought would give him the domination of the West, refused to involve himself in an impolitic struggle with Turkey. He refrained, therefore, from an open rupture with the Ottomans, who were embarrassed with their twofold war in Candia and Hungary, but sent 4,000 Frenchmen to

Candia, and protected the recruiting of numerous volunteers for the Venetian army; lastly, he prepared to give aid to the Emperor against the Ottomans.

Mazarin and Kupruli both died in the same year (1661), after having both exercised a veritable tutelage over the sovereigns of whom they were the Ministers, and resuscitated the power of the States they governed. Mazarin had to conquer the Fronde; Kupruli repressed the Janissaries, stifled an insurrection in Asia Minor, and pacified Upper Egypt. The first-named, finishing the work of Richelieu, abased both branches of the House of Austria, and aggrandized France on the East and South; the latter prepared the fall of Candia, refastened the links of vassalage which bound Transylvania and the Danubian Principalities to the Ottoman Empire, and commenced against Austria a war calculated to place Vienna in peril. But if he may be compared in some things with Mazarin, Kupruli still more closely resembled Richelieu alike by his energy and his cruelty. He caused the death, it is said, of more than 30,000 persons. On his death-bed, before expiring, he advised the Sultan to withdraw himself from the control of the women; not to shut himself up in the Seraglio; nor to allow the troops to become enervated by idleness, and never to choose a too wealthy Minister. Mahomet IV. requested of him, as a last service, to indicate the person whom he considered the most fitting to replace him. "I know none," replied the Grand Vizier, "more capable than my son Ahmed." So, Ahmed Kupruli inherited the functions and authority of his father (1661).

3. *War in Hungary.—Intervention of France.—Battle of St. Gothard.—Treaty of Vasvar.*

The Grand Vizier bequeathed to his son the termination of two wars. Venice and Austria in vain entered upon negotiations. Ahmed Kupruli crossed the Danube near to Gran, and laid siege to Neuhæusel. The capture of that fortress, which was the bulwark of Hungary, entailed the submission of the adjacent strongholds. At this time the Tartar hordes ravaged Hungary, Moravia, and Silesia, and carried nearly 80,000 Christians into slavery.

The Emperor Leopold was abandoned to his own forces; the States of Germany, which found themselves, subsequent to the Treaties of Westphalia, and especially since the League of the Rhine, under the protection of France, were unwilling to afford him any assistance. In order to save Hungary, Alexander VII., a Pontiff devoted to the House of Austria, conceived the project of a coalition of all the Christian States against the Turks. After the overture that was made to him, Louis XIV. sent an ambassador to Rome to represent to the Pope the reasons that ought to deter France from entering such a League, " such as the protection of religion in the Ottoman dominions, the interests of French subjects in the commerce of the Levant; lastly, the particular complaints of Louis XIV. against the Emperor; nevertheless, the very-Christian King rose above those reasons; he would enter into the League, and urge upon his allies of Germany the necessary arguments to induce them to join it." The "Great Monarch," in fact, and the League of the Rhine concluded a Treaty by which both parties were bound to place on foot 30,000 men each to march against the Turks. But the Emperor, at the anticipation alone of such large forces, grew uneasy at the sorry part he was enacting in Germany in face of the Protector of the League of the Rhine; and through his advice the Pope grew cold touching the coalition. Louis XIV. was irritated at the reception given to his offers—" offers which were such," wrote his Minister Lionne, " that any other Pope would have publicly rendered thanks to Heaven for them; after all," added he, "it is yet more His Holiness's affair than ours; it will be sufficient for His Majesty, for his own satisfaction and his discharge towards God, the having made every advance in relation to this League that a king, the eldest son of the Church and principal defender of religion, could make in a peril imminent to Christianity.

The successes of the Turks continued. The Emperor and the Pope again asked for succour from France, but only in the shape of money. Louis XIV. offered 24,000 of his own troops and 24,000 of his German allies. The Emperor refused them, saying openly that, with such an army, the King of France would be more the master of the Empire than himself. Louis XIV. offered an army less by one half. At length it was agreed to send into Hungary 6,000 Frenchmen and 24,000 men of the Rhine League, commanded by the Duke de la Feuillade and the Count de Coligny. A subsidy of 200,000 crowns was given to the Pope for the war; but a renewal of the project of a coalition was urged in vain. "It is a noble design," wrote the French ambassador from Rome, "which has vanished in smoke."

Whilst the French and the auxiliaries of the Rhine League marched towards Hungary, Hohenlohe, the Imperial general, and Zriny, Ban of the Croats, seized upon Presnitz, Babocsa, and Baris, and burned the town of Fünfkirchen with more than 500 villages. The Count de Strozzi obtained also some successes, but he perished in a skirmish upon the banks of the Muhr. The celebrated Montecuculli succeeded him in the command, and arrested the menacing tide of Mussulman invasion.

In 1664, Montecuculli was enabled to take the field with greater chance of success; and though the first operations of the campaign were in favour of the Turks, he at length stopped their advance by the memorable battle near St. Gothard, a Cistercian monastery on the borders of Hungary and Styria. Kupruli-Ahmed had advanced as far as the Raab; thrice he attempted to cross that river, and thrice he was repulsed. In the last combat, fought near the village of St. Gothard, Montecuculli having given the word "Death or Victory," the Christians, contrary to their usual practice, charged without waiting to be attacked; the Turks were routed and thrown into a disorderly flight, in which nearly 25,000 of them were slain or drowned in the Raab (1st of August, 1664). The 30,000 auxiliaries of France and Germany decided the success of that battle. It is related that, when the Grand Vizier saw the French gentlemen rushing forward in their ribbon-decked hats and white perukes, he cried out: " What are those young girls?" But, in the twinkling of an eye, the ranks of the Janissaries were pierced by those whom the Ottoman historians call the " men of steel;" and those who escaped from the defeat repeated long afterwards, in their warlike exercises, the cries uttered by the French on rushing into the *mêlée:* "Allons! allons! Tue! tue!"

But instead of pursuing the advantage, which seemed to open the road to the most extensive conquests, the Imperial Cabinet surprised all Europe by seizing the opportunity to make peace with the Porte. On the 10th of August, only a few days after the battle of St. Gothard, a Treaty was concluded at Vasvar for a twenty years' truce. This Treaty differed widely from that of Sitvatorok, concerning which Kupruli could not endure any allusion to be made. By it, Transylvania was to be evacuated by the Imperialists and by the Turks. Apafy was acknowledged by the Emperor and by the Sultan as Prince of that country, but remaining tributary to the Porte. Of the seven Hungarian " comitats " situate between Transylvania and the Theiss, three were to belong to the Emperor; the four that had been seized upon by Rakoczy to remain to the Ottomans. The Sultan kept Novigrad and Neuhæusel. Thus the Emperor abandoned to the Turks almost all their conquests, and, moreover, made the Sultan *a present*—in other words, paid him a tribute—of 200,000 florins.

4. *Hostilities against the Barbary Pirates.*

The troops sent by Louis XIV. to the aid of the Emperor returned to France after the ratification of the treaty of Vasvar, but the French squadrons at sea continued to cruise in the Mediterranean for the destruction of the Barbary pirates. It were long to enumerate the combats with the corsairs fought by Beaufort, d'Hocquincourt, Duquesne, Tourville, and d'Estrées; the capture and burning of their vessels; the expeditions directed against their towns; and it would take longer still to enumerate the attempts made to induce them to respect the rights of nations, the negotiations entered upon with them, the treaties signed and broken by them. It is incredible to what an extent the government of Louis XIV. made advances, submitted to insults, promised advantages, in order to afford some security to maritime commerce and force the Barbaresques to form some idea of civilization. It was Colbert who constrained his royal master to abase his pride before the necessities of Eastern commerce.

The government of Louis XIV. was not satisfied with sending expeditions against the Barbaresques, it was desirous of having a military establishment upon the coast of Africa, as the Spaniards had one at Oran. After having made, with the Order of Malta, the alliance projected by Richelieu, and which placed at its disposal the entire navy of the Knights, it despatched, under the command of the Duke of Beaufort, a fleet of thirty sail, which steered for Djigelli or Gigeri. That small place was seized upon, and a fort built there, the ruins of which are still to be seen. But then discord having ensued between the troops on land and the sea force, the Algerines profited by it to retake the town, and compel the French to retreat. In spite of this check, the enterprise against Gigeri created a great sensation. "It is a sample," said a contemporary journalist, "of what the infidels have to fear and the Christians to hope for." "It excited," says the Chevalier d'Arvieux,[*] "endless murmurs throughout the Ottoman Empire, in Syria, and in Egypt. . . . The Turks and the Moors cried for vengeance. They said openly that all the Franks who were in the Empire must be exterminated. Those who entered the harbours of Syria were loaded with insults and threatened with vengeance, both in their persons and their possessions, for the losses which the capture of Gigeri

[*] "Mémoires," tom. iii. p. 3.

had entailed. The English, the Dutch, and other Franks who were in the seaports kept aloof from us, and took care to say that they were not Frenchmen, and that they had taken no part in the capture of Gigeri. We were warned on all sides that we stood in an extreme danger, and that there was a likelihood that the Turks would make us experience the fury of another Sicilian Vespers."

The government of Louis XIV. had hoped that the expedition against Gigeri, the battle of St. Gothard, the succour given to the Venetians, would induce the Ottoman Porte to make reparation, and to seek for a renewal of the alliance; but the Divan concealed its resentment, affecting a careless and haughty imperturbability; it appeared neither to be moved by the departure of the French ambassador, nor to perceive the hostility of France, nor to fear a rupture; it contented itself by replying to the aggressions of its ancient ally by crippling her commerce and persecuting the Christians in the East. Matters had come to that point that the alliance must be renewed or entirely broken off. "War has been made in Europe," wrote d'Arvieux to Louis XIV., "for much less reasons, and I do not think it can be said that we are truly at peace with the Grand Seignior, if that alliance be not renewed upon the same footing as though nothing had ever taken place between your Majesty and him." Colbert, inheriting Mazarin's ideas, looked upon a war against the Turks as a catastrophe to be avoided at any price. In his opinion, it would turn aside France from its true interests in the East, ruin a portion of her commerce, launch her upon an unknown path, and which could not be hers. He further forced Louis XIV. to humble himself before that fatal necessity, and despatched to Constantinople two Secretaries of Embassy to inquire whether the Porte would be disposed to renew the capitulations, if it would receive with honour a new ambassador, and had no repugnance to see the younger M. de la Haye exercise those functions. Kupruli, feigning to forget Gigeri, St. Gothard, and Candia, replied that the friendship of the Porte for France was of too long standing to be changed by the insensate conduct of an ambassador, and he promised a fair reception to M. de la Haye.

The latter was in nowise the functionary capable of reconciling the two Powers; against it, besides the antecedents of his father, was his rancorous and passionate disposition, which made him hated even by his fellow-countrymen. He arrived in Constantinople in 1666, and "from the first," says Chardin, "he conducted himself with as much haughtiness as might be expected from a firm-minded Minister who sustains the character of ambassador of a powerful and formidable King. In the visits which he paid to the members of the Divan, he spoke only and incessantly of the grandeur of the King his master, and the power of his arms. This very much displeased the Vizier, who imagined that it was an intentional insult offered to him and the Grand Seignior in his own Court, and, with that prepossession, he treated the ambassador with a contempt outrageous enough." In an audience he gave him, he received him with much disdain, not looking at him, or rising from his place; when at length he turned round to speak to him, it was to reproach him for the succour that France had sent into Hungary and to Candia; then he dismissed him.

De la Haye, whom his compatriots accuse of the malignant proceedings of the Porte against France, supported that affront uncomplainingly; but as soon as he had quitted the palace, he sent to tell the Vizier that he certainly would not reckon the *rencontre* that had just taken place between them as an audience given by the Prime Minister of the Grand Seignior to the ambassador of the most puissant monarch of Christendom; that he demanded of him a fresh audience, but on condition that he should be received therein with all the homage due to the master whom he represented. The Vizier granted the audience, with the condition imposed upon it; but, by a caprice of brutal barbarity, he received the ambassador as for the first time. De la Haye, highly indignant, reproached him both for his insolence and for his want of faith, and he declared to him that, if he did not make him reparation, he had orders to hand back the capitulations and return to France. The Vizier in turn flew into a rage and replied by an insult. The ambassador took from the hands of his interpreter the copy of the capitulations, flung them to the Vizier and rose up to take his departure. Thereupon it is said (but the report alone of the Austrian ambassador mentions these details) that, the Vizier having treated him as a Jew and a dog, he placed his hand upon the hilt of his sword, when the *chiaoux* rushed upon him, struck him with a stool from which he had just risen, and gave him a box on the ear. That which appears certain is that on going out he was arrested and detained for three days in one of the chambers of the palace. During that interval, the Vizier deliberated with the Mufti and the Capudan-Pacha upon that imbroglio and the war which might ensue. The Grand Seignior being informed of what had happened, commanded Kupruli to reconcile himself with De la Haye. The latter, knowing that the Court of France was dissatisfied with his conduct, lent himself to all the arrangements; and it was determined that the two preceding audiences should be considered as null; that the ambassador should give no account of them to his master, and that, in a third audience, he should be received by the Grand Vizier with the customary ceremonies and honours. The audience took place; Kupruli overwhelmed De la Haye with kind attention, politeness and presents; but a good understanding was not re-established between the two Ministers, and France and the Porte continued, whilst preserving a friendly exterior, to annoy each other secretly.

De la Haye was ordered to demand the renewal of the capitulations and freedom for the French to trade with India by way of Egypt and the Red Sea. These demands were refused. The Genoese, who traded in the Levant under the French flag, had made use of the name of France to obtain from the Grand Seignior the liberty of trading directly with his subjects; they had been refused. Then they addressed themselves to England, and, under her protection, obtained capitulations analogous to those of the English and the Dutch. Louis XIV. ordered De la Haye to demand the revocation of those capitulations, as being a violation of the Treaty by which the Porte bound itself not to receive into Turkey any European nation save under the French flag. The Vizier replied to him : " That the Sublime Porte was open for withdrawal as well as arrival; that the King of France had no right to wish to hinder the Grand Seignior from making peace with old enemies and according them capitulations when they came to demand them of him ; that it ought to suffice His Majesty being acknowledged by the Porte as Padischah and as the first prince of Christendom, without pretending to prescribe in any way respecting other nations." De la Haye recriminated in offensive terms against the bad faith of the Ottoman Court; and reverting to the kind of favour which the Grand Seignior conferred on the King of France by treating him as the first Christian prince : " That title," said he, " my master is indebted for to God alone and to his victorious arms." The treaty made with the Genoese was maintained.

The Court of France was irritated at all these insults, and avenged itself for them by giving fresh succour to the Venetians.

5. *France succours Candia.—Capture of that place.*

The war in Hungary had created a diversion from that of Candia. When the treaty of Vasvar was signed, Kupruli-Ahmed resolved to terminate by a decisive blow the long-pending contest between the Ottoman Empire and the Republic of Venice. Embarking in May, 1666, he coasted along Asia Minor and arrived on the 3rd of November at Canea. His presence reanimated the ardour of the Turks, wearied by a war of twenty-two years, and the trenches were opened under the walls of Candia the 28th of May, 1667. The besieged sustained the attack of the Grand Vizier with an incredible obstinacy; and the Turks exhibited a no less fierce animosity. But as fast as they carried or destroyed some portion of the ramparts, new fortifications arose in their rear; it might be said, according to the expression of an historian, that the city only shut itself up closer before the besiegers. Kupruli, in that campaign, lost 8,000 men.

The following year, a troop of 1,200 French gentlemen, amongst whom were to be found some of the most illustrious names in the French monarchy, crossed the Mediterranean under the flag of Malta, and entered Candia under the command of the Duke de la Feuillade. These volunteers, animated by that wild and irrepressible valour which has frequently cost France as many defeats as victories, thought that it would be sufficient for them to make a sortie to effect the deliverance of Candia, and they demanded that it should be made. The governor Morosini, whose garrison was exhausted, refused. Thereupon they declared that they would make the sortie by themselves, unassisted. In fact, aided only by the Knights of Malta, they sallied out, headed by La Feuillade, who had a whip in his hand, and six monks carrying a crucifix; they spread a panic in the Turkish camp and slew some 1,200 of them; but surrounded very soon by thousands of the foe, they retreated, leaving a hundred of their band dead or wounded, and, discouraged by that unfortunate adventure, they re-embarked.

The renown of this chivalrous affair entailed upon the ambassador fresh insults and upon the French merchants in the Levant fresh extortions. Louis XIV. becoming weary of all this, ordered De la Haye to return to France, and despatched four vessels commanded by M. Dalmeiras to bring back with him all Frenchmen willing to return. The ambassador informed the Kaïmacan of this measure, telling him that he was only waiting for the French squadron and the *congé* of the Porte. The Kaïmacan inquired of the ambassador whether he had a successor. De la Haye replied that the King of France would no longer keep an embassy at the Porte, because that dignity had not been considered nor respected there as it ought to be; that he would leave a merchant to reside there, until reparation had been made for the insults offered France for long years past. The Divan took time ere they gave the *congé* asked for, in accord with De la Haye, who wished to retain his appointment. But a report ran that Louis XIV. was preparing a formidable succour for the deliverance of Candia, and that he had even decided upon open war against the Turks. The Grand Vizier became alarmed at this and pressed the siege of the city with forces exceeding 100,000 men.

In fact, Louis XIV., driven to extremity by the insults of the Porte, and wishing to make a parade in the eyes of Christendom of his religious zeal, was preparing a succour for Candia (January, 1669), composed of twelve battalions of infantry, 300 cavalry and a detachment from the King's household of 200 gentlemen volunteers, in all 6,000 men, whom a Turkish historian calls "6,000 swine having evil designs." That small army, commanded by the Duke de Navailles, was embarked in twenty-seven transports escorted by fifteen ships of war under command of the Duke de Beaufort; it hoisted, in order to keep up the appearance of neutrality, the standard of the Church, and had for its van-guard fourteen pontifical galleys. The first division, 4,500 strong, arrived in June, 1669, when Candia was reduced to the last extremities : the musketeers of the King's household would not disembark during the night, but landed in open daylight under fire of the Turks. Next day, and without waiting for the remainder of the army, a sortie was determined upon ; but Navailles, desirous of making it with his troops alone, refused the soldiers that Morosini offered to give him. The sortie was a vigorous one, the front line of the Turks being hurled back and terror spread through their army, when an explosion of some barrels of gunpowder, which took place in the ranks of the French, threw them into confusion and compelled a retreat. They left 500 men upon the field of battle, and amongst them was the Duke de Beaufort.

The second division arrived; but discouragement was already manifest in the royal army, which had recognized that the place was no longer defensible. However, the French Fleet joined itself to the Venetian Fleet in order to attack the Turkish camp, and cannonaded it for an entire day, without other result than the loss of a French ship, which blew up during the combat. Then Navailles, dissatisfied with the Venetians, reimbarked with his small army (21st of August) and returned to France. He was blamed by Louis XIV. for that precipitous return, and exiled from Court. The departure of the French was

MOUNT IDA, IN CRETE.

the signal for the surrender of the town. Morosini capitulated, and at the same time signed a peace with the Turks (September 6, 1669). The Republic lost the island of Crete, with the exception of three ports: Carabusa, Suda, and Spina-Longa.

"History," says Von Hammer, "mentions no stronghold the conquest of which cost so much treasure, time, and efforts as that of Candia. Twenty-five years passed in fighting for its possession, and during that time it had sustained three sieges, the last of which was prolonged for three whole years. The Turks had attempted fifty-six times to assault; they had pushed forty-five subterranean attacks. The besieged exploded 1,172 mines; the Turks firing three times as many. The Venetians lost 50,000 men; the Turks above 100,000."

Dearly as this victory had cost the Empire, the Sultan and his Court manifested the greatest joy at it. Kupruli-Ahmed shared with his companions in arms the glory of the success. "All," said he to them, "all of you have contributed to that conquest with all your soul and all your strength. May your faces shine with refulgence in both worlds! May the Padishah's bread be honestly earned by you! I shall represent before the eyes of our sublime master the grandeur of your services, and my attention shall be given to the bestowal of rewards according to your several ranks." The Sultan ratified the promises of the Grand Vizier, and lavished upon him the most signal proofs of his favour. It had been thought that Candia was the shoal against which the Ottoman power would be dashed to pieces. Thus Krupuli remarked after the capitulation: "The French have had pity upon us!"

6. *Fresh disagreement with France.*

The squadron of Dalmeiras had arrived, but De la Haye had not taken his departure. To maintain himself in his office, he laboured secretly and meanly to restore a good understanding between France and the Porte, and he deceived his own Court by telling it in his letters that he was treated with all customary respect. Finally, he allowed the squadron of Dalmeiras to set sail again for France, and went himself to Larissa, where the Ottoman Court was then sojourning, under pretext of taking leave of the Sultan; there he manœuvred in such wise that he decided the Divan to send an ambassador to Paris with a letter from the Sultan, in order to renew friendly relations between the two States. That mission was confided to a *mouteferrika* (officer of the guards) named Soliman, to whom the Porte granted only 2,000 crowns for his journey, and which was defrayed secretly, it is said, by the money of De la Haye. He embarked on board a French vessel, arrived in Paris, was received in solemn audience at St. Germain, and presented to the King (5th of December, 1669) his master's letter. "You know," said the Sultan, "that for a period very long past the Emperors of France, your predecessors, had contracted that ancient alliance with the sure and firm family of the Ottomans, that they have lived up to the present time so happily in such alliance, friendship, and sincerity that the nations and peoples have always enjoyed repose and tranquillity. That good understanding was increased to such a degree, that, having suffered neither any alteration nor change, it might be said that it had been established for the peace of the whole world, for the regulation and ordering of the affairs of men . . . ." And he complained of the recall of the ambassador, "who has always been," said he, "under the permanent shadow of our justice, with honour, whilst your subjects and merchants entering the havens of our empire, have enjoyed all the protection they required, and nothing has happened that should alter in the slightest degree the good faith, the friendship, the affection and the sincerity which have existed between us for so long a period."

Louis XIV. was satisfied neither with the Sultan's letter, nor with the quality and manners of his envoy, a coarse and vulgarly haughty individual, who expected that amends would be made, and received only vague and illusory words. The majority of the courtiers forced him to a rupture. "The Turks," said they, "are arrogantly prepossessed with the idea that their country is indispensably necessary to everybody; they are imbued with the vanity that the Porte is the asylum and the resource of all the princes on earth; their superstition leads them to believe that all the Christian nations ought to be subjected to them; and they do not scruple to tell us, whenever we complain of their injustice, that, should any one of us quit their country on one of his eyes being knocked out, he would return next day in order that they might tear out the other also."

"It seems," wrote d'Arvieux to Louis XIV.,"that if your Majesty would be treated as on an equality with the Grand Seignior, that the latter should not be allowed to send an ambassador to France who cannot answer for the treatment that ours should receive at the hands of the Grand Seignior; affairs would then go on much better. That, however, appears impossible, if it be considered that it is not at all the custom of the Turks to keep ambassadors in residence amongst their confederates. The Ottoman Emperors receive graciously all those whom the Christian princes send there, provided they have presents to offer, and that they find their account in the propositions which they come to make. In that way they consider it an honour and a singular grandeur to be sought by all, and to seek the friendship of none."

Louis, who was then in all the pride of youth and power, felt inclined to follow such counsels, although they might lead to war. But Colbert represented to him that the superiority which the Sultans affected over the Christian princes was rather a form common throughout the East than a reality; that it had no effective value, as events during the alliance had proved, since the Turks had rather been in the service of France than France in the service of the Turks; that it would not be wise for the sake of a few words to put at stake an alliance which had been a stumbling-block for the House of Austria, and which was envied by all their enemies. Louis yielded to these reasons; and it was decided that a fresh ambassador should be sent to the Porte to replace De la Haye, whose intrigues had become known; that a company for the Levant should be formed with twenty of the most notable merchants of Paris, Lyons, and Marseilles; that a school for French dragomans should be established at Constantinople, &c. At the same time, the commerce of those countries was regulated by special legislation; the consuls were for the most part unknown or foreigners; they were almost all replaced, and very severe instructions were given them that they should keep themselves in constant correspondence with the ambassador, to render him an account of the commerce of their port, of the number and quality of the French and foreign merchants, &c. The police of the consulates and their chanceries was regulated by a very minute ordinance. The ambassadors were forbidden to levy fines upon the French merchants, in virtue of ordinances which they themselves drew up. Finally, very severe orders were given to the military marine for the escort and the protection of merchant vessels.

7. *The Embassy of Nointel.—New Capitulations.*

The new ambassador was the Marquis de Nointel (1670), a learned magistrate and skilful antiquary, who had already travelled in the East, and who received from Colbert the most detailed and sage instructions. He was to demand the renewal of the capitulations with the following alterations: that the customs duty should be reduced from five to three per cent.; that the King of France should be recognized as the unique protector of the Catholics of the East; that French merchandise coming from India should have free passage by the Red Sea and across Egypt. This latter demand excited above all Colbert's solicitude, who devoted to the prosperity of French commerce an attention as active as it was enthusiastic. He regarded Egypt as the true route to India, and he desired thereby to ruin the trade of the English and the Dutch in Asia. "We must endeavour," he wrote to Nointel, "to make a Treaty with the Grand Seignior, by which it would be permitted us to have at Alexandria or at Grand Cairo vessels that might receive the merchandise that other vessels would bring by the Red Sea from Aden to Suez; which would shorten the voyage to the East Indies by more than 200 leagues."

Nointel arrived at Constantinople with a squadron of

men-of-war, which entered the harbour without saluting the Seraglio and in order of battle. The populace and the Ottoman sailors uttered furious cries, and a collision was probably about to take place, when the Sultana-Validé requested the commandant of the squadron to give the salute for herself; and immediately, the four French ships were dressed from stem to stern with every kind of banderole, silken and embroided banners and to shouts of *Vive le roi!* saluted the Seraglio with all their guns. This conduct displeased the Divan; and, when Nointel, after having made a pompous entry into the city, which excited fresh displeasure, had set forth the object of his mission, he was coldly received. Kupruli-Ahmed treated his demand as exorbitant; affected to believe that the ambassador exceeded his instructions, and required that a letter from the King should formally state the nature and extent of the claims of France. Also, when Nointel had his solemn audience of the Sultan, he saw in the manner and the words of his Ministers the desire to defy him. When he vaunted the puissance, the riches, the armies of his master: "Yes," replied the Vizier, "the Emperor of France is a great monarch, but his sword is yet new." As Nointel recalled the antiquity of the alliance between the French and Turks: "Yes," said the Vizier, "the French are our best friends, but we find them everywhere amongst our enemies." Lastly, on Nointel remarking that His Majesty had particularly at heart the passage by the Red Sea: "Can it be," said Kupruli, "that an Emperor so great as yours has so much at heart a mere mercantile matter?" However, the negotiation went on; but Nointel endeavoured in vain to place the affairs under the Sultan's eye, for it was thought in France that the personal resentment of the Vizier was the sole cause of the rupture: he could only treat through the mediation of the Greek Panajotti, first dragoman of the Porte, all-powerful with the Divan and the enemy of France. It was proposed to renew simply the ancient capitulations. He refused with some ill-humour, and uttered some threats. The Vizier replied that "His Highness did not enter into treaty nor into commerce with the other potentates of the world, having no interest to dispute with them; that these kind of capitulations were a grace and a favour which the Grand Seignior granted to his confederates; that His Majesty ought to be contented with them as accorded; finally, that the advantages guaranteed to foreigners by the Sublime Porte had never been conceded to violence, but to gentleness, and that, if he would not adhere to the renewal of the capitulations, he might withdraw into France."

At these tidings Louis XIV. flew into a great rage, and "it was deliberated," says Chardin, "whether the Porte should be broken with, or whether no notice should be taken of a treatment so unreasonable. However, in order to undertake nothing lightly in an affair of that importance, M. d'Oppède, first president of Aix, was ordered to assemble at Marseilles all the Levant merchants and others well acquainted with Turkish affairs, and to take their opinion upon that which many persons gave the Council to understand: that France might cease to trade with the Levant, at least during several years, and that it might easily do by sea so much harm to the Turks, that the Grand Seignior, to arrest it, would be constrained to grant the King all that His Majesty demanded. The opinion of the assembly was that those propositions were valid, that there was in Provence enough of the Levant merchandise to supply France with it for ten years, and that, if the King sent only ten ships into the Ægean Sea, and particularly into the Dardanelles, famine would in a very short time be felt in Constantinople, and there would be a rising in favour of the French.

All seemed disposed for war; a fleet was prepared, destined to sail for Constantinople to obtain, by force, the renewal of the alliance, and which should seize upon the chief islands of the Archipelago, in order to secure protection in future. The spirit of the crusades revived; several essays were published upon the opportunity of driving the Turks out of Europe, and Boileau only expressed the general belief when he said to the King:

VOL. I.   z

"Je t'attends dans six mois aux bords de l'Hellespont."
That was the popular opinion, and it was also the thought of men of genius, even among the Protestants.

The report soon spread at Constantinople that the King of France was arming 50 vessels and 30,000 men at Toulon: the Turks were filled with terror, the French announcing with bravado that they were going to burn Constantinople, seize upon the islands of the Archipelago, and drive the Ottomans out of Europe. But, at that moment, Louis XIV. was preparing to avenge himself upon the Dutch, and it was deliberated in Council, which war should be undertaken. That of Holland was the question of pre-eminence on the Ocean; that of Turkey, the question of pre-eminence on the Mediterranean; the insults of the Ottomans were real, those of Holland very nearly imaginary; but the first were little known, about the latter a great stir had been made: so, war with the Dutch was decided upon. But it was resolved that it should be made in such a fashion that the rebound should make itself felt in the East and render the Ottomans more tractable.

The Minister of Louis XIV., Lionne, wrote to Kupruli, "that the Emperor of France was astonished that he refused to give credence to his ambassador; that the Porte had never brought in doubt the truth and fidelity of the proposals of the French ambassador; that His Majesty would not explain himself through any other channel than that of M. de Nointel; that, if the Grand Seignior refused to give him credence and to treat him with the honour due to the envoy of the first Christian Monarch, the King orders his ambassador to embark in the vessel which carries that letter to Constantinople." The Vizier relented, negotiations were recommenced, but carried on slowly, confusedly, and with an ill-disguised malevolence. Nointel did not become disheartened: he had received from Colbert orders the most precise to maintain peace at any price. It resulted in an understanding with one another so far as the diminution of the customs duties, upon the restitution of the Holy Places, upon the recognition of the King of France as protector of the Christians in the East; but, upon the famous prerogative attached to the flag of France, Krupuli declared " that it was accorded to the English, the Dutch, the Venetians, Genoese and subjects of the House of Austria that foreigners who should come into Turkey under their own banner should be treated like them; and that he could not deprive them of the privilege." The negotiations were broken off several times; money was offered in vain; all depended upon Panajotti, who was sold to Austria and to England.

At length all the Levant rang with the news of the conquest of Holland. The French raised their heads, exalting the power of the Great King and threatening the Turks with his vengeance; the Dutch were dismayed, whilst the English rejoiced in their ruin. The Divan became alarmed to such a degree, that it caused the capitulations to be drawn up immediately, even upon the memoranda of Nointel, and which it sent to him formally signed (5th of June, 1673). The Sultan announced that result to Louis XIV. in a pompous letter full of professions of affectionate friendship.

In the new articles of the capitulations no question was raised of the passage to India by the Red Sea; the negotiation had succeeded with the Pacha of Egypt, to whom was given two per cent., as a transit duty, for all the merchandise that went from Suez to Alexandria; the Sultan had approved of that arrangement; but the Mufti and the Iman of Mecca were opposed to it, under pretext that the Christian vessels which would navigate the Red Sea might insult or carry away the tomb of Mahomet; moreover the English ambassador alleged at the Divan that the French had the project of seizing upon Egypt, and thus the affair miscarried. However, the Government of Louis XIV. did not lose sight of it: the proof exists in two memoirs of M. de Maillet, consul at Cairo in 1692, who sought the most likely means of renewing the negotiation, and who, in 1706, went into Abyssinia to enter upon commercial relations with that country and facilitate the communications of the French colonists of Bourbon and Madagascar with Suez and Egypt.

Thus was re-established between France and Turkey the alliance which, after having been an intimate one under Francis I. and Henry II., benevolent under the last Valois and Henry IV., had come to a veritable rupture at the commencement of the reign of Louis XIV.

Thanks to the sympathy of the Catholic population for "the very-Christian King" and the reconciliation of Mahomet IV. and Louis XIV., France recovered her former preponderance in the Levant. The alliance of the Turks with France had been, in its origin, wholly one of policy, and destined to abase the House of Austria; under the successors of Henry II., it had not retained that character, and had been solely directed to the interests of commerce and religion; from 1605 to 1673 it had undergone numerous violations and had been, so to speak, suspended. The struggle against the House of Austria being the knot of the entire policy of Louis XIV., and the pivot upon which all the events of his reign turned, the alliance of France with the Porte, when it had been restored under the relations of commerce and religion, tended to retake the character which it had under Francis I.; but then the miserable disagreements that had separated the two States during seventy years began to bear fruit. If the two allies could only have sincerely understood one another, if they could have actively joined their arms in an unique and definite object, they might have obtained almost without obstacle the domination of Europe, at the epoch when the House of Austria was in decadence, when England was sailing in tow of France, when Russia, as an European Power, did not exist. But, on one side, the ignorant and fanatical pride of the Osmanlis only inspired them with a passionate, blind and brutal policy, in which they obstinately insisted to march alone, without taking any account of the state of Europe, in defying the counsel and exhortations of their allies, full of contempt for the interests and policy of the Christians; on the other hand, the Catholic idea of Louis XIV., which made him commit so many errors in his policy with regard to the West, did not mislead him less in his policy with regard to the East; hating the Turks to the extent of desiring their destruction, he disliked a direct alliance with them; he looked upon them as instruments; he only sought to profit by the diversions operated by the Ottoman forces on the side of Germany. From that time the two allies were seen to act almost constantly isolated against their common enemy; France to lay down arms when Turkey began war, and Turkey to conclude peace when France entered upon a campaign. That great error has had the most fatal influence upon the destinies of the two States; it has not only prevented the ruin of the House of Austria, but prepared the greatness of Russia, brought about the decadence of the Ottomans, and thrown France upon a policy full of difficulty and danger, in which she still struggles at the present time.

CHAPTER IX.

FROM THE CAPTURE OF CANDIA TO THE PEACE OF CARLOWITZ (1669-1699).

1. *State of the Ottoman Empire after the Capture of Candia.—Submission of the Cossacks.—War in Poland. —Treaty of* 1676.

THE Ottoman Empire, under the administration of Ahmed Kupruli, had regained the height of its power. " If you consider," says an English historian of the time, " its origin, its progress, and its uninterrupted success, nothing is more admirable or more astonishing; if you contemplate its grandeur and its splendour, nothing more magnificent or more glorious; if you consider its power and its strength, nothing more terrible or more dangerous. Intoxicated with the draught of constant fortune, the Ottoman looks only with contempt on the other nations of the earth."* In reality, the Ottoman Empire, which comprehended at that epoch forty governments and four tributary countries, then encircled in Europe all Greece, Illyria, Mæsia, Macedonia, Pannonia, Thrace, and Dacia; the Kingdoms of Pyrrhus and Perseus; the States of the Treballi and the Bulgarians; in Africa, the Kingdom of the Ptolemies, with the territory of Carthage and Numidia; in Asia, the Kingdoms of Mithridates, Antiochus, Attalus, Prusias, Herod, and Tigranes; those of the obscure sovereigns of Cappadocia, Cilicia, and Comagena; the territories of the Iberians and the Scythians; and a portion of the Empire of the Parthians. Without reckoning the Greek Republics and the Tyrian Colony, there were twenty kingdoms included in those forty governments, from the Syrtes to the Caucasus, and to the countries watered by the Hydaspes.

* Knolle, preface to the "History of the Turks."

The voluntary submission of the Cossacks helped still further to increase for a time the limits, already so vast, of the Ottoman domination. The Cossacks inhabited the Ukraine, situated between Little Tartary, Poland, and Moscow. That country extended for about a hundred leagues from north to south, and nearly as far from east to west. It is divided into two almost equal portions by the Borysthenes, which traverses it from the north-west to the south-east. The most northern portion of the Ukraine is cultivated and rich; the most southern, which is situate near the 48th degree of latitude, is alike one of the most fertile and the most desert countries in the world; bad government stifles there the good with which nature desires to benefit man. The inhabitants of these cantons, neighbours of Little Tartary, neither plant nor sow, because the Tartars of Budziac and Precop, the Moldavians, all brigand people, would come and ravage their harvests. The Cossacks have always aspired to be free; but, being surrounded by Muscovy, the States of the Grand Seignior, and Poland, it was necessary for them to seek a protector, and consequently a master in one of those three States.* So long as the Tartars and the Turks menaced the liberty of Europe, the military institution of the Cossacks was useful and politic; they were upon the Borysthenes what the Knights of St. John of Jerusalem had been in the Isle of Rhodes; but when the Ottoman Porte had taken rank among the European Powers, and regular alliances were made with it, it became necessary to put a stop to the hostilities of the Cossacks; their incursions were nothing more than brigandage. The Kings of Poland, therefore, were urged to repress them. The troubles of Russia still occupied for some time their vagabond activity, but when it became necessary to be at peace with their neighbours, their turbulent race finding the domination of Poland irksome and galling, they endeavoured to secure the protection of the Turks.†

The Ottomans were still occupied with the siege of

* Voltaire, "History of Charles XII.," i. 4.
† "Des Progrès de la puissance Russe," p. 113.

Candia, when Doroszensko, hetman of the Cossacks, went to offer to Mahomet IV. the Suzerainty of the Ukraine. The Sultan gave him the investiture with the title of Sandjak-Bey. On hearing this, the neighbouring peoples became uneasy, fearing to be exposed by that alliance to all the inconveniences likely to be its natural result. The Cossacks inhabited a marshy country, intersected throughout by defiles. The Poles and Muscovites having until then lived on good terms with them, and derived great service therefrom, not only on account of their situation, but more especially because, being fond of brigandage, they overran the Ottoman frontiers, their new alliance would make all these advantages revert to the Turks. The King of Poland was only too conscious of this. It was of the last importance to retain these old friends or subjects, and to hinder them from throwing themselves into the arms of the Osmanli. Thus, before the Turks had had time to ensure the obedience of the Cossacks, a Polish army was sent into their country, and as they had still many partisans there, they penetrated as far as they chose, and lived in it at their discretion. Mahomet IV. might have regarded this proceeding as an infraction of treaties, and made it a pretext for declaring instant war against the King of Poland; but he thought it more reasonable to essay in the first instance the power of remonstrance. He sent a letter to the King, therefore, which concluded in these summary terms: "If you refuse to submit yourself to our mandate, and you are disposed to sustain your injustice by arms, our law denounces by our mouth death to your person, desolation to your kingdom, the slavery of your people; and all the world will impute these calamities solely to your wickedness and obstinacy."*

The King of Poland having refused to obey this summons, war was declared, and the Sultan placed himself at the head of his army. Setting out from Adrianople on the 5th of June, 1672, he crossed the Danube, traversed Moldavia, and encamped near Choczim, on the banks of

* Cantemir, tom. iii. p. 136.

the Dniester. The Tartars of the Crimea, led by the Khan Selim Gheraï, here effected a junction with the Turks. In August the Mussulmans crossed the Dniester, and sat down before Kaminiec. That place, which seemed impregnable, capitulated at the end of ten days. The city of Lemberg was taken shortly after. The King of Poland, in consternation, sued for peace, but only obtained it on disgraceful conditions by the treaty of Bucsacs (18th of September, 1672). By that treaty " He gave up Podolia to the Ottomans, the Ukraine to the Cossacks, bound himself to pay an annual tribute of 20,000 ducats and promised 80,000 crowns for the redemption of Lemberg. By way of compensation, the Tartars engaged to make no more irruptions into Poland."*

The Poles, excited by the Pope and the German Emperor, refused to ratify the treaty of Bucsacs. The Grand Chancellor wrote to Ahmed Kupruli, "that the King of Poland, having submitted to conditions of peace without the consent of the Republic, it declared them null, and would pay nothing, resolved to suffer a thousand deaths rather than the infamy attached to the name of tributary." Mahomet IV. again placed himself at the head of his troops, and retook the way to Poland. He was prevented by John Sobieski, General of the Republic, who crossed the Dniester, and, seconded by the Wallachians and Moldavians, defeated the Ottomans at Choczim, and pursued them as far as the gates of Kaminiec. The news of the death of Michael, King of Poland, recalled him to Warsaw; he then received the reward for his services that he had just rendered to the Republic and Christianity; the Diet proclaimed him King (1673).

The Porte did not learn without perturbation the election of Sobieski. Conquered by him when he was only one of the generals of the Republic, what had they not to dread from his ambition, now that the title of King gave him the power and the confidence to undertake everything? But soon the Polish nobility, more jealous of its liberties than of the national glory, took umbrage at

* Von Hammer, tom. iii. p. 149.

Sobieski's projects, and feared to give themselves a master if they left much longer all the forces of the State reunited in his hands. In vain did the King propose to set on foot an army equal to that of the Turks. Under pretext of economizing the money of the public treasury, the Diet refused to raise fresh troops, whilst the Sultan collected his soldiers from every quarter and demanded reinforcements from the Tartars of the Crimea.

On the approach of the Turks, the Poles abandoned the siege of Kaminiec (1674). To secure the submission of that place, the Sultan forced all the Christian inhabitants to quit it; he transported them beyond the Danube and the Balkans, and assigned them lands in the province of Kirk-Kilissia; they were replaced by 2,000 Sipahis.

France beheld with regret the war waging between Poland and Turkey—a war only profitable to the House of Austria: the Bishop of Marseilles, ambassador of Louis XIV. at Warsaw, vainly endeavoured to negotiate peace; his proposals were not listened to. The Tartar Khan had more success; he acted as mediator between Sobieski and Mahomet IV. A treaty was signed at Daoud Pacha, near Constantinople (27th of October, 1676), by which Kaminiec and Podolia remained to the Porte, as well as the Ukraine, with the exception of some towns.

2. *Death of Ahmed Kupruli* (1676); *Kara Mustapha succeeds him.—War with Russia.—Peace of Radzin* (1681).

A few days after the conclusion of that treaty Ahmed Kupruli died, having scarcely reached his forty-first year. He had borne during fifteen years the heaviest burthen of the Empire. "He was a man of tall stature; he had large and well-opened eyes, fair complexion, and in manner was modest, gracious, and full of dignity. He did not show himself blood-thirsty like his father, always combatted oppression and injustice, and raised himself so firmly against corruption, cupidity and all personal views, that presents, instead of disposing him in favour of a request, induced him to refuse it. His expansive and penetrating mind, his happy and ready memory, his sure and firm judgment, his sound understanding and just common sense conducted him to the truth by the shortest way. He spoke little and with reserve, after mature reflection, and always with a perfect knowledge of things. The science to which he had at first devoted himself, and which launched him in the career of legist, always followed him as faithful companion in the ranks of the army, and as far as the banks of the Raab and the Dniester, as amidst the ruins of Candia. The glory of Ahmed Kupruli was assured by the wars of Hungary, of Crete, of Poland, by the conquest of Neuhæusel, Candia, and Kaminiec, by the peace of Vasvar, that of Candia, and the treaties of Bucsacs and Daoud-Pacha. During three lustres, he knew how to aggrandize and pacify Turkey. After Sokolli, he was, beyond doubt, first among the Ministers who have directed the Ottoman Empire.*

He had for successor his brother-in-law, the Kaïmacan Kara Mustapha, who maintained himself in power during seven years (1676-83). The accession of that unworthy heir of the Kuprulis marked the commencement of the period of decadence. Puffed up with pride, he displayed the most scandalous ostentation; his harem contained more than 1,500 concubines, and at least as many female slaves to attend upon them, with 700 black eunuchs; his horses, dogs, and hawks for hunting were to be counted by thousands. Constantinople, Adrianople, and Belgrade owed, it is true, to his vanity some useful edifices—mosques, fountains, baths, and schools; but to meet all those expenses, Kara Mustapha had need of enormous sums, which he procured by the most shameful means and the most cruel extortions. He bargained with the European ambassadors for the renewal of the capitulations and even for audiences with the Sultan; he sold governments, dignities, justice; finally, we shall see what dreams of ambition he hoped to realize by the aid of his treasures.

* Von Hammer, tom. iii. p. 162.

Kara Mustapha manifested no more talent as a general than probity as an administrator. During the last war against Poland, Doroszensko, hetman of the Cossacks, had offered his aid to the Porte; but through defiance or disdain, the Turks had rejected his proposition. The hetman, either out of pique or revenge, submitted himself, with all his people, to the protectorate of Russia. On hearing this, Mahomet IV. drew from the prison of the Seven Towers Georges Kiemielniski, son of an old hetman, and nominated him in the place of Doroszensko. The Cossacks refused to recognize the authority of Kiemielniski. The Porte was then compelled to have recourse to arms; 40,000 men traversed Moldavia and Podolia, and advanced upon Cehryn, which place they had orders to besiege. At the same time, the Tartars hurried up from the Crimea. The Cossacks and Russians, to the number of 60,000, were entrenched near Cehryn; in order to hinder the junction of the two hostile armies, they put themselves in motion, fell upon the Tartars, and cut them in pieces. The Turks, terrified, recrossed the Bug (1677).

The Divan was ready to enter upon negotiations; but Kara Mustapha energetically opposed that course; and, as the Russians demanded the cession of the Ukraine as far as the Dneister, the Sultan listened to the warlike counsels of the Grand Vizier. Kara Mustapha himself took the command of the expedition; 30,000 Tartars sent by the Khan of the Crimea, and 4,000 Cossacks collected by Kiemielniski, joined with the Ottomans in the attack upon Cehryn. They only took it after a long and sanguinary siege (1678). To that was limited the success of that campaign. The retreat of the Turks almost resembled a rout: continually harassed by the Russians, who lay in wait for them at all the difficult passes, they lost a great portion of their artillery and baggage. The war dragged on its lengthened course till 1681. At last a peace was concluded at Radzin, through the mediation of the Khan of the Crimea.

The mere record of the wars between Russians and

Turks which have succeeded one another since 1677 at short intervals, is infinitely less instructive than the series of treaties settling the relations of Sultan and Czar. It is only in the face of these documents that we can clearly read the true objects of Russia, the pretexts which have been put forward as her objects, the tenacity of her purposes, and the degree in which she has advanced towards their fulfilment, or has been forced to recede from it for a time.

When the Russians and Turks first came into conflict, in the last half of the seventeenth century, it is not too much to say that they were two hordes of barbarians. But the Turks were barbarians on the decline. Their old energy was nearly spent, the superiority in armament which had been the secret of their conquests was lost, their political system was eaten through with internal corruption, and the elements of strength which it had contained were turning into sources of weakness. The Russians, on the other hand, were just beginning to be conscious of the impulses which centuries before had poured the Turks over Western Asia and Eastern Europe. They were sunk in barbarism and squalor, and they professed Christianity in the most superstitious form in which it had ever been clothed. But accident placed some men and women of genius at their head, and their Christianity, though altogether valueless for moral purposes, gave them a point of contact with Western Europe which has proved of the greatest advantage to them.

3. *War in Hungary.—Policy of Louis XIV.—Siege and Relief of Vienna.*

The Porte would not probably have consented to treat with Russia if its attention had not been called to another quarter by the affairs of Hungary. In that country the discontent caused by the oppressive Government and the fanatical persecution of Protestantism by the Austrian Cabinet had gone on increasing. At length, the Austrian domination had rendered itself thoroughly odious to the Hungarians. To hinder the progress of Protestantism, the Emperor Leopold, in the excess of his Catholic zeal, sent to the galleys a great number of preachers and ministers; and to all the evils of religious persecution were added the violence and devastations of the generals and the German administrators, who treated Hungary as a conquered province. The Hungarians in vain invoked the charters which consecrated their national liberties. To their most legitimate complaints Leopold replied by the infliction of punishments; he spared not even the families of the most illustrious; several magnates perished by the hands of the executioner. Such oppression was certain to bring about a revolt. In 1668 a conspiracy had been formed against Leopold by certain Hungarian leaders, which, however, was discovered and frustrated; and it was not till 1677, when the young Count Emmerich Tekeli, having escaped from prison, placed himself at the head of the malcontents, that these disturbances assumed any formidable importance. The Hungarians adopted his motto, *pro Deo et patria;* and Tekeli, who possessed much military talent, and was an uncompromising enemy of the House of Austria, having entered Upper Hungary with 12,000 men, defeated the Imperial forces, captured several towns, occupied the whole district of the Carpathian Mountains, and compelled the Austrian generals, Counts Wurmb and Leslie, to accept the truce he offered. The Emperor, enlightened by these reverses, at length comprehended the necessity for reforms, and towards the end of 1681, at the Diet of Oldenburg, did justice to the claims of Hungary. These concessions contented a portion of the magnates and weakened the party of independence; moreover, the treaty of Nimeguen, recently concluded with France, allowed the House of Austria to employ all her forces against the rebels. In this conjuncture Tekeli turned for aid towards the Turks, making an appeal to Mahomet IV.; and after the conclusion of the Turkish and Russian war in 1681, Kara Mustapha determined to assist the insurgents openly, their leader offering, in exchange, to acknowledge the suzerainty of the Porte. Tekeli sought also succour from France. Louis XIV. gave him subsidies, solicited the Sultan to send an army into Hungary, and caused an alliance between the Hungarians, Transylvanians, and Wallachians to be concluded against Austria (1682).

The truce concluded in 1665 between Austria and Turkey had not yet expired; the Porte could not therefore support Tekeli without violating the faith of treaties; but considerations of that nature had but little influence over the minds of the Grand Vizier and the Sultan; the war party carried the day. The Governor of Buda received orders to support Tekeli, who took the title of King. Count Albert of Caprara, Envoy Extraordinary of the Emperor, arrived shortly after at Constantinople to claim the maintenance of the truce. Kara Mustapha fixed the conditions of the peace thus : Austria should pay to the Porte an annual tribute of 500,000 florins; Leopoldstadt and Gutta should be demolished ; the island of Schutt, the fortress of Muran, and several other places should be put into the hands of Tekeli; all Hungarians should re-enter into possession of their belongings and privileges; a general amnesty should cover all the past. The Austrian envoy returned to Vienna (August, 1682). Some days after, the Sultan, as a signal for war, caused the horse-tails to be set up in front of the Seraglio, and great preparations were commenced which spread terror through Germany. Leopold now despatched a splendid embassy to Constantinople in the hope of renewing the Treaty of Vasvar, but without avail; the Turks only increased their demands.

Early in the spring of 1683 Sultan Mahomet marched forth from his capital with a large army, which at Belgrade he transferred to the command of Kara Mustapha. Tekeli formed a junction with the Turks at Essek. In vain did Ibrahim, the experienced Pacha of Buda, endeavour to persuade Kara Mustapha first of all to subdue the surrounding country, and to postpone until the following year the attack upon Vienna; his advice was scornfully rejected, and, indeed, the audacity of the Grand Vizier seemed justified by the scant resistance he had met with. He talked of renewing the conquests of Solyman: he assembled, it is said, 700,000 men, 100,000 horses, and 1,200 guns— an army more powerful than any the Turks had set on foot since the capture of Constantinople. All of which may be reduced to 150,000 barbarian troops without discipline, the last conquering army which the degenerate race of the Osmanli produced wherewith to invade Hungary.

Hostilities commenced in March, 1683; for the Turks, who had not been accustomed to enter upon a campaign before the summer season, had begun their march that year before the end of winter. Some prompt and easy successes exalted the ambition of Kara Mustapha; and, in spite of the contrary advice of Tekeli, Ibrahim Pacha, and several other personages, he determined to besiege Vienna. He accordingly advanced direct upon that capital and encamped under its walls on the 14th of July. It was just at the moment that Louis XIV. had captured Strasbourg, and at which his army appeared ready to cross the Rhine: all Europe was in alarm, believing that an agreement existed between France and the Porte for the conquest and dismemberment of Germany. But it was not so. The Turks, without giving France any previous warning, had of themselves made their invasion of Hungary; Louis XIV. was delighted at their success, but nevertheless disposed, if it went too far, to check them, in order to play the part of Saviour of Christendom.

It was fortunate for the Emperor Leopold that he had upon the frontiers of Poland an ally of indomitable courage in King John Sobieski, and that he found the German princes loyal and prompt on this occasion, contrary to their custom, in sending him succour. Moreover, in Duke Charles of Lorraine he met with a skilful general to lead his army. Consternation and confusion prevailed, however, in Vienna, whilst the Emperor with his Court fled to Linz. Many of the inhabitants followed him; but the rest, when the first moments of terror had passed, prepared for the defence, and the dilatoriness of the Turks, who amused themselves with pillaging the environs and neighbouring chateaux, allowed the Duke of Lorraine to throw 12,000 men as a garrison into the city; then, as he was unable with his slender force to bar the approach of the Turkish army, he kept aloof and waited for the King of Poland.

Leopold solicited succour on all sides, and the Pope made an appeal to the piety of the King of France. Louis XIV., on the contrary, was intriguing throughout Europe in order that the Christian princes should not quit their attitude of repose, and he only offered to the Diet of Ratisbon the aid of his arms on condition that it should recognize the recent usurpations decreed by the famous Chambers of Reunion, and that it should elect his son King of the Romans. He reckoned, if it should accept his offers, to determine the Turks to retreat and to effect a peace which, by bringing the Imperial Crown into his house, would have been the death-stroke for Austria. All these combinations miscarried through the devotedness of the Poles.

When Leopold supplicated Sobieski to come to his aid, Louis XIV. tried to divert him from it; he reassured him upon the projects of the Turks by a letter of the Sultan, he made him see his real enemies in Austria, Brandenbourg, and that power of the North, which the Dutch gazettes had begun to call *His Russian Majesty;* he reminded him in fine that the House of Austria, saved by the French on the day of St. Gothard, had testified its gratitude to them by allowing the victors to die of hunger and by envenoming their differences with the Porte. But it was all useless; hatred of the infidels prevailed, and the Polish squadrons hurried to the deliverance of Vienna.

Count Rudiger de Stahrenberg was made commandant of the city, and showed himself alike bold and energetic in everything that could contribute to its defence. The Turkish camp encircled Vienna and its suburbs, spreading over the country all round to the distance of six leagues. Two days afterwards, Kara Mustapha opened the trenches, and his artillery battered the walls in order to make a breach. Great efforts moreover were made in digging mines, with the design of blowing up bastions or portions of the wall, so that the city might be carried by assault, wherein the Turks hoped to find an immense booty. But the besieged made an obstinate defence, and repaired during the night the damage done on the previous day. During sixty days, forty mines and ten counter-mines were exploded; the Turks delivered eighteen assaults, the besieged made twenty-four sorties. Each inch of ground was only obtained by dint of a hard and long struggle, in which an equal stubbornness both in attack and defence was exhibited. The hottest fighting took place at the *Label* bastion, around which there was not a foot of ground that had not been steeped in the blood of friend or foe. However, by degrees the Turks gained a few paces; at the end of August, they were lodged in the ditches of the city; and on the 4th of September they sprung a mine under the *Bourg* bastion; one-half of the city was shaken thereby, and a breach was rent in the bastion wide enough for an assault to be delivered, but the enemy was repulsed. Next day the Turks attacked it with renewed courage, but the valour of the besieged baffled the assailants. On the 10th of September another mine was sprung under the same bastion, and the breach was so wide that a battalion might have entered it abreast. The danger was extreme, for the garrison was exhausted by fighting, sickness, and incessant labour. The Count de Stahrenberg despatched courier after courier to the Duke of Lorraine for succour. "There is not a moment to be lost, monseigneur," he wrote, "not a moment;" and Vienna, exhausted, saw not yet her liberators arrive. At length, on the 14th, when the whole city was in a stupor in the immediate expectation of an attack, a movement was observed in the enemy's camp which announced that succour was at hand. At five o'clock in the afternoon the Christian army was descried surmounting the Hill of Kahlen, and it made its presence known by a salvo of artillery. John Sobieski had arrived at the head of a valiant army. The electors of Saxony and of Bavaria with many princes, dukes, and margraves of Germany had brought with them fresh troops. Charles of Lorraine might then dare to march against the Moslems, although he had yet only 46,000 men. The army of Sobieski reached Klosternenbourg, Kœnigstetten, Saint-André, the valley of Hagen and Kirling, where it effected its junction with the Austrians and the Saxons who had arrived there in passing by Hœflin. On Sunday, the 15th of September, in the earliest rays of a fine autumnal day, the holy priest Marco d'Aviano celebrated mass in the chapel of Kahlenberg, and the King of Poland served him during the sacrifice. Afterwards, Sobieski made his son kneel down, and dubbed him a knight in remembrance of the great occasion on which he was going to be present; then, turning towards his officers, he reminded them of the victory of Choczim, adding that the triumph they were about to achieve under the walls of Vienna would not only save a city, but Christendom. Next morning the Christian army descended the Hill of Kahlen in order of battle. A salvo of five cannon-shot gave the signal for the fight. Sobieski commanded the right wing, the Duke of Lorraine the left, under whose orders served Prince Eugene of Savoy, then aged nineteen. The Elector of Bavaria was in the centre. The village of Naussdorf, situated upon the Danube, was attacked by the Saxon and Imperial troops which formed the left wing, and carried after an obstinate resistance. Towards noon, the King of Poland having descended into the plain with the right wing, at the head of his Polish cavalry, attacked the innumerable squadrons of Turkish horse. Flinging himself upon the enemy's centre with all the fury of a hurricane, he spread confusion in their ranks; but his courage carried him too far, he was surrounded, and was on the point of being overwhelmed by numbers. Then, shouting for aid, the German cavalry, which had followed him, charged the enemy at full gallop, delivered the King, and soon put the Turks to flight on all sides. The right wing had decided the victory; by seven o'clock in the evening the deliverance of Vienna was achieved. The bodies of more than 10,000 infidels strewed the field of battle.

But all those combats were mere preludes to the great battle which must decide the fortune of the war. For the Turkish camp with its thousands of tents could still be seen spreading around as far as eye could reach, and its artillery continued to play upon the city. The victorious commander-in-chief was holding a council of war to decide whether to give battle again on that same day, or wait till the morrow to give his troops an interval of rest, when a messenger came with the announcement that the enemy appeared to be in full flight; and it proved to be the fact. A panic had seized the Turks, and they fled in disorder, abandoning their camp and baggage; and soon even those who were attacking the city were seen in full flight with the rest of the army.

The booty found in the Turkish camp was immense: three hundred pieces of heavy artillery, five thousand tents, that of the Grand Vizier with all the military chests and the chancery. The treasure amounted to fifteen million crowns, the tent of the Vizier alone yielding four hundred thousand crowns. Two millions also were found in the military chest; arms studded with precious stones, the equipments of Kara Mustapha fell into the hands of the victors. In their flight, the Mussulmans threw away arms, baggage, and banners, with the exception of the Holy Standard of the Prophet, which, nevertheless, the Imperials pretended to have seized. The King of Poland received for his share four million florins; and in a letter to his wife, the sole delight of his soul, his dear and well-beloved Mariette, he speaks of that booty and of the happiness of having delivered Vienna. "All the enemy's camp," he wrote, "with the whole of his artillery and all his enormous riches, have fallen into our hands. We are driving before us a host of camels, mules, and Turkish prisoners."

Count Stahrenberg received the King of Poland in the magnificent tent of the Grand Vizier, and greeted him as a deliverer. Next day Sobieski, accompanied by the Elector of Bavaria and the different commanders, traversed the city on horseback, preceded by a great banner of cloth of gold and two tall gilded staves bearing the horse-tails which had been planted in front of the Grand Vizier's tent, as a symbol of supreme command. In the Loretto chapel of the Augustins, the hero threw himself upon his face before the altar and chanted the *Te Deum*. "Vienna was delivered; the flood of Ottomans, that had beaten against its walls one hundred and fifty-four years previously, had returned more furiously, more menacing still, against that dignified protectress of European civilization, but, this time, it had been repelled never to return thither again."*

Thus vanished the insane hopes of the Grand Vizier. If Demetrius Cantemir may be believed, Kara Mustapha had desired to capture Vienna to appropriate it to himself, and found in the West an empire of which he would have been the sovereign. "That subject," says the historian, "who only held his power from the Sultan, despised in his heart the Sultan himself; and, as he found himself at the head of all the disciplined troops of the empire, he looked upon his master as a shadow denuded of strength and substance, who, being very inferior in courage to him, could never oppose to him an army like that which was under his command. For all that concerned the Emperor of Germany, he appeared still less to be feared: being a prince bare and despoiled so soon as he should have lost Vienna. It was thus that Kara Mustapha reasoned within himself. Already he casts his eyes over the treasures which he has in his possession; with the money of the Sultan he has also brought his own; all that of the German princes is going to be his; for he believes that it is amassed in the city he is besieging. If he needs support, he reckons upon the different governors of Hungary as devoted to his interests; these are his creatures, whom he has put into their posts during the seven years of his vizierate, not one of those functionaries dare offer an obstacle to the elevation of his benefactor. Ibrahim Pacha, beylerbey of Buda, keeps him in suspense by reason of the influence that his fame gives him over the army and

* Von Hammer, tom. xii. p. 120.

over Hungary; he must be won over before all else, as
well as the chief officers of the Janissaries and the Sipahis.
Ibrahim shall be made King of Hungary. The different
provinces comprised in that kingdom shall be divided into
timars for appanage of the Sipahis, and all the rest of the
soldiery shall have establishments in the towns, as so
many new colonies; to them shall be assigned the lands of
the old inhabitants, who will be driven out or reduced to
slavery. He reserves for himself the title of Sultan, his
share shall be all Germany as far as the frontiers of
France, with Transylvania and Poland, which he intends
to render subject or at least make tributary the year
following." Such are the projects that Cantemir attributes to Kara Mustapha; the intervention of Sobieski
caused these chimerical plans quickly to vanish.

The Emperor Leopold, who returned to Vienna on the
16th of September, instead of expressing his thanks and
gratitude to the commanders who had rescued his capital,
received them with the haughty and repulsive coldness
prescribed by the etiquette of the Imperial Court. Sobieski nevertheless continued his services by pursuing the
retreating Turks. Awakened from his dream of self-exal-
tation, the Grand Vizier retook the road towards Turkey,
directing his steps to the Raab, where he rallied the
remnants of his army. Thence, he marched towards
Buda, and attacked by the way the Styrian town of
Lilienfeld; he was repulsed by the prelate Matthias Kal-
weis, and avenged himself for that fresh check by devastating Lower Styria. He crossed the Danube by a bridge
of boats at Parkany; but the Poles vigorously disputed
the passage with him, and he again lost more than 8,000
men taken or slain by the Christians. Shortly after, the
fortress of Gran opened its gates to Sobieski. The Grand
Vizier barbarously put to death the officers who had
signed the capitulation; he threw upon his generals the
responsibility of his reverses and thought to stifle in
blood the murmurs of his accusers. The army marched
in disorder, as though struck with a panic terror. Kara
Mustapha wished that a Jew whom he despatched to Bel-

grade should be escorted by a troop of horsemen. "I have no need of an escort," replied the Jew; "I have only to wear my cap in the German fashion, and not a Turk will touch me."

The enemies of the Grand Vizier, however, conspired to effect his ruin at Constantinople: and the results of the campaign justified the predictions of the party of peace. Mahomet IV., enraged at these disasters, sent his grand chamberlain to Belgrade with orders to bring back the head of the vizier (1683): it was, in fact, brought to the Sultan in a silver dish.

To Kara Mustapha succeeded the Kaïmacan Ibrahim Pacha. The latter did not accept without hesitation the charge of governing the Empire amidst the perils that threatened it on all sides. In fact, a great league called *the Holy Alliance* had just, thanks to the terror which the siege of Vienna had inspired, been formed against the Ottomans: it was composed, besides Austria, of the Venetians, Poles, and Russians. The Emperor Leopold had found the Venetians quite disposed for war; he won over Sobieski, who was still deaf to the instances of France; finally, he armed the Russians by soliciting them "to open the Black Sea and march upon Byzantium: Greece and Asia," said he, "awaited them." The Porte must then have repented of the insulting proceedings which had made them lose the sympathies of France, and which had been just repeated against her new ambassador.

4. *Power of France in the Mediterranean.*

Since the victories of Stromboli, Agousta and Palermo, where Duquesne destroyed the fleets of Holland and Spain, since the battle of Cape St. Vincent, since its alliance with the Order of Malta and the States of Italy, finally, since the renewal of capitulations with the Porte, the French flag had dominated in the Mediterranean. But there was an obstacle to that domination—piracy. The Barbary corsairs had profited by the war of 1672 to violate the treaties; the Sultan in vain recommended them to respect the vessels of his ally; the King of France vainly menaced them with total destruction; French ships were insulted, pillaged, carried away from the very shores of Provence. Then a war of extermination was recommenced against the African pirates, and the French squadrons were solely engaged in hunting them out in every quarter. One of these expeditions was on the point of bringing about a disagreement between France and the Porte.

Duquesne, pursuing eight vessels belonging to Tripoli, learned that they had taken refuge at Chios, and went to attack them in the harbour of that island (1681). The Turkish commandant ordered him to respect the territory of the Sultan, and, upon his refusal to clear out, fired upon his ships. Duquesne then bombarded the fort and laid it in ruins; and his cannon-balls carried devastation also into the town, where they destroyed two mosques; he only ceased firing at the prayers of the inhabitants, and on condition that it should be referred to the Grand Seignior. The Capudan-Pacha hurried thither with forty-two galleys. Duquesne declared to him that, if he did not compel the Tripolitains to make their submission to France, to carry out the capitulations concluded with the Porte, to deliver up their French slaves, he would burn the eight vessels belonging to Tripoli, the town of Chios and the Ottoman Fleet. The Capudan-Pacha desired to negotiate; but meanwhile the Court of Constantinople was in the greatest agitation: the Sultan declared that he would inflict vengeance for the insult perpetrated on the mosques of Chios, although he should demand it throughout the universe. The French ambassador then was the Marquis de Guilleragues, who had succeeded to Nointel in 1678, and who, for the last three years, had been quarrelling with the Vizier upon a question of etiquette. He was ordered to appear before that Minister, who declared to him that he had only one means of saving his own life and that of all the Franks; which was to offer a heavy sum of money in reparation of the damage caused by the

French cannonade. The ambassador replied that the Sultan was just and the King of France powerful; that, therefore, he regarded himself and his compatriots as being in perfect safety; and he refused to sign a document by which he would bind himself, in the name of his master, to make excuses to the Sultan and to give him pecuniary reparation. He was threatened with imprisonment in the castle of the Seven Towers. His answer to that threat was : "If I enter therein, I will not go out thence, unless the King my master come himself to open the doors for me." He was kept prisoner in one of the apartments of the Vizier.

Duquesne, however, arrived in the Dardanelles with ten vessels, and sent to inform the Divan that if violence were offered to the ambassador, and if the disputes about etiquette which existed between him and the Vizier were not adjusted to the entire satisfaction of France, he would proceed to fetch M. de Guilleragues out of Constantinople. The Vizier then proposed to the ambassador to arrange the affair by making, in his own name personally, a present to the Sultan. Guilleragues consented thereto, Duquesne being constrained by orders from the French Court, which was ignorant of these events, to suddenly quit the Archipelago. After several months' negotiations, in which the Ottoman Ministers unveiled their base cupidity by miserable discussions upon the value of the present, the ambassador was received in solemn audience by Mahomet IV. He offered him in his own name, and without making it a question of the Chios affair, a present of jewels and furniture of the value of 15,000 livres, and obtained in compensation the adjustment of the disputes about etiquette to his entire satisfaction, with all the firmans he demanded, whether for the merchants or for the missionaries. The Porte made a great fuss about this insignificant reparation. "It is a brilliant performance," said the narrative which it ordered to be circulated, "of which the people speak with the greatest delight. The report of it has spread into Persia, Armenia, to the Indies. Our friends, the tributaries, and the nations under the law of the Messiah have been informed touching it." Those same nations had tried to prevent a reconciliation. "Never," said the same narrative, "has there appeared so much eagerness on the part of the Christian ministers against him of France. The Venetians, the Dutch, and all the rest have excited, as much as it has been possible, the hatred of his Highness against the French, making every effort to engage us in a rupture with them; but the much-enlightened Vizier has contented himself with the reparation of the ambassador."

Duquesne had been recalled to France to prepare the vengeance which the Grand Monarque desired to inflict upon the Algerines. He appeared before their city with a fleet composed of sixteen ships, fifteen galleys, and five bomb-vessels, bombarded it during several days, but was compelled to withdraw in consequence of the bad season. He returned the year following, bombarded Algiers again during two months, and destroyed it almost entirely. The inhabitants, in consternation, sued for peace. Duquesne rejected all their propositions until they had delivered up all the Christian slaves, restored the French cannon left at Gigeri, and paid 1,200,000 piastres for the expenses of the war. Then an embassy, composed of the principal Algerines, went to Versailles to implore pardon of Louis XIV., and swore to respect henceforth "the capitulations of the Grand Seignior and the treaties made with France to the advantage of the French merchants" (25th April, 1684).

Tripoli had the same fate as Algiers. Duquesne threw 5,000 bombs into it (1686). Tunis hastened to sue for peace, and faithfully kept it. The squadron of Château-Renaud blocked all the ports of Morocco, and caused such losses to its navy that the Sultan sent an embassy to Louis XIV. to solicit from him a treaty of friendship and commerce. Lastly, piracy was pursued even against its indirect auxiliaries at Genoa. That Republic, sold to the enemies of France, furnished vessels to the Algerines and Spaniards. It had repudiated in the Levant the protection of the French flag; it was a lively insult to the ports of

Marseilles and Toulon: Genoa was piteously bombarded. Then France entirely dominated the Mediterranean.

5. *War against the Holy Alliance.—Deposition of Mahomet IV.* (1687).

In that situation, the Porte was menaced by the Holy Alliance—a league against the Turks under the protection of the Pope, and formed by the Emperor, the King of Poland, and the Republic of Venice, and it was resolved to procure, if possible, the accession to it of the Czar of Muscovy. The Venetians were induced to join the League in the hope of recovering their former possessions, and declared war against the Sultan. The war which ensued then, called the *Holy War*, lasted till the Peace of Carlowitz in 1699. Venice in this war put forth a strength that was little expected from that declining State. Many thousand Germans were enrolled in her army, commanded by Morosini, and by Count Königsmark, a Swede.

Thus threatened on all sides, the Porte drew near again to the French Cabinet, overwhelmed its ambassador with honours and kind attentions, satisfied all its demands concerning commerce, the Holy Places, the missions; but its pride hindered it from soliciting directly the alliance of the monarch who had just bombarded Algiers and Tripoli; it contented itself with asking his mediation to obtain peace. On the other hand, Louis XIV., who was still under the illusions of the truce of Ratisbon, desirous of inducing Leopold to change that truce into a lasting peace, dare not manifest his sentiments in favour of the Turks, and he contented himself with exciting the Poles to abandon the Holy Alliance, and the Hungarians to persist in their revolt. The result of these errors was at first that the Ottomans, attacked upon all their frontiers, experienced nothing save defeats; the consequence was, that Louis XIV. commenced the war when his allies of the East were unfortunate, and had already sued for peace to Austria.

The Duke of Lorraine, however, invaded Hungary, the Venetians attempted the conquest of the Morea, Sobieski menaced Moldavia. In order to resist this triple attack, the Divan placed on foot three armies.

The Duke of Lorraine seized upon Wissegrad, and, some days after, upon Waitzen, as the result of a brilliant victory; Pesth capitulated. The Turks, defeated a second time near Saint-André, retired to Buda. That city, heroically defended by Ibrahim Pacha, arrested the march of the Imperialists. The besieged attributed their deliverance to a miracle: twice they thought they saw the Prophet hovering, at the hour of prayer, above their ramparts. During the siege, the Duke of Lorraine defeated the Seraskier Suleiman Pacha; and, at the same time, the Generals Trauttmansdorf and Leslie, conquerors of the pachas of Bosnia and Gradiska, captured, in Croatia, Veroviz and some other fortresses (1683).

The following year, the Turks retook Waitzen; but they failed before Raab and Wissegrad; Ismaïl Pacha, beylerbey of Roumelia, retired before General Hausler. In the campaign of 1685, the Duke of Lorraine besieged Neuhæusel, and carried it by assault, after having raised the blockade of the fortress of Gran, whilst the Count of Herberstein devastated the territory of Licca, Corbavie, the valley of Udwina, and that Leslie burned Essek; lastly, the Turks abandoned the towns of Waitzen and Novigrad, and Tekeli fell back before General Schultz, and was, by order of the Grand Vizier, confined in the Seven Towers.

Meanwhile, the Venetians made some progress. The Proveditore Pietro Valiero was forced to raise the siege of Sign; but the Christians in the mountains of Dalmatia, Albania, and the Morea rose, joined their arms to those of the Republic, defeated their beys, and sent their heads to Venice. The islands of St. Maura and Previsa fell into the power of the Christians. In 1685, Morosini invested Coron and seized upon it, after having beaten the troops that had come to succour that place. He sent to the Senate a standard and two horse-tails, which were suspended as a trophy in a church at Venice. With the aid of the Maïnotes he took Zernata, Calamata and other fortresses; then, quitting the Morea, he made a descent into Albania. Kœnigsmark united with him, the following year, in conquering a great portion of Greece. They both took Navarino, Modon, Napoli de Romania, Arcadia, Patras, Lepanto, Corinth, Misitra, Athens, &c. The marble lions, which seemed to defend the entrance to the Piræus, were sent to Venice and placed before the gates of the Arsenal. The grateful Republic caused to be placed in the great hall of the Doge's palace the bust of Morosini, with this inscription: *The Senate to Morosini, the Peloponesiarch, from the Life* (1686).

The war was pushed with little vigour on the side of Poland. Sobieski tried in vain to draw into his alliance Constantin Cantemir, Voïvode of Moldavia; he was conquered by that prince near Bojau. The Seraskier Suleiman Pacha having obtained some other successes, Mahomet IV. confided to him the seals of the Empire.

Raised to the Grand Vizierate, Suleiman did not realize the hopes of the Ottomans. He showed much activity, but he had not the talent necessary in order to struggle against the Duke of Lorraine. That illustrious general commanded an army of 90,000 men. All Europe was represented in his camp by officers who wished to train in his school, and who thought it an honour to fight under the command of such a master against the barbarians; German, French, English, Spanish, and Italian nobles were to be seen around him. He began the siege of Buda on the 18th of June, 1686; the Governor, Abdi Pacha, refused to capitulate, and courageously sustained two formidable assaults; but, in a third attack, he perished upon the breach with more than 4,000 men, and the Imperialists, penetrating into the town, enveloped it in blood and fire (Sept. 2). Buda, the capital of Hungary, had belonged to the Turks during forty-five years: it was the rampart of Islamism, the pivot of the Holy War, the key of the Ottoman Empire. The capture of that city involved the surrender of a great number of other places.

Suleiman Pacha established his winter quarters at Belgrade, and tried to negotiate a truce; he soon recognized that peace was not possible, save on dishonourable conditions, and redoubled his energies to recommence the campaign. The Sultan imposed forced contributions throughout the Empire, and, by way of example, gave 500 purses out of his own private treasure. The Vizier, having assembled 60,000 men and 70 pieces of cannon, encountered the Christian army near Mohacs; a great battle took place in that locality, already celebrated by the disaster of the Hungarians; but, this time, the Ottomans succumbed; they lost 20,000 men with their artillery and baggage (Aug. 4, 1687). The reduction of Transylvania completed the measure of the Duke of Lorraine's glory and the discouragement of the Turks; they then abandoned Essek, Valpo, and fourteen strongholds in Sclavonia, Palota in Lower Hungary, and several places in Croatia.

At the same time, the Russians attacked the Tartars, and the King of Poland invaded Moldavia: he put it to pillage, and was only driven out of it by famine. The following year he besieged Kaminiec; but, the Turks and Tartars arriving with superior forces, he was constrained to retire.

The French ambassador, Guilleragues, having died in 1685, had for successor Girardin, who died in 1686. To Girardin succeeded Chateauneuf, who had instructions to instigate the Porte to continue the war against Austria, and to make peace with Poland. The Poles slackened, in fact, hostilities; but the moral support given by Louis XIV. to Mahomet IV. did not suffice to arrest the invasions of the Imperialists: against the Duke of Lorraine the Ottomans had need of effective and real succour; Louis, whom the league of Augsbourg already threatened, did not know the proper moment at which to begin an inevitable war, and gave the Austrians time to consummate the defeat of the Turks. If he had drawn upon the Rhine the forces of the House of Austria, the Ottoman Empire, saved by that diversion, might have sustained the struggle with advantage; reduced to his own resources, the Sultan experienced nothing but reverses; and the reverses, joining themselves to famine, brought sedition in their train. Turkey, raised up again momentarily from her decadence by the Kuprulis, saw a renewal, inwardly, of the deplorable excesses of military anarchy, when she had lost outwardly the prestige of her arms, and that, not being strong enough to resist alone her enemies, she waited in vain for the support of France.

After the unfortunate Hungarian expedition, the Janissaries and the Sipahis mutinied against the Grand Vizier, Suleiman Pacha, who tried to appease them by offering them money and provisions; but his weakness encouraged the revolt; he was summoned to give up the standard and the seals. To escape himself from that outburst of violence, he secretly reached Peterwardein, and thence he repaired to Belgrade. After his flight, the soldiers elected a Grand Vizier and addressed to the Sultan a solemn petition against Suleiman; Mahomet, terrified, granted their demands and sent them the head of his old Minister. But the soldiery, once set in motion, could not longer be stopped; it marched upon Constantinople to depose the Sultan himself. Everything was to be feared from its fury. The Kaïmacan Kupruli Mustapha sacrificed the Emperor to save the Empire. He signified to the Sultan, by the ulemas, the will of the nation and of the army. "Let the will of Allah be accomplished!" said the dethroned monarch, and, satisfied with preserving his life, he allowed himself to be shut up in the Seraglio, whence they drew forth his brother to succeed him (November 8, 1687). Mahomet IV. died disregarded five years afterwards.

6. Soliman II.—Continuation of the War.—Vizierate of Kupruli Mustapha.

Soliman II. had lived during forty-six years in the most absolute seclusion, wholly devoted to the study of law and religion. The news of his elevation to the throne struck him with terror. " In the name of the immortal Creator," he exclaimed, " wherefore come you thus to disturb my tranquillity ? Leave me, I conjure you, to pass in peace in my retirement the short span of life remaining to me ; I was born only to meditate upon what concerns the life eternal." It was represented to him that the determination of the viziers, the ulemas, the army, and the people could not be revoked; that to remit the sovereign power to the hands of Mahomet would be to expose the State to the greatest peril. " I would fain resign myself to the necessity, but I dread my brother," was his reply. He was dragged almost by main force from his apartment as far as the throne-room. There he looked around on all sides, trembling from head to foot, and muttering that the sight of his brother would be enough to cause his death. At length, after having undergone purification, he consented to receive the homage of the ulemas and the great dignitaries.

This revolution had scarcely been completed, when the Grand Vizier Siawusch entered Constantinople at the head of the rebellious soldiery, for the revolt had not yet been appeased. The Janissaries and Sipahis indeed became now more turbulent than ever. They demanded that the donative usual on the accession of a new Sultan should be increased, and that all such Ministers and placemen as they disapproved of should be banished. Soliman ordered the accession donative to be distributed amongst them, and appointed two chiefs of the rebels to the governments of Roumelia and Djedda. That was certes not the way to establish order. Some of the viziers having attempted to resist their demands, a fearful riot ensued, the Sipahis and Janissaries massacred their agas, the palaces of all the ministers were stormed, plundered, and burnt; and even the Grand Vizier Siawusch himself fell by the hands of those who had elected him. He defended himself for awhile with the utmost energy, but succumbed at last to numbers, his body being torn into shreds. The assassins then penetrated within the harem of the slain vizier, seized his wife and sister, cut off their noses, hands and feet, and afterwards dragged them naked through the streets. Their slaves suffered similar treatment at the hands of the brutal soldiery. After these horrible exploits, the rebels spread themselves through every quarter of Constantinople, massacreing and pillaging as they went. To arrest their fury, the ulema planted the sacred standard of the Prophet at the Seraglio gate, and called upon all faithful Mussulmans to aid them in the suppression of the revolt. The Janissaries and Sipahis were only thus at length controlled by the people rising against them (February, 1688), and order was gradually restored by the confinement of the soldiery to their barracks.

All those revolts turned to the profit of the Austrians. The aged Ismael Pacha was now entrusted with the seals of the Empire, and with the conduct of a war which seemed to menace the Osmanli Empire with destruction; for the campaign of 1688 was still more disastrous to the Turks than the preceding one. In Hungary, Caraffa subdued Erlau, Lippa and Munkacs, valiantly defended by the wife of Tekeli; in Bosnia, Gradiska was abandoned by its garrison; Cornaro took Knin in Dalmatia, and Morosini seized upon Thebes. The following year, the Ottomans, overcome by Veterani and by the Margrave Louis of Baden, further lost several important places in Hungary, Sclavonia and Bosnia; Belgrade surrendered to the Elector of Bavaria. But, in Greece, Morosini failed before Salonica and before Negropont, this last siege costing him a third of his army; the plague ravaged the camp of the Venetians and carried off Count Kœnigsmark. On the side of Poland, the Tartars obtained some successes; they devasted Volhynia, revictualled Kaminiec and advanced as far as Lemberg.

These latter advantages were far from compensating the reverses experienced by the Mussulmans in the valley of the Danube. Humbled by these reverses, the Porte, for the first time, resolved to negotiate, and was disposed to make very ample concessions. The Emperor, elated by his successes against the Turks, dreamt of nothing less than putting an end to the Turkish Empire in Europe, and effecting the union of the Greek and Latin Churches. The Porte accredited to the Emperor Zulfikar Effendi and the Greek Mavrocordato Ten months passed in discussions without result: Austria, Venice and Poland proposed inadmissible conditions. "However," says Cantemir, "the Turks would have accepted the peace, even at that price, if the very Christian sun had not communicated a ray of its light to the pale crescent already on the eve of waning, and had not prevented, by the diversion of its arms, the obscurity which the German troops were about to spread there. Then the King of France declared war against the Emperor, and caused to be recalled to the Rhine the forces that were triumphing on the Danube. However, not wishing to draw upon himself all the weight of the war, he made the Sultan understand, by his ambassador the Marquis de Chateauneuf, that he had 400,000 men ready to enter into action, and that, the year following, he would penetrate into the heart of Germany."

Hostilities recommenced; but the affairs of the Empire were conducted by an incapable Vizier, Mustapha of Rodosto, and the Turks experienced nothing but defeats: they were beaten at Kostanitza in Croatia, at Baloudjina in Servia, lastly at Nissa. That place was taken, with Widdin and several other towns. The Imperialists excited Servia to insurrection, on one side they descended upon Uskioup, menacing Macedonia; on another side they attacked the defile of Dragoman, in which they were repulsed. "Yet one more campaign," said a Kupruli, "and the enemy will encamp under the walls of Constantinople." These reverses, it is true, were compensated by some advantages against other enemies: thus the Tartars defeated the Russian General Galitzin; the Poles were repulsed from Kaminiec and Morosini changed into a blockade the siege of Malvoisia. In spite of these successes, the Empire seemed threatened with ruin; a solemn divan, held at Adrianople, resolved to confide the salvation of it to a third Kupruli.

Kupruli Mustapha showed himself worthy of bearing the name that his father Mahomet Kupruli and his brother Ahmed Kupruli had made illustrious. The Germans were almost masters of the routes to Constantinople, and the Venetians dominated in Greece. To the coalesced Christians the Ottoman Empire had only worn-out troops to oppose; money was wanting for the victualling and pay, notwithstanding the increase of taxation; disorder reigned everywhere, in the administration as in the army. The Grand Vizier undertook a general reform, and accomplished it in a very short time without having recourse to the terrible means his father had employed.

He began by filling the treasury chests, in order to secure the obedience of the soldiers and provide for the necessities of the war. "Before entering into action," says Cantemir, "Kupruli thought that it was advisable to take a review of the finances, desiring only to pour into the Sultan's coffers money legitimately raised from the people. He found the finances in as much confusion as were other matters; for, in time of peace the viziers and great functionaries squandered treasure recklessly; they gave, or rather sold, to some exemption from tribute, and they taxed others beyond their means. In time of war, the defterdars practised extortion, and invented a thousand onerous systems of raising money; the people were racked in so many ways that a chorus of murmurs arose against those iniquitous oppressions which cried to Heaven for vengeance. The Vizier applied himself, therefore, wholly to reform such abuses. He caused to be returned into the treasury all the sums that had been diverted by his predecessors, by the pachas, by the clerks, or farmers of taxes; lastly, he made new regulations for the levy of imposts, in order to establish a kind of equality between those taxed. He ordered that the Kharadj should have three classes: those among the rich were taxed at ten leonines a-head; those of lower condition at six; those of the lowest at three. He caused to be restored to the treasury the foundations or depôts of money that devotion had formerly bequeathed to the mosques. The Mufti regarded that usurpation as sacrilege; he replied that the wealth destined to religious uses ought to be employed in wars of religion;

that such was their true application, and that the interest of Mussulmans demanded that it should be made use of for the maintenance of those who defended the sacred edifices, rather than to nourish enemies and robbers." At the same time, Kupruli regulated the monetary circulation; he caused the superfluous gold and silver vessels of the Seraglio to be melted, and generously gave to the State all his own plate, which he replaced by vessels of copper.

When he had, by all these measures, secured the payment of the troops, he addressed them in a firman calculated to raise the courage of the most disheartened. "Since it has pleased His Highness to honour me with the dignity of Vizier, I have resolved to confide," said he, "the command of the army against the Germans only to myself. I declare that I will not receive any soldier enrolled by force; the service ought to be undertaken of good-will; it is good-will alone that God regards, and it is more meritorious than actions. But I must place before the eyes of all followers of the Mahometan religion the obligation of the precepts of God and his Prophet, which command that martyrdom should not be shunned, and success not despaired of when arms are taken up for defence of the law, and for the extirpation of infidels. Thus every Mussulman who believes himself bound by conscience to follow that law has only to come and enrol himself, if he is resolved to suffer all things for his faith. He, on the contrary, who doubts or fears to expose himself to martyrdom, or even who has indispensable affairs which may excuse him in the sight of God, the latter, I say, may in all liberty remain at home; there, living inoffensively, he will render himself equally agreeable to God, and endeavour to obtain by his prayers the success of the Imperial arms; and, when even he may be of the military profession, not only he shall neither be sought for nor punished, but even the Sultan will yet extend to him his favour, and he will receive his pay, as if he was in the army."

This firman produced all the effect that the Grand Vizier had expected from it: it aroused the people and the soldiers, especially in Asia. The Mussulmans assembled in crowds, stimulated at once by the point of honour and by the religious sentiment: no one desired to be looked upon as a coward or an infidel, and Krupuli had very soon an army more numerous than those which his predecessors had collected by dint of threats and severity.

Whilst appealing to the religious sentiments of the Mussulmans, Kupruli treated the Christian subjects with much humanity. By his *nisami-dschedid* (new regulation), he expressly forbade all violence towards them, and ordered that the troops traversing the Christian provinces should pay for grain and all provisions in ready money, at a reasonable price, and always by consent of the vendor. The Christian historian Cantemir, who was almost his contemporary, remarked in him a surprising degree of equity and wisdom which made him look upon all the subjects of the Sultan "with impartiality and without regard to difference of religion." Thus he granted to the Christians of Constantinople permission to rebuild their ancient churches. Some country folk having preferred a similar request to him, he hastened to sign their memorial. The officer charged with the drawing up of the firman, making use of the old form, specified that the church should be restored with the same wood, stones and lime of the ancient building. "They are fools who invented that formula," exclaimed Kupruli, "and greater fools still are they who follow it! These people desire to repair their temple; if it is so dilapidated that to repair it is impossible, let them build a new one. All that we need care about is, that they do it at their own expense, and not with money of the Mussulmans; and provided that they pay their tribute regularly, the rest does not concern us." Thus the Greeks often remarked, "Kupruli has built more churches than Justinian."

The Grand Vizier did not confine himself to the alleviation of the condition of the rayahs by protecting them against the violence and fanaticism of the Ottomans; he was the first statesman in Turkey who had laid down the principle of free trade and the suppression of all prohibitive measures. When he was advised to regulate sales and purchases he replied: "The Koran contains nothing thereon; sale and purchase ought to be left to the free will of both parties." That wise policy was especially profitable to the Christians and to the Jews, to whom the Turks abandoned almost wholly the concerns and benefits of commerce. Judicial reform was not less useful to the rayahs. "Justice," says an historian, "was nearly everywhere venal; false testimony was in some sort publicly authorized. The Grand Vizier discharged those who were weighted by bad practices, and without regard of persons he set the law again everywhere into vigorous action; and he was soon able to say with a legitimate pride: 'See what tolerance produces! I have augmented the power of the Padischah, and I have caused his government to be blessed by people who detested it.'"

His humanity preserved the Morea to the Empire, and contributed, more than the force of arms, to bring back that province into obedience. He appointed a Greek, Liberius Geratchari, prince of the Mainotes. That which urged him to this nomination was the example of Moldavia, where the Turks had not had the undermost part as in the other provinces; a palpable proof that a Christian governor was more fitting than a Mussulman to keep to their allegiance a people of the same religion as himself. Besides that, Liberius had made himself acceptable to him by another argument: he had depicted the Venetians as tyrants of the faith, affirming that their zeal to impose the Romish religion upon the Greeks of the Morea made them long for Ottoman domination; a prince of the Greek church could not therefore fail to bring them back to submission.* In fact, irritated by the persecutions of the Catholics and influenced by the amenity of the Grand Vizier, the Greeks of the Peloponnesus and of Attica abandoned the party of the Venetians, which they had at first warmly embraced; the Mainotes of themselves returned under the domination of the Porte.

To the successes obtained in Greece by a conciliating

* Cantemir, tom. iv. p. 25.

policy Kupruli Mustapha knew how to add other victories, more disputed, more costly, and not less necessary for the safety of the Empire. Whilst the Khan of the Crimea, Selim Gheraï, checked the insurrection of the Serbs and defeated, in the plains of Kossovo, a corps of the Christian army, he himself captured from the Imperialists Dragoman, Nissa, Widdin, Semendria, and lastly Belgrade, after twelve days of siege. Meanwhile Tekeli, aided by the Voïvode of Wallachia, entered Transylvania by the defile of Tœrsbourg, destroyed near Zernescht a corps of the German army, and took prisoner General Haüsler; in recompense, he was named Prince of Transylvania.

The Ottoman arms were less fortunate against the Venetians, who, in Dalmatia, seized upon Valona, and, in the Morea, on Napoli de Malvoisia; the Turks, nevertheless, took their revenge upon the field of battle, and made 3,700 prisoners, whom they slaughtered (1690). A few months afterwards Soliman II. died (June 23, 1691), and was succeeded by his brother Achmet II.

7. Reigns of Achmet II. and Mustapha II.—Peace of Carlowitz.

The new reign was disastrously inaugurated by a sanguinary defeat and by the death of the great man who governed the Empire. Kupruli Mustapha met the Imperial army, commanded by the Margrave of Baden, near Salankemen, the 19th of August, 1691. The Turks were completely defeated; 28,000 perished; amongst the dead was the Grand Vizier. Such was the end of the third Kupruli, of that intelligent, courageous and humane statesman who was regretted alike by rayahs and Turks; the people preserved his memory under the title of Kupruli *the Virtuous.*

After his death, the Divan, discouraged, listened to the propositions of the English and Dutch ambassadors, who offered their mediation between the belligerent Powers. Kupruli, without acceding to the demands of Louis XIV., who was desirous that they should not acknowledge William of Orange as King of England, had followed against the House of Austria the inspiration of the Court of France. The English influence prevailed with the new Grand Vizier, Ali Pacha; but Austria set forth claims so exorbitant, that in spite of the capture of Grosswardein by the Imperialists, the attempts to make peace failed completely. In 1692 and in 1693, the war was confined to the revictualling of Belgrade, to slight skirmishes in Dalmatia, and incursions of the Tartars into Poland. The following campaign was more serious: the Turks in vain besieged Peterwardein; they experienced some checks in Poland and Dalmatia; in the Archipelago the Venetians seized upon the island of Chios (1694). A short time afterwards Achmet II. died (February 6, 1695).

His successor, Mustapha II., an energetic prince, announced, at his accession, his intention of governing by himself and of pushing the war vigorously. Having determined to take command of his armies, he crossed the Danube, captured several places and began his career by a course of victories. In Hungary, he carried by assault Lippa and defeated near Lugos General Veterani; the Germans, taken between two fires by the Turks and the Tartars, could not stand long against very superior forces; Veterani wounded, was taken and beheaded (September, 22, 1695). The Tartars invaded Poland, and only stopped their march when under the walls of Lemberg. The Czar Peter I. raised the siege of Azof, after the loss of 30,000 men. At sea, the Ottomans, under the leadership of Mezzomorto, an old Tunisian pirate, defeated the Venetian fleet in two battles and reconquered the island of Chios (1695).

The success of that campaign revived the enthusiasm of the Mussulmans. Voluntary gifts provided pay for the army, and certain wealthy persons even equipped at their own cost a body of troops. The battle of Olasch gained by the Sultan, the incursions of the Tartars in Poland after the death of John Sobieski, the checks given to the Venetians in Dalmatia, compensated the loss of Azof, which the Czar besieged during two months with 60,000 regular troops and clouds of Kalmucks and Cossacks (1696).

But in the following year fortune changed face. Prince Eugene of Savoy, bred in the school of the Duke of Lorraine in the Hungarian war, was placed by the Emperor at the head of the Austrian army. After a series of skilful marches and counter-marches, he fell upon the Turks at the fords of the Theiss, near Zenta. 20,000 Ottomans were left on the field of battle; 10,000 perished in the river; the Grand Vizier was slain, and the Sultan put to flight. A few days afterwards the conquerors entered Bosnia (1697).

The Empire was in great peril, and it was once more a Kupruli who was summoned to save it. Mustapha gave the standard and the seals to Kupruli Hussein, nephew of Kupruli Mahomet. The new Grand Vizier, by clever expedients, provided for the most pressing needs, and the Ottoman army being enabled to put itself again in motion, the Austrians recrossed the Save and took up their winter quarters in Hungary.

Meanwhile Louis XIV., exhausted by the struggle which he had sustained against one-half of Europe, was at that moment meditating the desirableness of peace. Of this he apprised the Divan, and offered his intervention to obtain its admission to the negotiations he was about to open. That offer met with a decided refusal from the Sultan, who hoped to recover the provinces which he had lost during the war; and, moreover, he distrusted the ambassador who made those propositions on the part of France. That functionary was M. de Feriol, who had succeeded Chateauneuf. Badly instructed in the usages of the Porte, notwithstanding the seven campaigns he had made with the Turks, he had offended the Ottoman Court by his conceitedness of manner, and had insulted the Grand Seignior by presenting himself at an audience wearing a sword at his side.

Though Louis XIV. had signed the Treaty of Ryswyck (1698), yet he now advised the Divan to continue the war, urging that the peace which he had just concluded was only a truce, and that the approaching demise of Charles II. of Spain was about to re-open a struggle in which France would deploy all her strength against the House of Austria. The Porte was dissatisfied with the conduct of the French King, whom it regarded as abandoned by the other Powers of Europe. It listened to the solicitations of William of Orange, who won over by dint of gold, it was said, the members of the Divan to accept the mediation of England and Holland; and, finally, it made overtures of peace to Austria. Louis XIV. remonstrated with the Divan upon the error it was about to commit: representing that " Turkey conquered could only obtain peace under conditions upon which depended its very existence; for the Turks, in all their wars with the Christians, had never receded; and should they now do so, the prestige attached to their power would be dissipated." He therefore advised the Porte to prolong the war until France could take up arms again; and he engaged not to lay them down until Turkey had recovered Hungary and all her lost provinces. But these representations of the great monarch were transmitted by Feriol, a man in whom the Divan had no confidence, and even regarded as imbecile; moreover, the ambassadors of William had made themselves masters of the chief ministers, either through intrigue or fear. Louis XIV. was answered that France made peace at her own time and will, and that the Porte would do the same. Thereupon negotiations were opened through the mediation of England and Holland, which Feriol tried to traverse. " He set every engine to work to that end," says Cantemir, " but he did not succeed. The Divan ended even by inviting him not to give himself needless trouble; that peace was determined upon, and peace would be made." And it was, in fact, signed at Carlowitz (1699).

By that Treaty, Turkey ceded to Leopold Hungary and Transylvania, with its natural boundaries, from Podolia to Wallachia, reserving only the territory between the Theiss and the Marosk. In the Syrmium a conventional line was traced, marked out by a series of ditches or stakes, from the confluence of the Theiss with the Danube to the mouth of the Bossut in the Save. From that point the course of the Save forms a natural frontier, continued onwards by the Unna. Poland recovered Kaminiec, Podolia and the Ukraine. Russia retained Azof. Venice only gave up the conquests made by her to the north of the Gulf of Corinth, and almost the whole of Dalmatia; she evacuated Lepanto, but only after destroying its fortifications. All the tributes paid by the Christian Powers to the Ottoman Porte were abolished.

The loss of Hungary and Transylvania, of the Morea, Dalmatia, Podolia, the Ukraine and Azof, was the first great gap made in the Ottoman Empire. From that moment it ceased to be formidable to Europe. It found itself mixed up in all the affairs of the West—that Power which had owed its greatness to its isolation; in fine, instead of being dominated by the advice of its old and close ally, it had to submit to the influence of ambitious neighbours or interested friends. Its decadence could no longer be arrested; the Russians, by acquiring an entrance to the southern seas, had just commenced their European existence.

"The peace of Carlowitz," says Hammer, "restrained the Turks, on the side of Poland and Hungary, within the limits of the Dniester, the Save, and the Unna. That Treaty proclaimed significantly the decadence of the Ottoman Empire, which, suspended for awhile by the iron arm of Amurath III. and the sanguinary remedies of the elder Kupruli, could not be arrested afterwards by the politic wisdom of the Grand Vizier of the latter's family, nor hidden from the eyes of the world by the hosts of undisciplined soldiers thrust forward by the Porte in its distress. A century elapsed between the submission of Hungary to Turkish tyranny, and the establishment of the *nisami-dschedid* ('equitable reparation') by the wise and virtuous Mustapha Kupruli for the relief of the rayahs." A century more passed before that renovated institution, under the reign of Selim III., was vigorously applied on a more extended scale. If the example of the third Kupruli, in his measures of humanity on behalf of the Christian subjects of the Empire, had been followed up by the Grand Viziers, his successors; if the system of equitable reparation which he had conceived, and which tended to restore order and economy in the public administration, had been carried into effect, the existence of Turkey would not have been compromised. At the present day, by the irresistible effect of time, which changes all things, and which inevitably brings about everywhere progress as inevitable as necessary, the Mahometan dominator has no other alternative than of renouncing his power over the Christians, or of exercising it with more gentleness and moderation, according to the dictates of interest and prudence.

HISTORICAL INDEX.
VOL. I.

Abbas, Shah of Persia, breaking through all convention with the Turks, seizes upon Tebriz, Erivan and Kars ; extorts a treaty from the Porte, which renounced all its conquests since Selim, 283 ; extends his conquests during the military anarchy of the minority of Amurath IV., seizes upon Bagdad, and the Osmanli vainly try to retake that city, 299.

Abbassides,their usurpation in Asia ; with their Empire Islam takes a new form, 22 ; fatal policy of embodying a standing army of Turkish mercenaries, 29 ; their western provinces torn from them by the Ommiades and Fatimites, 30.

Abu-Bekr, elected to succeed Mahomet, his father-in-law, takes the title of *Kalife-y-recoul Allah*, vicar of the Prophet of God, 17.

Achmet I., Son of Mahomet III. ; his reign marks the first step towards decided decadence of the Empire ; ascending the throne in his fifteenth year, only attained manhood at the close of his reign ; two wars bequeathed him to sustain against the Imperialists in Hungary and the Shah of Persia, 283 ; his character and inclinations ; incapable of making proper choice of Ministers ; a power formed in the harem, whose interests were neither those of the Empire nor those of the Sultan, 292 ; general demoralization of army and navy, 293 ; unimportance of Achmet's reign, with whom Austria concluded the peace of Sitvatorok, 294.

Achmet II. succeeds his brother Solyman II. ; his reign disastrously inaugurated by a sanguinary defeat near Salankemen by the Imperialists, 375 ; gives place shortly afterwards to Mustapha II., 376.

Ahmed, son of Tholon, a Turkish chief, renders himself independent in Egypt, where three descendants reign after him, 31.

Ahmed Pacha, angered by the nomination of Ibrahim, Solyman's favourite, to the dignity of Grand Vizier, rebels, wins over the Mamelukes, seizes upon the Castle of Cairo, and assumes the title of Sultan of Egypt ; betrayed by one of his Viziers, and delivered up by the Arabs, he is put to death, 183.

Ahmed Pacha, Governor of Anatolia, overcome and slain by the rebels, 314.

Aladdin III., last of the Seljukides, dethroned by Ghazan, Khan of the Mongols, 52.

Aladdin, brother of Orchan, compiles a code of laws for the Ottoman Empire ; three points especially attract his attention—the coinage, costume, and the army ; originates the policy of a standing army, 57 ; establishes the sipahis and a renegade infantry, the nucleus of the Janissaries, 58.

Aladdin, Emir of Karamania, commences open hostilities against Amurath I. ; defeated by the latter near Iconium, and is granted peace through the intercession of the victor's daughter, wife of the Emir, 81 ; invades the Asiatic dominions of Bajazet I. ; is defeated in a decisive battle, taken and put to death, and the whole of his territory added to the Ottoman Empire, 86.

Albania, subjected temporarily by Stephen Douschan, takes part in all the wars of the Serbs against the Turks, 68; continual attacks of the Ottomans sustained by Scanderbeg, 132.

Alexander VI., (Borgia) Pope, proposes to Bajazet II. to keep his brother Djem captive for an annual payment of 40,000 ducats, or to get rid of him by murder for 300,000 ducats promptly paid down, 162; besieged by the French in the Castle of St. Angelo and constrained to deliver up his captive; gives him up, but poisoned, 163.

Almanzor, Abou-Giaffar, founder of Bagdad, 30.

Alp Arslan—*See* Arslan.

Al Rhadi, twentieth Khalife of the Abbassides, the last who deserved the title of *Commander of the Faithful*, 31.

Amastris (*Amasrah*), a Genoese colony, depopulated by Mahomet II., 132.

Amurath I., second son of Orchan, his reign of prodigious activity; organizes the Janissaries, 71; his successful expeditions and extensive conquests, 74; Adrianople surrenders to him, 75; after the capture of Philippopolis, makes peace with the Emperor Palæologus I., 75; his conquests in Thrace, Thessaly, Servia, and Bulgaria; promotes the aggrandizement of his Empire by the marriage of his son Bajazet to the Emir of Kermian's daughter; introduces an important modification in the military organization, 77; captures the city of Sophia, 79; punishes the rebellion of his son Sandschi with death, 80; defeats Aladdin, Emir of Karamania, near Iconium, 81; recalled to Europe by the revolt of Servia; is victorious at Kassova, but assassinated there by Milosch Kabilovitch, 83.

Amurath II., son of Mahomet I., his reign opens with civil war; on his refusal to confide his two brothers to the care of Manuel, that Emperor releases Mustapha from prison, incites him to rebellion and makes a treaty with him to restore to the Greeks the European territories of the Sultan, 105; the latter despatches Bajezid Pacha with an army to confront the rebels, but the Sultan's troops all passing over to Mustapha's side, the Pacha is massacred; Amurath, in turn, employs Michaelogli to seduce the cavalry of Mustapha, who being abandoned also by Djouneid, flees precipitately, is pursued by the Sultan, taken and hanged, 106; Manuel, seeking to disarm the Sultan's resentment, sends an embassy, to which the latter refuses to listen, and at once besieges Constantinople, burns the villages and crops in the environs, and massacre the inhabitants; a terrible assault fails, and on learning that his youngest brother had taken up arms against him, the Sultan raises the siege, 107; the accomplices of the rebel prince deliver him up to his brother, who causes him to be strangled; directs an expedition against the Prince of Kastemouni, obtains his renewed submission and the hand of his daughter. Djouneid having again revolted, and being unable to resist the Sultan's forces, shuts himself up in Hypsela; blockaded by sea and land, he surrenders, and is strangled with all his family by Hamsa Bey; Amurath reunites the territories of Mentesché and Tekieh to the Empire, diminishes those of Karaman by one-half, and receives by request the States of the aged Prince of Kermian, 108; having secured tranquillity on the Oriental side of Diarbekir, the Ottomans have no longer any rivals in Asia; intervenes in a war between the Serbs and Hungarians, and acquires a first station on the Danube; next deals blows against the Greeks calculated to bring about their ruin; attacks Thessalonica, ceded by Palæologus II. to the Venetians; that city is carried by assault, sacked, and all the inhabitants massacred or reduced to slavery; desirous of becoming master of the detached provinces of the Greek Empire before attacking Constantinople, he turns his arms against Albania, Servia, and Wallachia, which brings the Turks in contact with Hungary, 109; compels John Castriot, the Albanian ruler, to deliver up his four sons to him, and on his death takes possession of the country; compels Drakul (or *the Devil*), tyrant of Wallachia, to pay tribute and supply troops; attacks Brankowich, Prince of Servia, compels him to submit and give him his daughter in marriage; ravages Transylvania, and carries away 70,000 prisoners; besieges Semendria, captures it, and puts out the eyes of the Kral's son, who defended it; besieges Belgrade in vain for six months; defeated at Hermanstadt by Hunyade, with the loss of 20,000 men, 110;

and again at Vasag; he sues for peace after the disastrous "long campaign" at the hands of the Hungarian hero; restores Wallachia to Drakul, and Semendria, &c., to Brankowitch; and concludes a truce which places Servia and Wallachia under the suzerainty of Hungary; disgusted with power, on the death of his eldest son Aladdin, he abdicates, entrusting authority to his son Mahomet, then fourteen years old, and seeks retirement among the dervishes at Maguesia, 111; is speedily drawn from that retreat by the news of a crusade of German and Italian adventurers, which proposed to destroy the Ottoman power and drive the Turks into Asia; Bulgaria is devastated, and Varna besieged, 112; the Sultan defeats Hunyade and Drakul at Varna, and carries the Christian camp by assault, and massacres its defenders; resumes his projects against the remnants of the Byzantine Empire; imposing his alliance on the Duke of Athens; Amurath besieges, captures and burns Corinth, and sacks the Peloponnesus without mercy; next turns his efforts against Albania, and makes preparations for a decisive expedition against Scanderbeg, 113; but is diverted therefrom by the campaign of Hunyade in Servia, whom he defeats, 114; invades Albania with an immense army, but unsuccessfully, and next year besieges Croïa, which resists him heroically, and he is compelled to raise the siege; on returning to Adrianople he dies of apoplexy, 115.

Amurath III., son of Selim II., restrains the authority of the sagacious Vizier, Mohammed Sokolli, and yields everything to the influence of women and favourites; his character and habits, 255; on arriving at Constantinople causes his five brothers to be strangled during the night; issues a degree against the use of wine, whereupon the Sipahis and Janissaries mutiny, and insult and maltreat the Grand Vizier, 256; hostilities resumed with Hungary, and the Imperialists defeated near Kruppa; the heads of the chiefs in command sent to Constantinople and redeemed from the hands of the executioner by the Austrian Ambassador; peace formally renewed for eight years, but disturbed by perpetual aggressions between the Porte and the Emperor Rodolph II.; the attitude of the Porte nearly the same towards Poland—a nominal peace and actual hostilities; Poland treated like Transylvania, as a vassal and tributary State; the favourite Sultana, the Venetian Baffa, obtains the renewal of the capitulations with Venice and greater security for her commerce, 257; the alliance with France respected through the great influence of the French Ambassador with the Divan; an Embassy from the Sultan to Henry III. of France meets with a magnificent reception, 258; in spite of concessions and professions of friendship, Germigny, the ambassador, appreciates at its proper value the alliance and benevolence of the Turks, and foresees the decadence of the Empire, with no longer a Solyman to direct it, 259; Queen Elizabeth of England demands freedom of navigation and commerce for her subjects under their own flag, and the Sultan accedes to the demand, in spite of the lively opposition of the Ambassadors of France and Venice; the venality of the Porte: everything bartered for within and without, the Sultan being the first to set the example; treasure amassed by piracy, which no treaties could stop, 260; the piratical cities of Algiers, Tunis, and Tripoli transformed into regencies or pachalics, and made to pay an annual tribute; the victory won by the Pacha of Tripoli against the Portuguese in the battle of Alcazar Kebir, brings rich presents and a dominating influence in the Mogreb; the favourites labour at the ruin of Sokolli, who is assassinated, 261; rapid changes of grand viziers through rivalries and intrigues; the honour of the Ottoman arms sustained by Osman Pacha in Daghestan, who is named Vizier and Seraskier, 264; the veritable depositaries of power entirely concentrated in the harem—the mother and sisters of the Sultan, the Sultana Baffa and two Christian slaves the true sovereigns of the Empire; these influences incite Amurath to persecute the Christians, 265; England gains the influence which France had lost, 266; the Czar, Fœdor Ivanowitch, sends Ambassadors with rich presents; the Persian war begins afresh under command of Osman Pacha, who enters Tebriz, which is pillaged; but ill-health arrests his successes; is defeated near Schembi-

Ghazan by the Persian Prince Hamsa; suffers a second defeat, and dies a few days afterwards, 267 ; a furious revolt of the Janissaries at Constantinople, 268 ; their renewed insolence becoming intolerable, it was resolved to wage war in Hungary to get rid of them; war declared against Austria ; the indifferent success of a campaign and the revolt of Moldavia, Wallachia, and Transylvania, in which the Turks in those provinces were massacred, filling Amurath with consternation, he sends for the holy banner from Damascus ; death, however, relieves him from his anxieties, 270.

Amurath IV., eldest son of Achmet I., succeeds to the throne in his eleventh year; during the first ten years of his reign the Janissaries and Sipahis continue to harass and oppress the Empire ; Persia extends its conquests ; the Pacha of Erzeroum persists in his rebellion until he receives the government of Bosnia ; the Crimean Tartars rise, defeat the Ottomans, and take so many prisoners that a Turk is sold for a glass of b*u*za ; all these reverses caused by the spirit of faction and insubordination reigning in the army, 299; the Sultan strikes terror amongst them by the death of their ringleader, Redgeb Pacha, and from that moment his actual reign begins ; the end of that military anarchy brings back victory to the Osmanli ; Amurath resolves to invade Persia, and places himself at the head of the army ; takes Erivan, Tebriz, and besieges Bagdad ; wears the uniform of a Janissary, and works in the trenches like a common soldier ; Persia sues for peace, cedes Bagdad, and receives in exchange Erivan, 300 ; Amurath's character in manhood ; his ferocity and lust of murder ; his extreme severity tames the rebellious militia, but fails to restore the ancient valour to his troops, 301 ; the Ottoman armies fall back into their primitive condition, whilst the Christians rejoice at such decadence, 302 ; the Sultan is dominated by the influence of the Seraglio; law and right have little power over him in presence of gold ; he filled his coffers, placed his life in safety, and died calmly in his bed, but his reign of terror paralyzed the Empire, 303.

Andronicus the Elder, Greek Emperor, calls in the aid of Ottoman troops against his grandson, Andronicus the Younger ; but is defeated and constrained to share his crown with the rebel, 63.

Andronicus the Younger, having become sole Emperor, concludes with Orchan the first peace between the Greeks and Ottomans ; to shield himself from further invasion makes a league with the Sarou-Khan Emirs, 63.

Andronicus, son of Palæologus, attempts to wrest the supreme power from his father, and is punished with blindness, 79 ; recovers the sight of one eye and is assisted by Bajazet I. to dethrone the old Emperor on promise of a heavy tribute ; is in turn deposed, but receives the few other Byzantine cities, 84.

Apafy, Michael, nominee of the Porte, Transylvania abandoned to him by the Emperor Leopold, 323.

Aramon, d', ambassador of Henry II. (France), accompanies Solyman *the Great* in his Persian expedition ; opposes steadfastly the violence exercised by the Capudan-Pacha upon Scio, 224 ; and procures for the Christians the privileges which they have in part still preserved ; obtains the Sultan's consent that the Ottoman fleet should join that of the French, 225.

Arslan, Alp, the Seljukide, ruler of the East and West, his career of conquest, defeats Cæsar Romanus Diogenes at Konogo; treatment of his prisoner, 34 ; is assassinated, 35.

Arslan, David and Kilidje, found at Koniah (Iconium) the Sultanry of Roum, 36.

Asia, Western, its situation when the struggle between the East and West was recommenced by the Crusades, 37.

Aubusson, Pierre d', Grand Master of the Knights of Rhodes, valiantly repulses an attempt of the Turks to take the island by surprise, 147.

Baber founds the Mogul Empire of Delhi, 28.

Baffa, the Venetian, Sultana, her dominant influence with Amurath III. in the affairs of Venice ; obtains a renewal of the capitulations and greater security for its commerce, 257 ; her protection preserves peace with the Venetians, 267.

Bagdad, founded by Almanzor *the Victorious*, brother and successor of the first Abbasside, the seat of the Empire of Islam for 500 years, 22; Almanzor, Haroun-Al-Raschid and Al-Mamoun, the three great names of the Eastern Khalifate, 30; grandeur and fall of the Khalifate; its dismemberment by the Turkish Guards, 31.

Bajazet I., son of Amurath I., surnamed Ilderim (*the Lightning*); his first act on accession is the strangling of his only surviving brother Yacoub; his first warlike effort, the reduction of Servia; assists Andronicus, son of Palæologus, to dethrone the old Emperor and his son Manuel; restores them afterwards to the throne on their promise to pay tribute, 81; Philadelphia, with Sarou-Khan and Menteschė, fall under his sway and he makes inroad upon Karamania; his haughty message to Palæologus, 85; enforces submission of Bulgaria and Wallachia, and makes inroad upon Hungary; defeats Aladdin, Prince of Karaman, at Aktschaï, who is taken and put to death, and the whole country incorporated in the Empire; with the reduction of Kastemouni the whole of the ancient Seljukian Empire merges in the Ottoman, 86; snatches Thessalonica from the Greeks, and defeats a Christian fleet despatched thither from Italy; his domination of Europe appears to have reached its apogee, and he assumes the title of *Sultan*, 87; defeats Sigismund, King of Hungary, at Nicopolis, and slaughters his Christian prisoners, 89; besieges Constantinople for five years and a half; the siege raised on a promise of an augmented tribute, with other humiliating concessions, 90; new accessions through his extensive conquests; reduces the whole of Greece, and plants therein colonies of Turkomans from Central Asia; threatens Constantinople with a second siege, but is diverted from it by Tamerlane, 91; war with Tamerlane, by whom he is defeated and made prisoner at Angora; his treatment during captivity; story of the iron cage; dies in the camp of Tamerlane, 96; his large empire is dismembered, and the remains of it becomes a subject of contention to his three sons, 99.

Bajazet II., son of Mahomet II., on his proclamation as Sultan, the Janissaries demand an amnesty for their disorders, the accession bounty, the banishment of the favourite Mustapha Pacha, and the elevation of Ishak Bey to the vizierate, all of which he grants, and their tyranny is thus consecrated; character of Bajazet II. (called the Sofi); is thrown by the destinies of the Empire into wars almost perpetual; his brother Djem takes up arms against him, whom he defeats near Jenischehr; ransoms Broussa, which the Janissaries demand for pillage, 160; defeats Djem again at Konieh, who is obliged to flee a second time, and afterwards proposes an equal share of territory, but is refused by the Sultan; Keduk Ahmed, the conqueror of Kaffa and Otranto, put to death on account of his pride and popularity, 161; signs a treaty with the Knights of Rhodes to remain at peace with the order and to pay it an annual pension of 45,000 ducats for keeping Djem in custody, 162; the projected conquest of Constantinople and Jerusalem by Charles VIII. of France, spreads terror and hope throughout the East; the Pope, Venice, and Ferdinand of Naples, to oppose it, solicit the Sultan to make a descent upon Italy, who, instructed by the Venetians in all the details of the conspiracy, extinguished it in the blood of 40,000 Christians, 163; in Hungary and Bosnia a war of pillage and atrocities nearly permanent, in which Kinis, Jaxieh, Tekeli, and other Christian chiefs rival the pachas in ferocity; the Sultan renews the truce for five years concluded with the King of Hungary; Herzegovina subjected without resistance, and incorporated in the Ottoman Empire; turns his arms against Moldavia and seizes upon Kilia and Akerman; a serious war undertaken against the Sultan of Egypt; the Egyptians obtain a great victory between Adana and Tarsus and pillage the Ottoman camp; an honourable peace concluded between the two Mussulman princes, 164; war recommenced overtly with Hungary; an attempt to surprise Belgrade fails, but Transylvania, Croatia, Dalmatia, Illyria, Carniola and Styria desolated; the Turks defeated by the Hungarians at Villach, but take their revenge the year following, slaying 25,000 of the latter; first relations of the Ottoman Empire with Russia; Ivan III.

making friendly propositions to the Sultan through the medium of the Khan of the Crimea, 165; pacific relations entered into with Poland: concludes a treaty with John Albert, but that good understanding interrupted through both princes contending for the suzerainty of Moldavia; on John Albert invading that country, the Turks drive him out and make two irruptions into Poland, pillaging Jaroslav and burning several towns; rupture between the Porte and the Venetians; a naval combat, fought near Sapienza, opening the entrance of the Gulf of Lepanto to the fleet, the city surrenders; Iskender Pacha invades Friuli, crosses the Isonzo and ravages the Venetian territory, and appears under the walls of Vicenza; the Venetians seize upon Cephalonia, and burn, at Previsa, a squadron of forty Turkish ships, but later, lose Modon, Coron, and Navarino; two treaties concluded with Venice and Hungary, in which all the Christian States are comprised, 166; the last years of Bajazet's reign troubled by the ambitious pretensions of his sons; a struggle appearing imminent, the Sultan distributes the chief governments amongst his three sons—Korkud, Ahmed, and Selim; the ambition of the latter not being satisfied, he revolts and marches towards Roumelia; his father sends an army against him, which is forced to retire; the Sultan treats with his son, and Selim obtains the government of Semendria and Widdin, 167; on entering Adrianople as a sovereign, Selim is defeated near Tchorli and flees to the Crimea; the Janissaries force the Sultan to recall his son, and conduct him in triumph to Constantinople; Bajazet cedes the empire to Selim, and dies on his way to Dimotika, his birthplace, 168.

Bajazet, Prince, son of Solyman *the Great*, the plot of Lala Mustapha to effect his ruin; is incited to insult his brother Selim, 228; is threatened with disgrace by the Sultan by ordering him to exchange his government of Konieh for that of Amasia; burns his father's letters, and takes up arms, is conquered, and flees to Persia; delivered up to the agents of his brother, is murdered, with his five sons, and the throne thus secured to Selim, 229.

Bajazet *the Perclus*, last representative of the dynasty of the Isfendiars suddenly attacked by Bajazet I. shuts himself up in Sinope and treats with the conqueror, who leaves him that town and its territory; but, not thinking himself in safety, he flees and seeks a protector in Timour, 87.

Barbarossa (*Red Beard*), see Chaireddin.

Batou, grandson of Zinghis Khan, leader of the Golden Horde, overruns and barbarizes Russia, 28.

Bathori, Stephen, Võivode of Transylvania, with Paul Kinis, inflicts a memorable defeat on the Turks at Kenger-Mesæ, near Karlsbourg, 146.

Bektash, Hadji, a celebrated dervish, consecrates the corps of Janissaries, 71.

Bell-Ourosch, son of Voulkan, entitles himself Grand Duke of Servia, 67.

Bochari, Seid (called *Emir-Sultan*), Grand Sheik of Broussa, leads 500 dervishes to the siege of Constantinople on the promise of pillage, and who claim as their share the nuns of the convents therein; gives the signal for a desperate assault which lasts till sunset, when the Turks burn their machines and retire, the Greeks attributing their deliverance to the Virgin Mary having appeared on the walls, 107.

Bosnia created by Voulkan a State, sometimes independent of, sometimes vassal of, Hungary becomes an independent kingdom under the Ban Stephen Tvarko, 68.

Boujide, the, sovereigns of Persia, destroy the power of the Turkish guards to replace it by their own more systematic tyranny, 32.

Bragadino, Marc Antonio, valiantly defends Famagosta against Mustapha Pacha, who, in spite of the capitulation, has the barbarity to cause its defender to be flayed alive and quartered, 248.

Bulgarians, their Tartar origin; establish themselves in Mœsia towards end of 7th century; for three centuries the terror of the Byzantine Emperors; subdued by John Zimisces and converted to Christianity, they render themselves once more independent; Basil annexes them afresh to his Empire; they regain their independence and wage fierce war against the Franks; fall subsequently under the domination of the Serb Kings;

HISTORICAL INDEX. 387

again form a separate State under the Kral Sisman, and follow the Serbs in all their wars against the Turks, 69.

Burton, Edward, ambassador to the Porte from Queen Elizabeth, demands that cruisers might be allowed to molest the commerce of the Spaniards; his demands eluded without being positively rejected, 266.

Byzantine Empire, its caducity, 47; St. Chrysostom's description of a Byzantine Emperor; description of its people, 48; their venality and servility, 49; its losses at the period of Othoman's death, 56.

Cæsar Romanus Diogenes, the Byzantine Emperor, encouraged by the success of three campaigns against Alp Arslan, advances with 100,000 men into Media; Alp's overtures of peace being met by a demand that he should surrender his capital as a pledge of his sincerity, the Sultan arrays his cavalry on the plain of Konogo; at the close of the hard-fought battle, Romanus, left almost alone, is disarmed and led before Alp Arslan, who sets his foot upon the neck of the Emperor, but afterwards treats him with kindness, 34; Romanus is put to death by his subjects, 35.

Candia (*Crete*), siege of, one of the most remarkable in history; its acquisition costs the Turks twenty-five years fighting, 311-12; an attempt to relieve it by the Duke de Navailles in 1669 having failed, the garrison is compelled to capitulate; a peace terminates a struggle in which the Venetians lost 30,000 and the Turks more than 100,000 men, 331-32.

Cantacuzene, John, joint Emperor with John Palæologus vigorously repulses the attack of Orchan upon Constantinople, 63; profiting by the minority of John Palæologus, whilst regent he assumes the purple and declares himself colleague of the young Emperor; seeking absolute sovereignty, in order to carry on civil war, summons to his aid Umer Bey, Prince of Aïdin; the latter, recalled to Asia by an attack of the Venetians having abandoned his ally, Orchan intervenes, and demands of Cantacuzene, his daughter's hand, which is accorded him; in spite of the alliance and ties of relationship, a band of Ottomans ravage afresh the coast of Thrace; solicited by both parties, Orchan finds himself sole arbiter of the Greek Empire, 64; Cantacuzene in vain offers Orchan 40,000 ducats for the ransom of Gallipoli, 65.

Cantacuzene, Michael, surnamed *Sheitanogli*, "son of Satan"; his intrigues and enormous wealth; the splendour of his palace rivals the Seraglio; the fate of whole provinces in his hands; gains his influence through the favour of the Vizier Sokolli; incurs the wrath of Amurath III., and is hanged before the gate of his own palace, 261.

Capistrano, John, the Franciscan, preaches a crusade in Hungary against the Turks; determines the raising of the siege of Belgrade by heading a vigorous sortie, 130.

Carlowitz, Treaty of, entails the loss to the Turks of Hungary and Transylvania, the Morea, Dalmatia, Podolia, the Ukraine, and Azof—the first great gap made in the Ottoman Empire; from that moment it ceased to be formidable in Europe; its decadence could no longer be arrested; and the Russians, by acquiring an entrance to the southern seas, commence their European existence, 379.

Castriot, John, Prince of Albania, compelled to deliver up his four sons to Amurath II., who at Castriot's death takes possession of the country, 110.

Castriot, George, fourth son of John, called by the Turks "Iskender Bey" and by Europeans *Scanderbeg*, "the dragon of Albania," obtains the favour of Amurath II., and the command of 5,000 men in his army; but mindful of his religion and country, abandons the infidels after the first battle of the "long campaign"; kills the Sultan's secretary, and flees into Albania; with a band of 600 partizans forces the gates of Croïa and massacres the Turkish garrison; a general insurrection ensues, and in thirty days finds himself master of Albania; defeats four armies successively sent against him, 114; harasses the immense army of Amurath by incessant attacks whilst besieging Croïa; repulses the overtures of the Sultan, who tries to negotiate with him, 115; sustains with indefatigable perseverance the attacks of the Turks, and wins the admiration even of his enemies; Mahomet II.,

D D 2

offers him peace, and leaves him in tranquil possession of Epirus and Albania, 132; dies of fever at Alessio; his tomb opened by Mahomet II., who exhibits his remains to the admiring Moslems; pieces of his bones sought for with avidity to be converted into talismans, 139.

Cervantes, author of "Don Quixote," loses his left arm in the battle of Lepanto, 250.

Cesarini, Cardinal, papal legate, summons Ladislas, King of Hungary, to tear up the treaty (1444) which placed Servia and Wallachia under the suzerainty of Hungary; takes command of an army of German and Italian adventurers with the design of destroying the Ottoman power, 112; is slain at the battle of Varna, 113.

Chaireddin Barbarossa (*Red-beard*), admiral of Solyman's fleet; son of a Sipahi of Mitylene, devotes himself to piracy during the reign of Bajazet II.; enters the service of Mahommed, Sultan of Tunis; his piratical descents upon Cheroell, Bougia and Algiers; makes himself master of the latter by assassinating the Moorish prince; does homage for his conquest to the Sultan, and receives from him the title of Beylerbey of Algiers, which port becomes a nest of corsairs; disperses a Spanish squadron and carries away from Andalusia 70,000 moors; captures two sail of Doria's fleet and burns eighteen vessels off Messina, 205; created Capudan-pacha; equips a formidable fleet of eighty-four ships, with which he sacks Reggio, Fondi, and other Italian strongholds; steers for Africa and takes possession of Tunis in the Sultan's name; Charles V. resolves to take Tunis, but Barbarossa, despairing of defending the town, risks an encounter in the open; abandoned by his African auxiliaries is forced to flee; Tunis being pillaged by the conquerors, 30,000 inhabitants are massacred, and 50,000 Christian captives set free, 206; ravages the islands of the Archipelago and the Ægean, most of which fall to the Turks; then obtains a brilliant victory over a Christian fleet commanded by Andrea Doria, 213; captures Nice; his insolence at Toulon induces Francis I. to pay him 800,000 crowns to quit that harbour; again spreads terror and desolation along the Italian coasts, whence he carries off 14,000 Christians, the Corsair-captain's last notable exploit, 220.

Chardin, the traveller, his account of the Ottoman State at the commencement of the reign of Mahomet IV., 317.

Charles V., Emperor of Germany, his vast possessions on his accession, 185; accuses Francis I. (France) openly of treason against Christendom by his alliance with Solyman *the Great;* Francis formally denies the accusation and tells Charles V. that "he lied in his throat," 193; his first appearance at the head of his army against Solyman attended with considerable glory and success, 202; resolves to retake Tunis in the hope of dealing a mortal blow to the Turco-French alliance, and takes command of a powerful armament; carries the place after a month of continual fighting, 30,000 inhabitants massacred and 50,000 Christians released, 206; that feat fills up the measure of power and glory of the Emperor, 207; Charles and Ferdinand desirous of peace, become necessary for both through the revolt of the Lutheran princes, consent to pay the Porte an annual subsidy; a truce for five years concluded with the Sultan, the Emperor, and Ferdinand, 221; the Imperialists capture Szegedin, but are surprised before the town and cut in pieces, 223.

Charles VIII. of France, his projected crusade against Constantinople and Jerusalem; purchases from Thomas Palæologus his rights to the throne of the East; distributes arms and money throughout Macedonia, Greece and Albania, 162; and the route of the French is marked out from Otranto to Avlona, from Avlona to Byzantium; claims the person of Prince Djem, with whom he hopes to kindle war in the Turkish provinces; is hailed in Italy with the titles of "Defender of the Church" and "Liberator of the Faith," and spreads terror and hope throughout the East; the Pope, Venice, and Ferdinand of Naples, in order to oppose the French conquest, solicit the Sultan to make a descent upon Italy; Bajazet II., instructed by the Venetians in all the details of the conspiracy, extinguishes it in the blood of 40,000 Christians, 163.

Chelibi, Yakoub, only surviving brother of Bajazet I., murdered by him on his accession; this example of fratricide becomes a standing law of the Ottoman Empire, 84.

Christian era, that portion of it which preceded the birth of Islamism, 27.

Cicala, the renegade, a Turkish *Corps d'armée* defeated under his command by the Persian Prince Hamsa with the loss of 20,000 men, 267.

Condolmieri, Cardinal, commandant of the pontifical fleet, enters upon a crusade to drive the Turks into Asia, 112.

Constantine (Dragozes) the Greek Prince, defender of the Morea, sends ambassadors to Mahomet II. on his accession, 115.

Corvinus, Matthias, King of Hungary, makes a treaty with Wlad *the Devil* to attack the Ottomans, 135; flings Wlad into prison, 136.

Cossacks, the, of the Ukraine, their voluntary submission to Mahomet IV. increases for a time the already vast limits of the Ottoman domination; locality and extent of their country; from its position it becomes necessary to seek a protector; their military institution useful and politic so long as the Turks and Tartars menaced the liberty of Europe; their incursions becoming nothing more than brigandage, the kings of Poland are urged to repress them; finding the domination of Poland irksome and galling, they seek to secure the protection of the Turks, 343; upon this a Polish army is sent into their country, and war breaks out between the Sultan and the King of Poland, 344.

Dédé-Sultan (father and lord), a Turk of obscure birth, gives himself out as a prophet, and heads a revolt of dervishes near Smyrna, and goes about preaching equality, 103; mustering to the number of 10,000 strong at Mount Stylarios, they exterminate the first body of troops sent to disperse them; Dédé afterwards defeated in a sanguinary battle by Amurath, the Sultan's son, and put to the sword with all his adherents; this revolt involved an attempt of the Christian races to regain their independence, 104.

Devlet Sheraï, sole survivor of the race of Zinghis Khan, becomes founder of the Khans of the Crimea, 143.

Djighala Zadé, son of the renegade Cicala, made governor of the province of Bagdad, seizes upon Disfoul and several other strongholds, and defeats the governors of Loristan and Hamadan, 268.

Djem or Zizim, Prince, younger son of Mahomet II., governor of Karamania, his character; his understanding with the Vizier Karamani to conceal his father's death, but the truth being suspected, the Janissaries rise and put the Vizier to death, 159; the messenger to Djem intercepted, and warned in time: Bajazet causes himself to be proclaimed Sultan; Djem takes up arms, marches upon Broussa, defeats a corps of 2,000 Janissaries, and enters the city; his brother Bajazet advancing with an army to maintain his rights, Djem dividing his insufficient forces, is defeated near Jenischehr and seeks refuge with the Sultan of Egypt, 160; next year returns from Cairo to Aleppo, allies himself with Kasim Bey, last of the Karaman princes, and besieges Konieh; compelled to raise the siege by Keduk Ahmed; the governor of Angora is slain, and the rebel prince obliged to flee a second time; proposes to Bajazet an equal share of territory, is refused, and throws himself into the arms of the enemies of the Empire; sends a secret agent to the Grand Master of Rhodes to propose a treaty; is received in the island with great pomp, and a treaty concluded securing great advantages to the Order in the event of his becoming Sultan; is made however to take his departure for France, 161; some days after, the Knights sign a treaty with Bajazet II., who engages to remain at peace with the Order and pay it an annual pension of 45,000 ducats for keeping his brother in custody; the Pope, King of Hungary, and the Emperor, in vain demand that he should be set at liberty, hoping to make him assist in weakening the Ottoman Empire; arrives at Nice and thence successively transferred as a captive to various strongholds during seven years; delivered up at length to Pope Innocent VIII., and on his death, to Pope Alexander Borgia, who offers to get rid of him for 300,000 ducats, 162;

but gives up his captive poisoned, who dies at Naples; his love for the beautiful Helen of Sassenage; his captivity and the events consequent upon it contribute to multiply the relations of the Ottomans with Western Europe, 163.

Djouneïd, lieutenant of Solyman, son of Bajazet I., attempts to found an independent principality by seizing upon Ephesus, Smyrna, and Pergamus; confronted by Mahomet I. he sues for peace, and is afterwards made governor of Nicopolis, 102; supports the pretender Mustapha in his invasion of Thessaly, 104.

Doria, Andrea, the Genoese admiral of Charles V., seizes upon Coron, and excites the Greeks to revolt, 202; is compelled to put into Messina to escape from Barbarossa's fleet, 205.

Doroszensko, Hetman of the Cossacks, offers Mahomet IV. the suzerainty of the Ukraine; the Sultan gives him the investiture and title of Sandjak-Bey; that alliance causes war between the Porte and Poland, 344; during that war, the Hetman having offered his aid to the Porte, which, being rejected, out of pique or revenge, he submits himself, with all his people, to the protectorate of Russia; on hearing this, the Sultan draws from prison Georges Kiemielniski, son of an old Hetman, and nominates him in the place of Doroszensko, but the Cossacks refuse to recognize the authority of Kiemielniski; the Porte then invades Moldavia and Podolia, advances to besiege Cehryn, and the Tartars hurry up from the Crimea; the Cossacks and Russians, in order to hinder the junction of the two armies, fall upon the Tartars and cut them in pieces; the Turks, terrified, recross the Bug, 348.

Douschan, Stephen, the Servian conqueror and legislator, possesses by himself, or by his vassals the whole of what was Turkey in Europe; causes himself to be crowned, at Uskoup, Emperor of the Romans and Triballes, and conceives the project of destroying the Empire of the East; the Serb Empire dismembered under his successor, Ourosch V., 68.

Duquesne, the French Admiral, bombards Chios to compel the Tripolitan corsairs to make their submission to France and deliver up the French slaves; the Porte demands a heavy sum of money in reparation of damages, and in default of which threatens the life of the Ambassador and of all the Franks, 360; Duquesne arrives in the Dardanelles with ten ships, and the dispute is adjusted by the Ambassador personally making the Sultan a present, 361.

Emir al Omara (or *Chief of Chiefs*) the, supersedes the office of Vizier in the Khalifate, and becomes the real sovereign of the State.

Eugene, Prince of Savoy, in command of the Imperial army, after a series of skilful marches and counter-marches, falls upon the Turks at the fords of the Theiss, near Zenta, and signally defeats them; 10,000 perish in the river, the Grand Vizier is slain, the Sultan, Mustapha II., takes flight, and the conquerors enter Bosnia, 377.

Ferdinand, Archduke of Austria, (afterwards King of Hungary and Bohemia), brother of Charles V.; a French ambassador and his twelve attendants assassinated by the Pacha of Bosnia, with the privity, it is supposed, of Ferdinand, 187; claims the vacant throne of Hungary, 192; encounters a rival claimant, John Zapoly, at Tokay, and defeats him; vainly endeavours to bring over the Sultan to his interests, who imprisons his envoys, 193; sends an embassy to Solyman, which, after enduring the insults of the Grand Vizier, leads to nothing, 197-99; awaits at Linz the succours of the German princes to defend Vienna against 300,000 Turks; the defence one of the most brilliant feats in the history of Germany, 197; the Sultan refuses to acknowledge Ferdinand either as King of Hungary or of Bohemia, but simply as lieutenant of Charles V., 199; tries the effect of a new embassy at Nissa, but his envoys undergo humiliations strikingly in contrast with the magnificent reception of the French ambassador, 200; concludes a peace with the Porte, the first made by the house of Austria with the Ottomans, 203.

Ferhad Bey, commander of the Turkish army, causes the sieges of Tebriz and Tiflis to be raised; maintains a secret understanding with the Turcomans of the Persian army; fights the great battle of Grues, which lasts three days, ending in the defeat of the Persians, 267; invades Karabagh, takes Ghendjé, and converts it into a stronghold, 268.

Feriol, de, ambassador of Louis XIV., makes seven campaigns with the Turks, but offends the Ottoman Court by conceitedness, and insults the Sultan by presenting himself wearing a sword at his side, 377; tries to traverse the negotiations for peace with Austria, opened through the mediation of England and Holland, 378.

Feudal System, the Turkish; Mahomet II. introduces the old feudal usages of the Seljukian Empire, called the Timariot system; in some respects singularly parallel with the English feudal system; in conjunction with the tributes of Christian chiefdom, it mainly consolidated the Turkish power in Europe; contrasted favourably in some points with the Western system, 155; the Turkish feudality military and territorial; the decline of cultivation, credit and population not essentially due to the feudal system, 156; the old system has passed away without the substitution of anything better, but with the aggravation of its worst elements, 157.

Feuillade, the Duke de, with 1,200 French gentlemen, attempt by a sortie the deliverance of Candia; they spread a panic in the Turkish camp, and slay some 1,200, but, surrounded by thousands they retreat, leaving 100 dead or wounded, 329.

Fœdor Ivanovitch, Czar of Russia, sends ambassadors with rich presents to Amurath III., 267.

Germigny, Baron de, ambassador of Henry III. (France) acquires great influence with the Divan; rescues numerous Frenchmen sold into slavery and obtains reparation for pillage committed by the Barbary corsairs; regulates the new coral fishery of the Marseilles adventurers upon the coast of Tunis; obtains the nomination of a Greek patriarch and a Voïvode of Wallachia in spite of the opposition of favourites; favours with his protection the affairs and subjects of the Pope, of the Emperor, of the Signory of Venice, the Republic of Ragusa, the Grand Master of Malta, and the renewal of the privileges of the Holy Places of Jerusalem and Sinai, &c. Germany, however, appreciates at its proper value the alliance and good-will of the Turks, foreseeing the decadence of the Empire with no longer a Solyman to direct it, 259; presents a Memorial to the Sultan on the wrongs of his nation, which is sent back with a threatening reply; the closing of the churches brings his irritation to a climax; their reopening purchased by presents, 265-6.

Ghazan, King of the Mongols, dethrones Aladdin III., last of the Seljukides, 52.

Gheraï, Mohammed, Khan of the Crimea, withdraws his aid in spite of remonstrances from Osman Pacha in Daghestan; by his desertion, draws upon himself the displeasure of the Porte, is deposed, but offering resistance is taken with arms in hand and put to death; his brother Islam Gheraï replacing him, 264.

Gratiani, Caspar, Voïvode of Moldavia, courts the favour of Sigismund III. of Poland by sending him intercepted letters addressed to Bethlem Gabor; is deposed on its discovery, but being assisted by the Poles with an army, he fights an obstinate battle near Jassy against Iskander Pacha; is defeated and perishes in the retreat, 296.

Greek Empire, the, its effete condition in the middle of the fifteenth century; Constantinople existing only by sufferance of the Turks until it yields to the arms of Mahomet II.; with its fall the curtain falls on the nations of antiquity, and the final establishment of the Turks in Europe forms the first great episode of Modern History, 123.

Greeks, the Byzantine, their corruption and degeneracy, 40; purchase peace of the Barbarians instead of fighting them, 50; their corruption of Christianity, 51.

Greek Fire, use of the, 50, 120.

Hamsa, the Persian Prince, defeats the renegade Cicala near Schembi-Ghazan, with a loss to the Ottomans of 20,000 men, 267.

Hamsa Bey, brother of Bajczid Pacha, causes the arch-rebel Djouneid, with all his family, to be strangled in prison, 108.

Harebone (or Harburn), ambassador of Queen Elizabeth (England), charged to demand from Amurath III. freedom of commerce for English ships in Ottoman waters; which is acceded to in spite of the opposition of the ambassadors of France and Venice, 260.

Haroun Al-Raschid, Khalife of Bagdad, his relations with Charlemagne; one of the three great names of the Eastern Khalifate, 23, 30.

Hassan (called *the Old Man of the Mountain*), chief and prophet of the Sect of the *Bathenians* or *Assassins;* three Khalifes slain by his adherents, as well as several heroes of the Crusades, 40; the Mongols track them to their retreats and their last chief surrenders himself into the hands of the great Khan of Mangou, fourth successor of Zinghis, 41.

Haye, De la, French Ambassador, affronts the Grand Vizier Kupruli Mahommed, 317; this personal slight is the cause of divers insults offered to the French during some twenty years; the Vizier finds an occasion for giving vent to his resentment during the war in Candia; orders the son of De la Haye to decipher certain correspondence, who refusing is maltreated and flung into a dungeon, 319; Mazarin demands amends and the dismissal of the Vizier; Blondel the envoy, unable to obtain an audience of the Sultan, returns with his letters; Mazarin anxious to prevent a rupture recalls De la Haye, 319.

Haye, De la, son of the above, is promised by Ahmed Kupruli, the new Vizier, a fair reception as French ambassador in 1666; his haughty demeanour displeases Kupruli, who dismisses him with disdain and reproaches; De la Hay demands a fresh audience, which leads to another altercation during which the ambassador is struck, arrested and detained for three days; the affair is compromised by a third audience, where Kupruli overwhelms De la Haye with kind attentions, politeness and presents, 327; he labours secretly and meanly to maintain himself in office, 332.

Henry II. (France) takes care to keep up friendly relations with the Porte, the alliance being almost solely directed to the interests of commerce and protection of Christians in the East, 224; his sons, guided by their astute mother, Catherine de' Medici, follow the policy of their grandfather, Francis I., 225.

Henry III. (France) deserting his throne of Poland to return to France, thus miscarries the sole chance of securing the accession of Poland to the Turco-French alliance, an accession that would not only have checked the aggrandisement of Austria, but hindered the rise of Russia, 256; an embassy from Amurath III. receives a magnificent reception; Henry's want of a navy compels him to send his ambassadors in a Venetian vessel, 258.

Hohenlohe, general of the Emperor Leopold I. (Germany), and Zriny, Ban of the Croats, seize upon Presnitz, Babosca, and Baris, and burn the town of Fünfkirchen with more than 500 villages, 322.

Holy League, the, an alliance between Pope Pius V., Philip II. of Spain, and the Venetians against Selim II., 248; another league against the Turks formed by Innocent XI., the Emperor Leopold, John Sobieski, the Czar Ivan Alexiowitsch, and the Republic of Venice; the war proclaimed against Mahomet IV., called the Holy War, lasts till the peace of Carlowitz, 363.

Hunyade (or Hunniades), John Corvinus, surnamed *the White Knight*, Voïvode of Transylvania, arrests the invasions of the Turks during 20 years; raised by his merits to command the Hungarian armies, Ladislas owed to him his throne; defends Hermanstadt against the Turks, kills 20,000, and drives the rest beyond the Danube, 110; and sends the heads of the Turkish generals to the Kral of Servia; achieves a victory at Vasagas as complete as the first against 80,000 Turks; his "long campaign" still more disastrous to the Ottomans, and Amurath is compelled to sue to him for peace; a truce of ten years places Servia and Wallachia under the suzerainty of Hungary, 111; joins a crusade with King Ladislas, Drakul, and a body of German and Italian adventurers with the design of destroying the Ottoman power; is defeated and put to flight by Amurath II. in the battle of Varna, 113; invades and ravages Servia, wages a terrible and unequal struggle for three days with Amurath at Kassova, but, betrayed by the Wallachians, is compelled to flee, 115; in the campaign of Mahomet II. against Servia, assists the Kral Georges to defeat the Turks, and obtains a truce, 129; Hunyade with an army throws himself into Belgrade besieged by the Sultan, destroys the Turkish flotilla and repulses every assault; at length a vigorous sortie throws the Ottoman camp into disorder and determines the raising of the siege; Mahomet II. withdraws wounded, leaving 24,000 dead and all his artillery; the saviours of the city only shortly survive their triumph; Hunyade succumbs at the end of fifteen days, 130.

Ibrahim Pacha, vizier of Solyman *the Great*, a Christian by birth, and son of a sailor of Parga; his education and mental qualities; becomes page and favourite of Solyman and afterwards first Vizier; his nomination angers Ahmed Pacha, who, rushing into open rebellion, is delivered up by the Arabs and put to death, 183; possesses the ring worn by Francis I. at Pavia, 187; is won over to the interests of King John Zapoly after the battle of Tokay, 193; appointed Seraskier, directs the siege of Vienna, 197; ordered to reduce Bagdad and bring back to obedience the Khan of Bidlis; receives the submission of places about Lake Van, and enters Tebriz without obstacle, 204; concludes an alliance with France which, under the form of a commercial treaty, was in fact a political league—his last policical act; wrings from the Sultan first the deposition and next the condemnation to death of the Defterdar Iskender Tchelebi, whose wealth and fame gave him umbrage; assumes the significant title of *Seraskier-Sultan*, at which presumption the offended Sultan orders him to be strangled, 211.

Ibrahim I., youngest son of Achmet I. and brother of Amurath IV., humours the House of Austria, enjoins Rakoczy, Prince of Transylvania, to discontinue war against the Emperor and break with Sweden; recaptures Azof from the Cossacks; all his efforts directed against the Republic of Venice; his son having been captured at sea and detained in Candia by the Venetian commander, the Sultan resolves to exterminate all the Christians in his States; confines the ambassadors to their houses, closes the offices of the Frank merchants, and lays an embargo on their ships, 310; directs a great expedition against Candia, the acquisition of which costs twenty-five years' fighting; the Turks fail before Candia and in their attacks on Dalmatia; the religious zeal of the Catholic world finds vent in cries for war against the infidels, 311; the vices of the Sultan rather than the courage of the Candians retard the capture of the city; the favourite Sultanas devour the revenues of the State and dispose at will of every appointment; the army weary of this shameful tyranny, the spirit of revolt is again aroused; the Janissaries depose Ibrahim, and the principal dignitaries cause him to be strangled, 312.

Ibrahim, Grand Vizier of Mahomet IV., succeeds Kara Mustapha; hesitates to accept the charge of governing the Empire amidst the perils threatening it on all sides, 359; arrests the march of the Imperialists by heroically defending Buda; orders Tekeli to be confined in the Seven Towers, 364.

Iskander Pacha, governor of Silistria, defeats a Polish army under Caspar Gratiani in a great battle near Jassy, 296.

Jews, the, occupy an important position in the Empire; monopolize most branches of commerce, 283.

John, son of Andronicus, succeeds to the throne of Constantinople on the abdication of Manuel; Bajazet I. reappears under the walls and haughtily orders the gates to be opened; Christian-like answer of the Byzantines; the Sultan is diverted from undertaking a second siege by the approach of Timour, 91; John, finding himself incapable of defending Constantinople against Amurath II. cedes it to the Venetians, 109.

John, Don, of Austria, the victory of Lepanto creates the reputation of, 250.

Jurisich, Nicholas, at the head of only 700 men, inflicts a humiliating disgrace upon Solyman *the Great*, who is repulsed before the little town of Güns in eleven assaults and at length obliged to accept a capitulation, 201.

Jurked Pacha, governor of Amasia, makes himself master by treason of the most turbulent chiefs on the Oriental side of Diarbekir, and secures tranquillity upon that frontier, 108.

Kabilovitch Milosch, a noble Serb, assassinates Amurath I. during the battle of Kassova, and overtaken in flight is cut in pieces, 82.

Kara Mustapha, the Kaimacan, succeeds his brother-in-law, Ahmed Kupruli, as grand vizier; maintains himself in power during seven years; the accession of that unworthy heir of the Kuprulis marks the beginning of the period of decadence; his pride and most scandalous ostentation; to meet his lavish expenditure needed enormous sums, which he procured by the most shameful means and cruel extortions; his venality; he sells governments, dignities, and justice, 347; manifests no more talent as a general than probity as an administrator; opposes the opening of negotiations with the victorious Russians and Cossacks, and takes command of an expedition against them; Cehryn only taken after a long and murderous siege; continually harassed by the Russians, the retreat of the Turks resembles a rout; they lose a great portion of their artillery and baggage; a peace at last concluded at Radzin, 348; resolves to openly aid the Hungarian malcontents under Count Emmerich Tekeli, who enters into a formal treaty with the Porte, and several conquests are effected; fixes the heavy conditions of a peace with Austria; takes command of a large but disorderly army transferred to him by the Sultan at Belgrade and talks of renewing the conquests of Solyman, 351; some prompt and easy successes exalt his ambition, and contrary to the advice of Tekeli and others, he resolves to besiege Vienna; advances direct upon that capital and encamps under its walls, 352; through his dilatoriness the Duke of Lorraine throws 12,000 men into the city; he meets with a sturdy resistance, and, when on the point of delivering an assault, a fresh army under John Sobieski arrives to the succour of Vienna; Kara Mustapha opens the trenches but encounters an obstinate defence, 354; the King of Poland, the Elector of Bavaria and the Duke of Lorraine having joined forces, the Turks are put to flight on all sides, leaving 10,000 dead on the field, 355; seized with a panic, they abandon their camp and baggage, the booty amounting to 15,000,000 crowns, 356; campaign terminated by the capture of Gran, which had been almost a century and a half in the hands of the Turks, 358; Mahomet IV. enraged at these reverses, causes Kara Mustapha to be beheaded at Belgrade, and his head taken to the Sultan on a silver dish, 359.

Kasim Bey, last of the princes of Karaman, joins Prince Djem in besieging Konieh; makes submission to Bajazet II., and all Karamania is pacified, 161.

Kasim Pacha, replaces Ahmed Pacha, put to death as a rebel in the government of Egypt, 183.

Katzianer, general of Ferdinand of Austria, his disastrous defeat by the Ottoman cavalry; is thrown into prison at Vienna; makes his escape, essays to sell himself to the Turks but perishes by assassination before he could consummate his treason, 214.

Keduk Ahmed, conqueror of Kaffa and Otranto, compels Prince Djem to raise the siege of Konieh; but rendering himself odious to Bajazet II. alike by his pride and popularity, is put to death, 161.

Kiemielniski, George, son of an old Hetman of the Cossacks, is drawn from prison by Mahomet IV, and nominated in the place of Doroszensako, but the Cossacks refuse to recognize his authority; joins in the attack on Cehryn, taken only after a long and sanguinary siege, 348.

Kinis, Paul, Count of Temesvar, long a terror to the Turks inflicts upon them a memorable defeat near Kenger-Mesæ, 146.

Konigsmark, Count, a Swede, commands a large force of Germans in the Venetian army in the *Holy War* against the Turks, 363.

Korân, the, intended at first only for Arabia, Mahomet's native country, 7; Mussulman society springs from it in its entirety, 8; its dogmas and precepts, 9-10; its errors, 11; the triple error contained in its code the ruin of all the Empires that Islam has successively raised, 15.

Kruppa, battle of, the Imperialists defeated in the, their heads sent to Constantinople, where the Austrian ambassador is compelled to redeem them from the hands of the executioner, 257.

Kupruli, Mahommed, Grand Vizier of Mahomet IV., situation of the Empire on his being raised to that post, 317; takes offence at not receiving the customary visit and presents from the French ambassador De la Haye, and a serious rupture is the result; becomes infuriated by a correspondence in cipher intercepted by a renegade, which discloses the secret assistance given by France to the Venetians; orders the ambassador's son, on his refusal to decipher the letters, to be maltreated, 318; and afterwards thrown into a dungeon; detains De la Haye at Adrianople under strict watch until after his return from the war in Transylvania; anxious to prevent a rupture, Mazarin sends an envoy with a letter from Louis XIV.; Kupruli receives him superciliously and threatens to send away De la Haye ignominiously; the envoy returns with his letters; Mazarin recalls De la Haye, 319; Mazarin and Kupruli both die in the same year; a comparison between the two ministers, who both exercised a veritable tutelage over their sovereigns and raised up again the States they governed; Kupruli's death-bed advice to the Sultan; Mahomet's last request to his Grand Vizier, 320.

Kupruli, Ahmed, son of Kupruli Mahommed, inherits the functions and authority of his father, who bequeaths to him the termination of two wars; Venice and Austria in vain open negotiations; Ahmed crosses the Danube, lays siege to Neuhœusel, 320, and captures that stronghold, the bulwark of Hungary, and which entails the submission of the adjacent fortresses, 321; the menacing tide of Mussulman invasion arrested by the celebrated Montecuculli, who defeats the Turks in the battle of St. Gothard, and throws them into a disorderly flight, in which nearly 25,000 were slain or drowned in the Raab, 322; a treaty concluded at Vasvar for a twenty years' truce, 323; after an attempt to relieve Candia with a large French force under the Duke de Navailles, the garrison is compelled to capitulate, 331; Kupruli shares in the glory of this success and the Sultan lavishes upon him the most signal proofs of his favour, 332; the Vizier's haughty treatment of the French ambassador Nointel so enrages Louis XIV. that a fleet is prepared to obtain by force a renewal of the alliance; Kupruli relents, and negotiations are recommenced but broken off several times, until the Great King threatening the Turks with his vengeance, the Divan greatly alarmed, causes the capitulations to be drawn up even upon the memoranda of Nointel, 339; the Empire under the administration of Kupruli having regained the summit of its power, he dies a few days after signing the Treaty of Daoud, which closed the war between Poland and Turkey, having borne during fifteen years the heaviest burthen of government; after Sokolli the first among the ministers who have directed the Ottoman Empire, 346.

Kupruli, Mustapha, *the Virtuous*, on his appointment as Grand Vizier, shows himself worthy of the illustrious name he bears, 371; infuses vigour into the government, reforms abuses, regulates anew the taxation and restores the finances; having secured payment of the troops, very soon raises an army more numerous than those which his predecessors had collected by dints of threats and severity; treats the Christian subjects with much humanity and grants them permission to rebuild their ancient churches; the first statesman in Turkey who had laid down the principle of free trade and the suppression of all prohibitive measures, 373; his amenity has the effect of causing the Greeks to abandon the party of the Venetians, 374; with the assistance of Tekeli, the Turks recover almost all they had previously lost; Belgrade retaken, to the great alarm of the Viennese, and divisions push on to Temesvar, Waradin and even into Transylvania; but next year Kupruli is completely defeated by Louis of Baden at Salan Kemen and slain, 375.

Kuprull, Hussein, surnamed *the Wise*, nephew of Kupruli Mahommed, summoned to save the Empire in great peril when Mustapha II. gives him the seals; by clever expedients provides for the most pressing needs, and the army succeeds in driving the Austrians across the Save, 377.

Khodabende, Shah of Persia, father of the great Shah Abbas, compelled by his son to abdicate, 268.

Ladislas, King of Poland, owes the throne of Hungary to the heroic Hunyade, 110; summoned by Cardinal Cesarini to tear up the treaty which placed Servia and Wallachia under the suzerainty of Hungary; enters upon a crusade to destroy the Ottoman power; after devastating Bulgaria and besieging Varna, is slain by a Janissary in the battle of Varna, 113.

Lala Mustapha, former preceptor of Prince Bajazet, becomes confidant of his younger brother Selim and grandmaster of his Court; plots to effect the ruin of the elder brother; undertakes to put arms into Bajazet's hands, and provokes him to send Selim an insulting letter, together with a distaff and female vestments, 228; Solyman irritated, threatens Bajazet with disgrace, who takes up arms, but being conquered, flees into Persia; his extradition being demanded, the Shah remits him to the agents of Selim, who murder him with his five sons, thus securing the throne to Selim, who becomes sole heir of Solyman *the Great*, 229.

Leopold I. Emperor of Germany; after the memorable victory of St. Gothard, won by Montecuculli over the Turks, the Imperial cabinet, instead of pursuing that advantage which opened the road to most extensive conquests, surprises all Europe by making peace with the Porte, a treaty for a twenty years' truce being concluded a few days after at Vasvar; the Emperor abandons to the Turks all their conquests, and withdraws his support from Rakoczy and Kemeni, thus abandoning Transylvania to Apafy, the nominee of the Porte, and makes the Sultan *a present* of 200,000 florins, 323; through the fanatical persecution of Protestantism by Leopold a conspiracy is formed by certain Hungarian leaders, headed by Count Tekeli; the Imperial forces are defeated and several towns captured, and the Austrian Generals, Wurmb and Leslie, compelled to accept the truce he offers, 350; on Kara Mustapha besieging Vienna, Leopold, with his Court, flees to Linz, 252; after the relief of Vienna by King John Sobieski and the Duke of Lorraine, the Emperor instead of expressing his thanks and gratitude, receives those commanders with haughty and repulsive coldness, 358; joins the *Holy League* against the Turks, 359; places Prince Eugene at the head of his army, who signally defeats the Turks near Zenta, 377.

Lionne, Minister of Louis XIV. "his letter upon the advances made by that king; to the League of the Rhine against the Turks," 321.

Louis of Baden, Margrave, with an Imperialist army, overruns great part of Bosnia, 369; after the successful campaign of 1689 against the Turks, he advises continuance of the war, and carries it from Bosnia into Servia; inflicts several severe defeats upon the infidels; occupies the passes of the Balkans from the borders of Roumelia to the Herzegovina, and captures all the Danube fortresses from Widdin to Nicopolis; opposes a Turkish army of more than double the number of his own, and completely defeats them near Salankemen, in which battle Mustapha Kupruli is slain, 375.

Louis XIV. (France) having captured Strasbourg, all Europe is in alarm, thinking that France and the Porte are agreed upon the conquest and dismemberment of Germany, 352; advises the Divan to continue the war against Austria, but the Porte, dissatisfied with the French King, listens to the solicitations of the Prince of Orange, and accepts the mediation of England and Holland, which brings about the Peace of Carlowitz, 378.

Loredano, the Venetian commander, delivers Lepanto from the Turks with his fleet, 106.

Lorraine, Charles Duke of, leads skilfully the army of the Emperor Leopold against the Turks at the siege of Vienna, 352; takes advantage of the dilatoriness of the infidels to throw 12,000 men into the city, 353; joined by Sobieski, they attack and put to flight the innumerable squadrons of Turkish cavalry, 355; with the aid of Sobieski, inflicts signal defeat upon the Turks at Parkany, 358; invades Hungary, seizes upon Wissegrad and Waitzen, as the result of a brilliant victory Pesth capitulates; defeats the Seraskier Suleiman Pacha before Buda; besieges Neuhœusel and carries it by assault; raises the blockade of Gran, 364; takes Buda by assault, which had been during forty-five years in the hands of the Osmanli, 365; completely defeats the Turks in the battle of Mohacs, who lose 20,000 men, artillery and baggage; the reduction of Transylvania completes the measure of the Duke's glory and the discouragement of the Turks, 366.

Mahmud of Ghizni, the mighty destroyer, his alarm at the progress of the Turks, 32.

Mahomet announces himself as sent from God to explain the laws of Moses and of Christ, 7; the character of Islamism, 9; at first preaches his doctrine at Mecca; is persecuted, condemned to death, and takes refuge in Medina, 15; his rejection by Khosroes, 29; his tribe and family obtain the sovereignty of Mecca and the guardianship of the Caaba, and a series of events is set in motion in the heart of Arabia of a most stupendous nature, 28; he dies at the moment when he was preparing to enter Syria at the head of an army, 16.

Mahomet I., Sultan, son of Bajazet, established himself at Amasia, 98; struggles with his brother Mousa for ascendancy in Asia; aids the Emperor Manuel to defend Constantinople, 99; advances against Mousa, who, after sustaining four defeats, disappears and lives awhile in obscurity, 100; becomes, by the death of his brothers, undisputed Sultan and sole master of the empire; re-establishes order and peace interiorly after twelve years of anarchy and civil war; in eight years of sway succeeds in effacing the traces of misrule left in the empire; his policy of peace; restores to the Greek Emperor the places Mousa had torn from him; renews the commercial treaty with the Venetians, and frees the princes of Wallachia and Servia from all tribute; represses the revolts of Prince Karaman and Djouneïd in Asia, and forces them to sue for pardon and peace; despatches an expedition against the Duke of Naxos, Lord of the Cyclades—whence springs the first hostilities between Venice and the Ottomans, 102; that war promptly terminated by a treaty ratified at Venice by a Turkish ambassador—the first who had appeared in Christendom; revolt of the Smyrna dervishes crushed by a sanguinary battle near Ephesus by Amurath, son of Mahomet, and Bajezid Pacha, 103-4; the Sultan dies of apoplexy at Gallipoli; his death kept secret, and the mutinous Janissaries, deceived by a trick, defile before his corpse, and permit the peaceful accession of his heir, 105.

Mahomet II., son of Amurath II., receives on his accession an embassy from the Greek Emperor, to whom he testifies his pacific intentions, and renews existing treaties with his Christian allies; concludes a truce with Hunyade, and crosses over into Asia to make war upon the Prince of Karaman; on a threat from Constantine of setting Solyman's grandson, his captive, at liberty, the young Sultan determines to make an end of Constantinople; returns to Europe, and, to starve out the city, builds a formidable fortress on the Bosphorus; the Emperor, terrified, sends a humble embassy, offering to pay tribute, and entreating that the country around may be spared; in answer, the Sultan orders his sipahis to feed their horses on the crops of the Greeks, through which a quarrel arises which proves the beginning of war, 116; his ardour and restlessness in making preparations for the siege prevent him from sleeping, 117; the Genoese of Galata treacherously enter into a treaty with the Sultan; he invests Constantinople by land with 200,000 Osmanli, but at first little progress is made, 119; the Sultan witnesses the disgraceful defeat of his fleet, and revenges the affront on the admiral, who is bastinadoed, deprived of his possessions and exiled; singular project of conveying his vessels overland, 120; he promises life and liberty to the besieged if the city capitulated, to the Emperor peaceful possession of the Morea, but his offers are rejected; orders a general assault, 121; and takes the city by a stratagem, 122; inaugurates the reign of Islam in his new capital; exposes the head of the Emperor Constantine upon the square of the Augusteon, 125; puts 2,000 inhabitants to the sword and has many thousands sold into slavery; supplies the vacancy thus created by a Turkish population; celebrates his triumph by orgies and bloody executions, 126; in the consolidation of his empire is guided by politic and enlightened counsels; his renewal of the Greek patriarchate gives rise to the population of Greek nobles called Phanariots; drafts families from Servia, the Morea, Genoese colonies, Trebizonde, Sinope, and Adrianople to repeople the capital; confiscates the lands of the great Greek families, and transforms them into *timars*, 128; the rapid development of Ottoman power the work of less than thirty years; Greece, Wallachia, Servia, Bosnia, Albania, the Crimea, and principal isles of the Archipelago, completely subjected; the Turkish Empire very nearly attains its definitive limits in Europe; punishes his Vizier, Khalil Pacha, convicted of connivance with the Greeks, with death; makes war upon Servia, seizes upon Ostrowitz, but miscarries before Semendria; his army defeated by the Kral Georges, assisted by Hunyade, who obtain a truce; recommences the war and besieges Belgrade, 129; is wounded and raises the siege, leaving his dead and all his artillery under the walls; the conquest of Servia is completed, and it is reduced to a province of the Ottoman Empire, 130; the subjection of Greece consummated; the Morea frightfully devastated, its inhabitants pitilessly massacred, and the Turks rule undividedly all the Greek peninsula, and put the isles of the Archipelago to ransom, 131; Scanderbeg having defeated successively three armies, the Sultan offers him peace, and leaves him in tranquil possession of Epirus and Albania; expedition against Trebizonde and Sinope, 182; the Comnenes made prisoners and put to death; the Empress Helena, having witnessed the massacre of her children, dies from grief and misery, 133; attempts the reduction of Bosnia and Wallachia, and overruns the Herzegovina; disguised as a monk, enters Bosnia to inspect the fortresses, is discovered, brought before King Stephen, and honourably dismissed; tries to get rid of his enemy Wlad by cunning, who seizes the Sultan's envoys and empales them; exasperated at this, reascends the Danube, takes Kilia and Braïla, and pursues Wlad, who surprises the Sultan's camp and nearly takes him prisoner; next, directs his march upon Bucharest, and is horror-stricken at the sight of 20,000 Turks and Bulgarians empaled by Wlad on the plain of Prælatu, 135; Jaicza captured, and all Bosnia falls to the Turks; definitively unites Wallachia to the Empire by establishing Radul, brother of Wlad, in his stead, 136; marches against Albania, but compelled by Scanderbeg to retire; Venice menaced by the Osmanli, 139; conquers Karamania, deposes the Grand Vizier Mahmoud and causes him to be put to death, 141; Croatia, Carniola, and Styria, invaded and ravaged by savage bands of Turks, 142; seeking to compel Stephen IV. of Moldavia to pay tribute, an Ottoman army of 100,000 thoroughly routed by 40,000 Moldavians; the Crimea conquered and Mengli Sheraï installed there as the Sultan's vassal and tributary, 143; Stephen IV. draws the Turkish army into the forest of Roboeni and thoroughly routs it with the loss of 30,000 men, 144; an attempt on Croïa repulsed, and Lepanto being delivered by Loredano, a treaty made with Venice, 145; after dreadful ravages in Slavonia, Hungary, and Transylvania, the Turks sustain a memorable defeat at Kenger-Messæ; three of the Ionian islands wrested from the despot of Arta, 146; an attempt to take Rhodes by surprise, repulsed by Pierre d'Aubusson, 147; death, character, and institutions of Mahomet II., 148.

Mahomet III., son of Amurath III. by the Sultana Baffa, the Venetian, the last heir of the Turkish throne who enjoyed before accession an independent government; his accession marked by the most horrible application of the fratricidal law of Mahomet II.; he orders his nineteen brothers to be strangled; the first campaign highly unfavourable to the Turks; Sinan, the Grand Vizier, attempting to gain possession of Wallachia, is driven back with great slaughter by Michael *the Brave*, 273; war in Hungary; treatment of the Christians by the viziers, 275; Michael *the Brave*, 276; relations of Mahomet III. with France, 277-279; the two next campaigns highly adverse to the

HISTORICAL INDEX. 399

Turks; the operations of the Seraskier Saturdschi so unfortunate as to cost him his dismissal and his life; the war carried on feebly for six years longer with varying success, 279; even the death of the Sultan had little effect upon it; Mahomet III. is quietly succeeded by his son, Achmet I., then scarcely seven years of age, 280.

Mahomet IV., son of the Sultan Ibrahim, succeeds him when scarcely seven years old; at first the State is governed by the women and eunuchs, who fill up the highest posts at their pleasure; his long reign may be divided into three periods—the first, filled with seditions and reverses; in the second, Ahmed Kupruli re-establishes the affairs of the Empire; in the third troubles recommence, and the Ottoman power, shaken within and without, totters to its decline; after the murder of Ibrahim, the Porte experiences anew the domination of the soldiery; the Janissaries at first suppress an insurrection of Itchoglans and Sipahis, but make the young Sultan pay dearly for their guardianship; during the war against Venice they compromise the honour of the Crescent by revolts in presence even of the enemy; they refuse to continue the siege of Candia; another sedition costs the life of the Sultan's grandfather; irritated at the delay in the payment of their arrears, 313; they call for death to the members of the Divan; the Sultan obeys, delivers to the executioner his dearest servants, and the whole administration is overthrown; the Grand Vizier next deposed; revolts break out in the Asiatic provinces; the governor of Anatolia is overcome and slain by the rebels; so long as internal anarchy prevails, the Sultan obtains no advantage without the realm; Admiral Moncenigo obtains a complete victory over the Turkish fleet, and, by a strict blockade of the Hellespont, Constantinople is almost famished; Mahommed Kupruli made Grand Vizier, restores order and discipline; suppresses a military mutiny by capital punishments, and hangs the Greek patriarch accused of treason; the war against the Venetians vigorously resumed; the isles of Tenedos and Lemnos reconquered, but these successes are balanced by a victory obtained by the Republic near Milo, 314; diplomatic rupture with France caused by De la Haye, the ambassador, giving offence to the new Vizier, Kupruli, 317; certain despatches from the Venetians to the Ambassador having been delivered up to the Vizier by a renegade, Kupruli orders De la Haye to repair to Adrianople; the latter being ill is represented by his son, 318; who on refusing to decipher the despatches, is maltreated and thrown into a dungeon, whilst the secretaries and interpreters of the embassy are menaced with torments and even death; on Mazarin demanding amends and the dismissal of the Vizier, Kupruli receives the envoy superciliously and threatens to send away De la Haye ignominiously; the rupture seems complete, but Mazarin refusing to involve himself in an impolitic struggle with Turkey, recalls De la Haye, 319; the Sultan, having remonstrated in vain with the King of Poland against his invasion of the Ukraine, declares war against him, and, in conjunction with the Tartars of the Crimea, besieges and captures Kaminiec and Lemberg; the king sues for peace, but only obtains it by the disgraceful conditions of the treaty of Bucsacs; the Poles refusing to ratify the treaty, the Sultan at the head of his army retakes the way to Poland, but is defeated at Choczim by Sobieski, 345; the Tartar Khan serving as a mediator between Sobieski and the Sultan, a treaty is signed at Daoud, 346; a war disastrous to the Porte waged with the Russians for five years is terminated by the treaty of Radzin, 348; a formal treaty entered into with Tekeli, and several conquests effected against the Austrians, 350; the Sultan having marched with a large army to Belgrade, there transfers it to Kara Mustapha, who rashly resolves to besiege Vienna, 351; the Turks encounter a signal defeat, flee in disorder, abandoning their camp and baggage, and a booty estimated at fifteen million crowns, 356; the Sultan enraged at a succession of reverses causes Kara Mustapha to be beheaded; the league against the Turks, called the *Holy War*, ensues, lasting till the Peace of Carlowitz, 359; fresh reverses in Hungary, and Buda taken by the Duke of Lorraine, 364-5; Athens besieged and its Acropolis partially destroyed by explosion of the Turkish powder magazine, 365; the Vizier, Suleiman Pasha, defeated by the Christian army near Mohacs with a loss of 20,000 men, with their artillery and baggage, and the reduction of Transylvania completes the measure of the Duke of Lorraine's glory and the discouragement of the Turks, 366; after the unfortunate Hungarian expedition, the Janissaries and Sipahis mutiny against the Grand Vizier, who is summoned to give up the standard and seals; to escape that outburst he flees secretly to Peterwardein and thence to Belgrade; the soldiers elect a Grand Vizier and address a solemn petition against Suleiman; Mahomet terrified, grants their demands, and sends them the head of his old minister; but the soldiery could no longer be stopped; they march upon Constantinople and depose the Sultan himself; he is confined in the Seraglio, whence they draw forth his brother Soliman to succeed him; Mahomet IV. dies disregarded five years afterwards, 367.

Malek-Adhel, Sultan of Cairo, reunites under his domination the inheritances of the sons of Saladin, the valorous Sultan of Egypt and chivalrous foe of Richard *Cœur de Lion*, 38.

Malek Shah, son of Alp Arslan, the Seljukian Empire attains its highest pitch of splendour under him; it falls to pieces at his death, 35, 36.

Mameluke dynasty, the, established in Egypt since the middle of the thirteenth century, assailed by Selim I., and defeated after a sanguinary struggle, lasting three days and nights, from street to street in Cairo; almost all are massacred, and with them 30,000 of the inhabitants; the last Mameluke Sultan, Touman Bey, hanged at the gate of Cairo, 175.

Mangou, the great Khan of the Mongols, fourth successor of Zinghis, is converted to Christianity by the prayers and entreaties of the King of Armenia; occupies himself with destroying the sect of the *Assassins*, which had made the western princes tremble during two centuries, 40; tracked to their retreats, their last chief comes to surrender himself into the hands of Mangou, 41.

Manuel, son of Palæologus I., agrees to abdicate the Byzantine throne in favour of John, son of Andronicus and content himself with the Morea, 91; recovers the throne and enters into an alliance with Solyman, son of Bajazet I., who surrenders to him a portion of the Ottoman conquests in Europe, 99; Mousa, brother of Solyman, having laid siege to Constantinople, the Emperor invites Mahomet, Mousa's brother, to aid him, 101; the places recently torn from him by Mousa restored by Mahomet I. on his accession, 102; offended by the refusal of Amurath II. to confide his two brothers to his care, he releases from prison the pretender Mustapha, the latter engaging by treaty to restore to the Greeks Gallipoli, Thessaly, etc., 105; essays in vain to disarm the resentment of Amurath, who besieges Constantinople; incites the Sultan's youngest brother to rebellion, 107.

Massoud, son of Mahmud of Ghizni, utterly defeated at Zendecan by Togrul Bey, the Turkish chief, and this decisive action shatters into fragments the colossal empire of the Ghiznevides, 33.

Maximilian, the Archduke, hastens with Sigismund, Prince of Transylvania, to recover Erlau, and fights a sanguinary battle with the Turks for three days on the plain of Keresztes; the Christians sustain great loss, and, seized with a panic, take to disorderly flight; 50,000 Germans or Hungarians perish, 275.

Mazarin, Jules, Prime Minister of Louis XIV., his wily policy alike towards the Turks and Venetians; but is unwilling that the Turks should dominate the Mediterranean by the possession of Candia; sends an ambassador extraordinary to offer the Divan the mediation of France, which is haughtily rejected; offers to the Venetians the co-operation of the French navy on such conditions that the Senate refuses the offer; sends to Venice a subsidy of 10,000 crowns, but secretly, and in his own name; sends nine ships to fight under the Venetian flag, 311; and allows more than 50,000 soldiers to be recruited in France, and accept the pay of Venice, 312; anxious to prevent a diplomatic rupture arising out of the misunderstanding between the Vizier and the

HISTORICAL INDEX. 401

French ambassador, sends a letter from Louis XIV., demanding amends and the dismissal of Kupruli; the envoy, received superciliously, is unable to obtain an audience of the Sultan, and returns with his letters; Mazarin recalls De la Haye, and entrusts the affairs of France at Constantinople to Roboly, a merchant, who remains in charge till 1665; urged by England, Holland and Austria to declare war, he refuses to involve himself in an impolitic struggle with Turkey, but sends 4,000 Frenchmen to Candia, and prepares to aid the Emperor against the Ottomans, 319; a comparison of Mazarin with Kupruli, 320.

Mengli Sherai, son of Devlet, installed Khan of the Crimea by Mahomet II. as his vassal and tributary, 143.

Michael, King of Poland, invades the Ukraine to hinder the Cossacks throwing themselves into the arms of the Osmanli; refusing to obey the mandate of Mahomet IV., the Sultan, in conjunction with the Tartars of the Crimea, besieges Kaminiec, which capitulates, and Lemberg being taken also, Michael sues for peace, and obtains it by the disgraceful treaty of Bucsacs, 345.

Miridites, the, with the Archbishop of Durazzo, head a conspiracy against Bajazet II., 163.

Mirza Mahömet, grandson of Timour, pillages and destroys Broussa, Nicæa and other places in Asia Minor, 98.

Mohacz, the sanguinary battle of, won by Solyman I., in which perished the Hungarian nationality; its great influence upon the destinies of Europe, 191.

Moncenigo, the Venetian Admiral, obtains a complete victory over the Turkish fleet in the Dardanelles; seizes upon Tenedos, Samothracia, and Lemnos, and by a strict blockade almost famishes Constantinople; loses his life in an indecisive battle fought near the Hellespont, 314.

Montassem, third son of Haroun-Al-Raschid, and twenty-seventh Khalife of Bagdad, forms a body-guard of Turkish mercenaries; his policy fatally erroneous, as they despise the feebleness of the Khalifate, whilst they grasp at its riches; retires in disgust from Bagdad and founds Samara; becomes the chief agent in the destruction of the Khalifate, 30-1.

Montecuculli, commander-in-chief of the army of Leopold I. (Germany), succeeds Count de Strozzi in Hungary, and arrests the tide of Mussulman invasion; defeats the Turks in the memorable battle of St. Gothard, in which they are utterly routed, and nearly 25,000 of them slain or drowned in the Raab, 322.

Morosini, governor of Candia, refuses to allow a band of volunteers under command of the Duke de la Feuillade to make a sortie, the garrison being exhausted, 329; on the departure of the French under the Duke de Navailles, Candia being no longer defendable, Morosini capitulates, and signs a peace with the Turks, 331.

Mousa, son of Bajazet I., establishes himself at Broussa, 99; struggles with Mahomet for ascendency in Asia, and with his brother Solyman in Europe; is defeated, but with a recruited army is welcomed at Adrianople, and on the flight and death of Solyman, takes possession of the throne, 100; effects some conquests in the Byzantine dominions, and lays siege to Constantinople; compelled to raise the siege, and, Mahomet having advanced against him, he sustains a total defeat, and dies in a marsh during his flight, 101.

Murad Pacha, by his indomitable energy, succeeds in terminating a long and murderous struggle against Persia, allied with numerous Asiatic populations, and gains thereby the surname of *Restorer of the Empire*, 283.

Mustapha, a pretender to the throne, giving himself out to be the fourth son of Bajazet I., supported by Marcea Voïvode of Wallachia and Djouneïd, invades Thessaly, 104; is overcome near Thessalonica and kept prisoner by the Emperor Manuel; on the accession of Amurath II. is released and incited by Manuel to rebel against that Sultan, 105; at the head of a Greek army takes Gallipoli, and thence, accompanied by Djouneïd, marches upon Adrianople; is confronted by Bajezid Pacha, Amurath's general, whose troops all pass over to the pretender's side and massacre Bajezid; crosses the straits to encounter the forces of Amurath; deserted by Djouneïd and his army, he flees to Lampsacus and thence to Gallipoli;

VOL. I.   E E is pursued by Amurath and defeated; flees to Adrianople, where he robs the treasury and resumes his flight towards Wallachia; is seized upon by his followers, brought back to Adrianople, and hanged upon a tower of that city by Amurath II., 106.

Mustapha Pacha, his rivalry with Sinan Pacha for the Vizierate; on the seals being given by Amurath III. to Sinan, he dies some days after, either of grief or suicide, 263.

Mustapha I., the imbecile brother of Achmet I., is raised from a dungeon to the throne; his pastime to throw gold to the fishes of the Bosphorus; after three months' possession of the sceptre, is led back to prison—replaced by his nephew Osman, 295; on the murder of Osman, is once more set upon the throne; after being for fifteen months the plaything of the soldiery, is deposed in favour of Amurath, eldest son of Achmet, 299.

Mustapha II., on succeeding his brother, Achmet II., as Sultan, energetically heads his army, crosses the Danube, captures several places; carries by assault Lippa in Hungary, and defeats General Veterani near Lugos; the success of that campaign revives the enthusiasm of the Mussulmans, 376.

Naoouh Pacha dares propose to Achmet I. to purchase the Vizierate; points out to him the general demoralisation of the public service, 293.

Navailles, Duke de, attempts to relieve Candia with a large French force, but fails, and the garrison is forced to capitulate, 331.

Nemania, Stephen, recognized by the Greek Emperors as independent Prince of Servia, and becomes founder of a dynasty which lasts 300 years, 67.

Octal-Kahn, son of Zinghis; under him the Karismians, conquered and driven back by the Mongols, throw themselves upon Syria, ravage it, seize upon Jerusalem and massacre all its inhabitants, 38.

Oghuz-Kahn, a descendant of Turk, the common ancestor of all the Turks; the legend of his six sons, 26.

Ommiades, the, usurp the western provinces of the Eastern Khalifate, 21.

Orban, an Hungarian ironfounder, constructs, for the siege of Constantinople, the most enormous cannon of which history makes mention, 117; it bursts and kills its inventor, 119.

Orchan, son of Othoman, appoints his brother Aladdin Vizier; transfers the seat of government to Broussa, 56; defeats the Emperor Andronicus the younger, and captures Nicæa, 58; his series of conquests, 59; his attempt upon Constantinople vigorously repulsed by John Cantacuzene, 63; Orchan's marriage with the latter's daughter, the bond of an important alliance; he finds himself sole arbiter of the Greek Empire; aiding the Venetians causes an open rupture with Cantacuzene; sides with John Palæologus against the latter, 64; the capture of the fortress of Tzympe gives the Turks their first permanent footing in Europe; sends forces under his son Solyman to aid Cantacuzene against Palæologus, 65; the Turks extend their dominions from the Propontis to the Danube; as a lawgiver and author of the Constitution, Orchan is regarded as the Numa of the Ottomans, and by his policy universally respected as the head of the Moslem faith, 66.

Orthoguel, son of Soliman Shah, renders aid in battle to Alaeddin, Seljukide Sultan, against the Mongols and Greeks; is rewarded with territory which becomes the cradle of the Ottoman power, 45.

Osman or Othoman (*leg-breaker*), founder of the Ottoman dynasty, 45; its grandeur said to have been miraculously announced to him; his dream; marries the beautiful Malkatoun, 46; founds a new empire upon the ruins of the Seljukian and Byzantine dynasties; stains the commencement of his reign by the murder of his uncle Deindar, 53; his victorious career, character, and death, 55.

Osman II., eldest son of Achmet I., saluted Padischa by the venal soldiery; his character, 295; the success of Iskander Pacha incites him to attempt the conquest of Poland against the advice of his ministers; marches against Sigismund III.; his first assault on the Poles successful, but a mutiny breaks out, and the Sultan retreats; his scheme to destroy the refractory Janissaries prematurely betrayed; they revolt and attack the Seraglio, 297; drag forth Mustapha from his dungeon and salute him Padischa; Constantinople is abandoned to plunder and devastation; the youthful Sultan dragged to the Seven Towers, is there strangled—the first Ottoman Emperor assassinated by his subjects, 298.

Osman Pacha sustains the honour of the Ottoman arms in Daghestan; destroys the Persian army and submission of the country secured; received on his return with extraordinary honour by Amurath III. and named Vizier and Seraskier, 264; begins the Persian war again with renewed activity; the Ottomans enter Tebriz as conquerors, and pillage it during three days and nights; but the ill-health of the Vizier arrests his successes; constrained to effect his retreat, and disabled from directing the army, is attacked, suffers defeat, and dies a few days afterwards, 267.

Ottoman Turks, the, their origin; the Osmanli a branch of the Turks in the larger meaning of the word, 25; their conversion to Islamism, 27; when permanently established in Constantinople, 29; their first passage into Europe and early contests with the Greeks, 62; progress of their arms, 66.

Ottoman Navy, its decay towards the close of the 16th century, 281.

Ourosch V., the Serb empire dismembered under the attacks of his vassals, who sought to render themselves independent, 68.

Palæologus, John, Emperor of Constantinople, his struggle with Cantacuzene; his troops defeated by Solyman, son of Orchan, 65; sends his son Theodore to serve in the Ottoman camp as a proof of his submission to Amurath I.; conspiracy of his eldest son Andronicus with Sandschi, son of Amurath, to depose their respective fathers, 79; is dethroned by his son Andronicus assisted by Bajazet I.; is restored by the latter under humiliating conditions, 84; forms a plan of fortifying Constantinople, but required to abandon the project by Bajazet; dies, leaving his son Manuel in possession of the throne, 85.

Palæologus II., John, finding himself incapable of defending Thessalonica, cedes that city to the Venetians, 109; ——, Constantine (Dragozes), not receiving the promised pension for the maintenance of Solyman's grandson, imprudently threatens to set his prisoner at liberty; irritated at that menace, Mahomet II. thinks only of making an end of Constantinople; the Emperor, terrified, sends an humble embassy to Mahomet, offering to pay tribute, which offer is unheeded; sends a last message of defiance, 116; all the energy of the Byzantines expended in miserable religious discords, 118; state of Constantinople when invested by Mahomet II.; the Emperor animates his people by fighting in person on the ramparts, 119; on Mahomet offering life and liberty to the inhabitants if the city capitulated, Constantine refuses the offer, preferring rather to bury himself in its ruins, 121; on the assailants breaking their way through the Caligaria Gate, the Emperor rushes in desperation among their ranks and falls beneath a sabre of a Janissary, 122; his head exposed upon the Augusteon, 125.

Palæologus, Thomas, a son of, sells to Charles VIII. of France his rights to the throne of the East, 162.

Piri Pacha, Grand Vizier of Selim I. and Solyman *the Great*, 172; Selim's cruel reply to Piri's request to give him notice when the Sultan wished to get rid of him, 177; invests Belgrade, 180; is deposed in favour of Solyman's favourite, Ibrahim, 183.

Radhi, Al, an imbecile Khalife of Bagdad, 20th of the Abbassides and 39th of the successors of Mahomet, dies in 940, and the temporal power of the Khalifes terminates with him, 31.

Ragazzoni, his description of the depression and degradation of the Christians in Turkey in 1571, 282.

Roumains, the, become tributary to the Hungarians; regain their independence under Radoul *the Black*, but fall again under Hungarian domination, 69.

Roxalana, a Russian slave, whom Solyman *the Great*, by pre-eminent distinction, acknowledges as his legitimate wife (Khourum Sultana); obtains an extraordinary ascendancy over him; successfully strives for the

E E 2

succession to the throne of her son Selim; the Persian campaign undertaken at her instigation, in order to display the military talents of her son-in-law, Rustem, made commander-in-chief, 226.

Russia, first relations of the Ottoman Empire with; in 1492, Ivan III., Grand Duke of Moscow, the veritable creator of the Russian Empire, makes friendly propositions to Bajazet II. through the medium of the Khan of the Crimea; in 1495 a Muscovite ambassador appears at Constantinople, 165; and four years after a second envoy obtains commercial privileges for the Russian merchants, 166.

Rustem Pacha, third Vizier of Solyman *the Great*, becomes son-in-law to that Sultan by marriage with the daughter of the Sultana Roxalana, and is raised from favour to favour to the highest dignity of the Empire; is made commander-in-chief to conduct the Persian campaign; renders his benefactress a repulsive service, 226.

Saturdschi, the Seraskier, his campaign of 1598 so highly adverse to the Turkish arms as to cost him his dismissal and his life, 279.

Sava, Prince of Servia, son of Stephen Nemania, founds the patriarchate, 67.

Scanderbeg,—see Castriot, George.

Selim I., *the Inflexible*, son of Bajazet II., raised to the throne by the Janissaries, distributes fifty ducats per man amongst them on his accession, 168; Ahmed, his brother, endeavouring to assert his claims by arms, is defeated, captured, and executed; and that he may have no rival near the throne, puts to death his younger brother Korkud, and causes five of his nephews to be slain before his eyes at Broussa, 169; Ismaïl, the Shiite leader, half warrior, half prophet, at the head of his adherents harasses the Ottoman frontiers; Selim has an exact census taken of them with the most profound secrecy, and then orders a general massacre; 40,000 heretics perish in one day, 171; the Sultan defeats Ismaïl in the valley of Tchaldiran, and seizes upon the Schah's treasures in Tebriz; after reducing several fortresses he traverses Georgia and Armenia, and passes the winter in Amasia; conquers, in two years, Northern Mesopotamia and a considerable part of Persia; next, reduces Syria, and then turns his arms against Egypt, 173; subdues Touman Bey, the last Sultan of the Mamelukes, and has him hanged at the gate of Cairo; carries away the treasures of the Mameluke Sultans, and takes with him a colony of artizans, whom he establishes at Constantinople; enforces from Mahomet XII. the last representative of the Abbasside Kalifes, the rights and distinctive ensigns of the Khalifate—the standard, sword and mantle of the Prophet, 175; the rapidity and magnitude of his conquests excite the alarm of the European potentates; Venice and Hungary conciliate the Porte and renew the peace entered into with the Sultan's father; the Venetians transfer to him the tribute previously paid to the Sultan of Egypt for the possession of Cyprus; Pope Leo X. decrees a new crusade against the infidels, but with no result save a profitable compact between himself and the French King, 176; Selim's last enterprise is directed against Rhodes, which he was not destined to accomplish; dies of the plague at Tschorli; the fame of this great conqueror sullied by acts of the most impious cruelty; yet, in spite of sanguinary follies and crimes, he is reckoned amongst the great men of the Ottoman Empire, 177.

Selim II., *the Drunkard*, son of Solyman the Great and Roxalana; his share in the plot to ruin his brother Bajazet, who is given up by the Shah of Persia, and murdered with his five sons, 229; on his accession he exhausts the treasury by gratifications to the Janissaries, Seraglio officers, and the Ulema; the first of the Ottoman Sultans who proves to be unworthy of the throne; leaves all the cares of government to his Vizier Sokolli; after concluding a peace with Austria, 242, the Sultan directs his attention to the conquest of Cyprus and Arabia, by which his reign is chiefly distinguished, 245; curious motive assigned for undertaking the Cyprian war, 246; the Venetians defend Nicosia and Famagosta against the Turkish forces under Mustapha Pacha; Nicosia taken and the inhabitants massacred, 247; Famagosta opposes a stubborn resistance under

Marc Antonio Bragadino, and repulses six assaults; want of munitions compels him at length to capitulate; the Turks shamefully violate the capitulation, the valiant Bragadino being flayed alive and quartered by Mustapha; these atrocities provoke an alliance against the Sultan called the Holy League, concluded between Pope Pius V., Philip II. of Spain, the Venetians and one or two minor powers, 248; the Christians of the League attack the Osmanli fleet near Lepanto, and defeat the Turks with terrible loss of men and ships; the most signal disaster that had yet befallen the Ottoman arms, 249-50; a peace being finally concluded, Venice surrenders Cyprus, and consents to pay a double tribute for Zante, 253; a naval force leaves Constantinople to snatch Tunis from the grasp of the Spaniards, which is taken by assault, 254; this expedition is the last important act of Selim's reign, who dies from the effect of a debauch; towards the close of this reign begin the first disputes of the Porte with Russia, 255.

Seljukide Sultans, the, their ferocious ardour for war and conquest, 34; the empire attains its highest pitch of splendour under Malek Shah; at his death it is divided between the four chief Seljukian dynasties, 36.

Serbs, the, clear the way to Constantinople for the Turks by their conquests, 68.

"Seven Towers," the ancient Byzantine castle called the, description of, 281.

Siawusch Pacha, Grand Vizier of Soliman II., after the deposition of Mahomet IV. by the army, he enters Constantinople at the head of the rebellious troops; the Janissaries and Sipahis becoming more turbulent than ever, demand an increased accession-donative, which being resisted, a furious riot ensues, in which the palaces of the ministers are stormed, plundered, and burnt, and the Grand Vizier himself falls by the hands of those who elected him, his body being torn into shreds, and horrible cruelties inflicted upon his wife, sister, and slaves, 368.

Sigismond, King of Hungary, aided by French and German allies, besieges Nicopolis with a view of crushing the rising Ottoman Empire, but is defeated by Bajazet I.; escapes in the Venetian and Rhodian fleet to Dalmatia, 89.

Sigismond Bathory, Prince of Transylvania, is defeated with the Archduke Maximilian by the Turks at Keresztes in a battle which lasts three days, an event which creates the greatest alarm throughout Europe, 275.

Siman, Bedreddin, a learned jurisconsult and theologian, promoter of certain strange dogmas, the preaching of which causes an insurrection near Smyrna, 103; rapidly raises a force in the Hæmus mountains; is defeated by the Turkish army near Seres, and hanged, 104.

Sobieski, John, King of Poland; the Poles refusing to ratify the treaty of Bucsacs, or become tributary to the Porte, Mahomet IV. again invades Poland; Sobieski, General of the Republic, crosses the Dniester, and seconded by the Wallachians and Moldavians, defeats the Ottomans at Choczim, and pursues them as far as the Gates of Kaminiec; Michael, King of Poland, dying at that moment, Sobieski receives the reward for his services to the Republic and Christianity by the Diet proclaiming him King, 345; the Turks proving a second time successful against Kaminiec, France in vain attempts to negotiate a peace; the Tartar Khan then serves as a mediator, and a treaty is signed at Daoud, by which Kaminieo, Podolia, and the Ukraine remain to the Porte, except some towns, 346; Sobieski, at the head of a valiant army, aids the Emperor Leopold at the siege of Vienna by the Turks; heading a charge, is carried too far, and nearly overwhelmed by numbers, but puts the enemy to flight on all sides, 355; inflicts upon them another signal defeat at Parkany, and ends the campaign by the capture of Gran, held almost a century and a half by the Ottomans, 358.

Sokolli, Vizier of Selim *the Drunkard*, preserves the traditions of the reign of Solyman *the Great*, and maintains the dignity of the Empire in its foreign relations, 242; after the battle of Lepanto repairs the losses of the Ottoman marine with marvellous promptitude, 252; his authority restrained unfortunately by Amurath III., 255; the Sultan's favourites work the Vizier's ruin; his nephew Mustapha Pacha, Governor of Ofen, is executed, and Sokolli assassinated in his palace, 261.

Soliman Shah, son of Kaialp, driven into Armenia by the invasion of Zinghis, is drowned in the Euphrates; his descendants settle in the narrow canton in Asia Minor, which was the cradle of the Ottoman power, 45.

Soliman, kinsman of Malek Shah, conquers Asia Minor from the Greeks; forms an alliance with one of the two Greek competitors for the Byzantine throne, helps to set him on the throne, and rewards himself by taking possession of all the Greek provinces of Asia; by his Mahommedan zeal earns the title of *Gazi*, the *Holy Champion;* attempting to free himself from the suzerainty of the Seljukides is overcome and slain, 36.

Solyman, son of Orchan, captures a fortress in Thrace, and the Turks first obtain a permanent footing in Europe, 65; fixes his residence at Gallipoli, and extends his conquests until arrested by a fatal accident, 66.

Solyman, son of Bajazet I., establishes himself at Adrianople; enters into an alliance with the Emperor Manuel, and surrenders to him a portion of the Ottoman conquests in Europe, 99; takes the title of *Sultan* in Asia, and enters upon a long and desperate rivalry with his brother Mahomet; attacked in his own states by the allied Princes of Servia and Wallachia, is constrained to abandon Asia; whilst Solyman gives himself up in the Seraglio of Adrianople to his sensual proclivities, Mousa appears suddenly at the gates of that city with his recruited army; that pressing danger cannot tear Solyman from his inaction, 100; his emirs, indignant, abandon him; he is constrained to flee, and is slain on the road to Constantinople by the peasants, 101.

Solyman, *the Great*, son of Selim I., his first acts show his love of justice and his generosity; one revolt alone troubles the commencement of his reign—that of Djanberdi, who is, after causing the massacre of 5,000 Janissaries, defeated, given up by his followers and put to death; hostilities resumed with Hungary; the garrison of Czabacz makes an heroic resistance, but is exterminated, and Solyman enters the town between two ranges of heads stuck upon stakes; next presses operations against Belgrade, which, shattered by his artillery, capitulates after repulsing more than twenty assaults; it becomes thenceforth the strongest bulwark of the Empire; having regained his capital receives the ambassadors and felicitations of the Grand Duke of Russia and other princes; peace renewed with the Venetians and a commercial treaty concluded with them; resumes the projects of his father against Rhodes by besieging that island, 180; after several assaults, repulsed with heroic obstinacy by the knights; stimulated by the example of the aged Grand Master, the Turks retreat with loss of 15,000 men; after two months more of continual fighting, the Sultan offers the knights a capitulation, but the Janissaries treacherously seize upon and pillage the town; Solyman gives the Grand Master an honourable reception, and the knights find a refuge in Malta, which Charles V. cedes to them, 182; the Grand Vizier, Piri Pacha, deposed, and his post given to the Sultan's favourite, Ibrahim Pacha; chagrined at this nomination, Ahmed Pacha throws himself into open rebellion, and assumes the title of Sultan of Egypt; an army of 30,000 Janissaries being sent against him, he is betrayed by one of his viziers, delivered up by the Arabs and put to death, 183; the Janissaries revolt through long inaction, but are appeased and punished by the Sultan, 184; new policy of France towards the Ottoman Empire, 185; a French embassy intercepted by the Sandjak of Bosnia, and the ambassador murdered, together with his twelve attendants, with the supposed privity of Ferdinand of Austria, 187; Solyman makes preparations for invading Hungary, and concludes an armistice with the King of Poland; an alliance contracted between France and the Porte, 189; Francis I. presses Solyman to invade Hungary, to which the Sultan assents; anarchy in Hungary, 190; Solyman captures Peterwardein; is confronted by the young King Louis at Mohacz with greatly inferior forces, who is defeated and perishes in the river marshes; this battle has great influence over the destinies of Europe; the Sultan receives at Fældwald the keys of Buda;

Wissegrad and Gran successfully resist, and the Hungarian entrenched camp costs the Turks more men than did the battle of Mohacz, 191; the number of Hungarians massacred in this campaign computed at 200,000; after promising them John Zapoly for their king, the Sultan, laden with booty, retakes the way to his capital; the Turcomans of Cilicia revolt on account of the brutalities and exactions of the Turkish agents; the war continues in Hungary, and the submission of Croatia, Slavonia, and Dalmatia effected, 192; Zapoly, defeated by Ferdinand of Austria, implores succour of the Porte, and receives a formal promise from the Sultan to be put in possession of Hungary; new relations of Francis I. and Solyman, 193; second expedition against Hungary, when Ferdinand of Austria humbles himself; King John Zapoly, at the head of the magnates, does homage to the Sultan on the plain of Mohacz; Buda capitulates after a resistance of five days, and its garrison is massacred by the Janissaries, 196; Solyman next besieges Vienna, 197; every assault repulsed, and the Turks at length retreat in the night, after committing their usual barbarities and wasting the country, 198; his third expedition against Hungary; the Sultan begins his march with Oriental pomp, 199; his imposing reception of a French embassy at Belgrade, 200; his march through Hungary resembles a progress in his own dominions; but the little town of Güns inflicts upon him the most humiliating disgrace ever experienced by the pride of Oriental despotism since that of Xerxes, 201; after investing Gratz, which was well defended, Solyman reluctantly abandons an enterprize for which he had made such vast preparations, 202; concludes a peace with Ferdinand's envoys, by which that Emperor was to retain all he held in Hungary, and make what terms he pleased with Zapoly, 203; under the appearance of a commercial treaty, a political league is concluded between Francis I. and the Sultan for the conquest of Naples; Solyman assembles a large force in Albania for a descent upon Italy, but Francis not making his appearance there, the Sultan does not follow up the invasion, 213; the war in Hungary renewed, and Solyman enters Buda without resistance, 215; new Franco-Turkish alliance, 219; the Sultan besieges Gran, which surrenders, 220; the death of Francis I. hastens the conclusion of a treaty between Charles V., King Ferdinand, and the Sultan; war in Asia, 221; the flames of war rekindled in Hungary; the Imperialists surprised before Szegedin and cut in pieces, 223; Temesvar taken, and all the Banat returns under Ottoman domination, 224; the Turkish fleet join the French fleet—the last time, until the present century, that the French and Turks fight in the same ranks; but the alliance between the two Powers ceases to be effective, direct, and offensive, 225; the Sultana Roxalana, 226; murder of Prince Mustapha, 227; revolt and murder of Prince Bajazet, 229; war with Hungary renewed, 230-1; the enterprise against Szigeth costs the Sultan his life; his death concealed for three weeks, 233; character of Solyman *the Great*, 234; his *Institutions*, 235-7; he himself commenced the decadence of his Empire, 238.

Solyman II. saluted as Padischa in place of his brother Mahomet IV., after living during forty-six years in the most absolute seclusion, 367; the news of his elevation strikes him with terror; is dragged almost by main force to the throne room to receive the homage of the Ulema and great dignitaries; the Janissaries demand an increased accession-donative, which being resisted, they commit the most sanguinary atrocities, murder the Grand Vizier, storm, plunder, and burn the palaces of the ministers, 368; the standard of the Prophet is raised by the Ulema, and the people rising against the rebels, the revolt is suppressed; the aged Ismael Pacha is entrusted with the seals and the conduct of a war which threatens the Ottoman Empire with destruction; Belgrade taken, and a great part of Bosnia overrun by the Imperialists, 369; the affairs of the Empire conducted by an incapable Vizier, Mustapha of Rodosto, the Turks experience nothing but defeats; the Divan resolved to confide the salvation of the Empire to Kupruli Mustapha, 370; his energetic yet enlightened measures, 371-3; his humanity pro-serves the Morea to the Empire, 374; to his successes in Greece he adds other victories, but proves less successful against the Venetians in Dalmatia; death of Solyman II., 375.

Spahi, the word originally denoted the lowest class of Timariot, 155.

Ssafis or Sofis. An important revolution, at once political and religious, is accomplished in the East, which reawakens the sleeping quarrel of the Shiites and Sunnites, and raises upon the ruins of the Tartar and Turkoman Empires the new Persian Empire of the *Ssafis*, 169.

Stahrenberg, Count Rudiger de, made commandant of Vienna, makes a bold and active defence against the Turks, until the garrison, exhausted by fighting, sickness, and incessant labour, is succoured by the Christian army under John Sobieski, 354; receives the King of Poland in the magnificent tent of the Grand Vizier and greets him as a deliverer, 356.

Stephen, Prince of Servia, obtains from Rome the title of *King*, at which Emeric, King of Hungary, takes offence, and drives him out of Servia, 67.

Stephen Ourosch III., re-establishes the dynasty of Nemania, which takes fresh lustre under him, 67.

Stephen Douschan, his glorious reign; very nearly replacing the Greek by a Serb Empire, rendering abortive the Ottoman power; the extent of his dominions; is crowned at Uskioup "Emperor of the Romans and of the Triballi"; besieges Constantinople, and forces the Emperor Andronicus to sue for peace; dies during a second expedition thither, 68.

Stephen IV. of Moldavia, by his victories and talents, embellishes that country with its noblest pages, 142; defeats successively the Hungarians, Poles and Tartars; refuses to pay Mahomet II. tribute, and puts an army of 100,000 Turks to thorough rout near Racovitza, but causes his prisoners to be empaled, 143; acquires like Hunyade and Scanderbeg the renown of champion of Christianity, and is called by the Pope "the Athlete of Christ"; retreating before a formidable army led by Mahomet II., he draws it into a forest near Robœni, and thoroughly defeats it with a loss of 30,000 men, 144.

Tekeli, Count Emmerich, an uncompromising enemy of the House of Austria, places himself at the head of the malcontent Hungarian leaders; discontented with the Emperor Leopold's fanatical persecution of Protestantism, enters Upper Hungary, defeats the Imperial forces, captures several towns, occupies the whole district of the Carpathian Mountains, and compels the Austrian generals Wurmb and Leslie to accept the truce he offered; in spite of the Liberal offers made him by the Emperor, he enters into a treaty with the Porte, and in conjunction with the Turks effects several conquests; the governor of Buda has orders to aid Tekeli, who assumes the title of King, against Austria; advises Kara Mustapha not to besiege Vienna, 351-2; aided by the Voïvode of Wallachia enters Transylvania and destroys a corps of the German army, and in recompense is named Prince of Transylvania, 375.

Togrul Beg, grandson of Seljuk, Emir of Turkestán, defeats the Khálife Massoud at Zendecan, which decisive action shatters into fragments the colossal Empire of the Ghiznevides and commences the prosperity of the Seljukides, who are about to absorb the other tribes and dominate all the East; enters Khorassan and overthrows the chief of the Boujides, commander of the Khalife's army; that victory opens to Togrul the way to Bagdad, which he enters unopposed and compels the Abbasside prince to confer upon him the title of *Sultan*, and wrests from him the guardianship of the Boujides to impose his own; receives the title of Emir al Omara, and reigns from Bokhara to Syria, from the vicinity of the Indus to the Black Sea, in the name of the monarch whom he had reinstated; at his death bequeaths the vast Empire he had conquered to his nephew Alp Arslan, 33.

Torghud (called by Europeans Dragut), the Corsair, sustains the reputation of the Ottoman navy, and renders himself as formidable to the Christians as his predecessor Barbarossa, 224; his fleet joins that of the French under Paulin—the last time until the present century that the French and Turks were seen fighting in the same ranks, 225.

Treaty between Mahomet II. and

HISTORICAL INDEX. 409

Venice, 145 ; the first between the Porte and Austria, 203 ; with Francis I., 207; between Solyman I., Charles V., and Ferdinand of Austria, 221; of Carlowitz, 378.

Touman Bey, Sultan of the Mamelukes, subdued and put to death at Cairo by command of Selim I., 175.

Turban, the distinctive sign of peoples and castes, 57.

Turkish guards, growth of their power and sway ; their rivalry with the Syrians, 30.

Voulkan, raises Servia and Bosnia, 67.

Wlad or Bladus, called by his subjects *The Devil* (Drakul), by the Hungarians *the Executioner*, and by the Turks *the Empaler*, overthrows and puts to death Dan, his kinsman, Hospodar of Wallachia ; defeats the Turkish troops sent against him, and preserves his throne on condition of paying tribute, and supplying forces to the Sultan, 110 ; joins a band of German and Italian adventurers leagued with the Hungarians in a crusade to drive the Turks into Asia, who are defeated by Amurath II. at Varna, 113 ; Wlad's atrocities and number of his victims; Mahomet II. makes preparations to attack him, to bring Wallachia under Ottoman domination ; signs treaties almost simultaneously with the Sultan and the King of Hungary, binding himself with the latter to attack the Turks ; Mahomet, with the view to get rid of his enemy by cunning, sends Hamsa Pacha to draw him into a conference ; divining their object, Wlad empales the envoy with all his suite, enters Bulgaria, destroying and massacring all along his route, and carrying away 25,000 captives ; other ambassadors being sent to him, on their refusal to take off their turbans, he causes them to be nailed to their heads ; exasperated at this, Mahomet pursues him with a large fleet and army ; devastating all before him, Wlad surprises the Ottoman camp, very nearly taking or slaying the Sultan, 135 ; the latter, on reaching the plain of Prælatu, near Bucharest, stands horror-stricken at the sight of 20,000 Turks and Bulgarians empaled ; at length, after desolating the country during several months, the ferocious Wlad flees into Hungary, where Matthias Corvinus flings him into prison, and the Sultan establishes his brother Radul in his stead ; Wallachia is definitively reunited to the Ottoman Empire ; Wlad reappears, terrifies the country by his cruelties, and comes to his end by assassination, 136.

Zapoly, John, voïvode of Transylvania, his pretensions to the throne of Hungary ; is opposed by Ferdinand of Austria, 192 ; the two rivals encounter at Tokay, where Zapoly is conquered ; gains over the Vizier Ibrahim to his interests, and Solyman *the Great* enters into a treaty of alliance with him, 193.

Zimisces, John, Emperor of Byzantium, subdues the Bulgarians and converts them to Christianity, 69.

Zinghis Khan, unites all the Mongolian hordes under his authority and resolves to lead them to the conquest of the world ; having subdued Tartary the north of China and India, directs his march towards the west and overthrows the Karismian Empire, 38.

WOODFALL & KINDER, Print rs, Milford Lane, Strand, London, W.C.
VOL. I.

www.ingramcontent.com/pod-product-compliance
Lightning Source LLC
Chambersburg PA
CBHW022103290426
44112CB00008B/531